Legal Modernism

Law, Meaning, and Violence

The scope of Law, Meaning, and Violence is defined by the wide-ranging scholarly debates signaled by each of the words in the title. Those debates have taken place among and between lawyers, anthropologists, political theorists, sociologists, and historians, as well as literary and cultural critics. This series is intended to recognize the importance of such ongoing conversations about law, meaning, and violence as well as to encourage and further them.

Series Editors:

Martha Minow, Harvard Law School
Michael Ryan, Northeastern University
Austin Sarat, Amherst College

Legal Modernism

David Luban

Ann Arbor

THE UNIVERSITY OF MICHIGAN PRESS

First paperback edition 1997
Copyright © by the University of Michigan 1994
All rights reserved
Published in the United States of America by
The University of Michigan Press
Manufactured in the United States of America

2000 1999 1998 1997   4 3 2 1

A CIP catalog record for this book is available from the British Library.

Library of Congress Cataloging-in-Publication Data

Luban, David, 1949–
    Legal modernism / David Luban.
        p.   cm. — (Law, meaning, and violence)
    Includes bibliographical references and index.
    ISBN 0-472-10380-6 (alk. paper)
    1. Law—Philosophy. 2. Critical legal studies. 3. Modernism.
I. Title. II. Series.
K355.L83 1994
340′.1—dc20   93-44830
                                                           CIP

ISBN 0-472-08439-9 (pbk. : alk. paper)

For Douglas MacLean and Michael Sukale

Idea for an Arcanum

To present history as a trial in which man as an advocate for mute nature makes a complaint against the nonappearance of the promised Messiah. The court, however, decides to hear witnesses for the future. Here appear the poet who senses it, the sculptor who sees it, the musician who hears it, and the philosopher who knows it. Their testimony thus diverges, though all of them testify to his coming. The court does not dare admit its indecision. Hence there is no end of new complaints or new witnesses. There is torture and martyrdom. The jury benches are occupied by the living, who listen to the human prosecutor and the witnesses with equal mistrust. The jurors' seats are inherited by their sons. At length they grow afraid they may be driven from their benches. Finally all the jurors take flight, and only the prosecutor and witnesses remain.

Walter Benjamin, letter to Gershom Scholem, November 1927

Contents

Preface

The history of this book is the history of friendships and conversations. I first began to think about what makes modernity different when I was a graduate student at Yale in the early 1970s. Surrounded by the student movement, the Vietnam war, and the counterculture in its brief creative phase, there was not much else that a political philosopher of my generation *could* think about. My views were shaped by my fellow students, but particularly by Jon Bordo, who persuaded me that to understand the events around us, which seemed so overwhelming in their immediate significance, I must delve into the thought, practice, and art of the early modern era. I began to study the Copernican revolution, guided by Professor Fred Oscanyan, and set to work on a dissertation about Descartes and modernity. The dissertation was abandoned for a different topic, and nothing remains but a drawer full of manuscripts; however, some of its ideas appear in the introduction to this book.

Beginning in 1974, I was able to develop my ideas further in a four-year period of intense collaboration with Michael Sukale and Douglas MacLean, to whom this book is dedicated. The chapter on Hannah Arendt was composed in 1978, but I did not return to the theme of modernity until 1986, when the Canadian Association of Law Teachers invited me to address its annual meeting on the relationship between law, the humanities, and the Critical Legal Studies movement. The result was the title chapter.

In between, I wrote "Some Greek Trials" and "The Legacies of Nuremberg." The former was inspired by the powerful 1980 Schaubühne performance of the *Oresteia* in Berlin and grew out of conversations with Helgard Kremin about that performance. It has benefited greatly from the comments of three classicists, Daniel Blickman, Peter Burian, and James Lesher (none of whom, however, agree with all my conclusions). The latter was written to commemorate the fortieth anniversary of the Nuremberg trials, though it did not appear in print until two years later. I wrote "Difference Made Legal" for a *Michigan Law Review* symposium on the legal significance of narrative. "Legal Traditionalism" was inspired by Anthony Kronman's splendid paper

"Precedent and Tradition," while "Doubts about the New Pragmatism" began as a long letter to Thomas Grey about his "Holmes and Legal Pragmatism." Grey has generously corresponded with me about pragmatism ever since—and remains unpersuaded by my arguments.

Among the debts this book incurs, some are literary rather than personal. They are, specifically, debts to Martin Luther King, Jr.'s "Letter from Birmingham City Jail"; to Walter Benjamin's "Theses on the Philosophy of History"; to Stanley Cavell's *Must We Mean What We Say?*; to Michael Fried's "Art and Objecthood"; to the writings of Hannah Arendt; and to a 1974 essay by Jon Bordo on the Isenheim Altarpiece of Grünewald—an essay I have read dozens of times but that, so far as I know, remains untitled and unpublished.

Law teachers and philosophers are a remarkably generous group, and these chapters have all benefited from the comments of many colleagues. Especially I must thank Robin West, whose friendship and intelligence have aided me in the composition of every essay from 1986 on. In addition, I am grateful to Austin Sarat, who insisted that I write the introduction and conclusion to the book and whose penetrating questions more or less dictated their content. Others whose comments have improved various chapters include Richard Boldt, David Bogen, Keith Campbell, Richard Delgado, Robert Fullinwider, William Galston, Theresa Glennon, Paul Kahn, Mike Kelly, Charles Larmore, Jerry Levinson, Martha Minow, Richard Mohr, Richard Pildes, Thomas Pogge, Richard Posner, Peter Quint, Deborah Rhode, Mark Sagoff, Kim Lane Scheppele, William Simon, Jana Singer, Rachel Sommerville, Gerardieu Spann, Pierre Schlag, Jerry Segal, John Stick, Alan Strudler, Mark Tushnet, Robert Wachbroit, David Wasserman, Michael Williams, Steve Winter, and Greg Young.

I must express my deep gratitude to the Morton and Sophia Macht Foundation and the Macht family for their generous support and friendship; to the Guggenheim Foundation, which awarded me a fellowship in 1989; and to the University of Melbourne, for a research fellowship that enabled me to compose the introduction in the congenial surroundings of the Melbourne philosophy department.

I am particularly grateful to Colin Day and Malcolm Litchfield of the University of Michigan Press, as well as to the Press's copyediting department, for their commitment and meticulous attention to my book. They have ensured that its remaining inadequacies are truly those of the author. Arthur Evenchik assisted heroically with the proofreading.

Above all, this book exists because of Judy Lichtenberg, my wife and colleague, who talked me through the whole thing and whose skeptical comments have continually saved me from the worst of my philosophical excesses; it exists also because of our children, Daniel and Rachel, whose love has sustained me and whose tolerance has been remarkable under the circumstances.

As I have indicated, several of these chapters appeared originally as articles, though all have been revised, some quite substantially, for this book. Chapters 1 and 5 were originally published in 84 *Michigan Law Review* 1656 (1986) and 87 *Michigan Law Review* 2152 (1989) and are reprinted by permission of that journal. Chapter 2 originally appeared in 43 *Stanford Law Review* 1035 (1991). Copyright © 1991 by the Board of Trustees of the Leland Stanford Junior University, who, with the Fred B. Rothman Company, have granted permission for its use. Chapter 4 originally appeared as "Explaining Dark Times: Hannah Arendt's Theory of Theory" in 50 *Social Research* 215 (1983); chapter 7 appeared in 54 *Social Research* 779 (1987); both are reprinted by permission of that journal. Chapter 6 is based on an article that originally appeared in 54 *Tennessee Law Review* 279 (1987) and is reproduced here by permission of the Tennessee Law Review Association, Inc., 1505 W. Cumberland, Knoxville, Tennessee 37996–1800.

Introduction:
We Copernicans

The Senselessness of Legal Theory

In 1987 Ronald Reagan nominated Federal Appellate Judge Robert
Bork, a former Yale law professor and solicitor general, to the U. S.
Supreme Court. Bork was a prominent conservative well known for his
vitriolic criticisms of the right to privacy, of civil rights legislation, and
of Supreme Court decisions striking down bans on contraception and
desegregating the Washington, D.C., public schools. Opponents mobilized a potent anti-Bork campaign, and by the time the Senate Judiciary
Committee convened hearings on the Bork nomination, it had exploded
into a headline-grabbing political battle.

During the Senate hearings, George Priest, a distinguished Yale
law professor, testified on Bork's behalf. Priest ventured a remarkable
argument in Bork's defense—an argument that raises profound questions about the nature of contemporary legal theory and, ultimately,
about law itself.

Priest conceded that "Bork's academic writings are slashing. They
are hypercritical. They are extreme."[1] His antitrust writings "challenge
that there is any wisdom at all in 85 years of Supreme Court precedent,
and they focus single mindedly on one set of concerns—consumer
welfare—to the exclusion of all others."[2] Nevertheless, Priest maintained, these writings should not be taken as an indicator of Bork's
judicial temperament.

The reason, according to Priest, lies in the difference between the
role of the scholar and that of the judge. The judge must be open-
minded, moderate, and respectful of previous authority. Since World
War II, however,

---

1. Testimony of George Priest, in 2 *Hearings Before the Committee on the Judiciary of
the United States Senate, on the Nomination of Robert H. Bork to be Associate Justice of the
Supreme Court of the United States*, 100th Cong., 1st Sess. 2435 (1989).

2. *Id.* at 2437.

there has been a vast change in the style of modern legal scholarship. . . . Those scholars competing in the front rank on the frontier of legal scholarship have very self-consciously adopted the style of research and scholarship of the natural sciences. This scientific style consists of the development of a generalized theory that provides a unifying method for thinking about phenomena, and then the further demonstration that the new theory or conception is superior to all previously accepted theories or concepts; and just as in the sciences, this style generates and has generated a fierce competition among the most ambitious of legal scholars.

The competition among these scholars is over who will announce and who can confirm some dominant theory of the law, and these scholars compete much like athletes seeking records or much like 17th and 18th century explorers seeking new discoveries. They compete to promote new theories and new ideas around which fields of law will be reorganized. . . .

This scholarly style leads quite obviously to conceptual exaggeration, but it is an exaggeration with a purpose. The scholar pursuing the importance of an idea can only learn its full importance when the idea is pressed to an extreme which exposes the idea to the harshest possible light.[3]

According to Priest, it was this scholarly style, and not Judge Bork's temperament or personal beliefs, that accounted for the extraordinary intemperance of his published writings.

Once Bork became a judge, however, his approach adapted to his new role, or so Priest suggested. Bork's judicial opinions "are reasonable and moderate and generally respectful of previous authority."[4]

Then came Priest's astonishing comment on Bork's transformation:

Most importantly, though, I think one can say that Judge Bork's opinions demonstrate in themselves no academic achievement. On the basis of his judicial writings, Judge Bork could not obtain appointment in any major American law school. Though I admire his academic work, his previous academic work, and though I support his appointment to the Supreme Court, *his abandonment of this slashing and extreme style in favor of a judicious incremental approach to thinking about the law I think disqualifies him for a reappointment at Yale Law School, if he were to seek it.*[5]

---

3. *Id.* at 2435–36.
4. *Id.* at 2437.
5. *Id.* (emphasis added).

This is an extraordinary assessment of contemporary legal scholarship. First, and most obviously, it concedes that there is an enormous gap between the academic study of legal practices and the practices themselves. Many legal academics worry about this gap and seek ways to bridge it. They lament that their writings are irrelevant to the bench or the bar. Not Priest, however, who revels in the distance between legal theory and legal practice. For Priest, the very fact that Bork has now adopted the role of judge stigmatizes him. Judicial thinking amounts to a kind of pollution that banishes him from Yale Law School.

Two words in Priest's testimony are particularly arresting. "Judge Bork's judicial opinions are . . . reasonable and moderate and generally respectful of previous authority. *Most importantly,* though, I think one can say that Judge Bork's opinions demonstrate in themselves no academic achievement."

Most importantly. The fact that Bork's opinions demonstrate no academic achievement is more important than the fact that they are reasonable. From the point of view of the citizen, who will be governed by the law enunciated by judges, it is of paramount importance that the law be reasonable. Not so to the legal scholar, for whom academic achievement (slashing, extreme) is the most important value—not just in academic writings, evidently, but in law itself, at least law that is made by judges. Let truth triumph though the world perish.

Second, Priest believes the appropriate form of investigating legal phenomena to be "emulation of the style of scholarship in the natural sciences."[6] This he understands as a struggle that is at once the battle for personal supremacy of fiercely ambitious scientists ("scholars compete much like athletes") and the investigation of hypotheses under the stress of blanket assertion unsullied by qualification ("The scholar . . . can only learn its full importance when the idea is pressed to an extreme which exposes the idea to the harshest possible light."). For Priest, the serious legal scholar is a would-be scientist, and the scientific method is a ruthless game of king of the mountain.

Third is a certain understanding of what the truth about legal structures must be. If "reasonable and moderate" ideas disqualify one from the serious pursuit of truth, it follows that reasonable and moderate ideas cannot be true. The truth about legal structures must be radically different from the way they manifest themselves in practice. Priest's argument implies a kind of "Copernican reversal": legal phenomena, like the apparent motion of the Sun, are not what they seem.

6. *Id.* at 2436.

Only this can explain why a good judge is necessarily a bad scholar. The judge adopts "a judicious incremental approach to thinking about the law." The judge thinks case by case, focusing heavily on the particular facts of the case and abstracting only to the extent minimally necessary to render judgment in a way that respects the integrity of the law. The judge views the case through conventional categories; every case is largely what it seems to be. The scholar, by contrast, seeks "a generalized theory that provides a unifying method for thinking about phenomena." He abstracts to the maximum degree possible. He explains phenomena by theories that propose a hidden order beneath surface confusion.

Let me emphasize that Priest does not speak for all legal scholars. Even within Yale Law School, Professor Anthony Kronman has eloquently defended the importance of practical wisdom, Priest's "judicious incremental approach," against the self-asserting theoretical exuberance that Priest extols.[7] Philosophers of science may protest Priest's assumption that the methods of the natural sciences equally suit the social sciences; the "theory envy" with which social scientists regard physics is notorious. Physical scientists will wince at the epistemological confusion that leads Priest to equate theory testing with intellectual one-upsmanship. And indeed, many legal scholars I know were embarrassed by what they took to be the overall strangeness of Priest's testimony—embarrassed because they feared that the general public would conclude that legal academics had left their senses.

Now it might be thought that Priest's remarks were motivated by the political need to explain away Bork's record. But, in words of G. H. Hardy, I am "driven to the more uncharitable conclusion that he really believes them true."[8] For, in a very real way, leaving their senses is precisely what legal academics have done. I have described Priest's underlying assumption that legal reality is far different from legal appearance as a Copernican reversal. Though some legal academics were embarrassed by the Alice in Wonderland image Priest painted of elite law professors preening themselves over their lack of judgment, they nevertheless agree that legal phenomena are not what they seem.

If everything is precisely as it seems, there would be little justification for the existence of legal scholarship, the professional career of intellectual investigation of law. For over a century, legal scholars have endeavored to penetrate beneath the surface of legal phenomena to understand what actually makes the legal world tick. This enterprise

---

7. Anthony T. Kronman, *The Lost Lawyer* (1993).
8. G. H. Hardy, 7 *Collected Papers of G. H. Hardy* 611 (1979).

would be pointless unless understanding can be won by leaving one's senses—by using the power of thought to uncover heliocentric realities beneath geocentric appearances.

I have said that Priest's testimony raises profound questions not only about contemporary legal scholarship but about law itself. That is because, after all, legal scholars may be right. Perhaps law is very different from what it seems to be. Perhaps, as the legal realists argued, law is really predictions of official behavior on the basis of variables that only social scientists are fully competent to identify. Perhaps, as Priest's own colleagues in the law and economics movement argue, law is really a self-conscious or unconscious effort to improve economic efficiency. Perhaps Marx was right, and law is an ideological superstructure designed to promote the interests of the economically dominant class. Perhaps those feminists are right who regard law as an instrument that reinforces patriarchal domination not only through oppressive rules but also through an abstracted and antirelational style of understanding social existence. Perhaps postmodernists are right, and law *is* nothing apart from whatever the dominant interpretation of law says that it is.

This is a disturbing line of thought. Most of us are unable to offer a snappy definition of law, yet we usually feel that we understand tolerably well what it is that lawyers, judges, legislators, and police do and what roles they play in the social world. If legal scholars are right, however, we understand all that only in the way we "understand" that the Sun moves around the earth—that is, we understand nothing at all. All we can say is that law and legal phenomena are important pieces of our social world, though we don't really know what they are, nor where their importance lies, nor what their importance consists in, nor even what the phenomena are that we are talking about. It is enough to make us feel that we have left our senses.

There is an interesting aesthetic counterpart to Priest's view of law and legal theory. In his well-known polemic "Who Cares If You Listen?," composer Milton Babbitt argued that contemporary musicians should have no regrets about the fact that "advanced" compositions of the postwar period had lost their general audience.[9] Babbitt was referring to the so-called New Music, influenced by Anton Webern, that was composed according to principles of total serialization (of melody, harmony, rhythm, and instrumentation), or that incorporated aleatoric (random) elements, or that was synthesized on electronic tape.

9. Milton Babbitt, "Who Cares If You Listen?," 8 *High Fidelity Magazine* 38 (1958), *reprinted in The American Composer Speaks: A Historical Anthology, 1770–1965* 235–44 (Gilbert Chase ed. 1966). Babbitt wrote in 1958, close to the high-water mark for "difficult" new music.

To the uninformed ear, the New Music often sounded like little more than arrhythmic eruptions of tweeting and burping. Critics charged that the New Music had degenerated to the point where it was intelligible only to other professional composers of New Music. Sounds were organized according to theoretical ideas that could not actually be heard in the music, or at any rate not by a listener who did not have the score and the theory in hand. The theories, moreover, originated primarily as responses to developments within composition itself; their imperatives were professional rather than aesthetic.

Babbitt's response was an aggressive, "So much the better!" He argued that in a scientific age, it is neither necessary nor even appropriate for high culture to be intelligible to the general public. Composing, according to Babbitt, has a closer kinship to science than to popular art. It is pursued by a professionalized community, its connection to esoteric theory is a matter for pride rather than embarrassment, and, as in science, the only appropriate judges of new music are the composer's professional peers. They are the only audience that matters. In effect, Babbitt echoed Mark Twain's ironic remark about Wagner, that his music is better than it sounds; only Babbitt echoed it without a trace of irony.

The parallels between Babbitt's views and Priest's should be plain. Legal theory, like New Music, aspires to be a science. Legal theory, like New Music (and particle physics), awards no points for public legibility. Indeed, public legibility signals that the theorist, like the musician, lacks seriousness. Legal theory looks for structures hidden beneath the surface of things, and it is in structures hidden beneath the surface of things that the rewards of New Music likewise lie. Developments in legal theory, like developments in New Music, respond to contemporaneous work within the profession, not extraprofessional demands or criteria. This is true despite the fact that nonprofessionals typically assume that law and music cannot be esoteric, cannot differ radically from the way they seem.[10]

I find the parallel between Priest and Babbitt illuminating and striking, but not for the reasons that they offer. Both Priest and Babbitt

---

10. Babbitt is aware of the parallel. "It often has been remarked that only in politics and the 'arts' does the layman regard himself as an expert, with the right to have his opinion heard." *Id.* at 239. But he has no patience with this view: "Like all communication, this music presupposes a suitably equipped receptor. I am aware that 'tradition' has it that the lay listener, by virtue of some undefined, transcendental faculty, always is able to arrive at a musical judgment absolute in its wisdom if not always permanent in its validity. I regret my inability to accord this declaration of faith the respect due its advanced age." *Id.* at 238–39.

regard the postwar transformation of their fields as a sign that the fields have become sciences.[11] I, on the other hand, wish to suggest that music is, and remains, an art and that the desire to transform art to science is simply one possible response to the fact that art in the twentieth century has entered into a *modernist predicament.*

Likewise, I believe that legal theory is more like art than like science and that it, too, has entered a modernist predicament, very similar to the cultural crisis that gave rise to artistic modernism early in the twentieth century. The essays in this book explore some central strands in contemporary legal theory with this parallel in mind.

Artistic Modernism

Artistic modernism emerged from a drastic loss of confidence in the capacity of the reigning traditions, such as representational painting and tonal music, to sustain work of major quality. The arts in nineteenth-century Europe had seemed to their practitioners to be powered by an inner dynamic that compelled them toward increasing intensity and complexity of expression. Painting from Manet to van Gogh and Cézanne, music from Beethoven to Debussy and Mahler, the novel from Goethe to Dostoevsky and Flaubert, poetry from Wordsworth to Rimbaud and Rilke, all seemed to advance according to an evolutionary logic that now imposed impossible demands on artists: to exhibit the next developmental step in the technical and expressive possibilities of their medium, even though the media seemed already to have been pressed to the maximum.

To remain within the existing horizon was to become epigonal or academic. It was a kind of moral inauthenticity inconsistent with the demands of high art. Perhaps the modernists deceived themselves about this; after all, Richard Strauss wrote unsurpassable masterpieces in the late 1940s using the harmonic language of a half-century before. Yet Strauss—aristocratic, ill at ease in modern life, instinctively reactionary—is perhaps an exception that proves the rule. It is no coincidence that *Metamorphosen,* his most concentrated postwar master-

---

11. "The unprecedented divergence between contemporary serious music and its listeners, on the one hand, and traditional music and its following on the other . . . is a result of a half-century of revolution in musical thought, a revolution whose nature and consequences can be compared only with, and in many respects are closely analogous to, those of the mid-nineteenth-century revolution in mathematics and the twentieth-century revolution in theoretical physics." *Id.* at 236. As an example of the scientific turn in music, one might consider Babbitt's description of his own 1974 *Arie da Capo for 5 Players:* "models of similar, interval-preserving, registrally uninterpreted pitch-class and metrically-durationally uninterpreted time-point aggregate arrays."

piece, was written as a funeral dirge for his beloved Munich opera house, bombed by the Allies during the death throes of the Nazi movement that Strauss had fatally and uncritically supported. In music as in life, Strauss apparently never perceived that the old world's passage could not be stayed, whereas the early modernists never forgot it.

It is significant that all the early modernists created masterpieces within the late nineteenth-century idiom before they broke with it. Yet much as we may love Picasso's Rose and Blue paintings, Schoenberg's *Gurre-Lieder* and *Verklärte Nacht*, or Stravinsky's *Firebird*, their creators found it necessary in the end to break with the traditions they represented. They felt themselves enervated by the conventions of traditional art, conventions that they believed they must violate to succeed as artists. They could no longer stay within the tradition because the tradition itself demanded innovation and yet left nowhere to go.

Early modernism went beyond the observation that traditional painting, writing, or composition had come to a dead end. Artistic modernists believed as a moral matter that the traditions had lost their validity, or even that they had always operated beyond their authority. That was how Stravinsky responded to romanticism; Graham to the classical ballet; Kandinsky and Picasso to Renaissance spatiality; Proust, Joyce, and Kafka to the traditional novel; Artaud and Brecht to the cathartic theater prescribed by Aristotle.[12] As a result, they were suspicious of the artistic public that delighted in traditional works. They knew that high art must be more than sentimental stimulation but suspected that sentimental stimulation was exactly what their audiences craved. Acknowledging that his spare, five-minute-long *Orchestral Variations* might prove inaccessible to a concert audience accustomed to "the prolix speech of the music that provides the pablum of our concert life," Stravinsky added, "therein lies a difficulty, mine with you no less than yours with me."[13] Though modernist art sometimes sunk to *épater les bourgeois*, its real aim was to exhibit the relationship of art and audience as a problem, and in that way to restore morality to it.

The early modernists found themselves face to face with Kant's question, "By what right?" Taking art with the utmost seriousness, they believed that any set of artistic conventions, be it Renaissance spatiality or traditional harmony, demands justification. Lacking justification, the

---

12. Schoenberg famously declared that there was still great music to be written in C major, but this was surely disingenuous, for in his theory, his pedagogy, and his harmonic practice, he clearly regarded the turns to atonality and dodecaphony as inevitable. *See* Charles Rosen, *Schoenberg* (1975).

13. Igor Stravinsky & Robert Craft, *Themes and Conclusions* 63 (1972).

convention can sustain only humbug, all the worse in moral terms if audiences love it. We should not forget that, from the early modernists' point of view, the stakes in art are incalculably large. One way or another, the founders of modernism would have agreed with Nietzsche that art justifies existence. In that case, offering inauthentic art would be as disastrous as announcing a false messiah. To fail at Beauty was equally to fail at Truth and the Good. Consequently, the early modernists drew no sharp distinction between aesthetic justification on the one hand and cognitive or moral justification on the other.

But where was this justification to come from? Faced with the Kantian question, "By what right?" four alternatives present themselves. These prove central to the argument of this book, for in its first three chapters I claim that the need to choose among these same four alternatives shapes much of contemporary legal theory.

1. *Avant-gardism.* First, one can answer, "By no right!" and launch an obliteration campaign against the tradition. This was the response of Dada and Duchamp, of the Sex Pistols and segments of today's cultural left. Adopting Clement Greenberg's term, I shall call this response *avant-gardism,*[14] the instinctive (and by now fatally routine) rejection of everything that is not avant-garde. In the first chapter of this book, I argue that the so-called nihilist wing of Critical Legal Studies (CLS) represents the avant-gardist response to the modernist predicament of legal theory.

2. *Traditionalism.* Second, one can withhold the tradition from scrutiny, regarding the incessant demand to pose Kant's question as a Jacobin pathology rather than a cultural necessity. The Burkean rejection of Enlightenment critique was the response of T. S. Eliot and C. S. Lewis and is widely represented today by conservative aesthetes and publicists. Traditionalism forms a major strand in legal theory, and in the second chapter I assess the traditionalist response as it is exemplified in the neo-Burkean theory of Anthony Kronman.

3. *Pragmatism and postmodernism.* Third, one may evade the Kantian question by deflating the claims of art or the centrality of the tradition that generated those claims. Maybe art need not represent Truth and the Good; maybe the demand for authenticity on the terms set by the tradition is nothing more than a contingent cultural construction. If so, "By what right?" is no longer a question of any interest.

Brecht insisted that theater should be useful and instructive, not transcendent or shattering; proponents of *Gebrauchsmusik*, like architects such as Gropius and Le Corbusier, believed that beauty arises out

---

14. Clement Greenberg, "Counter-Avant-Garde," *Art International,* May 20, 1971, at 16.

of art's intelligible social function.[15] This is the pragmatic strain in modernism, but what might be called the postmodern strain also adopts the deflationary strategy. In his celebrated 1936 essay "The Work of Art in the Age of Mechanical Reproduction," Walter Benjamin maintained what Andy Warhol would later illustrate—that the "aura" of art, traditionally associated with its uniqueness, its seriousness, and its "cult value," was soon to be a thing of the past. Benjamin's essay, which stresses the iterability and "decentering" of mechanically reproducible art such as photographs and film, strikingly anticipates themes that would later preoccupy Jacques Derrida and his followers; in important respects, Benjamin and Warhol were the first theoretician and the first practitioner of postmodernism. Warhol and his successors aimed to obliterate the distinctions between high art, low art, and nonart and thereby to make the Kantian question, "By what right?" irrelevant. And obviously, the smug, postmodern self-confidence of today's culture industry that art is (and always was) nothing but entertainment has become the ruling orthodoxy, to such an extent that the concerns of the early modernists can strike us now as nearly unintelligible.[16]

Within legal theory, this deflationary strategy in response to the Kantian question is best exemplified in the current turn toward pragmatism, which subordinates the demands of theory to the exigencies of future-directed problem solving. In a sense, pragmatism forms the natural complement to traditionalism, for both of them duck the Kantian question, the traditionalist by retreating to the past, to antecedents, and the pragmatist by retreating (I use the word advisedly) to the future, to consequences. The traditionalist believes that it is out of order to pose Kant's question, while the pragmatist believes that it is unnecessary to answer it. Together with avant-gardism, traditionalism and pragmatism seem to exhaust the possibilities.

---

15. I believe that the scientism of Babbitt and Priest can best be understood as one strain of the pragmatic evasion of Kant's question. As Kuhn has argued, a defining characteristic of a mature science is that the question, "By what right?" seems uninteresting or beside the point; at any rate, it is not a genuine scientific question, the way that problem solving within the discipline is genuine. Scientism in art and legal theory aspires to elevate its disciplines to the status of a mature science, in which the Kantian question no longer arises.

16. The phenomenon is particularly visible within popular music since the 1960s, which has in many ways reenacted the history of early modernism. The most advanced bands of the 1960s—the Beatles, the Doors, the Grateful Dead, the Jefferson Airplane, Bob Dylan—had enormous artistic ambitions, and redemptive visions, comparable to those of the early modernists. By contrast, today's reigning acts create their effects by exulting in prefabricated, glitzy, entertainment-*über-alles* spectacles.

4. *The way of the modernists: neo-Kantian modernism.* Crucially, however, the founders of modernism discovered a path distinct from all of these. Intellectually, modernist culture arises from an intensification of the Enlightenment demand that we cast off the claims of dogmatic authority; politically, it arises from our drastic loss of confidence in the ability of public institutions to cast light on human affairs (or so I argue in chapter 4). Spiritually and emotionally, the modernist predicament appears in the form of a heightened awareness that all our beliefs and routines are conditioned by background presuppositions, coupled with a dismaying realization that those presuppositions may well be arbitrary.[17] Feeling at once bound by the givens of our culture and yet distanced and estranged from them, we are likely to experience our modernist predicament as a sense of homelessness.

Modernism thus places us in a complex, highly self-conscious relationship to our own activities and history—a relationship in which (in the words of Brecht) "we know that we're only tenants, provisional ones / And after us will come: nothing worth talking about."[18] Unable to persevere in the premodernist enterprise once we have come face to face with its arbitrariness, and yet lacking the resources to found a substitute tradition from the ground up, the founders of modernism responded by using "the characteristic methods of a discipline to criticize the discipline itself," to quote Clement Greenberg's famous definition of modernism.[19] Greenberg locates the source of this enterprise in Kant, and in chapter 1 I call it neo-Kantian modernism (to distinguish it from avant-gardism). The imperative of responding creatively to our history becomes itself the principal theme of modernism. Within contemporary legal theory, I identify neo-Kantian modernism with the nonnihilist writers within CLS.

Modernism, on the neo-Kantian understanding, finds a revivifying alternative to avant-gardism, traditionalism, and pragmatism by turning the modernist predicament on itself. It amounts to a dialectical self-criticism of each discipline. The modernist predicament—the newly problematic relationship between us and traditional art—becomes itself the subject matter of modernist art. Subsequently, our relationship to modernist art becomes the new subject matter, and so on, as each artistic generation poses the Kantian question, "By what right?" to its immediate predecessors in what might be called iterated Enlighten-

---

17. Here I am adopting the argument of Roberto Mangabeira Unger, *Passion: An Essay on Personality* (1984).

18. Bertolt Brecht, "Of Poor B.B.," *Poems 1913–1956* 108 (1976).

19. Greenberg, "Modernist Painting," in *The New Art* 67–68 (Gregory Battcock rev. ed. 1973).

ment. No doubt there is a hint of futility in this process; but it is an incontrovertible fact that through it, modernist art generated an astonishing sequence of masterpieces.

My thesis is that legal theory, and even law itself, has entered a similarly modernist situation. What can this mean? In art, I have said, the modernist situation concerns the inability of traditional artistic practice to secure work of the same quality as the masterpieces of the tradition; it is a predicament centering on the quest for artistic quality. What, then, is the counterpart within legal theory of artistic quality?

This is no easy question, for the aims of legal theory are themselves a matter of intense controversy, which itself I take to be a symptom of the modernist predicament. (The same, incidentally, is true in the artistic counterpart.) But surely this much can be said: Legal theory aims descriptively at an understanding of what law is and what it does, and legal theory aims morally at the articulation and pursuit of justice. The counterparts within legal theory of artistic quality are therefore truth (about law) and justice. These are the *intellectual* and the *moral* problems of legal theory.

On the moral side, it seems plain that legal theorists and contemporary legal culture have experienced a striking loss of confidence that we understand the demands of justice, though our yearning for a legal system that delivers justice is for that very reason perhaps more intense than ever. And this I take to constitute an aspect of the modernist predicament: as Roberto Unger puts it, "a basic, common experience in modern society . . . . : the sense of being surrounded by injustice without knowing where justice lies."[20] From the widespread public apprehension that the U.S. Supreme Court engages in overt political partisanship, to the Holmesian view, echoed by contemporary lawyers such as Robert Bork, that moral concepts have no place in the law, to our cultural ambivalence about whether recourse to the law is a salutary pursuit of rights or a dangerous undermining of the sense of community, the dissociation of legality from justice is a striking phenomenon.

The intellectual problem of legal theory may be superficially summed up in a Kuhnian cliché: legal theory lacks a paradigm. Economists and feminists, sociologists and doctrinalists, centralists and pluralists, positivists and purposivists, are unable even to agree on the boundaries of the object they are studying, let alone the propositions that are true of that object.

---

20. Unger, *Law in Modern Society: Toward a Criticism of Social Theory* 175 (1976).

At first this problem—if it is a problem—may seem to have little to do with Unger's "sense of being surrounded by injustice without knowing where justice lies." But I will argue in chapters 4 and 5 that the intellectual and moral confusions of legal theory are deeply connected: both arise from the incapacity of legal theory to illuminate the meaning of legal events, and this in turn results from the modern substitution of a *scientific* ideal of understanding for a fundamentally *narrative* ideal. Elaborating an argument of Hannah Arendt, in chapter 4 I locate the problem in the underdetermination of social-scientific laws by their data, coupled with the insistence that only social-scientific laws constitute a proper explanation of legal phenomena. If nothing will provide intellectual satisfaction except scientific laws, and scientific laws won't provide intellectual satisfaction, it is small wonder that "the mind of man wanders in obscurity," as Arendt was wont to quote from Tocqueville.

The analogy between this difficulty and artistic modernism is straightforward: both the arts and social science pose challenges that they provide insufficient resources to fulfill. Arendt argued in addition that the decline of narrative models for understanding political events, with the concomitant rise of scientific models for understanding them, are themselves products of modernity, and I agree. In chapter 5, I stress some of the ways in which narrative techniques are absolutely central to legal argument.

It may seem preposterous to liken legal theory to cultural events as momentous (in their way) as the turn of the arts to modernism. Legal theory is an entirely academic discipline that is as conventional as any and perhaps more tedious than most. And it seems doubly preposterous to suggest that legal culture itself now finds itself in a modernist predicament. Yet that is the claim that these essays assume the burden of establishing. In the remainder of this introduction I wish to sketch the argument against whose background I wrote the essays. First, I use the metaphor of the Copernican revolution to examine the centuries-long process that by the end of the nineteenth century had produced the modernist predicament. This section argues that one central achievement of modernity lies in the replacement of canonical narratives, such as epics and scriptures, by scientific theories as our fundamental mode of understanding our place in the world. Focusing on Oliver Wendell Holmes as a case study, I draw out the implications of this achievement for legal theory. Holmes, like Priest and many other contemporary legal theorists, predicted that law was due for its own Copernican revolution; as he once put it, "Science is gradually drawing legal history into its

sphere. . . . The law has got to be stated over again; and I venture to say
that in fifty years we shall have it in a form of which no man could have
dreamed fifty years ago."[21] The drive to formulate a legal science, I
believe, results in a particular theory of what a good legal system
should be—a theory that I call *statist liberalism.* One of my aims
throughout this book is to criticize statist liberalism and defend a communitarian liberal alternative that in my view better realizes the promise of modernism.

My argument, developed in the following sections, is that Holmes
guessed wrong, that forms of explanation that work in the natural
sciences simply don't tell us what we want to know about human
affairs. In a sense, that fact *is* the modernist predicament. Focusing on
ideas of Walter Benjamin, I suggest that we need narrative as well as
causal explanations to make sense of political and legal experience. In
the final sections, I discuss the relationship between my own views and
those of CLS and argue briefly that the issue of legal modernism is
central to our larger legal culture as well as to legal theory.

Narrative and Understanding

The importance of narrative for law and legal theory is obvious: law is
built of stories. Trials involve testimony, conflicting stories, efforts to
produce a coherent narrative of past events. But legal interpretation is
also steeped in story. To understand an ambiguous statute, judges must
reconstruct the history of a problem that a past legislature confronted
and aimed to solve. To interpret constitutional provisions, judges find
occasion to retell the tale of the republic's founding. To state a string of
precedents is to reconstruct a history of rational progress interweaving
the subtly different factual narratives of a number of cases.

Contemporary appreciation of the importance of narrative to law
probably dates from the late Robert Cover's remarkable article "*Nomos*
and Narrative." In chapter 5 I take as an epigraph this passage from
Cover:

> No set of legal institutions or prescriptions exists apart from the
> narratives that locate it and give it meaning. For every constitution
> there is an epic, for each decalogue a scripture. Once understood in
> the context of the narratives that give it meaning, law becomes not

21. Oliver Wendell Holmes, "The Use of Law Schools," in *Collected Legal Papers* 35,
41–42 (1920).

merely a system of rules to be observed, but a world in which we live.[22]

Cover singles out two special cases of narrative: epic and scripture. The singular importance of these lies in their public and authoritative character. Epics, like scriptures, are the common property of a culture, and when they are alive (that is, not yet relegated to "literature"), they radiate political and moral authority. We may add to these other public and authoritative narratives: tales of the founding (Romulus and Remus, Madison and Jefferson), mythology, fables, even fairy tales. Cover's point is that legal rules wither when they are abstracted from the culture's authoritative narratives. Placed within such a narrative, however, law creates a *nomos*, a normative world. Let us consider why this might be so.

In preliterate Greece, nobles would gather to hear the epics sung by itinerant bards, using these occasions to memorize large stretches of the poetry. According to Eric Havelock's influential account in *A Preface to Plato*, these were occasions of immense significance. The epics contained a vast trove of cultural information—information about the proper rituals to use in a variety of circumstances, about virtue and vice, about the usages of war and the construction of boats, about animal husbandry and the conventions of hospitality. The epics constituted what Havelock calls the "Homeric encyclopedia"—a repository of cultural information whose narrative intensity, meter, repetitive verbal formulae, and diction made it easy for a nonliterate Greek to memorize.[23] Memorizing the epics provided access to otherwise unavailable aspects of the culture. Walter Benjamin remarks that "every real story . . . contains, openly or covertly, something useful. The usefulness may, in one case, consist in a moral; in another, in some practical advice; in a third, in a proverb or maxim."[24] To this he adds that the genuine story operates by exerting a "claim to a place in the memory of the listener," so that it becomes part of the listener's own experience, inclining him or her to repeat it to someone else someday.[25] Where the quality of novels is to be read, the quality of stories is to be (re)told.

In this sense, Havelock's illuminating metaphor of a cultural encyclopedia is apt to mislead, for our relation to the stuff of memory is

---

22. Robert Cover, "The Supreme Court, 1982 Term—Foreword: *Nomos* and Narrative," 97 *Harvard Law Review* 4, 4–5 (1983).

23. E. A. Havelock, *A Preface to Plato* 61–84 (1963).

24. Walter Benjamin, "The Storyteller," in *Illuminations* 83, 86 (Hannah Arendt ed. Harry Zohn trans. 1969).

25. *Id.* at 91.

more intimate and fundamental than our relation to a reference work that we consult, replace on the shelf, and forget about. Benjamin tells us that stories are to become part of our own experience. It is this deeper relation—the incorporation of the content of a story into one's own experience—that a civilization's epics and scriptures presuppose.

We should not conclude from Havelock's account that this deeper relationship to epics and scriptures was confined to preliterate societies. For one thing, even in literate societies books were not readily available before the sixteenth century. In the Middle Ages students of Islamic law prepared themselves for advanced study by memorizing the entire Koran, and a twelfth-century Baghdad scholar advised students to memorize every book they read so they would not be dependent on books.[26] But even in contemporary society the ability to read, far from substituting for the internal cultural encyclopedia, may itself presuppose a reservoir of cultural knowledge that is part of one's own pre-reflective experience. The newly popular notion of cultural literacy is based on the insight that understanding the printed word requires the ability to recognize a large number of fragmentary particulars of cultural and literary history.

This last point is worth dwelling on. Cultural literacy is a theory of how one learns to read, claiming that literacy rests on the ability to recognize references to a vast number of contingent cultural and historical facts (though not necessarily to know anything substantive about them). These facts are the cultural (rather than semantic) elements whose combinations and rearrangements make up printed discourse. Though they may first have been encountered and learned through reading, they have become presuppositions of further reading, and thus our relation to them is different and more basic than our relation to most of what we read.

An epistemological analogy might help to explain this relationship. In *On Certainty*, Wittgenstein observed that it would be odd to use the expression "I know . . . " in connection with the most fundamental facts about ourselves. "I know that I am David Luban"; "I know that I have never been to the moon"; "I know that my skull is not empty"; "I know that I have a hand"—all these are anomalous uses of the expression "I know." But it's not that I *don't* know facts like "I have a hand"; nor is it that we cannot imagine unusual contexts in which these sentences would be appropriate things for me to say. The point is rather that our relationship to these facts is of a different character than our relationship to mere empirical knowledge. At one point Wittgenstein likens

---

26. Albert Hourani, *A History of the Arab Peoples* 164–65 (1991).

these facts to the hinge around which the door (of empirical knowledge) turns;[27] at another point, to the riverbed over which the river (once again, of empirical knowledge) flows.[28] If we couldn't count on these, we couldn't count on anything; the door would not turn and the river would not flow. At the same time, however, "riverbed" propositions assume that function only within a system of empirical knowledge that transforms them as it evolves: the flowing river carves and reconfigures its own channel.

Riverbed propositions thus have a twofold character. In one sense they are items of contingent knowledge, but in another sense they are more basic than knowledge—in Kantian terms, they are necessary conditions of the possibility of knowledge.

Our relationship with the stuff of authoritative stories is surely not as intimate as our relationship to the facts that Wittgenstein is talking about, but I am suggesting that there are similarities and that in important respects epics and scriptures, like the reservoir of factual knowledge required for cultural literacy, served "hinge" or "riverbed" functions within traditional cultures. They were, in a word, *canonical*.

In addition, of course, traditional culture oriented itself by its epics and scriptures. Believing in their historical truthfulness, a culture explained its own existence as the inheritor of a divinely ordained history. Living within the tradition meant that one was living according to a cosmic master plan. One's life might be hard or cruel, perhaps not even worth living, but it was not senseless. One was the bearer of the legacy of Arjuna or Abraham, Romulus or Theseus, Dendid or Jesus or Muhammed.

Modernity as Copernican Revolution

Canonical narratives knit together the normative worlds of traditional cultures; they are, in a sense, the verbal form that tradition assumes. Modernism, on the other hand, grows out of the apprehension that traditional culture has come to the end of its rope. Though modernity can be understood in a variety of ways, it will prove convenient for my purposes to focus on a single aspect of the transition from traditional to modern culture, namely the replacement of traditional narrative by scientific knowledge as the paradigmatic manner in which we understand the world.

---

27. Ludwig Wittgenstein, *On Certainty* §§ 341–43 (G. E. M. Anscombe & G. H. von Wright eds. Denis Paul & G. E. M. Anscombe transs. 1969).
28. *Id.* at §§ 95–97.

To explain the destructive power that modernity has had on traditional narrative, I shall employ a familiar metaphor for modernity, one
suggested by my earlier discussion of contemporary legal theory. That
is the metaphor of the Copernican revolution.[29] Copernicanism provides an apt metaphor for modernity in several ways.

First, the Copernican cosmology has been repeatedly used as an
emblem of our modern sense of uprootedness, of homelessness. Copernicus translated us, in Alexander Koyré's phrase, from a closed world
to an infinite universe. It was this aspect that most impressed Nietzsche,
who anticipated that the Copernican deflation of human stature would
end in outright nihilism: "Since Copernicus man seems to have got
himself on an inclined plane—now he is slipping faster and faster away
from the center into—what? into nothingness? into a *penetrating* sense
of his nothingness'?"[30] And again: "Since Copernicus man has been
rolling from the center toward X."[31] Modernity sets us the task of
relocating ourselves and rediscovering—or perhaps reinventing—our
sense of worth against a background of cosmic indifference to us. Oliver
Wendell Holmes put the point brutally: "I don't believe in the infinite
importance of man—I see no reason to believe that a shudder could go
through the sky if the whole ant heap were kerosened."[32] And again,
"Doesn't this squashy sentimentality of a big minority of our people
about human life make you puke? . . . of people . . . who think that . . .
the universe is no longer predatory. Oh bring in a basin."[33] Holmes, the
patriarch of modern American legal thought, was, like Nietzsche, a
philosophical heir to Copernicus.

Second, Copernicanism stands as a trope for the path of rationalism and Enlightenment, the replacement of dogmatic authority with the
authority of reason. As Kant put it,

29. I am certainly not going to do the metaphor justice here. The reader should
consult Hans Blumenberg's magnificent study of the meaning of the Copernican revolution: Hans Blumenberg, *The Genesis of the Copernican World* (Robert M. Wallace trans.
1987).

30. Friedrich Nietzsche, Third Essay, in *Toward a Genealogy of Morals,* § 25, at 155
(Walter Kaufmann ed. Walter Kaufmann & R. J. Hollingdale transs. 1967).

31. Friedrich Nietzsche, *The Will to Power* § 1, at 8 (Walter Kaufmann ed. Walter
Kaufmann & R. J. Hollingdale transs. 1967).

32. Letter from Holmes to Harold Laski (July 21, 1921), *reprinted in The Holmes-
Laski Letters 1916–1935* 351 (Mark DeWolfe Howe ed. 1953) [hereinafter *Holmes-Laski*].
Almost the identical remark appears in a letter from Holmes to Morris Cohen (May 27,
1917), *reprinted in* "The Holmes-Cohen Correspondence," 9 *Journal of the History of Ideas* 1,
9 (Felix Cohen ed. 1948).

33. Letter from Holmes to John Wigmore (Nov. 1915), *quoted in* Sheldon Novick,
Honorable Justice 469n (1989).

Enlightenment is man's emergence from his self-incurred immaturity. Immaturity is the inability to use one's own understanding without the guidance of another. . . . The motto of enlightenment is therefore: *Sapere aude!* [Dare to be wise!] Have courage to use your own understanding![34]

"Dare to be wise!" sets the terms of how we are to accomplish modernity's task of relocating ourselves: we must rely not on past traditions but solely on the resources of our own understanding.

In this respect Copernicanism represents not our homelessness and inconsequentiality but our power and pride. As Lichtenberg, whom Blumenberg calls "the most thoroughgoing of the eighteenth century Copernicans,"[35] wrote of the telescope,

Without extracting humiliating reflections about man from this— reflections which, if he needs them, he can find close at hand—let us rather admire the spirit of the creature that was able to procure this knowledge by means of a bit of glass that it ground with dust. . . .[36]

Though Copernicanism may have sent us rolling from the center toward X, it hardly left us humbled in our exile; it filled us, on the contrary, with a kind of intellectual hubris. Our exile, after all, was the consequence of a stunning intellectual triumph, not of a defeat. As Lichtenberg put it in his biography of Copernicus, "Armed with reason and geometry . . . [Copernicus] finally turned the victory, by one decisive blow, to the side of truth."[37]

Third, Copernicus taught us to mistrust common sense, to view it as merely a belief system resting on criticizable presuppositions. Copernicanism insists that we abstract from the standpoint of the everyday world of sense and speech. In the most literal way, we are to view our world as though we were positioned elsewhere.[38] Positioning ourselves in thought as though we were seated directly above the sun, we discern a simple pattern of the planetary motions that is denied to us on earth. Copernicus and Galileo thereby force upon us an acute awareness of

---

34. Immanuel Kant, "An Answer to the Question: 'What Is Enlightenment?'" in *Kant's Political Writings* 54 (Hans Reiss ed. H. B. Nisbet trans. 1970).

35. Blumenberg, *supra* note 29, at 286.

36. Georg Christoph Lichtenberg, "Über das Weltgebäude," in 6 *Vermischte Schriften* 193–94, *quoted in* Blumenberg, *supra* note 29, at 619.

37. *Quoted in* Blumenberg, *supra* note 29, at 313.

38. So argues Hannah Arendt, "The Conquest of Space and the Stature of Man," in *Between Past and Future* 273–80 (rev. ed. 1968).

perspectival phenomena. They make us aware of the extent to which our experience is wholly conditioned by our point of view, and they compel us to acknowledge that other points of view are not only possible but may in some cases permit an understanding superior to our own.

Fourth, and central to the argument I have been developing, Copernicanism provided us with a new ideal of understanding: it replaced the world given to us in epics and scriptures with a world described by scientific laws. Predictive law replaced canonical narrative as the preferred mode of understanding.

Rather than attempt to provide a full intellectual history of this process, I shall examine it in the next section through a series of snapshots—exemplary historical episodes that may stand in for the more complex and profound process by which traditional narrative was marginalized. These are the first published response to Copernicus's theory, and writings of Descartes and Kant.

The Overthrow of Traditional Narrative

Osiander's Preface

It is one of the legendary episodes in the history of science that Copernicus received his newly printed copy of *De revolutionibus*, the treatise in which he announced his heliocentric theory, on his deathbed in 1543. Yet the treatise he held was not entirely his own. The manuscript had been given to Andreas Osiander, a Nuremberg clergyman and mathematician, to supervise its printing; and Osiander, unbeknownst to Copernicus, had changed the title of the book and added an anonymous preface entitled "To the Reader Concerning the Hypotheses of This Work."

Copernicus himself entertained no doubts about the straightforward and literal truth of his theory, but Osiander was deeply concerned over its heterodox religious implications and inserted the preface to defuse the scandal by deflating the book's truth claims. By this quirk of history, Osiander's preface won a place as the first philosophical reflection on the Copernican revolution. Here is what it says:

> [I]t is the duty of an astronomer to compose the history of the celestial motions through careful and skillful observation. Then turning to the causes of these motions or hypotheses about them, he must conceive and devise, since he cannot in any way attain to the true causes, such hypotheses as, being assumed, enable the

motions to be calculated correctly from the principles of geometry, for the future as well as the past. . . . [T]hese hypotheses need not be true nor even probable; if they provide a calculus consistent with the observations, that alone is sufficient. . . . And if any causes are devised by the imagination, as indeed very many are, they are not put forward to convince anyone that they are true, but merely to provide a correct basis for calculation. Now when from time to time there are offered for one and the same motion different hypotheses (as eccentricity and an epicycle for the sun's motion), the astronomer will accept above all others the one which is the easiest to grasp. The philosopher will perhaps rather seek the semblance of the truth. But neither of them will understand or state anything certain, unless it has been divinely revealed to him. Let us therefore permit these new hypotheses to become known together with the ancient hypotheses, which are no more probable; let us do so especially because the new hypotheses are admirable and also simple, and bring with them a huge treasure of very skillful observations. So far as hypotheses are concerned, let no one expect anything certain from astronomy, which cannot furnish it, lest he accept as the truth ideas conceived for another purpose, and depart from this study a greater fool than when he entered it. Farewell.[39]

Osiander's motive for disavowing the literal truth of Copernicus's theory may have been theological and political, but the argument itself consists of remarkably modern epistemological ideas. These include the Humean distinction between "true causes" and hypotheses that serve to order and organize the data; the reliance on instrumental and aesthetic criteria for theory choice (predictive power combined with simplicity); the insistence that true causes cannot be known (as Kant will later insist that things-in-themselves cannot be known); and the protopragmatist claims that astronomy does not seek certainty and that astronomical hypotheses are devised for a fundamentally practical purpose altogether different than finding truth.

  Underlying the entire argument is the perspectivalist notion that so far as truth is concerned, all hypotheses are created equal. They are mere fictions introduced for computational convenience. In that sense, seemingly contradictory hypotheses do not actually conflict; in particular, Copernicus's hypotheses do not conflict with the received geocentric tradition. At first, then, it appears that Osiander's deflation of

---

39. *Quoted in Three Copernican Treatises* 24–25 (Edward Rosen trans. 1959). For a fascinating discussion of the Osiander episode, see Blumenberg, *supra* note 29, at 290–315.

Copernicus's truth claims to avoid ruffling orthodox feathers represents intellectual conservatism, against the more radical view of Copernicus himself.

But taken to its logical conclusion, Osiander's position is just as destructive of the tradition. For if Copernicus's claims are mere hypotheses, so are the geocentric views that they replace. Osiander's argument places geocentrism among the "ancient hypotheses, which are no more probable."

Inasmuch as the traditional narratives that organized Western civilization are implicitly geocentric, they are likewise reduced to "ancient hypotheses, which are no more probable." God's parting of the heavens and the earth, the palpable and literal reality of incorruptible heaven, Joshua halting the sun in its daily motion, the music of the spheres, can no longer form the unquestioned background of daily life.

Though Osiander intended his argument to insulate Copernicus's theory from questioning, the effect is the opposite—not just for Copernicus's theory but for the traditional views it displaces as well. To call something a hypothesis is to move it from background to foreground, where it will inevitably be questioned and perhaps rejected, as Christianity had rejected the older geocentric narrative—or hypothesis—of Phoebus Apollo's chariot pulling the sun across the sky.

To treat the culture's authoritative narratives as "ancient hypotheses . . . no more probable" is in one sense the fundamental step that modernity takes out of the world of premodern tradition. The river leaves its channel; the door comes unhinged.

Descartes's *Discourse*

The devaluation of traditional narrative flits quickly by in Osiander's preface. To slow the action and watch the process unfold in greater detail, we must turn ahead a century to Descartes, the exemplary modern thinker. Descartes draws out the implications of Osiander's momentous change in outlook in his *Discourse on Method,* the work in which he makes most explicit what motivates his paradigmatically modern program. (I believe that the *Discourse* is even more significant than the *Meditations;* and the argument of the *Meditations* is incorporated in summary form in part 4 of the *Discourse.*) That Descartes had read and accepted Osiander's preface seems evident from a passage in the treatise on optics he appended to the *Discourse.* Explaining his method, Descartes tells us that he is

> imitating . . . the Astronomers who, although their assumptions are almost all false or uncertain, nevertheless, because these as-

sumptions refer to different observations which they have made, never cease to draw many very true and well-assured conclusions from them.[40]

The passage straightforwardly paraphrases the preface to *De revolutionibus* (which Descartes almost certainly assumed was written by Copernicus himself). As we shall see, the idea of false but useful hypotheses—including what he calls "fables and histories," that is, traditional narratives—plays a central role in the *Discourse*. Indeed, the idea virtually defines the literary form of the *Discourse*.

The *Discourse* takes the form of Descartes's intellectual autobiography, which he characterizes as a "history—or, if you prefer, a fable."[41] Though it is easy to overlook this brief remark, it is among the most significant in the *Discourse*, for within the next few paragraphs Descartes explicitly couples histories with fables three more times and in effect gives us directions on how to read his book.

First, he tells us that "the delicacy of fables revives the spirit" while "the memorable actions of history exalt it."[42] Then he says that shortly after his education was completed, he gave up reading histories and fables, for "conversing with men of past ages is somewhat like traveling," and "when one spends too much time traveling, one must eventually become a stranger to one's own country."[43] Finally, he cautions that "fables portray many events as possible when in fact they are not; and even if the most faithful histories neither change nor augment the value of things to make them more worthy of being read, they almost always omit the basest and least illustrious circumstances."[44]

Descartes could hardly be more explicit in warning us, first, that his account is frankly hortatory in intent (it should revive and exalt the spirit); second, that it should not be read literally—it may have omitted the basest circumstances from the story of his life or presented as possible that which is not; third, that it should be read as a modern counterpart to the histories and fables of the ancients.

---

40. René Descartes, *Discourse on Method, Optics, Geometry, and Meteorology* 66–67 (Paul J. Olscamp trans. 1965).

41. *Id.* at 5. Here and subsequently I shall also cite to the more common Haldane and Ross translation. The present passage appears in 1 *The Philosophical Works of Descartes* 83 (Elizabeth S. Haldane & G. R. T. Ross trans. 1911) [hereinafter *HR*].

42. Descartes, *supra* note 40, at 6. I have corrected Olscamp's translation; he uses the word *myths* for the French word *fables*. Cf. 1 *HR* 84.

43. Descartes, *supra* note 40, at 7.

44. *Id.* at 7. Again, I have corrected Olscamp's translation of *fable* as *myth*. Cf. 1 *HR* 84–85.

It is, in a sense, a modern substitute for the canonical narratives of the tradition. Astoundingly, Descartes proposes to replace the cultural encyclopedia with the fable or history of his own life.

Yet it is a fable or history of an entirely novel sort. In the opening paragraphs of the *Discourse*, Descartes explicitly warns his reader to accept nothing on Descartes's authority alone; this warning is also implicit in his cautions about the unreliability of histories and fables. By means of these self-undermining admonitions, Descartes transposes the traditional genres of history and fable into an Enlightenment key: he presents his own life as an *exemplary* tale, but not as an *authoritative* tale. The message of Descartes's example is to think for yourself, rather than following the message of examples. Dare to be wise! In true modernist style he invites the critique of his own critique.

It is necessary to create such a modern substitute for the histories and fables of the ancients, Descartes tells us, once one notices that "many things . . . were commonly accepted by other great peoples, although they seemed extravagant and ridiculous to us."[45] This suggests that things *we* commonly accept might be equally extravagant and ridiculous—Osiander's perspectivalist insight that our time-honored beliefs should be regarded as simply one set of hypotheses among many ancient hypotheses no more probable.

Indeed, this perspectivalist insight was already implicit in Descartes's cunning analogy, quoted above, between "conversing with men of past ages"—his metaphor for studying histories and fables—and traveling abroad. The analogy allows Descartes to identify immersion in one's own tradition with a voyage that "makes one a stranger in one's own country"! This is surely one of the most stunning rhetorical reversals on record. One's own tradition is like a foreign land: only the present, and indeed one's own mind, is native territory.

Descartes, therefore, "learned to have no very firm belief in anything that had been taught to me only by example and custom."[46] Yet example and custom are precisely the two forms of teaching available to traditionalist culture.

Traditionalist culture is, after all, a mélange of examples (histories, fables, scriptures) and customs amassed in haphazard strata like the layers of an ancient city unearthed in an archaeological dig. It is this very image that Descartes next discusses, in one of the *Discourse*'s most celebrated passages.

---

45. Descartes, *supra* note 40, at 10; 1 *HR* 87.
46. Descartes, *supra* note 40, at 1; 1 *HR* 87.

[O]ften there is not as much perfection in works composed of many pieces, and made by many masters, as in those on which one man alone has worked. . . . Thus those ancient towns which were nothing but hamlets in the beginning, and in the course of time have become great cities, are ordinarily so badly planned, compared to those regular districts that an engineer lays out on a plain according to his own imagination, that although when we consider each of their buildings by itself, we often find as much or more beauty as in those of the latter, nevertheless when we see how they are arranged—here a large building, there a small—and how their streets are crooked and uneven, we would say that it was chance, rather than the wills of some rational men, which so disposed them.[47]

For Descartes, the legacy of the past is nothing but an obstacle to the beauty that a single mind can create on a tabula rasa. He adds, "It is difficult to do good things when working with nothing but the works of others."[48] At this point, as at so many others, Descartes anticipates Kantian enlightenment, humanity's "emergence from . . . self-incurred . . . inability to use one's own understanding without the guidance of another."[49]

The climax in Descartes's reconstructed fable or history occurs in part 5 of the *Discourse*. Having derived his method and completed the metaphysical preliminaries that make up the *Meditations*, Descartes proceeds in part 5 to rewrite the history of the creation as it is given in Holy Scripture. (One hears Osiander's phrases echoing, "Let us therefore permit these new hypotheses to become known together with the ancient hypotheses. . . .")

I . . . resolved to . . . speak . . . of what would happen in a new world, if God were now to create somewhere, in imaginary space, enough matter to compose it, and if he agitated the parts of this matter diversely and without order, so that he made of it a chaos as confused as the poets can imagine, and if afterwards he did nothing else except lend his ordinary support to nature, and left it to act according to the laws which he established.[50]

Of course, this imaginary world is really our world, as Descartes emphasizes when he writes that "even if God had created many worlds,

47. Descartes, *supra* note 40, at 11; 1 HR 87–88.
48. Descartes, *supra* note 40, at 11–12; 1 HR 88.
49. Kant, *supra* note 34.
50. Descartes, *supra* note 40, at 35; 1 HR 107.

there would have been none of them where these laws failed to be observed."[51]

In true biblical fashion, Descartes begins with a discussion of the nature of light (Genesis 1:3–4, 14–17):

> I undertook to do no more than expose quite amply . . . what I conceived the nature of light to be. . . . After that, I showed how the greatest part of the matter of this chaos must, according to these laws, become disposed and arranged in a certain way, which would make it similar to our heavens; how, meanwhile, some of its parts must compose an earth, some compose planets and comets, and some others a sun and fixed stars.[52]

Following the order of Genesis, Descartes goes on to explain the nature of inanimate bodies, then plants, then animals, and finally humanity. He locates the difference between humanity and the other animals in the capacity for language and thus for reason. Just as Adam took over the stewardship of creation by naming the animals in Eden (Genesis 1:19–20), Descartes teaches that the method of right reasoning will enable us to find a new philosophy, "a practical one, through which, knowing the force and action of fire, water, air, the stars, the heavens, and all the other bodies which surround us," we can "make ourselves the masters and possessors, as it were, of nature."[53] Here he echoes the biblical promise that humanity will "have dominion over the fish of the sea, and over the fowl of the air, and over the cattle, and over all the earth, and over every creeping thing that creepeth upon the earth" (Genesis 1:26, 28–29). Or rather, Descartes replaces the biblical promise with a new scripture and a new covenant.

In sum, Descartes's warnings about the epistemological shortcomings of fables and histories undermine the claim of epics and scriptures to be canonical, or even reliable. His substitution of his own autobiography, coupled with warnings that admonish readers to treat it merely as an inspiration to their own inquiry, replaces tradition with the ideal of enlightenment; and his "disenchanted" scientific version of the Book of Genesis introduces a new paradigm of knowledge, the scientific explanation, that aims on explicitly pragmatic grounds to displace narrative at the epistemological summit.

---

51. ". . . il n'y en saurait avoir aucun où elles manquassent d'être observées." Descartes, *supra* note 40, at 36; 1 *HR* 108.
52. Descartes, *supra* note 40, at 35–36; 1 *HR* 107–8.
53. Descartes, *supra* note 40, at 50; 1 *HR* 119.

Kant's "Conjectural Beginning of Human History"

Curiously, Kant came subsequently to adopt Descartes's literary genre of a rewritten and "disenchanted" Book of Genesis in his 1786 essay "The Conjectural Beginning of Human History"—an essay that is remarkable in many ways but not least because it demonstrates the extent to which traditional narrative had become devalued.

Kant's aim in the essay, he tells us, is "a historical account of the first development of freedom from its original predisposition in human nature," an account that "one may attempt to establish . . . on the basis of pure conjecture."[54] Immediately after announcing this aim, however, Kant warns us that

> conjectures cannot make too high a claim on one's assent. They cannot announce themselves as serious business, but at best only as a permissible exercise of the imagination guided by reason, undertaken for the sake of relaxation and mental health.[55]

Therefore, "Because I here venture on a mere pleasure trip, I may hope to be favored with the permission to use, as a map for my trip, a sacred document; and also to fancy that my trip—undertaken on the wings of the imagination, albeit not without a clue rationally derived from experience—may take the very route sketched out in that document."[56]

What follows, then, is a speculative history of the development of human reason and the early stages of human culture, mapped onto Genesis 2–6, that is, from shortly after the creation of Adam and Eve to shortly before the Flood.[57] Kant's account forms a remarkable counterpoint to Descartes's, for, like Descartes, Kant rewrites Genesis in a way that dispenses with divine agency and interprets the story of the Fall as nothing less than the internally powered natural history of reason itself. For Kant, moreover, the loss of paradise is no fall but rather the transition from animality to humanity and the beginning of a glorious destiny, the progress of reason toward Enlightenment.[58]

Though much else in Kant's account is equally interesting, I want to turn from the substance of his argument to its treatment of traditional narrative. The main point to observe is this: *everything that Kant says*

---

54. "Conjectural Beginning," in Kant, *On History* 53 (Lewis White Beck ed. Emil Fackenheim trans. 1963).

55. *Id.*

56. *Id.* at 53–54.

57. For pertinent analysis of the substance of Kant's argument, see William A. Galston, *Kant and the Problem of History* 70–102 (1975).

58. Kant, *supra* note 54, at 59–60.

*about the epistemological status of his rewrite of Genesis holds for the original
as well.* For both of them depict a stage in human development for
which no genuine and authenticated records exist. Above all, scripture
is now mere conjecture—Osiander's "ancient hypotheses." And as
such, scripture "cannot make too high a claim on one's assent," for
conjectures are not "serious business." They "are no match for a history
which reports the same events as an actually recorded occurrence, and
which is accepted as such a report."[59] Indeed, scripture is now nothing
more than a map that the imagination may use for a pleasure trip.

At this point, traditional narrative has reached its epistemological
nadir. It is too unscientific to serve as anything more than a stimulus to
the imagination, useful only as an allegory for the natural history of
reason.

Modernity in Legal Theory: The Case of Holmes

Within legal theory, the effect of Copernican scientific rationalism was
to discredit the two traditional modes of securing the legitimacy of legal
authority. These are the derivation of law from an authoritative narrative (a national epic, a scripture, a reservoir of precedents) and the
derivation of natural law by philosophical argument from an underlying moral order. I have been discussing the former; let us now consider
the latter.

As we have seen, the Copernican revolution led to a reassessment
of our place in the order of things, translating us from a closed, geo- and
anthropocentric world to an infinite and indifferent universe—a universe, moreover, in which we are not only insignificant but are also
mere natural phenomena among other natural phenomena. These cosmological facts raise the possibility that there simply *is* no moral order
from which natural law could be derived.

Moreover, the perspectival character of knowledge inherent in
Copernicanism raises two epistemological suspicions: first, that since,
as Nietzsche nicely puts it, "[W]e cannot look around our own corner,"[60] we will never be able to discover an objective moral order even if
it exists; second, that whatever moral order we think we have found is
really one that we have made ourselves.

To see these modernist themes at work in legal theory close up, we
need go no further than the writings of Oliver Wendell Holmes, whom I
propose to take as a case study of the modernist predicament in law.
Holmes is a crucial case in point, for he stands at the fountainhead of

59. *Id.* at 53.
60. Nietzsche, *The Gay Science* § 374 (Walter Kaufmann ed. 1974).

American legal theory: he was prominent among the founders of legal realism, American-style positivism, and legal pragmatism. His views on judicial restraint have influenced theorists as well as judges ever since; and his famous dicta that the life of the law is not logic but experience and that "the black-letter man may be the man of the present, but the man of the future is the man of statistics and the master of economics"[61] inspired both sociological jurisprudence and the economic analysis of law.

Both the epistemological and cosmological arguments against anchoring law in an objective moral order appear prominently in the writings of Holmes. Holmes was a thoroughgoing perspectivalist who insisted that he could not be sure "that my *can't helps* which I call . . . truth are cosmic *can't helps*"[62] nor that "ultimates for me are cosmic ultimates."[63] And Holmes employed the cosmological argument in his essay on natural law, arguing that value judgments are arbitrary because the universe is indifferent to what we hold dear. "I see no basis for a philosophy that tells us what we should want to want."[64] In this sense, at any rate, Holmes was a moral nihilist; indeed, he often advances the nihilist's typical reduction of value judgments to tastes and brute preferences:

> [O]ne's own moral and aesthetic preferences are more or less arbitrary, although none the less dogmatic on that account. Do you like sugar in your coffee or don't you?[65]

> I understand by human rights what a given crowd will fight for (successfully). . . . When men differ in taste as to the kind of world they want the only thing to do is to go to work killing.[66]

> Deep-seated preferences can not be argued about . . . and therefore, when differences are sufficiently far reaching, we try to kill the other man rather than let him have his way.[67]

---

61. Holmes, "The Path of the Law," in *Collected Legal Papers, supra* note 21, at 191.

62. Letter from Holmes to John Wu (June 16, 1923), *reprinted in Justice Holmes to Doctor Wu: An Intimate Correspondence, 1921–1932* 14 (n.d.) [hereinafter *Holmes-Wu*].

63. Letter from Holmes to Wu (May 5, 1926), *id.* at 36.

64. Holmes, "Natural Law," *Collected Legal Papers, supra* note 21, at 314.

65. Letter from Holmes to Lady Pollock (Sept. 6, 1902), *reprinted in* 1 *Holmes-Pollock Letters: The Correspondence of Mr Justice Holmes and Sir Frederick Pollock 1874–1932* 105 (Mark DeWolfe Howe ed. 1942) [hereinafter *Holmes-Pollock*].

66. Letter from Holmes to Laski (Dec. 3, 1917), *reprinted in Holmes-Laski, supra* note 32, at 115–16.

67. Holmes, "Natural Law," in *Collected Legal Papers, supra* note 21, at 312.

I don't see that . . . [reason] stands any differently from my preference of champagne to ditch water.[68]

In these views, Holmes anticipates many contemporary legal theorists.[69] The crucial conclusion that Holmes drew from the nonexistence
(or unknowability) of an objective moral order is that the foundation of
legal order is purely and simply force: "The proximate test of good
government is that the dominant power has its way."[70] Holmes admitted to Cohen that "I do in a sense worship the inevitable . . ."[71] and to
Laski that "I do accept 'a rough equation of isness and oughtness.'"[72]
He returned to this theme again and again in his writings and correspondence. The identification of law with force underlies Holmes's
attachment to judicial restraint in the face of the wishes of the legislature, which possesses "the power of Parliament—i.e., absolute
power."[73] And it appears in his famous free speech opinions, which
defend free debate on the ground that it is essential for discovering the
wishes of the dominant power in society.

There can be little doubt that Holmes believed that his "rough
equation of isness and oughtness" follows inevitably once we take a
scientific view of legal phenomena: his polemic in "The Path of the
Law," his best-known essay, against analyzing the law in moral terms
positions itself explicitly on the high ground of science battling
superstition.

Indeed, his injunction in that essay to view the law from the standpoint of the "bad man," who asks only whether the force of the state is

---

68. Letter from Holmes to Cohen (Sept. 10, 1918), *reprinted in* "The Holmes-Cohen
Correspondence," *supra* note 32, at 12.

69. See, for example, Robert Bork, "Neutral Principles and Some First Amendment
Problems," 47 *Indiana Law Journal* 1, 10 (1971), which defends the "Equal Gratification
Principle," according to which "[t]here is no principled way to decide that one man's
gratification is more worthy than another. . . . There is no way of deciding these matters
other than by reference to some system of moral or ethical values that has no objective or
intrinsic validity of its own and about which men can and do differ."

70. Holmes, "Montesquieu," in *Collected Legal Papers, supra* note 21, at 258. See also
Holmes's very similar arguments in "The Gas-Stokers' Strike," 44 *Harvard Law Review*
796 (1931).

71. Letter from Holmes to Cohen (Jan. 30, 1921), *reprinted in* "The Holmes-Cohen
Correspondence," *supra* note 32, at 27.

72. Letter from Holmes to Laski (June 1, 1927), *reprinted in Holmes-Laski, supra* note
32, at 948.

73. Letter from Holmes to James Bradley Thayer (Nov. 2, 1893), Holmes papers,
Box 35, Folder 4, Harvard Law School, Cambridge, Mass. I discuss the connection
between Holmes's philosophical views and his theory of judicial restraint in "Justice
Holmes and Judicial Virtue," in *Virtue* 235 (John W. Chapman & William A. Galston eds.
1992). The text of the letter to Thayer is quoted in full in *id.* at 262 n.58.

likely to hinder his schemes, seems self-consciously modeled on the Copernican revolution. Viewing law morally is Ptolemaic, whereas the bad man's point of view offers us the authentic heliocentric perspective on legal phenomena. Only by understanding law from the bad man's point of view can you "catch . . . a glimpse of its unfathomable process, a hint of universal law."[74] We understand human law, evidently, by finding universal laws underlying it—laws that must ultimately refer to the forces that are the only ultimate actualities.

Given such intellectual ambitions, it is hardly surprising that Holmes's judicial opinions typically abjure narrative richness in their factual recitals, paring cases down as far as possible to bare legal principles. As Holmes wrote to Frankfurter, "I am afraid that I wish to know as little [about a case] as I can safely go on."[75] His dictum that "[g]reat cases, like hard cases, make bad law"[76] signals plainly that the local significance of a case simply makes no difference from a legal point of view: cases are "called great, not by reason of their real importance in shaping the law of the future, but because of some accident of immediate overwhelming interest. . . ."[77]

Several commentators have remarked on his extraordinary sense of disengagement and detachment in judging; Yosal Rogat entitled his well known article about Holmes "The Judge as Spectator."[78] Holmes viewed judging as a job, as a craft, as a kind of soldierly duty, but not as a public calling. This no doubt makes Holmes a rather unusual judge; but his aloof and intellectualized view of the law makes him a paradigm of the modern legal scholar. Ironically, Holmes as a judge resembled George Priest's portrait of the legal scholar more closely than Priest's depiction of the judge. In this sense, Holmes was truly a prophetic figure: the very traits that made Holmes an atypical jurist define the nature of contemporary legal scholarship.

Statist and Communitarian Liberalism

I do not maintain that Holmes's infatuation with force typifies all modern legal theory, but it in many respects offers a paradigm of how legal

---

74. Holmes, "The Path of the Law," in *Collected Legal Papers, supra* note 21, at 202.

75. Letter from Holmes to Frankfurter (Dec. 3, 1925), *quoted in* Philippa Strum, *Louis D. Brandeis: Justice for the People* 311 (1984).

76. Northern Securities Co. v. United States, 193 U.S. 197, 400 (1904) (Holmes, J., dissenting).

77. *Id.*

78. Yosal Rogat, "The Judge as Spectator," 31 *University of Chicago Law Review* 213 (1964); *see also* Thomas C. Grey, "Holmes and Legal Pragmatism," 41 *Stanford Law Review* 787 (1989).

theorists think. In place of canonical narratives and arguments about natural law, theorists from the nineteenth century on sought to anchor authority in something objective, something scientific, something "there."

The connection between legal positivism, which locates authority solely in the ascertainable pronouncements of the sovereign state, and scientific positivism, which mistrusts entities whose existence cannot be empirically verified, is too well known to require comment. More noteworthy is the fact that legal positivism has seemed so obviously correct to secular theorists from Austin on, even in the face of decisive objections.[79] I take this to indicate the tremendous pull that the notorious "normative force of the actual" exerts on legal theorists in the scientific age. (As usual, Holmes put the point pungently: "I don't believe much in anything that is, but I believe a damned sight less in anything that isn't."[80]) Positivism alone seems to ground authority in something actual.

I believe that something like an official account of the legal order has emerged from the various nineteenth- and twentieth-century efforts to fashion a legal science. The centerpiece of this account is the sovereign state, which issues top-down directives and creates a scheme of rights aimed first and foremost at securing social order. The state's interpretations of these directives and rights are the sole authoritative interpretations, and they impose legal obligations with which individuals are responsible for complying. Steady social progress will result from top-down legislative actions coupled with more perfect adherence to the law.[81] The state aims primarily at the protection of its citizens, not at their participation, though of course rights of participation and mobilization may be among those protected. And the state should recognize the so-called rule-of-law virtues, including neutrality and limits on official discretion, partly because the rule of law improves the efficiency with which the state's directives are administered[82] but partly because, in line with its statist preoccupations, this view perceives the main danger in society to lie with the abuse of state power rather than with private oppression. I call this official account *statist liberalism*. Though statist liberals need not worship force quite as overtly as does Holmes, I

---

79. The crispest and most devastating such argument that I know of is Lon Fuller's critique of positivism in *The Law in Quest of Itself* (1940).

80. Letter from Holmes to Wigmore (Dec. 4, 1910), *quoted in* Grey, *supra* note 78, at 812.

81. Kant argued both these points explicitly in "The Strife of the Faculties," in *On History, supra* note 54, at 151–52.

82. *See* Joseph Raz, "The Rule of Law and Its Virtue," 93 *Law Quarterly Review* 195, 198 (1977), *reprinted in* Raz, *The Authority of Law* (1979).

think it is plain that statist liberalism is fundamentally a doctrine that anchors legal authority in force just as surely as does Holmes.

These essays defend an alternative view that I call *communitarian liberalism*, which I base on the thought and practice of Martin Luther King. While retaining the importance of rights and the rule of law, communitarian liberalism makes relationships among citizens, rather than between citizens and the state, the primary focus of a legal order. It regards justice, not order, as the paramount legal value and does not privilege official interpretations of law over alternatives percolating through the society. Social progress will result not from top-down legislative directives but from direct political action within the community that impels fundamentally inertial (or inert) legislatures to act. Communitarian liberals admit group responsibility, not just individual responsibility, into the law, and they are concerned just as much with the private oppression of one group by another as they are by the oppressive misuse of state power. Because they downplay the authority of the state, communitarian liberals also attach little significance to national sovereignty and find human rights as important as state-created rights. My version of communitarian liberalism is thus a cosmopolitan view. In this I differ markedly from many contemporary communitarians, who repudiate cosmopolitanism and embrace the hallucination that human beings attain fulfillment only within ethnically, racially, or religiously homogeneous communities. Finally, communitarian liberalism puts a premium on political participation.

Though I think communitarian liberalism appealing in its own right, part of its attraction undeniably lies in the inadequacies of the statist alternative, which I explore at length in chapters 5, 6, and 7. Yet criticizing statism as a political theory is bound to remain unconvincing as long as we remain wedded to a picture according to which we can understand legality, normatively as well as descriptively, only through causal laws linking official actions to social effects. For this reason it is crucial to see the limits of causal explanation in legal and political affairs and to insist on the ineliminability of narrative, which compels us to attend to law's communitarian side just as surely as causal explanation compels us to attend to the forces mobilized by the state.

Stories as Explanations

Kant's Prophetic History

Holmes understood that scientific explanation, not epic and scripture, forms the canonical source of knowledge in modern societies. Yet the fact that narratives have lost their canonical status does not mean that narrative plays no role in explanation. In particular, narrative offers our most important mode of understanding social, political, and legal events.

This is due in part to the fact that predicting individual historical events (and, in most cases, even statistical trends) is so hopelessly beyond our abilities that when it comes to human affairs we are more inclined to take as our central cognitive task coming to terms with the past rather than predicting the future. It is due also to the enormous role of the accidental and fortuitous in history; as Sidney Morgenbesser has observed, "To explain why a man slipped on a banana peel we do not need a general theory of slipping."[83] And, I suggest in chapter 4, it is due to the fact of human freedom—or, as one might put it in methodological terms, the ineliminability of the concept of intention from explanations in the social sciences.[84]

As one might expect, this final point is quite congenial to Kant, the preeminent philosopher of freedom. Though Kant's "Conjectural Beginnings" completes the demotion of traditional narrative implicit in Osiander's preface, Kant also turns the Copernican metaphor to different purposes and points the way toward a renewed appreciation of narrative as a mode of understanding human affairs. In a sense, Kant journeys straight through Copernican modernity to its further side.

In one of his final works, *The Strife of the Faculties*, Kant considers whether the future development of humanity is predictable on the basis of experience. He concludes that the question cannot be answered by direct examination of the course of human affairs, for "we are dealing with beings that act freely, . . . of whom it may not be predicted what they will do."[85] In another essay, Kant acknowledges that we can find precise statistical or actuarial regularities in human behavior but points out that that will not help us in predicting any concrete events.[86] Hu-

---

83. "Scientific Explanation," in 14 *International Encyclopedia of the Social Sciences* 122 (David Sills ed. 1968).

84. On this point, see Jon Elster, *Ulysses and the Sirens: Studies in Rationality and Irrationality* 1–35 (rev. ed. 1984). And on the irreducibility of intentions to beliefs and desires, see Michael Bratman, *Intentions, Plans, and Practical Reason* (1987).

That Holmes believed in the possibility of eliminating talk of intention from social scientific explanation doubtless derives from the fact that he was a hard determinist: "Just as when certain rays meet and cross there is white light at the meeting point, but the rays go on after the meeting as they did before, so, when certain other streams of energy cross, the meeting point can frame a syllogism or wag its tail." Letter from Holmes to Wu (May 5, 1926), *Holmes-Wu, supra* note 62, at 35–36.

85. Kant, "The Strife of the Faculties," in *On History, supra* note 54, at 140.

86. Kant, "Idea of a Universal History from a Cosmopolitan Point of View," in *On History, supra* note 54, at 11.

man freedom cannot be captured in causal laws; knowing the annual birth rate for their age cohort will not help a couple decide whether or when to have children, nor will it enable an observer to predict their decision. Moreover, in its general tendencies, humanity seems sometimes to be advancing in the direction of greater culture and civilization, at other times relapsing into barbarism, in a pattern that seems thoroughly haphazard and unpredictable.

Remarkably, however, to Kant this suggests a Copernican strategy:

> If the course of human affairs seems so senseless to us, perhaps it lies in a poor choice of position from which we regard it. Viewed from the earth, the planets sometimes move backwards, sometimes forward, and sometimes not at all. But if the standpoint selected is the sun, an act which only reason can perform, according to the Copernican hypothesis they move constantly in their regular course.[87]

It is interesting to note the difference in outlook between Kant and Nietzsche: For Nietzsche, it is Copernicus who placed us on an inclined plane to nowhere, to nihilism; but for Kant, it is pre-Copernican thinking that renders the course of human affairs haphazard and meaningless and thereby poses the gravest threat to our sense of the value of life. In one work, Kant claimed that if human affairs are as haphazard as they appear, life "in the long run . . . becomes a farce."[88] And elsewhere he insisted that "such a spectacle would force us to turn away in revulsion. . . ."[89]

Unfortunately, however, the fact of human freedom means that the heliocentric point from which human history would assume a sensible pattern is inaccessible to us. It is accessible only to Providence, "which is situated beyond all human wisdom, and which likewise extends to the free actions of man."[90]

Kant's Copernican turn, then, concludes in an irony of reason: on the one hand, human affairs appear haphazard only because of our Ptolemaic perspective on them; on the other, the fact of human freedom forecloses us from the heliocentric perspective that alone would enable us to perceive the regularities that underlie social life.

---

87. Kant, *supra* note 85, at 140.
88. Kant, "Theory and Practice," in *Kant's Political Writings, supra* note 34, at 88.
89. Kant, "Idea of a Universal History," in *On History, supra* note 54, at 25.
90. Kant, "The Strife of the Faculties," in *On History, supra* note 54, at 142.

Remembrance of Things Past

This is where stories come in. The most obvious distinguishing feature of a story is that it relates a contingent series of events in a temporal sequence. Though the story may suggest explanations of why the events took place as they did, the fundamental point is simply that they did take place (though in a fictional story they took place in a fictional world). The story is the ideal vehicle for communicating the brute contingency of facts.

In particular, it is the ideal vehicle for communicating contingent facts that may be causally overdetermined, as I believe political events typically are. As I argue in chapter 4, if events are overdetermined, then the choice of explanatory laws is underdetermined, so the effort to seek meaning in scientific explanations of the events is doomed to failure.

This point is easiest to appreciate when we consider the distinction between foreground and background conditions in causal explanations. I strike a match and it bursts into flame; but it will not do so unless it is dry, and the atmosphere contains oxygen, and the laws of chemistry obtain, and innumerable similar assumptions hold. Each of these, like my striking of the match, is a *contributing condition* of the match bursting into flame.[91] In one respect, all contributing conditions are created equal: nothing intrinsic signals that striking the match, rather than the laws of chemistry obtaining, is the cause of ignition. It is only for pragmatic purposes that we distinguish foreground contributing conditions (e.g., striking the match) from background contributing conditions (e.g., the presence of oxygen) and adopt the convention of awarding causal honors to the foreground conditions alone.

When we turn from physical to social science, however, we encounter the brute fact of human plurality, the multiplicity of individual

---

91. To be more precise, each is a so-called INUS condition: an *I*nsufficient but *N*ecessary part of an *U*nnecessary but *S*ufficient condition of the match bursting into flame. The argument and terminology come from J. L. Mackie, "Causes and Conditions," 2 *American Philosophical Quarterly* 245 (1965). It is easiest to grasp the notion of INUS conditions by working through an example clause by clause. The whole complex of match-striking-under-appropriate-conditions is *sufficient* for the match to ignite, since we are stipulating that under these conditions it *does* ignite. But the complex is *unnecessary*, inasmuch as a different complex of events (throwing the match into a furnace, for example) could also cause it to ignite. Each component of the match-striking-under-appropriate-conditions complex—the dryness of the match, for example—is *necessary* for the complex to ignite the match, since if any component is taken away the match will not light; but no component is *sufficient*, since the other components are equally necessary. Hence, the dryness of the match is an insufficient but necessary part of an unnecessary but sufficient condition of the match igniting. *See also* H. L. A. Hart & Tony Honoré, *Causation in the Law* 32–38 (2d ed. 1985).

perspectives on a given event. From each participant's perspective, the activities of some other participants (often his or her own activities) occupy the foreground while those of many others recede to the background. This phenomenon of plurality—it is equivalent to Kant's assumption of human freedom—guarantees that no single causal explanation can hope to elicit general agreement. Plurality ensures that we will not be able to agree on how contributing conditions should be discriminated into mere background conditions and genuine causes.

Historians are accustomed to the parallel difficulty that different units of analysis and explanation can be brought to the foreground in explaining the same events.[92] Is the cause of a social phenomenon located in particular past events, as chroniclers typically suppose? In the actions of great men, as Carlyle believed? Or in class structure, as Marx argued? Or in the growth of the idea of freedom, as in Hegel? Or in technology, as Lynn White ingeniously argued when he attributed the rise of feudal society to the invention of the stirrup?[93] Or in geography, as Montesquieu and Fernand Braudel both suggest? Each of these may well constitute a contributing condition of the phenomenon, but there seems to be no way to adjudicate the debate over which belongs in the foreground; and that, too, is a consequence of human freedom. Faced with inherent ambiguity, causal explanations of past events seem unable to shed light on the present.

This perhaps helps us to see more clearly the nature of the modernist predicament. At bottom, the problem arises from what I take to be our basic existential need to make sense of what befalls us and what we do. Remarking in a speech that "[w]e are all very near despair,"[94] Holmes once catalogued the basic requirements of daily life as follows: "victuals—procreation—rest and eternal terror."[95] The canonical narratives enabled us to make sense of our lives (in the face of eternal terror) by locating them in a tradition. The Copernican revolution frayed and ultimately unraveled the authority of tradition, offering us causal patterns—"a glimpse of . . . unfathomable process, a hint of universal law"—in its place. But in the "human sciences," we cannot agree on the meaning of those patterns because we cannot discriminate foreground from background conditions in a way that seems valid from

---

92. This point has been well argued in Michel Foucault, *The Archaeology of Knowledge* (Alan Sheridan trans. 1971).

93. Lynn White, Jr., *Medieval Technology and Social Change* 1–39 (1962).

94. Holmes, "Speech at a Dinner Given to Chief Justice Holmes," in *Collected Legal Papers, supra* note 21, at 248.

95. Letter from Holmes to Frederick Pollock (Aug. 21, 1919), *reprinted in* 2 *Holmes-Pollock, supra* note 65, at 22.

all perspectives. Neither tradition nor universal law provides a meaning-giving context for what we do and suffer.

If, however, we cannot find meaning by embedding events in a larger pattern, it at least remains to us to remember and recollect, and this we do by telling and retelling stories. If the story does not win its significance through its place in a larger pattern, either a tradition or a causal explanation, it may do so because of its capacity to arouse our wonder at the sheer shape of contingency. Benjamin puts the matter beautifully: the story

> does not expend itself. It preserves and concentrates its strength and is capable of releasing it even after a long time. . . . [A] story from ancient Egypt is still capable after thousands of years of arousing astonishment and thoughtfulness. It resembles the seeds of grain which have lain for centuries in the chambers of the pyramids shut up air-tight and have retained their germinative powers to this day.[96]

Just as I took Holmes as a paradigm of the modernist predicament in legal theory, I regard Benjamin as a paradigm of the modernist response to that predicament.

In his "Theses on the Philosophy of History," Benjamin argues that traditionalism is nothing but a mirror image of the dogmatic modern belief in steady progress that underlies pragmatism as well as statist liberalism. Both presuppose that history unfolds through a medium of homogeneous, empty time.[97] Benjamin argues that our greater or lesser identification with different moments of the past, achieved through recollection and narration, implies that historical time is neither homogeneous nor empty. Historical time is not the same as clock time. I take up this argument in some detail in chapter 5. It signals a modernist view of the past—modernist, because it rejects the historicist notion that the past can be understood only in terms of tradition, while at the same time acknowledging that we cannot turn our back on the past. Instead, Benjamin invented a unique form of remembrance of the past— wrenching fragments of the past out of context and thereby destroying their familiar meaning, to dislodge us from our complacency and compel us to think.[98] If modernism consists in using the characteristic meth-

---

96. Benjamin, "The Storyteller," in *Illuminations, supra* note 24, at 90.

97. Benjamin, "Theses," in *Illuminations, supra* note 24, at 261, Thesis 13.

98. I am following Arendt's interpretation of Benjamin in her "Introduction: Walter Benjamin: 1892–1940," in Benjamin, *Illuminations, supra* note 24, at 38–51. For further useful interpretation of Benjamin's "Theses," see Jürgen Habermas, *The Philosophical Discourse of Modernity* 11–16 (Frederick G. Lawrence trans. 1987).

ods of a discipline to criticize the discipline itself, Benjamin's use of remembrance to distance us from tradition is thoroughly modernist. An obsessive focus on the past becomes the fulcrum for dislodging our attachment to the past.

Benjamin perceived that he stood in the midst of a civilization crashing into ruin; a German Jew who ended his own life to avoid capture by the Nazis, he likened himself to "one who keeps afloat on a shipwreck by climbing to the top of a mast that is already crumbling."[99] Benjamin's apprehension that his was the last generation of the European Jewish tradition made him a prototypical modernist, but he was at the same time a characteristically Jewish thinker. Jewish theology deeply influenced Benjamin, just as it did his literary hero Kafka. The driving force of Judaism is not the anticipation of heaven but remembrance—of the covenant, the Sabbath, the exodus; of the patriarchs, matriarchs, and martyrs; of parents; of the Law.

Yet Kafka, though a thoroughly Jewish writer, is not *just* a Jewish writer, and neither is Benjamin. Jews, after all, have had to confront the problem of finding a place in the modern world despite the destruction of our tradition. The Jewish response, of vigilant remembrance and storytelling, in this respect offers one significant paradigm (but of course only one) for modernism. Arnold Zable describes the survivors' endless reminiscences of Old World Jewish life as "a legacy of fragments, of jewels and ashes."[100] Storytelling is the stubborn effort to retain this legacy when no tradition remains to give it a home.

The aim in storytelling is not merely commemorative, however; it is also political. For Benjamin, the political significance of storytelling becomes clear once we realize two things: first, that resistance to oppression is "nourished by the image of enslaved ancestors rather than that of liberated grandchildren";[101] second, "that *even the dead* will not be safe from the enemy if he wins."[102] Everyone who has heard neo-

---

99. Letter from Benjamin to Gershom Scholem (April 17, 1931), *quoted in* Arendt, "Introduction," in *Illuminations, supra* note 24, at 19.

100. As he rides the Trans-Siberian Railway to Poland, on a visit to the home city of his ancestors, Zable reflects, "What was it they were trying to convey, our elders, when they told us their stories? . . . [T]hey talked endlessly about the past, sometimes lovingly, sometimes with great venom. Their stories were like the Siberian night sky as it appears now above the train, streaking starlight between spaces of darkness; and this is where their tales petered out, into an infinite darkness they called the Annihilation. They left a legacy of fragments, of jewels and ashes, and forests of severed family trees which their children now explore and try somehow to restore." Arnold Zable, *Jewels and Ashes* 23–24 (1991).

101. Benjamin, "Theses," in *Illuminations, supra* note 24, at 260, Thesis 12.

102. *Id.* at 255, Thesis 6.

Nazis sneer, "Six million lies!" must understand this fully. At one point Zable visits an old soldier who is now the caretaker of the Krakow Jewish cemetery:

> "This is where we all come when all is said and done", mutters the old soldier. "Our bodies are stripped, cleaned, tidied up, carried through the door and, so, it is over; we become mere memory. The memory fades and is transformed into history. In time the history is distorted, denied, impossible to believe, and we are reduced to absolutely nothing, zero, not even a figment of the imagination."[103]

Or, as Benjamin warns, "Every image of the past that is not recognized by the present as one of its own concerns threatens to disappear irretrievably."[104]

Benjamin believed that traditionalists inevitably empathize with victors and rulers and that "cultural treasures" are in actuality spoils of victory whose origin we "cannot contemplate without horror." The political task of the storyteller is consequently to "brush history against the grain."[105] I take Robert Cover to be arguing the same point when he insists, in "*Nomos* and Narrative," that the narratives by which the U. S. Supreme Court gives meaning to the Constitution have no more claim to validity than the narratives of groups such as the Amish and Mennonites. The Supreme Court obviously has force on its side, and from a statist point of view that fact distinguishes it from other interpreters. Like Benjamin and Cover, I mean to suggest that resistance to superior force lies in recollection and storytelling, the practice of *samizdat*.

Critical Legal Studies

Who within legal theory can claim to be Benjamin's heir? That lot, I believe, falls to the Critical Legal Studies movement, which alone seems aware of the modernist predicament in the contemporary legal context and takes up Benjamin's strange work of critique through recollection—though I suspect that few of the Critics would describe their work in these terms. Indeed, the views I defend in this book differ in many respects from the main line of work in CLS, and it is therefore worthwhile to explain how my views relate to those usually associated with CLS.

Critical Legal Studies is perhaps best known for its efforts to show that legal decisions, which apologists depict as inevitable consequences

---

103. Zable, *supra* note 100, at 171.
104. Benjamin, "Theses," in *Illuminations, supra* note 24, at 255, Thesis 5.
105. *Id.* at 256, Thesis 7.

of legal authority, in fact represent contingent (and contestable) political choices. According to the Critics, every legal doctrine is coupled with a counterdoctrine that underwrites its exceptions. In closely balanced cases, the choice between a doctrine and its complement escapes the sense of arbitrariness only by a selective and tendentious presentation of the facts calculated to invoke one principle rather than the other. The use of precedents is likewise tendentious, typically turning on analogies that seem plausible only from the perspective of power (the perspective of whites rather than African-Americans, of men rather than women, of capital rather than labor). In reality, the Critics insist, closely balanced cases are much less determinate than official legal reasoning makes out.

Some Critics believe that every case is closely balanced and thus that every case is indeterminate. But not me. It seems plain to me that there are easy legal questions that admit of determinate right answers. These questions usually do not occur to us, precisely because they are so easy that no one would dream of litigating or disputing them. Can I withhold rent from my landlord because he is ugly? Can I recover damages from you because it offends me that the square root of two is irrational? Could the holding in *Brown v. Board of Education* be based on the Third Amendment (or the constitution of Sweden)? These are easy questions with determinate answers. For that matter, even hard questions can have determinate answers: that it is difficult to sort out the balance of reasons in a case surely does not show that it cannot be persuasively done. Critics often claim that when both a principle and a counterprinciple apply to a single question, the result is a "contradiction," so that the answer is necessarily indeterminate. But that is wrong. Receiving my paycheck, I face the conflict between spending my money and saving my money, principle and counterprinciple, yet that is hardly a contradiction, and it surely does not mean that rational budgeting is impossible.

Why, then, have Critics thought that all legal questions are indeterminate? Sometimes Critics base their indeterminacy arguments on contemporary theories in the philosophy of language that purport to show that all linguistic meaning is indeterminate. I regard all such theories as philosophical snake oil. As I point out in chapter 1, if linguistic meaning is truly indeterminate, speech of any kind would be impossible, and the Critics' argument would turn into sheer solipsism.

More often, I think, Critics maintain their indeterminacy thesis because they have been impressed by the difficulty of legal questions posed in real pieces of litigation. By focusing on actual litigated cases, especially cases that parties have thought it worthwhile to appeal, Critics base the argument for indeterminacy on a biased sample consisting largely of genuinely difficult issues.[106] Sociologists of law sometimes speak of a pyramid of disputing, where the vast majority of disputes occupy the base and only a small number at the apex intrude into the formal legal system. Disputes at the base will concern easy questions more often than will disputes at the apex. The actual range of litigated legal questions, and grounds for deciding them, is in fact extraordinarily narrow, and most legal rules give rise to no genuine interpretive disagreements.

Thus, I reject those views within CLS that endorse radical indeterminacy.[107] In my view, the CLS critique of legal reasoning makes sense only in cases that are closely balanced. How, in such cases, are we to understand what it is that the Critics are up to?

In chapter 5, I suggest that official legal reasoning often turns on a tendentious presentation of cases from the standpoint of dominant interests. I offer an extended example, dissecting the Supreme Court's opinion in *Walker v. City of Birmingham* upholding Martin Luther King's imprisonment for violating an unconstitutional court order. In its opinion, the Court retells the events leading up to King's arrest entirely from the point of view of hostile government authorities, omitting significant facts and ignoring inconvenient pieces of the history underlying the Court's precedents—for example, that they arose from discredited union-busting tactics. Having chosen the narrative standpoint of authority, the outcome of the case is never in question.

Though *Walker* by no means represents an invariable pattern, it is hardly atypical; and, as the Critics have demonstrated again and again, the result is law that systematically favors whites over racial minorities, men over women, capital over labor, and government over individuals.

The only way to respond is to retell the case from the perspective of the subordinate rather than the dominant interests. Though Critics often deck their arguments in an elaborate carapace of abstraction, the critical effort is at bottom narrative. I understand it as a process of

---

106. For a clear presentation of these and related arguments, see Frederick Schauer, "Easy Cases," 58 *Southern California Law Review* 399 (1985).

I do not mean to suggest that easy cases never go to trial. Sometimes open-and-shut cases go to trial because the settlement process has broken down, through stubbornness or strategic miscalculation. *See* Samuel R. Gross & Kent D. Syverud, "Getting to No: A Study of Settlement Negotiations and the Selection of Cases for Trial," 90 *Michigan Law Review* 319 (1991). Thus, even the population of tried cases may well include easy cases.

107. For an important discussion of the indeterminacy thesis, see Kenneth Kress, "Legal Indeterminacy," 77 *California Law Review* 283 (1989).

sifting through the fragments of history that judges leave on the cutting-room floor. That is, the work of Critical Legal Studies amounts on my interpretation to a Benjamin-like procedure of retrieving episodes and stories that official doctrine obscures.

The point, I wish to emphasize, is not to oppose a dominant tradition with a countertradition, though I think that some Critical scholars do make that their aim. Traditions and countertraditions now exist largely in our imaginations. The point is rather to find a plural, dispersed, and occasional set of stories, a collection rather than a tradition, that has the power to set us thinking. That is how I should like to regard my own aim in the book's final three chapters.

Substantively, these essays are at once radical and conservative. With the Critics, I agree that we currently find ourselves in a predicament in which traditional forms of philosophical and legal reasoning fail. With the Critics, I criticize statist and authoritarian legal theories, which regard social order as the paramount legal value and detest disruptive attempts to obtain justice.

Yet (in contrast to CLS) I also believe that modernist legal philosophy leads to many standard liberal and legalist conclusions: that we cannot and should not discard the vocabulary of legal rights and human rights, that the rule-of-law virtues are indispensable conditions of decency, that fair social cooperation often creates moral obligations to obey the law, that arguments about justice are not merely ideological or instrumental, and that impersonal inquiry into justice has a legitimate place in the universe of legal theory.

American Law without Tradition

In this final section, I wish to move the argument I have offered so far out of the realm of legal theory and connect it with the larger legal culture. I believe that in many ways contemporary America represents an object lesson in the modernist predicament.

The Jewish tradition vanished in the five years of the Holocaust, but Jews are not the only survivors of shattered traditions in America. African-Americans endured the assault on family, community, and self of the Middle Passage and enslavement; Irish-Americans lost their homeland in the Potato Famine. Salvadorans fled the death squads; Nicaraguans, the civil war; Southeast Asians, three decades of slaughters upon slaughters by Americans as well as indigenous armies.

The experiences of these groups differ markedly from those of the Founders, many of whose ancestors fled religious persecutions but who never suffered the traumatic destruction of home and tradition.[108] The Founders brought English legal traditions with them and created what was in many respects a traditionalist legal culture, what Thomas Shaffer has recently called the gentleman's culture.[109]

Inasmuch as it resulted from a revolution, of course, the founding of the American republic marked a radical break with the past. As Jefferson's rhetoric in the Declaration of Independence suggests, however, our political history of dependence, maturation, and independence from the parents mimics the life history of every human being. In this respect, the story of the American founding is a story of continuity and in no way signals the destruction of tradition. In fact, the revolution did virtually nothing to weaken the cultural link between Britain and the young American republic.

The fact that the American Founders retained their orientation to tradition posed a challenge to each of the outsider communities I have mentioned. Left only with fragments of their own traditions and confronting a self-assured American establishment that frequently assumes that the responsibility for adaptation lies solely with the refugees, these immigrants had to choose between assimilation and loss of the past (on the one hand) and an unequal struggle to maintain a tradition that no longer exists (on the other). The distinction between insiders and outsiders, Americans and new arrivals, pervaded American society as well as American law for much of the nation's history.

By now, however, that distinction has become an anachronism, as well as a political challenge. The erstwhile outsider communities have come to constitute so significant a part of America, culturally as well as demographically, that it scarcely makes sense to think of the erstwhile insiders as the majority culture. The loss of tradition, not tradition, now represents the norm. In this sense, today's American culture confronts the modernist predicament, with essentially the same range of alternatives that faced early modernism. There is avant-gardism, represented by the flight into counterculture, into separatism, or into gang life and the underworld. There is sentimental traditionalism, represented by exaggerated identification with ethnicity or religious fundamentalism.

---

108. Thomas Shaffer and Mary Shaffer argue that Italian-Americans also differed in this respect from the immigrant groups I have just named, and the same might be said of many others, including many East Europeans, Japanese, and Chinese. "Southern Italians, like other late immigrants, did not come here to escape oppression. . . . They came here for money; the Italians came intending to return. They were not leaving their culture; they were trying to preserve it." *American Lawyers and Their Communities: Ethics in the Legal Profession* 133–34 (1991).

109. *Id.* at 30–47; *see also id.* at 135, where Shaffer and Shaffer refer to "the gentlemanly . . . moralities of American Puritanism and of Jeffersonian republicanism."

There is pragmatic assimilation, which in the case of many minority groups means acquiescence to a long-term second-class status. There is the postmodern embrace of consumerism as the highest good. Or there is the modernist alternative of trying to forge a community out of the disconnected fragments of traditions—the "jewels and ashes" that our stories represent.

It is not only the polyglot character of American society that makes our culture modernist, however. In his compelling analysis of contemporary legal culture, Lawrence Friedman rightly stresses the significance of rapid technological and social change.[110] As the rate of change accelerates, the sheer density of events increases; as the density of events increases, our time horizons shorten and memory recedes more quickly. This phenomenon is familiar in rapidly progressing sciences such as molecular biology and particle physics, where practitioners regard 1970 as the distant past. No tradition can survive in a society whose collective memory reaches back only a decade or two; even in the sciences it has become a truism that the explosion of knowledge prevents very much from being known. Physicists joke that at its current rate of growth their primary professional journal will soon be expanding faster than light—which would not violate relativity, because the journal transmits no information.

A pluralism of disrupted traditions, coupled with rapid social change, has thus thrown our society into Copernican upheaval, the sense of dislocation coupled with hubris and a hypersensitivity to perspectival phenomena that I analyzed earlier. Dislocation sets us the task of finding identities; hubris tells us that we can forge them for ourselves; perspectivalism tells us that many such identities are possible.

The result is a popular and legal culture organized around what Friedman calls *expressive individualism*. Where nineteenth-century individualism focused on self-control and self-reliance, ours identifies the good life with the availability of the maximum number of unconstrained options, so that we are able to express our individuality in whatever way we choose:

> [T]he state, the legal system, and organized society in general . . . seem . . . dedicated to one fundamental goal: to permit, foster, and protect the self, the person, the individual. A basic social creed justifies this aim: each person is unique, each person is or ought to be free, each one of us has or ought to have the right to create or

---

110. Lawrence M. Friedman, *The Republic of Choice: Law, Authority, and Culture* 51–60 (1990).

build up a way of life for ourselves, and to do it through free, open, and untrammeled choice.[111]

We live in the republic of choice, which is equally the "life-style society." In it, even traditionalism is a life-style that is as freely chosen as any other: Islamic fundamentalism takes its place on the cultural menu alongside body building and militant sadomasochism.[112]

Friedman's hypothesis explains a phenomenon that has seemed contradictory to some observers, namely our commitment to individualist ideology (reflected, for example, in the heated denial that *we*, whoever we are, are responsible for the misfortune of *them*—Hispanics, the urban underclass, ex-wives and the children we had by them, future generations) coupled with a profound sense of entitlement to the goods of the welfare state. From the standpoint of expressive individualism, there is no contradiction here at all. Our denial of responsibility flows from our sense that individual autonomy must be unconstrained; our sense of entitlement flows from our sense that we have a right to whatever it takes to express ourselves in the life-style of our choice.

Supposing Friedman's description of our culture is accurate—and I think it is—is this a culture in the grip of the modernist predicament? In one obvious sense the answer is *yes*, but in another it is *no*. It is *yes* because of the characteristically modernist emphasis we place on the ethical importance of autonomous self-creation. It is *no* because of our culture's remarkable absence of modernist angst, its self-confidence and self-congratulation (which go side by side with the contemporary disavowal of all responsibilities). In a sense, ours is a modernist society shorn of the early modernists' anxieties, which were born of the suspicion that prefabricated life-styles are just as unacceptable as vanished traditions.

This is an important difference between us and the early modernists, because if we can enjoy the goods of modernity but avoid the evils—despair and eternal terror, in Holmes's words—then modernism hardly counts as a *predicament*.

I write from the apprehension that expressive individualism can only defer, not solve, the problems of modernism. Take the phenomenon I just described, our powerfully felt sense of entitlement coupled

---

111. *Id.* at 8–9.

112. "Even 'conformity,' so-called, is at bottom a matter of choice; people choose the group they wish to conform to. . . . The very concept of 'conformity' is distinctly modern. It implies that it is possible *not* to conform. In a truly traditional culture, there is no such concept as 'conformity,' since actual conformity to community norms is taken for granted. . . . The modern conformists, in short, though they may act like sheep, have at least chosen their flock of affiliation." *Id.* at 128.

with an equally powerful disavowal of responsibilities. Both are inevitable products of expressive individualism; the problem is that rights without responsibilities can exist only in a world of fairy-tale bounty. The extraordinary binge of borrowing in the 1980s may have been necessary to finance the life-styles that have become our sole avenue of self-expression, but it also generated record bankruptcies and public deficits in the 1990s—a palpable sign that the republic of choice is built on the shakiest of material foundations.

In electoral politics, expressive individualism is manifest in the self-destructive unwillingness of voters to tax themselves or to accept any cuts in entitlements. ("The taxpayer shouldn't have to pay for it; the government should pay for it!" as I have heard the voters' views caricatured.) In family life, expressive individualism leads to relationships that swamp under their double load of unconstrained autonomy and children neglected by parents unwilling to accept adult responsibilities. In our moral lives, it has nurtured the error of seeking selfhood in independence rather than in attachment and vulnerability.[113]

Moreover, as Friedman argues, contemporary culture has transferred authority from political and legal institutions to celebrities, "the living embodiment of choice in style of life."[114] Political leaders are now celebrities—second in importance to what Friedman calls "heroes of popular culture," but celebrities nonetheless. As such, they owe their authority not to charisma but to image and familiarity. The predictable result of this transformation has been the much-lamented degradation of politics to mass marketing, with ever-lower rates of participation and commitment on the part of citizens. In many respects the political system of expressive individualism appears to be shutting itself off.

The great virtue of expressive individualism is its acknowledgment of human plurality, its hospitality to a large culture that is a federation of smaller cultures. At the same time, however, expressive individualism offers no materials by which the larger culture can achieve that federation. I write these words soon after the 1992 Los Angeles riots have led many Americans to despair over the possibility of a genuine racial community; I write while Yugoslavs annihilate each other in civil war, Czechs and Slovaks gloomily contemplate the possibility that they are next, and radical race-hate parties garner significant support in England, France, Germany, and elsewhere. That these are

---

113. I develop the argument against autonomy in David Luban, "Partisanship, Betrayal and Autonomy in the Lawyer-Client Relationship: A Reply to Stephen Ellmann," 90 *Columbia Law Review* 1004, 1035–43 (1990); *see especially id.* at 1041–42.

114. Friedman, *supra* note 110, at 129.

manifestations of the modernist predicament may be seen from Friedman's very plausible explanation:

> [C]hoice and expressive individualism tend to destroy tribal *custom*, but tribal *identity* survives. . . . A person in our mobile world can erase most or even all of his tribal identity, through conscious choice, but he can also choose to exalt or rediscover it. He can raise it to a higher level of intensity, just as adherents of born-again religions—*chosen* religions—can burn with a flame more intense than adherents of casual, traditional, or inherited religion. . . . Modern individualism, at its core, rejects passive acceptance of fate, a soft acquiescence in one's given life-station. It fosters pluralism, and at the same time, carried to extremes, it can destroy the ethical basis on which a plural society rests.[115]

For all these reasons, my sense is that expressive individualism can do nothing more than temporarily paper over the modernist predicament.

The alternative I have sketched here offers no panacea. I write from the sense that statist liberalism cannot foster community, while antiliberal communitarianism falsely identifies community with tribe. Instead of the force of the state, Holmes's adulation of victors, I suggest that we strain to hear the voices of the defeated. In place of facile explanations, I follow Benjamin in offering the power of memory.

---

115. *Id.* at 204–5.

Part 1
Theories

Chapter 1

Legal Modernism

What are the roots of Critical Legal Studies? "The immediate intellectual background . . . is the . . . achievement of early twentieth century modernism,"[1] writes Roberto Unger in his CLS manifesto; he elaborates this modernist connection in his deep and subtle book *Passion*.[2] Mark Tushnet likewise observes that "CLS is . . . the form that modernism takes in legal thought."[3] Other CLS members also draw parallels between their endeavor and artistic modernism.

Obviously, CLS is first and foremost a movement of left-leaning legal scholars; it is also associated with distinctive theoretical claims about law. But it should be equally obvious that CLS involves sensibilities and affinities that are strikingly similar to those of an artistic avant-garde. Moreover, CLS lives in a complicated relationship to its past and to its institutional setting—it simultaneously rejects and builds upon mainstream legal theory, simultaneously reviles and depends upon the legal academy. These ambivalences are strikingly similar to the relationships of artistic modernists to premodern art (on the one hand) and to the commercial art world (on the other).

Social facts like these are never merely superficial; thus, they provide ample reason to consider carefully CLS's connection with artistic modernism. That is my purpose in this chapter. The thesis that I want to explore here is roughly this: CLS is to legal theory as modernist art was to traditional art. CLS is legal modernism.

Five Features of Modernism

I begin by cataloguing five characteristics of modern art that CLS writing evidently shares.

---

1. Roberto Mangabeira Unger, "The Critical Legal Studies Movement," 96 *Harvard Law Review* 561, 587 (1983); *see also id.* at 660–62. Republished in book form as Unger, *The Critical Legal Studies Movement* (1986).

2. Unger, *Passion: An Essay on Human Personality* (1984).

3. Mark Tushnet, "Critical Legal Studies: An Introduction to Its Origins and Underpinnings," 36 *Journal of Legal Education* 505, 517 (1986).

1. *It makes people angry.* In 1907 Matisse visited Picasso in his studio
to look at Picasso's latest painting, the epochal *Demoiselles d'Avignon*,
the prototype of Cubism. Matisse thought it was a hoax, a spoof on the
whole modern movement, and swore that he would "sink Picasso."[4]
Similarly, the premiere of Stravinsky's *Le Sacre du Printemps* produced a
riot (and one critic labeled the work *"Massacre du Printemps"*[5]).

2. *It leaves an important hunger unsatisfied.* When Braque saw
Demoiselles d'Avignon in 1908, he commented, "It is as though we were
supposed to exchange our usual diet for one of tow and paraffin."[6] As
Leo Steinberg describes it, "There is a sense of loss, of sudden exile, of
something willfully denied—sometimes a feeling that one's accumulated culture or experience is hopelessly devalued, leaving one exposed
to spiritual destitution."[7]

3. *It bursts into public surrounded by manifestos, polemics, criticisms,
labels, and words, words, words.* The phenomenon need hardly be remarked upon; it was savagely lampooned by Tom Wolfe in *The Painted
Word,*[8] a book whose title tells all. According to Wolfe, Pollock exists
only as an illustrator of Greenberg's theories, just as de Kooning illustrates Rosenberg's, and Johns illustrates Steinberg's. Artistic subject
and critical predicate have been reversed. More sympathetically,
Stanley Cavell writes, "Often one does not know whether interest is
elicited and sustained primarily by the object or by what can be said
about the object. My suggestion is not that this is bad, but that it is
definitive of a modernist situation."[9]

Nobody would disagree that these are three characteristics of modernism. The next two are more controversial.

4. *The characteristic failing of modernist work, when it fails, is not that it
is bad but that it is fraudulent,*[10] by which I mean this: art is always the
working of a medium—objects, pigments, sounds, words—but not

4. Leo Steinberg, "Contemporary Art and the Plight of Its Public," in *Other Criteria:
Confrontations with Twentieth-Century Art* 4 (1972).

5. *Quoted in* Nicolas Slonimsky, *A Lexicon of Musical Invective: Critical Assaults on
Composers Since Beethoven's Time* 197 (2d ed. 1965). Stravinsky, however, gave as well as
he got, describing Glazunov as "Carl Philipp Emanuel Rimsky-Korsakov." And Poulenc
relates that no Parisian modernist dared listen to Vienna school music, because
Stravinsky referred to *Wozzeck* as *"une musique boche"* and to Mahler as *"Malheur."* Igor
Stravinsky & Robert Craft, *Retrospectives and Conclusions* 193 (1969).

6. Steinberg, *supra* note 4, at 6.

7. *Id.* at 7.

8. Tom Wolfe, *The Painted Word* (1975).

9. Stanley Cavell, "Music Discomposed," in *Must We Mean What We Say?* 207
(1969).

10. *Id.* at 188–89.

every working of a medium is art. To offer something as a work of art is to claim that the medium has in some way been transfigured, that it is now more than objects, pigments, sounds, or words. If that claim is false, then the work is a fraud, for it holds itself out as art when it is not. Clement Greenberg described the sculpture of Anne Truitt as art that "flirt[s] with the look of nonart,"[11] and this description holds to some extent, I think, for all modernism, at least when we first see it. It sometimes crosses the line into nonart; and since it nevertheless holds itself out as art, it is a fraud. As Cavell puts it:

> If you look at a Pollock drip painting or at a canvas consisting of eight parallel stripes of paint, and what you are looking for is *composition* (matters of balance, form, reference among the parts, etc.), the result is absurdly trivial: a child could do it; I could do it. The question, therefore, if it is art, must be: How is this to be seen? What is the painter doing? The problem, one could say, is not one of escaping inspiration, but of determining how a man could be inspired to do *this*, why he feels *this* necessary or satisfactory, how he can *mean* this. Suppose you conclude that he cannot. Then that will mean . . . that you conclude that this is not art, and this man is not an artist; that in failing to mean what he's done, he is fraudulent.[12]

John Cage's *4'33"* (the notorious silent "piano" piece) crosses the line into nonart, as (in my opinion) do Ad Reinhardt's all-over-black paintings and Duchamp's urinal. Aleatoric music, like some conceptual and pop art, is fraudulent.

I do not mean to imply that fraudulence is the *only* way modernist art can fail, that modernist art admits of no judgments of quality. Obviously, dull or minor Cubist works were painted, unimaginative and tedious serial music was composed. My claim is only that the charge of fraudulence is the most characteristic accusation leveled against modernist works, especially at first. (And some modernist works, such as Duchamp's urinal, cannot *conceivably* be criticized in terms of quality rather than fraudulence.)

Finally, most controversially:

5. *The artist herself cannot know beyond a doubt that she is creating art rather than nonart or fraudulent art.* No matter how sure his own eye, Pollock could not know that his all-over drip paintings were paintings, nor could Schoenberg know that *Pierrot Lunaire* was music. By defini-

---

11. Clement Greenberg, "Recentness of Sculpture," in *Minimal Art: A Critical Anthology* 185 (Gregory Battcock ed. 1968).

12. Cavell, *supra* note 9, at 203.

tion, a fraud can take you in, and the artist is no less gullible than her audience. The artist may sincerely intend a piece to be art, but neither *being an artist* nor *sincerely intending* is sufficient to grant one more insight into what one's art has become than any other member of the community possesses.

To put it another way, modernism throws into question the essence of the art, or rather, throws into question whether the art has an essence, and opens up a number of directions in which the art can be reconstituted and recharacterized. Only if, in the bright light of the public and the fullness of time, the work sustains the level of conviction that the art of the past sustained will it prove to be an instance of its art (painting, music, legal theory) at all (by showing us something that, all along, the art was).

My first suggestion, then, is that CLS is legal modernism because it makes people angry; it leaves a hunger unsatisfied (e.g., for "serious" doctrinal analysis or practicable alternative proposals); it thrives in an atmosphere of polemic and manifesto and autocommentary; its characteristic mode of failure is quackery rather than mediocrity; and the members of the CLS movement themselves don't know—I say can't know—when they are worth taking seriously.

Neo-Kantian Modernism

The five characteristics I have just outlined constitute an *external* or symptomatic description of modernism—they concern the way modernist work is received and the way it presents itself. More important (perhaps) is an internal description of modernism. This, of course, is a subject over which much ink has been spilled, and it will scarcely be possible to find a noncontroversial internal description of modernism. (Modernism is like Marxism in that deadlier enmities form within the movement over the question of what the movement is and what it means than over anything else, including how to deal with external threats.)

I propose to distinguish two ways of characterizing modernism, one concerned with the content of modernist art, the other with its form.

For the content, I rely on Unger. He lists writers whom he considers modernism's paradigms: Proust, Joyce, Woolf, Kraus, Beckett, Bely, Kafka, Musil, Céline, Eliot, and Montale, and (among philosophers) Heidegger and Sartre;[13] he describes their primary themes in three theses:

1. "[O]ur dealings with other individuals have primacy over the search for an impersonal reality or good. And among all en-

---

13. Unger, *supra* note 2, at 33.

counters [modernists] ascribe special importance to those that put in question the relation between the requirements of self-assertion" (by which Unger means, between the requirement to open ourselves to others and the requirement to protect ourselves from them).[14]

2. "[T]he conviction that the person transcends his contexts";[15] "the intolerance of all limits."[16]

3. "The modernists often combine an acknowledgment of the supreme importance of personal love with a skepticism about the possibility of achieving it or, more generally, of gaining access to another mind."[17]

These theses stress the themes of homelessness (in the world, among other people, in one's roles) and isolation. I shall refer to this account of modernism's content as the *exile motif*—the notion of exile encompasses isolation as well as homelessness. (So does the over-worked word *alienation*, but it has come to mean so many things that I shall not make it mean one more.)

More important than the content-based account of modernism, however, is the theory of modernist form, in the wide sense that includes language (vocabulary) as well as organization (syntax). One is more likely to think of the formal experiments of Joyce and Kafka and Woolf—of stream-of-consciousness and difficult language and allusiveness and dreamlikeness and the freeing-up of plotline—than of the exile motif. In music, one thinks of tone rows and folk rhythms and dissonance; in the visual arts, of abstraction and surrealism.

In what follows, I shall be relying on a theory of modernism developed by Clement Greenberg and Michael Fried (writing about the visual arts) and Stanley Cavell (writing about music).[18] Greenberg states the basic theory thus:

> I identify Modernism with the intensification, almost the exacerbation, of [the] self-critical tendency that began with the philosopher Kant. . . .
>
> The essence of Modernism lies, as I see it, in the use of the characteristic methods of a discipline to criticize the discipline

---

14. *Id.* at 35.
15. *Id.* at 36.
16. *Id.*
17. *Id.* at 38.
18. I do not mean to imply that Greenberg, Fried, and Cavell agree in their views. Fried offers some important criticisms of Greenberg in Michael Fried, "How Modernism Works: A Response to T. J. Clark," in *The Politics of Interpretation* 221, 226–29 (W. J. T. Mitchell ed. 1983).

itself—not in order to subvert it, but to entrench it more firmly in its area of competence. . . .

The arts could save themselves from . . . leveling down only by demonstrating that the kind of experience they provided was valuable in its own right and not to be obtained from any other kind of activity. . . .

Each art had to determine, through the operations peculiar to itself, the effects peculiar and exclusive to itself.[19]

Similarly, Cavell writes, "Whatever painting may be about, modernist painting is about *painting,* about what it means to use a limited two-dimensional surface in ways establishing the coherence and interest we demand of art."[20]

The Greenberg-Fried-Cavell approach to modernism is often deemed "formalist." I think this is a misnomer, since the self-criticism of an art often manifests itself in a piece's content. The use of allusions to premodernist work, for example, is a typical modernist device: think of Manet's ironic allusion to Titian's sumptuous nude *Venus of Urbino* in his *Olympia*—a painting of a nude prostitute in the identical posture. This is surely not a formal device.[21] In line with Greenberg's initial characterization, I shall call the Greenberg-Fried-Cavell theory *neo-Kantian* rather than formalist.[22]

---

19. Greenberg, "Modernist Painting," in *The New Art* 67–68 (Gregory Battcock rev. ed. 1973).

20. Cavell, *supra* note 9, at 207; *see also id.* at 219–20 (for an elaboration in the direction of the Greenberg excerpt); Fried, "Introduction" to *Three American Painters* (Fogg Art Museum 1965).

21. Greenberg helped propagate the notion that his theory is "formalist." *See* Greenberg, "Necessity of Formalism," 3 *New Literary History* 171, 173–74 (1971).

For a discussion of Manet's use of allusion, see Fried, "Manet's Sources: Aspects of His Art, 1859–1865," *Artforum,* March 1969, at 28 [hereinafter Fried, "Manet's Sources"]. The allusion to Titian's *Venus* is analyzed in Theodore Reff, *Manet: Olympia* 54–61 (1976). An interesting recent discussion of Olympia is T. J. Clark, *The Painting of Modern Life: Paris in the Art of Manet and His Followers* 79–146 (1984). Fried and Clark consider their approaches to be competitors—see their debate: Clark, "Clement Greenberg's Theory of Art," in *The Politics of Interpretation, supra* note 18, at 203; Clark, "Arguments about Modernism: A Reply to Michael Fried," in *The Politics of Interpretation, supra* note 18, at 239; Fried, *supra* note 18—but neither of them need disagree with the other about whether the allusion to Titian is a nonformal self-criticism of art.

22. Indeed, Greenberg's notion of modernism as the attempt to lay bare the necessary conditions for the possibility of each separate art bears a distant resemblance to the philosophy of symbolic forms of the neo-Kantian philosopher Cassirer. *See* Ernst Cassirer, *The Philosophy of Symbolic Forms* (1953–57) (vol. 1, *Language;* vol. 2, *Mythical Thought;* vol. 3, *The Phenomenology of Knowledge*); Cassirer, *An Essay on Man* (1944).

Venus of Urbino, by Titian. (Credit: Alinari/Art Resource, New York.)

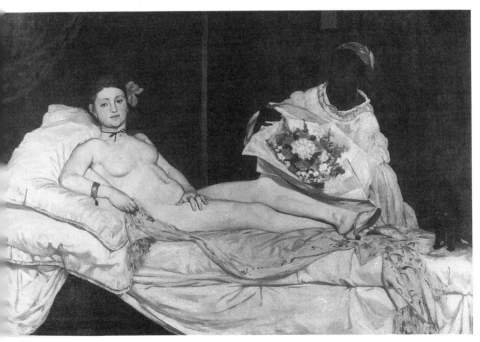

Olympia, by Edouard Manet. (Credit: Giraudon/Art Resource, New York.)

Let us see how the theory works by considering an example. A neo-Kantian account might explain the emergence of abstraction as a criticism, within painting, of the traditional conception of painting as pictorial—that is, of the idea that a necessary condition for the possibility of an object's being a painting is that it represent something.[23] By abandoning representation, Kandinsky's *Improvisations*—the first abstract easel paintings—make us see that representation was merely a convention, a limitation. For the *Improvisations* are clearly paintings of the highest quality even though they are neither pictorial nor merely decorative.

The *Improvisations*, in other words, contain the criticism of pictorial painting in them as if it were a subject matter. I must add one important qualification, however. The neo-Kantian theory of modernism is a relatively conservative one, in two ways. First, the self-criticism of an art is not simply a negation or rejection of it; it is a dialectical—though not a necessary—development of the art within the art. Modernist art is the determinate negation of premodernism. (The *Improvisations* appear to us now as a logical development and extension of the representational pictures Kandinsky and Gabriele Münter were painting in Murnau after 1908. That the turn to abstraction, though logical, was not necessary is illustrated by the fact that Münter never made the turn but nevertheless continued to deepen as an artist.)

Second, neo-Kantian modernism still seeks to live up to the quality achieved by the great premodernist works. Though modernism is suspicious of the capacity of the premodernist tradition to sustain significant art any longer, it is not suspicious of the significance of premodernist art. (Though, as we shall see, it harbors intense suspicions about the morality of premodernist art.)

For, on the neo-Kantian theory, the self-criticism of an art cannot rest content merely with abandoning conventions. Abandoning a convention is only half the demonstration that the art can get along without it: the other half, of course, is that the modernist work convinces us that it is still an instance of the art. The abstract painting must provide us with aesthetic rewards comparable to (though different from) those of a traditionalist painting. There will remain, I have said, some aesthetic

23. Greenberg himself gives a more complex account, his famous "theory of flatness" nicely mocked by Wolfe: Old Master painting, representing depth on a flat surface, dissembled about the essential flatness of the surface, making painting "sculptural." Modernist painting emphasizes the flatness of the canvas, and the abandonment of representation follows as a corollary of the abandonment of the third dimension. Greenberg, *supra* note 19, at 68–70; *see also* Greenberg, "Abstract, Representational, and So Forth," "Modernist Sculpture, Its Pictorial Past," "Byzantine Parallels," and "On the Role of Nature in Modernist Painting," in *Art and Culture* 133, 158, 167, 171 (1961).

hunger that the abstract painting does not satisfy; but as it works on us over time—and it had better not take too much time—it creates and fulfills new modes of aesthetic wanting. Otherwise it has failed—not just as a painting but as painting. Thus the neo-Kantian account continues to respect the art's tradition.

The Treachery of Images

There is a connection between the neo-Kantian account of modernist form and Unger's insistence that the exile motif is its content. The abstract artist does not criticize representational painting merely because it involves a mistaken thesis about what paintings are (i.e., necessarily pictorial). The abstract artist confronts representational painting with the much stronger charge that it *lies* about the world. It lies by using the illusionist techniques that since Brunelleschi have been its chief point of pride, in order to pretend that it is not painting, i.e., not just "flatness and the delimitation of flatness."[24] "Realistic, illusionist art had dissembled the medium, using art to conceal art. Modernism used art to call attention to art."[25] Pictorial painting is not a mistake, it is a lie. (Magritte illustrated this theme in one of modern art's most famous works, *The Treachery of Images,* depicting a highly realistic pipe beneath which is inscribed the French caption, "This is not a pipe.")

More than that: it is not just a lie about what a painting is but also about what the painting's beholder is, about the ontological relation-

---

24. Greenberg, "After Abstract Expressionism," *Art International,* Oct. 25, 1962, at 24, 30. I believe Greenberg's "theory of flatness" is directed primarily at Bernard Berenson's claim, in his celebrated 1896 essay "The Florentine Painters," that the aesthetic worth of painting resides primarily in its representation of "tactile values." Bernard Berenson, *Italian Painters of the Renaissance* 40–43 (1957). This illustrates how modernism amounts to an internal, or dialectical, criticism of traditional painting: Greenberg agrees with Berenson that the great achievement of Florentine painting lay in the representation of "tactile values"; his disagreement is over Berenson's value judgment, which Greenberg takes to be an endorsement of deception.

25. Greenberg, *supra* note 19, at 68. Brunelleschi had demonstrated his invention of linear perspective in a remarkable way, which illustrates what the modernist is complaining about. He painted the Florentine Baptistery mirror-reversed on a board, drilled a hole in the board, placed burnished silver on top of the painting (to reflect sky and moving clouds), and set the whole contrivance directly in front of the Baptistery itself, facing the Baptistery. The beholder would first look at the Baptistery, and then look through the hole in the back of the painting, holding a mirror to the painting. In the mirror, he would see the Baptistery itself; the perfection of the illusion was the proof of perspective. *See* Samuel Edgerton, *The Renaissance Rediscovery of Linear Perspective* 124–52 (1975) (an account by Manetti, a contemporary of Brunelleschi, is quoted at 127–29). I am indebted to Michael Sukale for allowing me to read an English version of his essay "Brunelleschi's Visual Demonstration," 92 *Iyyun* 129 (1980).

ship between painting and beholder.[26] The illusionist picture pretends to be a window into the scene depicted, a scene that goes on oblivious of the beholder. A traditionalist takes this pretense to be a mark of quality in the painting. Thus, Diderot wrote in praise of Van Dyck:

> If, when one paints a picture, one supposes there to be spectators, all is lost. The painter steps out of his canvas, as an actor who talks to the gallery steps out of his scene. It is in pretending that there is no one in the world except the personages in the picture that Van Dyck is sublime.[27]

But to the modernist, this pretense is morally unacceptable. The representational painter turns the beholder into a voyeur. By falsifying the nature of the painting, the painter enables the voyeur-beholder to forget herself, her predicament (a beholder confronting flatness and the delimitation of flatness).[28] A modernist painting aims to acknowledge the beholder.

To see what acknowledging the beholder means, one might look at Manet's *Old Musician* in the National Gallery of Art in Washington. Manet is often taken to be the first modernist, and this incredible masterwork plainly acknowledges the relation between painting and beholder in a novel way. The tableau includes a strange assortment of characters who, though paired, are in a state of frozen isolation from, and indifference toward, each other. The shallow space, the abstract color-field landscape, and the lack of modeling—the Old Musician's face alone is strongly modeled—all call attention to the flatness of the canvas in just the way the neo-Kantians emphasize. Similarly, the artificial bisection of the right-hand figure by the edge makes us aware of the canvas as bounded. Moreover, Manet gives the space what depth it has in the most perfunctory of ways. Take away the stage props—the grape vine in the upper-left corner, the shadows in the foreground, and the Old Musician's knapsack—and the figures will flatten and pop out like a chain of paper dolls. These are Manet's formal devices.

---

26. This way of framing the issue comes from Fried, particularly his great essay "Art and Objecthood," in *Minimal Art: A Critical Anthology* 116 (Gregory Battcock ed. 1968), and Fried, *Absorption and Theatricality: Painting and Beholder in the Age of Diderot* (1980).

27. "Si quand on fait un tableau, on suppose des spectateurs, tout est perdu. Le peintre sort de sa toile, comme l'acteur qui parle au parterre sort de la scène. En supposant qu'il n'y a personne au monde que les personnages du tableau, celui de Vandick est sublime." *Quoted in* Fried, *Absorption and Theatricality, supra* note 26, at 149.

28. Obviously, such a sweeping account of representational painting must be false in the details. For a compelling argument that seventeenth-century Dutch painting differed from Italian painting in its representational assumptions, see Svetlana Alpers, *The Art of Describing* (1983).

The Old Musician, by Edouard Manet. (Chester Dale Collection, copyright © 1993 National Gallery of Art, Washington.)

The depicted characters are figures from—that is, allusions to—paintings by Velasquez, Watteau, LeNain, and Manet himself.[29] Art is thus the content of this painting (the Old Musician is, of course, an artist). The inscrutability of the figures emphasizes the problematic, mediated character of our relation to the depicted scene. The boy next to the Old Musician and the two right-hand figures in particular appear to have been captured as it were "between poses," as in a snapshot taken a second too late. The scene thus has no narrative unity, and the only thing that holds it together is the seated figure of the Old Musician himself, gazing out at us, meeting our gaze, inviting us to make what we can of the painting, acknowledging our presence as nothing in painting ever had before. Manet seems explicitly to pose the painting-beholder relationship as the solution to a riddle, leaving us to guess what the riddle itself is.[30] Encountering the figure of the Old Musician is

---

29. Fried, "Manet's Sources," *supra* note 21, at 29–33.
30. *Id.* at 69 n.27.

like encountering a demiurge who causes us to understand that it is
only the painter's art that sustains the painting, causes us to understand
that we are seeing only a painting. And that is what makes it modernist.

Such modernist preoccupations lend themselves especially well to
incorporating the exile motif, which appears with astonishing literal-
ness in *The Old Musician*. Seven silent, unsmiling figures looking in
seven different directions, past rather than at each other: what could
more strongly evoke human isolation? They are, moreover, a band of
vagabonds on the road. The clothing of the two right-hand figures
conveys a sense of formerly comfortable living fallen on hard times; the
(motherless?) infant is cared for by a waif. We see this troupe as a band
of refugees, as displaced persons; and that is how Manet paints modernist homelessness.[31]

At the same time, *The Old Musician* seems more universal in its
meaning than a depiction of *these* people's isolation and homelessness.
The painting, in its overall inscrutability, asks to be read as an allegory. I
cannot keep myself from seeing the graybeard musician as God, silently
inviting us to ponder His creation. But then He is a God whose creatures freeze into enigmatic immobility when the animating violin falls
silent. And now it *has* fallen silent—for us, for the beholders who have
come too soon or too late to hear the Old Musician play. If some such
allegorizing interpretation bears up, the painting-beholder relationship
in *The Old Musician* becomes an almost terrifying evocation of the exile
motif writ large.

In all these ways *The Old Musician* illustrates how modernist formal
devices lend themselves to modernist content. The modernist moral
critique of traditional painting is that painting, art in general, has become a form of escapism. And, if it were not the case that some aspects
of our lives are hard to face up to, why would we need escape? The exile
is able to find solace in art; but for the modernist, such solace is purchased at the price of truth. The truth of the exile motif is our homelessness and isolation, and the painter of modern life will need to find ways
to acknowledge the beholder and the beholder's predicament.

In short, by incorporating the critique of painting into the painting
itself, modernism makes us unable to forget that what we behold is a
painting, hence unable to forget that we are its beholders, hence unable

---

31. It is perhaps not incidental that Manet's model for the musician was the leader
of a gypsy band, living in a neighborhood of Polish political refugees near the painter's
studio. Reff, *Manet and Modern Paris* 174 (1982). Interestingly, the musician appears to
have been modeled as well on an ancient statue of the philosopher Chrysippos, which
Manet sketched in the Louvre in 1860. George L. Mauner, *Manet Peintre-Philosophe: A
Study of the Painter's Themes* 50 (1975). A gypsy-philosopher seems precisely suited to an
exploration of the exile motif.

to forget ourselves, hence unable—the modernist hopes—to evade who we are. Who we are, according to the modernist, are exiles. Modernism stresses that this is our condition by exiling the beholder from the world of beautiful illusion created by premodernist art. And this is the connection between the exile motif and the neo-Kantian account of modernism.

Fried's account of this connection is worth quoting at length:

> Manet's ambitions are fundamentally realistic. He starts out aspiring to the objective transcription of reality, of a world to which one wholly belongs, such as he finds in the work of Velasquez and Hals. But where Velasquez and Hals took for granted their relation to the worlds they belonged to and observed and painted, Manet is sharply conscious that his own relation to reality is far more problematic. And to paint his world with the same fullness of response, the same passion for truth, that he finds in the work of Velasquez and Hals, means that he is forced to paint not merely his world but his problematic relation to it: his own awareness of himself as *in* and yet *not of* the world. In this sense Manet is the first post-Kantian painter: the first painter whose awareness of himself raises problems of extreme difficulty that cannot be ignored: the first painter for whom consciousness itself is the great subject of his art. . . . [T]he painting itself is conceived as a kind of *tableau vivant* . . . constructed so as to dramatize not a particular event so much as the beholder's alienation from that event. . . . [B]ut Manet's desire to make the estranging quality of self-awareness an essential part of the content of his work—a desire which, as we have seen, is at bottom realistic—has an important consequence: namely, that self-awareness in *this* particular situation necessarily entails the awareness that what one is looking at is, after all, merely a painting. And this awareness too must be made an essential part of the work itself. . . .[32]

32. Fried continues, "For this reason Manet emphasizes certain characteristics which have nothing to do with verisimilitude but which assert that the painting in question is exactly that: a painting. For example, Manet emphasizes the flatness of the picture-surface by eschewing modelling and . . . refusing to depict depth convincingly, calls attention to the limits of the canvas by truncating extended forms with the framing-edge, and underscores the rectangular shape of the picture-support by aligning with it, more or less conspicuously, various elements within the painting." Fried, *supra* note 20, at 49 n.3. This footnote bears careful reading in its entirety. Note that in the final sentence Fried is not discussing *The Old Musician*, to which, we have seen, the comments apply, but the other two paintings with which Manet is said to have begun modernism: *Déjeuner sur l'Herbe* and *Olympia*.

To put it another way, modernist art is, very literally, iconoclastic. Its preeminent concern is to remind us, for honesty's sake, that art is only art. It reminds us of this by calling attention to the conventions that constitute the art, and it does this by abandoning or unmasking those conventions. In this sense, modernism is a movement whose concern is to deny us the solace of art. (And CLS is modernist to the extent that it tries to deny us the solace of liberal legal theory.) For this reason its natural content is a grim spiritual state.

In this respect, there is nothing specially modern in modernism. Older artists have had iconoclastic concerns and have expressed them in the same ways: calling attention to the artificiality of painting by displaying its constitutive conventions and using this formal device to present an anxious, spiritually demanding content. These, I think, were the concerns of the great Florentine Mannerists of the early sixteenth century (Pontormo, Rosso, Bronzino). In such paintings as Pontormo's eerie Carmignano *Visitation* or his *Joseph in Egypt* in London's National Gallery, Rosso's *Moses and the Daughters of Jethro* in the Uffizi or his bizarre Louvre *Pietà*, or Bronzino's waxworks portraits, we find the modernist combination of disturbing content and a manner of painting that compels us to confront explicitly the (ontological) fact that it is painting.

Similar concerns preoccupied the great Bavarian church builders, the Zimmermans, the Asams, Balthasar Neumann:

> [Bavarian rococo] does not let us forget that what the painter furnishes is no more than theatre. To make this reminder explicit and to exhibit the theatricality of their art, the painters of the Bavarian rococo liked to introduce curtains into their already theatrical compositions. Divine transcendence becomes manifest only as a play within a play.[33]

(Recall Greenberg: "Modernism used art to call attention to art.")

Roll Over Beethoven

Modernist wine need not, then, appear in modernist bottles. Heidegger's *Being and Time* is perhaps the definitive philosophical exploration of the exile motif. Formally, however, it is not particularly modernistic: it is a classic ponderous professorial production, which fits comfortably

---

33. Karsten Harries, *The Bavarian Rococo Church* 125 (1983). *See id.* at 146–55 for further interesting discussion.

Visitation, by Jacopo Pontormo. (Credit: Alinari/Art Resource, New York.)

on the shelf beside Kant's *Critique of Pure Reason* and Hegel's *Science of Logic.* Wittgenstein's *Philosophical Investigations,* on the other hand, is modernist in form as well as theme, abjuring the linear philosophical argument and neat two-, three-, and four-term distinctions of the traditionalist treatise for a book of "philosophical remarks," "really only an album"[34]—the famously teasing dialogues, analogies, and aphorisms that have bewitched and befuddled two generations of philosophers.

The same distinction operates within CLS. Most CLS work treats the modernist exile motif, but in the standard, nonmodernist form of law review articles. Unger's *Passion,* however, like his manifesto *The Critical Legal Studies Movement,* undertakes a few modernist gestures. *Passion* has no footnotes whatever, nor real chapter titles, nor, for that matter, section headings. Many readers find this annoying, and some are very irritated indeed. ("Who does he think he is, that he doesn't refer to any other writers at all?") Even if one does not have this reaction, the lack of signposts makes it very dense going, rather like the multipage run-on sentences and lack of paragraphing and chapter headings in Thomas Bernhard's modernist novels.

Though I think that these formal features are of strictly secondary importance in Unger, they may be given a neo-Kantian modernist interpretation. On the neo-Kantian view, remember, a modernist painting calls attention to presuppositions of painting by violating them—violating illusionism through abstraction, for example. When Unger leaves out all the paraphernalia of legal scholarship, he invites us to ask what purpose it serves. Why must every thought be footnoted? (Is it because scholars are supposed to derive their ideas from a tradition rather than secluding themselves with their own thoughts?) Why are we afraid of argument without precedent? (Is it because lawyers commit the category mistake of equating legal theory with legal opinions, reifying the past in our thinking as we do in appellate decisions?) Why must thought be organized in outline form, with neat section headings? (Is it because a more plastic way of thinking is supposed to be unrigorous? Is it because we need slogans and labels for thoughts before we are able to recognize them?)

In general, it seems to me that Unger's austere way of proceeding is an attempt to rip down the landmarks and prepackagings that we use to negate the strangeness of thought and avoid confronting it on its own terms. If I am right, then, these formal devices are modernist in the second neo-Kantian sense as well: they attempt explicitly to acknowl-

---

34. Ludwig Wittgenstein, *Philosophical Investigations* ix (G. E. M. Anscombe trans. 1953).

edge the very problematic relationship between book and reader (beholder), by forcing the reader out of the voyeuristic mode in which we
customarily appropriate scholarship.

Passion is, nevertheless, largely traditionalist in form. It is an explicit treatment of the modernist exile motif; but mostly it is a traditional
book of philosophy or, perhaps, speculative psychology. I would now
like to consider the one CLS piece I know of that is through-and-
through modernist, Peter Gabel and Duncan Kennedy's "article" "Roll
Over Beethoven."[35]

"Roll Over Beethoven" is a dialogue between "Peter" and "Duncan," apparently the transcript of a conversation between the article's
authors. It is exhausting to read—fifty-four pages that often sounds like
a pair of old acid-heads chewing over a passage in Sartre. (One finds
sentences such as this: "Peter: It is not inconsistent to, on the one hand,
realize the projective temporal character of human existence, in which
no one is identity, and the living subject is continually not what he or
she is by moving into the next moment in a creative and constitutive
way."[36])

Roughly put, the topic of the conversation is the role of theory in
the CLS movement, Duncan accusing Peter of "betraying our program
by conceptualizing it,"[37] and Peter replying that "we can be explicit
about what it is that human beings are trying to do."[38] But this is very
rough: the conversation is complex, passing from one topic to another
in the improvisatory manner of real conversations. About halfway
through, it turns to the topic of rights, and various themes interweave
from that point on.

The tone of much of the conversation is campy, even precious.
Duncan demonstrates his impatience with the language of theory by
replacing Peter's term "unalienated relatedness" with "intersubjective
zap" and "making the kettle boil,"[39] remarking that if you don't watch
out, "the body snatchers are always nearby, and you wake up and
they're all pods. The whole conceptual structure has been turned into a
cluster of pods."[40] Academicians apparently are the body snatchers.

"Roll Over Beethoven" certainly satisfies the external criteria of
modernism. It makes people mad. (Legend has it that a well-known
professor was so upset when Kennedy presented "Roll Over

---

35. Peter Gabel & Duncan Kennedy, "Roll Over Beethoven," 37 *Stanford Law
Review* 1 (1984).
36. *Id.* at 19.
37. *Id.* at 1.
38. *Id.* at 5.
39. *Id.* at 4–5.
40. *Id.* at 7.

Beethoven" at the Columbia Legal Theory Workshop that he totaled his car on the way home.) If you're looking for scholarship, you will leave "Roll Over Beethoven" hungry; you might remark, as two well-known abstract painters did at Jasper Johns's first show, "If this is painting, I might as well give up," and "Well, I am still involved with the dream."[41]

Furthermore, "Roll Over Beethoven" appears with the maximum hype (it is the first article in the *Stanford Law Review* CLS symposium issue—the largest-selling single law review issue in history, incidentally—which is a batch of polemics and autocommentaries that would have been completely familiar in tone and purpose to the protagonists and antagonists of early modernism's art wars). It can impress readers as a complete fraud. And one can be confident that its authors are in no better position than any other reader to judge whether that is what it is.

My own initial reaction to "Roll Over Beethoven" was that it was a pile of crap. How dare they waste my time with a self-indulgent rap session! I was able to read only the first half of the article—it *is* tiring—then dipped into a few more pages to assure myself that it was all of a piece, then made fun of it to everyone within earshot. It's boring. It's rude. If Duncan Kennedy weren't notorious (and from Harvard), no journal would touch it without tongs. Gabel ought to burn his library of phenomenology and take a cold shower. Anyone can turn on a tape-recorder and reel off a lot of pretentious flapdoodle.

You recognize a classic reaction to modernism. Anyone can do a drip painting. Anyone can make random percussion sounds. It isn't real art, or music, or legal theory, or philosophy, or, or, or. . . .

I reread "Roll Over Beethoven." On second reading, it no longer struck me as insolent. Instead, I was amazed at how courageous the authors were for exposing so much of themselves, putting an intimate conversation out in public. Besides, a lot of what they are saying is quite important, quite true. But why do it that way?

I decided to read "Roll Over Beethoven" as a piece of neo-Kantian modernism. And points like the following began to stand out.

1. Why is a transcript a form of scholarship inferior to a didactic, heavily footnoted article? The purpose of scholarship is the communication and exploration of thought; why is the solitary research effort a better form of such endeavor than an intense conversation between two scholars who have a lot in common? "Roll Over Beethoven" throws into question the (quite un-Socratic!) presupposition of traditional scholarship that a monologue is a better vehicle of

---

41. Steinberg, *supra* note 4, at 13.

thought than a dialogue. And a dialogue, in turn, implies a kind of ethical relationship between its interlocutors quite different from the author-reader relationship. (And it is too, too perfect that the editors of the *Stanford Law Review* added their own footnotes to try to tame their unruly article—footnotes explaining, for example, that "body snatchers" and "pods" are references to the film *Invasion of the Body Snatchers.*)

2. "Roll Over Beethoven" confronts us with the question of whether it actually is the transcript of a taped conversation between its authors, rather than a composed dialogue between the literary personae "Peter" and "Duncan"—whether, to put it another way, it is a (mere?) mechanical production or the product of composition and virtuosity. The invidious contrast raised by this question is, of course, the site of a battle that photography had to win in the last century to be accepted as art and that a variety of modernist productions have fought ever since; and overcoming the contrast may well have changed forever our concept of what an art object is.[42]

The contrast, however, must be overcome anew every time a mechanical production process raises the worry that a piece is fraudulent. In the case of "Roll Over Beethoven," it seems to me that the contrast between mechanical production and virtuoso composition makes no difference. I do not believe that we would respect rather than revile the work if we learned that it was through-composed rather than taped and transcribed. Nor (on the other side of the ledger) would it invalidate the moral point of the dialogue form if we learned that the article was carefully written, rather than spontaneously uttered in the heat of conversation. This, I think, shows that it is a successful modernist piece. Like the first art photographs (or the film *My Dinner with André*,[43] which "Roll Over Beethoven" in many ways resembles), it demonstrates its nonfraudulence by making the question seem irrelevant. To overstate the matter, "Roll Over Beethoven" begins to change the whole way we think of a scholarly article.

3. The dialogue form perfectly exemplifies the first of Unger's modernist theses I quoted earlier: "[O]ur dealings with other individuals have primacy over the search for an impersonal reality or good. And among all encounters [modernists] ascribe special importance to those

---

42. The great discussion of this issue is Walter Benjamin, "The Work of Art in the Age of Mechanical Reproduction," in *Illuminations* 219–53 (1969). *See also* Benjamin, "Walter Benjamin's Short History of Photography," *Artforum*, Feb. 1977, at 46, 46–47.

43. New Yorker Films, 1981.

that put in question the relation between the requirements of self-assertion."[44]

4. Many people find one of "Roll Over Beethoven"'s most irritating features to be its serene presumption that the reader is interested in the minutiae of CLS internal debates and uncritically committed to the same radical values as CLS. (The piece is monumentally uninteresting to those for whom this presumption is false.) But—and this is a question that I take the piece to be inviting—what makes "Roll Over Beethoven" different in this respect from more standard law review fare? Most law review articles, after all, presume that the reader is interested in the minutiae of standard technocratic policy debates and is uncritically committed to the blandly centrist values they presuppose. It is just that we have become so habituated to these presumptions that we do not notice them. "Roll Over Beethoven" makes us notice them.

5. The subject of much of "Roll Over Beethoven" is the exile motif, the unfulfilled desire for solidarity, for unalienated relatedness, for intersubjective zap. In part the dialogical form of "Roll Over Beethoven" is supposed to illustrate what it is that we're missing, but in part it is supposed to illustrate that "Duncan" and "Peter" are missing it too.

In one crucial passage in the dialogue, Duncan and Peter are discussing a conversation some people had at CLS summer camp(!). Peter takes that conversation to be illustrative of the kettle boiling: "Everyone in the room was participating, intensely interested, and there." Duncan replies noncommittally, 8I remember it clearly";[45] Peter goes on with an analysis; and Duncan comes back as follows: "Here's what I remember about what made it a wonderful and dramatic occasion. I think this may be quite different from your memory of it. My memory may be wrong. I think the discussion was actually not a satisfactory discussion; people were not feeling good. . . ."[46] (He then goes on to explain what eventually made it animated.)

Nothing is more jarring than having someone tell you that an important memory is haywire. Indeed, if anything could count as a theme for early modernist literature, it is the elusiveness and importance of memory, the uncontrollable and unpredictable window it offers us, the solitude of being trapped in memory, as well as the solitude of being debarred from it. At this moment in the conversation, Duncan and Peter vividly confront a major component of the exile motif—in Unger's

44. Unger, *supra* note 2, at 35.
45. Gabel & Kennedy, *supra* note 35, at 12.
46. *Id.* at 13.

words previously cited, "skepticism about the possibility . . . of gaining access to another mind" (or even one's own mind).[47]

6. The dialogue form of "Roll Over Beethoven" invites the reader to question his or her own relationship to the conversation in the article. They are talking, I am (merely?) reading/beholding/eavesdropping. Is reading/beholding/eavesdropping—the partaking of the fruits of others' theoretical labor at a distance—itself a kind of estrangement? (Notice that this question is one construal of the subject matter of the dialogue: form and content fit perfectly together.) "Roll Over Beethoven" acknowledges the beholder in a modernist—that is, iconoclastic—way.

Much more could be said about "Roll Over Beethoven," but there is little need to labor the point further. In my view, "Roll Over Beethoven" is a successful modernist achievement. It keeps working on you after you have set it aside.

Avant-Gardist Modernism and the Critique of Rights

Modernism is self-critical and iconoclastic. Under its neo-Kantian interpretation, however, I have claimed that it amounts to much more (or less) than an undifferentiated negation of the premodernist tradition. It is a determinate negation of premodern art, accepting premodernism's claim to quality, denying only its power to maintain conviction now, aiming to attain premodernism's level of achievement by disassembling its constitutive conventions piecemeal.

There is another interpretation of modernism, however, one that is more in line with the leftist and counterculture sensibilities of CLS but that I wish to criticize and warn against. For want of a better term, I shall use Greenberg's and call this the "avant-gardist interpretation."[48] (Greenberg means the word *avant-gardist*—as distinct from *avant-garde*—pejoratively.)

Avant-gardism wants to bury the past, not criticize it. It proceeds from the premise that respect for the achievements of premodernism is itself suspect—perhaps because respect is produced by suspect ideology or because premodernist achievements are too implicated in cultural values that the avant-gardist wants to smash. Avant-gardism relishes the Shock of the New because it relishes shock and it relishes novelty. It doesn't trust anything over thirty.

---

47. Unger, *supra* note 2, at 38.
48. Greenberg, "Counter-Avant-Garde," *Art International*, May 20, 1971, at 16.

Avant-gardists practice a version of modernism that Unger criticizes as a "heresy" from the authentic modernist teaching.

> Their divinization of the self has often led them to pass from the conviction that the person transcends his contexts to the intolerance of all limits, whether the constraints of the body or those of society. . . . [The individual] can assert his independence only by a perpetual war against the fact of contextuality, a war that he cannot hope to win but that he must continue to wage.[49]

(Unger himself calls in *Passion* for a modernist reconstruction of a very traditional picture of personality and in *The Critical Legal Studies Movement* for a "deviationist" reconstruction of extant legal doctrine. This willingness to make the premodernist past his starting point marks these as neo-Kantian rather than avant-gardist works.)

The avant-gardist interpretation sees modernism primarily as cultural-revolutionary context-smashing—as the attempt to do away with art rather than find new ways to make it. It does not care to disassemble an art's constitutive conventions, so that through their absence we can understand what their presence meant; it simply wants to destroy them. Growing out of Dada and Surrealism, avant-gardism achieved something of a mass following in the 1960s and 1970s in the form of Happenings, multimedia art, some Pop Art, some rock, some punk and New Wave.

I will shortly consider the impulse to avant-gardism a bit more deeply and suggest that this impulse is realized in some of the postmodernist theory CLS scholars use. First, however, I want to ask why the avant-gardist interpretation of modernism is attractive to those of left political views, including CLS.

One of the attractions of avant-gardism to leftists is its association with the cultural-revolutionary political sensibilities of the 1960s. I do mean "sensibilities," for avant-gardism was evinced more in the style of the 1960s than in the substance of the political issues leftists addressed (Vietnam, race, women's liberation).

As an example of this sensibility, one might consider the Situationist International (SI), a small post-Surrealist group that began in France in 1958 and made a deep imprint on the colossal upheaval of May 1968. The SI, through its journal and the prolixity of its theoreticians, left

---

49. Unger, *supra* note 2, at 36.

behind it a formidable body of dense radical theory;[50] but, as the Situationists themselves would have wanted it, it is through their slogans and style that the SI is remembered. It was the Situationists who gave Parisian students, prying up cobblestones to make barricades, their slogan *"Sous le pavé, la plage"* ("Under the paving stones, the beach!"). They covered the walls of the universities with other slogans inspired by artistic modernism: "The sky will not be blue again until we reinvent it"; "Power to the imagination!"; "Poetry in the streets." One finds a good deal of Situationist language in Unger, who frequently appeals to us to "invent" or "imagine" new forms of social existence, as though the rightful successor to law will be art.

More memorably, the SI created what became the cliché format of leftist publications (employed by CLS members in the alternative newspaper they distributed at the 1984 convention of the Association of American Law Schools): Pop-style single cartoon-strip panels, fragments of old drawings, collages of advertising slogans snipped out of context. The mix of Pop, mass-culture icons, and black humor that we associate with 1960s leftism emerged in large part out of the obscurities of aesthetic theories forged in the furnaces of post-Surrealism in the late 1950s. And for those whose political sympathies lie with the residues of 1960s leftism, it is natural to find affinities with its avant-gardist roots.

A second point of affinity between avant-gardism and a leftist political sensibility may be found in the aesthetic doctrines of the Frankfurt school, so-called Critical Theory. Critical Theory has influenced CLS, as the similarity in names suggests, and it accords avant-gardism an important political role. This may be seen in the most influential book by the Frankfurt school's most influential member, Herbert

---

50. *See, e.g.,* Guy Debord, *La société du spectacle* (1968); Raul Vaneigem, *Traité de savoir-vivre à l'usage des jeunes générations* (1967). The issues of the journal are republished in *Internationale situationniste 1958–69* (1975). Unhappily, most of the English translations of Situationist works were issued by small anarchist presses and are hard to obtain. The largest English-language collection of SI writings is *Situationist International Anthology* (Ken Knabb ed. 1981), published by the Bureau of Public Secrets, P.O. Box 1044, Berkeley, California 94701. Debord's *Society of the Spectacle* was published by Black & Red, Box 9546, Detroit, Michigan 48202. I don't know whether either of these publishers still exists. As a matter of principle, neither publisher copyrighted its translations, and I will be delighted to send photocopies to interested readers. No doubt it is obvious that, my criticisms notwithstanding, I have an abiding affection for the Situationists, and I remain convinced that Debord's *Society of the Spectacle* is a genuine masterpiece. Recently, Debord returned to print with *Comments on the Society of the Spectacle* (Malcolm Imrie trans. 1990).

Marcuse's *One-Dimensional Man*,[51] one of the must-read texts of the
New Left.

Marcuse's basic argument is well known. The "technological rationality" of advanced capitalism swallows up all modes of discourse,
including oppositional discourse. It provides spurious legitimation by
means of a soulless hellfire of advertising images that canalize all our
urges for a truly human freedom into desires for commodities that
capitalism can satisfy. By making even opposition one dimensional, it
ensures that truly fundamental opposition cannot gain a toehold. And
since rationality has become one dimensional, it follows that our last
hope, true opposition or negation, must assume the guise of the
irrational.

Art plays a crucial role, for "art contains the rationality of negation.
In its advanced positions, it is the Great Refusal—the protest against
that which is."[52] This, according to Marcuse, has always been true, even
in the case of premodernist art that was in harmony with its society's
ideals: "[A]lienation characterizes affirmative as well as negative art."[53]
But now, in one-dimensional society, "[a]rtistic alienation succumbs,
together with other modes of negation, to the process of technological
rationality."[54] And that is where the avant-garde comes in. It is the final
revolutionary stronghold against one-dimensionality:

> [C]ontradiction . . . must have a medium of communication. The
> struggle for this medium, or rather the struggle against its absorp-
> tion into the predominant one-dimensionality, shows forth in the
> avant-garde efforts to create an estrangement which would make
> the artistic truth again communicable.[55]

In itself, there is nothing in this last sentence incompatible with a
neo-Kantian interpretation of the avant-garde; the sentence amounts
only to an explanation of why it has become necessary to go modernist.
What is avant-gardist in the aesthetics of *One-Dimensional Man* is rather
the demand that the artist always remain oppositional (ideally, "art
would become a technique for destroying this business and this
misery"[56])—the dread of co-optation that becomes the badge of the

51. Herbert Marcuse, *One-Dimensional Man: Studies in the Ideology of Advanced
Industrial Society* (1964).
52. *Id.* at 63.
53. *Id.*
54. *Id.* at 66.
55. *Id.* at 66.
56. *Id.* at 239.

Great Refusal. Marcuse ends his book romantically, with a veritable Oath of the Horatii:

> The critical theory of society possesses no concepts which could bridge the gap between the present and its future; holding no promise and showing no success, it remains negative. Thus it wants to remain loyal to those who, without hope, have given and give their life to the Great Refusal.[57]

This theme is strikingly echoed in CLS by Mark Tushnet, who writes: "One sides with the party of humanity because it is defined as the party in opposition to what exists."[58] And again, "And what if things change? If there is no transcendent humanity, when things change all that will be left is to remain in opposition."[59]

Marcuse's views are not entirely consistent with avant-gardism, for Marcuse grants validity to premodernist art; he is respectful of an art's past in a way that avant-gardists are not.[60] But—and this is a third affinity between avant-gardism and the left—Marxism is in obvious ways the most important leftist theory, and Marxism itself suspects that to respect the past even a little is to be swindled by an ideology that will merely deflect and co-opt the revolutionary impulse. In Marx's words,

> The tradition of all the dead generations weighs like a nightmare on the brain of the living. And just when they seem engaged in revolutionising themselves and things, in creating something that has never yet existed, precisely in such periods of revolutionary crisis they anxiously conjure up the spirits of the past. . . .
>   The social revolution . . . cannot draw its poetry from the past, but only from the future.[61]

Within CLS, I believe that this avant-gardist impulse is reflected in the practice of "trashing" traditional legal theory[62] but even more strik-

---

57. *Id.* at 257.

58. Tushnet, "An Essay on Rights," 62 *Texas Law Review* 1363, 1398 (1984).

59. *Id.* at 1402.

60. How little sympathy Marcuse actually had for avant-gardism and cultural revolution may be seen from Marcuse, "Art and Revolution," in *Counterrevolution and Revolt* 79 (1972); Marcuse, *The Aesthetic Dimension: Toward a Critique of Marxist Aesthetics* (1978). I take these works to be partial abandonments of the aesthetic views expressed in *One-Dimensional Man.*

61. Karl Marx, *The Eighteenth Brumaire of Louis Bonaparte* 13, 16 (1957) (1st ed. New York 1852).

62. I take the term from Mark Kelman, "Trashing," 36 *Stanford Law Review* 293 (1984).

ingly in the wholesale rejection of the concept of rights as—in Mark Tushnet's words—"affirmatively harmful to the party of humanity."[63] The appeal to rights is simply another nightmare on the brain of the living, another attempt to draw poetry from the past. And, the avant-gardist believes, there was no poetry in the past worth talking about.

I wish to pursue the topic of CLS's critique of rights a bit further, even though my primary aim in this chapter is not to engage with substantive CLS positions. It may be objected that my assimilation of the rights critique to avant-gardism begs the question. Perhaps the moral vocabulary of rights really is unnecessary and harmful; perhaps rights-talk is more like racism and sexism—things our culture would be well rid of—than it is like art or music.[64] In that case, the assault on rights is part of a legitimately neo-Kantian (rather than avant-gardist) modernist program. But I do not think that it is.

The primary aim of the CLS critique of rights is to debunk the idea that legal rights are politically neutral—that they form a fixed and determinate coin of the realm, by means of which the business of legal controversy may be transacted without bias grounded in either the identity or the group membership of the parties. CLS critics wish to stress that judges typically manipulate the vocabulary of legal rights to favor existing hierarchies.

Suppose we agree that that is true; there would then be several routes we could take to explain the phenomenon. One route is to conclude that when this happens the judges are violating their duty, because they are ideologically or personally biased against certain groups, or because (as Tocqueville believed) lawyers are better friends of order than of liberty, or because in their interest balancing the interests of powerful groups always take precedence over those of the less powerful. A second route is to argue (in the fashion of Beard) that the particu-

---

63. Tushnet, *supra* note 58, at 1384; *see also* Gabel, "The Phenomenology of Rights-Consciousness and the Pact of the Withdrawn Selves," 62 *Texas Law Review* 1563 (1984). The gap between the radical theorist's rejection of rights and the practical needs of radical politics is well illustrated by Staughton Lynd's worry that if CLS is correct and rights-talk is abandoned it will be impossible to achieve some very important ends of political organization. Lynd, "Communal Rights," 62 *Texas Law Review* 1417 (1984) (see especially pages 1417–29). Similarly, Patricia Williams has suggested that the pursuit of rights remains an important goal for African-Americans. Patricia Williams, "Alchemical Notes: Reconstructing Ideals from Deconstructed Rights," 22 *Harvard Civil Rights–Civil Liberties Law Review* 401 (1987). Williams's essay was among the first to manifest the difference in outlooks that makes critical race theory a distinctive movement within the legal left, in some ways antagonistic to the aims of CLS.

64. I owe this formulation to Robin West.

lar set of legal rights in (say) the U. S. Constitution is biased in any or all of these ways.

CLS rights critics, however, choose a more audacious and theoretically rarefied route, and therein lies their avant-gardism. They claim that the problem lies neither in the judges nor in the particular schedule of legal rights currently in effect but rather in the vocabulary of rights as such. In claiming this, they are at once committed to discarding eight hundred years of legal and moral language and to suggesting that controversy could be conducted in some alternative vocabulary.

The idea of scuttling whole segments of our vocabulary—the poetry of the past—has recently enjoyed considerable attention. But what does it mean to abolish the whole language of rights? What would a new language look like?

To address these questions, we need to ask what communicative purposes the language of rights serves. I believe the answer is this: the claim to have a right to a substance is simply the speaker's way of asserting an especially strong claim to that substance.[65]

That is, we may (roughly) analyze a claim couched in rights-talk as follows:

"*A* has a right to *S*" means that

1. there are valid reasons for guaranteeing that *A* gets *S*;
2. these reasons are among the strongest reasons we acknowledge (i.e., in most but not all contexts, they are decisive reasons); and
3. these reasons are relatively long-term (i.e., they are not the ad hoc creatures of political expediency or momentary or fortuitous constellations of events).[66]

And that is all: my claim that I have a right to a substance is a claim that there are very strong, long-term reasons for guaranteeing me that substance.

Notice what this analysis does not say. It does not say that the right-bearer is an individual, so it is neither individualistic nor biased against group rights. It does not say that rights are absolute. It does not say that rights are ahistorical (only that when they change, it will not be overnight). It does not say that rights are (like) property of their possessors, nor that rights are things. The analysis does not elevate claims of rights into dubious premises of political arguments; rather, it insists that they

---

65. I follow Henry Shue in defining the "substance" of a right as "whatever the right is a right to." Henry Shue, *Basic Rights: Subsistence, Affluence, and U.S. Foreign Policy* 15 (1980).

66. *Id.* at 13. Shue's analysis of a right is somewhat different.

are conclusions of such arguments. And so, people who talk rights-talk are not committed to individualism, absolutism, ahistoricism, property-worship, reification, or obfuscation. On the contrary, it is the rights critics who appear to be misled by a form of speech into reifying fictitious entities.

If I am right that the communicative function of a rights claim is to assert that there are very strong, long-term reasons for guaranteeing us the right's substance, what does it mean to abolish rights talk? Does it mean getting rid of the word *right*, the vocabulary of rights? In that case, we shall simply need to invent a new word to register claims that there are very strong, long-term reasons for guaranteeing us a substance.

Since there is evidently no point to a merely nominal change, the rights critique must instead mean something more fundamental: that there should *be* no rights, i.e., that there are no strong, long-term reasons we can invoke for guaranteeing us any substances. The demand for a priori guarantees against political change is itself unreasonable, and no substance should be held immune, even relatively immune, from political conflict over its distribution. That I take to be very close to the CLS critics' bottom line on rights, but then I return to my initial conviction that it is an avant-gardist vision. For now every fixed form of life becomes fluid, and no distribution can ever be taken for granted. Stable or dependable contexts as such, and the history that gives rise to them, are the enemy. All that is solid melts into air.

Avant-Gardism and French Postmodernism

It is probably evident that I am no fan of the avant-gardist interpretation of modernism. What are my reasons?

The most important, of course, is that I revere too much of the past—too much art, too much history, too many ideals and institutions—to have any real sympathy with the avant-gardist sensibility. That, however, is not an argument, and I do not offer it as one. Clearly it begs the avant-gardist's question. And one can surely understand why someone who has keenly experienced our culture's pervasive patriarchy or racism might abominate its cultural products, which are shot through with the offending attitudes.

Nevertheless, it seems to me that it is virtually impossible for a person to live sanely in (to use Unger's words that I have cited above) "a perpetual war against the fact of contextuality, a war that he cannot hope to win but that he must continue to wage."[67] Our lives, our experience, our language, and our modes of relationship are permeated with

---

67. Unger, *supra* note 2, at 36.

contexts given by the past, and permanent context smashing is not merely spiritually exhausting, it is destructive of sense. To reject the whole of one's culture is to be out of one's mind.

It is hardly a coincidence that avant-gardism's pantheon is heavily stacked with mad artists and thinkers (Hölderlin, Nietzsche, Lautréamont, Sade, Artaud).[68] The Situationists were pleased to number the crazed poet Ivan Chtcheglov in their charter membership.[69] One thing that I find distressing in avant-gardism is that it toys too readily with the desirability of extreme experience; lunacy may be Politically Correct. As Marcuse argues, "[T]he realm of the irrational becomes the home of the really rational—of the ideas which may 'promote the art of life.'"[70] A passage from Michel Foucault elaborates this theme:

> After Sade and Goya, and since them, unreason has belonged to whatever is decisive, for the modern world, in any work of art. . . . Ruse and new triumph of madness: the world that thought to measure and justify madness through psychology must justify itself before madness, since in its struggles and agonies it measures itself by the excess of works like those of Nietzsche, of Van Gogh, of Artaud.[71]

Now, one may well admire or even love the works of Nietzsche or van Gogh; one may also believe that without their madness these works could not exist. But plainly that does not imply that manic intensity is a state one should seek, any more than the fact that Schubert was inspired to write great music by the knowledge that he was dying implies that mortal illness is a state one should seek.

Some will object that I greatly exaggerate the importance of avant-gardist toying with madness, but that is to mistake the point. Few would deny that avant-gardism makes the quest for extraordinary spiritual states, the rhetoric of violence, and contempt for bourgeois normality centerpieces of its worldview; and my point is that when you have done that, unwanted consequences pursue you no matter what your intentions.

---

68. Wholly characteristic of avant-gardism's infatuation with insanity is Gilles Deleuze & Felix Guattari, *Anti-Oedipus: Capitalism and Schizophrenia* (1977). In fact, avant-gardist leftism vacillates between denouncing our society for creating schizophrenics and glorying in the schizophrenic experience. *See* R. D. Laing, *The Politics of Experience* (1967); Michel Foucault, *Madness and Civilization: A History of Insanity in the Age of Reason* (1965).

69. Ivan Chtcheglov, "Lettres de loin," 9 *Internationale situationniste* 38 (1964).

70. Marcuse, *supra* note 51, at 247.

71. Foucault, *supra* note 68, at 285, 289.

I am moved to raise these concerns in part by the great interest
evinced by CLS theorists in postmodernist French philosophy, especially the work of Foucault and Jacques Derrida. For it seems to me that
French postmodernism is a primary culprit in the game of glib flirtation
with a rhetoric of extremity and violence. Foucault, in particular, chose
to write in a very menacing idiom; one need think only of the apocalyp-
tic conclusion of *The Order of Things:*

> [M]an is an invention of recent date. And one perhaps nearing its
> end.
>   If . . . some event of which we can at the moment do no more
> than sense the possibility . . . were to cause [our categories of
> knowledge] to crumble, . . . then one can certainly wager that man
> would be erased, like a face drawn in sand at the edge of the sea.[72]

A similar example is Derrida's essay "Tympan," which is written in
a dense and incomprehensible prose permeated with imagery of rape,[73]
of forcible cunnilingus,[74] of bursting the philosopher's palate from
within his mouth,[75] of vocal cords being shattered and earwigs piercing
the eardrum.[76] (It also includes the mandatory, inevitable, tedious references to Lautréamont's *Chants de Maldoror*[77] and to Artaud.[78])

Why write like this? "Tympan" offers an important clue to understanding the root impulse of avant-gardism. Derrida takes as his text in
this essay three self-satisfied passages from Hegel suggesting that philosophy includes everything else within it. Derrida finds this unbearable, and his purpose in writing "Tympan" is to exemplify a kind of
discourse that philosophers cannot "hear" as philosophy and thus "to

---

72. Foucault, *The Order of Things: An Archaeology of the Human Sciences* 387 (1970).
On Foucault's love affair with *thanatos, see* James Miller, *The Passion of Michel Foucault* 20
(1993).

73. Jacques Derrida, "Tympan," in *Margins of Philosophy* xxv–xxix (1982). This
passage is an extended sexual double entendre based on images of a printing press
puncturing fastened-down silk, which "watches over its margins as virgin . . . space." *Id.*
at xxvii.

74. *Id.* at xviii n.9: "[T]he bloodiness of a disseminated writing comes to separate
the lips, to violate the embouchure of philosophy, putting its tongue into movement. . . ." That the "lips" referred to are the "small lips of the vulva" as well as the lips
of the mouth is explained at xvii n.9, as well as at xiv n.6.

75. "To luxate, to tympanize philosophical autism is never an operation . . . without some carnage of language. Thus it breaks open the roof, the closed spiral unity of the
palate. . . . It is no longer *a* tongue." *Id.* at xv n.8.

76. *Id.* at xvi–xviii (Learis's poem in the margin).

77. *Id.* at xiii.

78. *Id.* at xv n.8.

luxate [dislocate] the philosophical ear."[79] (Hence the images of violence performed on the head.)

Derrida's problem is that Hegel is right: philosophers cannot "hear" any criticisms without turning them into philosophical theses; thus, the attempt to criticize the very idea of philosophical theses is doomed from the outset because philosophy has stacked the deck. Derrida's solution is to carve out an idiom so odd and obscure that it cannot be rationally reconstructed into philosophical theses and to make it an attack on philosophy through the repeated use of violent images directed at philosophy.

At work here is the impulse to do work in philosophy that is not just some more philosophy, that cannot be pigeonholed, incorporated into philosophy's history, co-opted, work that cannot become last week's news, that will never be supplanted by something else, never *aufgehoben*.[80]

This is a deep motivation of avant-gardism. The first issue of the Situationists' journal was bound in sandpaper covers, so that you couldn't put it on your bookshelf without damaging the books next to it. An unshelvable book! An unassimilable piece of philosophy! An unco-optable political movement! A painting that can never become a footnote in an art history dissertation! A social structure in which complacency is impossible! It is exciting prospects like these that inflame the avant-gardist imagination.

The root impulse of avant-gardism, I believe, is the impulse to end history, or at least one's epoch in it—to achieve the achievement that ends all achievements. Derrida wants to finish off metaphysics ("phallogocentrism," as he calls it in his ugly jargon). Foucault wants to terminate subjectivity. Successive generations of avant-gardist artists want to end art. CLS rights critics want to abolish legalism.

CLS theorists often promote this way of thinking as necessary utopianism. I think of it as a kind of messianic impulse in modernism. The modernist, unable to rest content with the contexts in which we live, wants finally to be redeemed from all contextuality. No intermediate way station between us and the messiah is bearable.

---

79. *Id.* at xv. I have been greatly helped in understanding "Tympan" by reading (and discussing with her) Deborah Hellman's Dartmouth College thesis on Derrida.

80. I shall not dwell on what also seems plain: that Derrida has adopted this manner of writing out of a more-than-ordinary professorial vanity, a desire to triumph over his critics by mocking the whole idea of reasoned disagreement, thereby changing the rules of give-and-take to eliminate its in-built possibility of discovering that one is wrong.

This (quite understandable) impulse is deceptive, however, because we would feel it whether or not the messiah was imminent. Kant noted the bitterness of the idea of gradual progress, the idea

> that the earlier generations appear to carry through their toilsome labor only for the sake of the later . . . and yet that only the latest of the generations should have the good fortune to inhabit the building on which a long line of their ancestors had . . . labored without being permitted to partake of the fortune they had prepared.[81]

It is precisely this melancholy thought that kindles the messianic yearning, the inevitable yearning to be that "latest of the generations."

The impulse is dangerous because it leads us to treat the messianic moment as a goal at which we can aim. But since such a moment by definition involves a drastic rupture with all the preexisting contexts we use to make sense of things, we cannot take it as a goal because it has no content at all. Our aims are of necessity modeled on what we can know, and that, like it or not, entails giving the ghost of dead generations its due—modeling one's achievement on past achievements, aiming at amelioration rather than annihilation, leaving open the possibility of being co-opted.[82] (I take this neo-Kantian caution to be one of Unger's main points in *Passion* and *The Critical Legal Studies Movement*.)

For all these reasons, then, I think we should favor the neo-Kantian over the avant-gardist interpretation of modernism. I do not deny avant-gardism's allure; I urge only that, by hurling us into combat to revalue all values, avant-gardism imposes unlivable, deceptive, and spiritually destructive requirements on us.

The Situationist International shrank as its members were expelled for ideological deviations. Legend has it that it dissolved when the last two members met in a café and agreed to expel themselves because they, too, had sold out.

Avant-Gardism and Theatricality

One of the more obscure of the Situationist slogans was "Create situations!" The first issue of their journal defined a "constructed situation"

---

81. Immanuel Kant, "Idea for a Universal History from a Cosmopolitan Point of View," in *On History* 14 (Lewis White Beck trans. 1963).

82. I draw the argument of this paragraph from Benjamin, "Theologico-Political Fragment," in *Reflections* 312 (Peter Demetz ed. 1978): "From the standpoint of history [the Kingdom of God] is not the goal, but the end. . . . The order of the profane should be erected on the idea of happiness."

as a "moment of life, concretely and deliberately constructed by the collective organization of a unitary ambiance and a play of events."[83] Situationism was to be a kind of multimedia guerrilla theater.

But there is something wrong with being theatrical outside the theater—or even in the theater, if we are to believe the modernist theorists Brecht and Artaud. Think, for example, of what we mean when we accuse a friend of posturing, of being theatrical, in personal life. One of the most important facts about artworks is that (in Cavell's words) "we treat them in special ways, invest them with a value which normal people otherwise reserve only for other people—and with the same kind of scorn and outrage."[84] It is because art matters to us in ways that people matter to us, and because one way an artwork (like a person) can betray us is by posturing, that the theatricality of art is an important issue.

Fried argues in his crucial neo-Kantian essay "Art and Objecthood" for two theses: "1) The success, even the survival of the arts has come increasingly to depend on their ability to defeat theatre. . . . 2) Art degenerates as it approaches the condition of theatre."[85] This seems mysterious, until we realize that the theater is defined by two conditions: it involves playacting, and it depends for its success on self-consciousness, even hyperawareness, of the way the performance looks to the audience. And Fried's criticism can be understood thus: When a work of modernist art rests its claim to our attentiveness on theatrical effects, it operates merely by manipulating our situation; it achieves notoriety without achieving quality. It fails in the way that I have suggested is characteristic of modernist art: it is (not mediocre but) fraudulent.

One can readily imagine examples of purely theatrical modernist works: a sculpture that depends for its effectiveness on sheer size, a light so bright that you can't look at it, music that has nothing going for it but high volume. Each of these may attract attention in the art gallery or concert hall; each may be defended with passionate aesthetic arguments; but, in the end, each depends for its effectiveness on something that is aesthetically irrelevant. Though it can compel our attention, theatrical art does not reward our attentiveness.

Avant-gardist work, I believe, is inherently theatrical; it glories and exults in the theatrical, for its claim to status as a political force is that it confronts us in our situations—it (re)creates situations. But, if the neo-Kantian arguments I have advanced in this chapter are sound, this is no

83. 1 *Internationale situationniste* 13 (my translation).
84. Cavell, *supra* note 9, at 198.
85. Fried, "Art and Objecthood," *supra* note 26, at 139, 141.

virtue. This point bears emphasis. I have claimed that modernism's mode of failure is inauthenticity or theatricality; and I am now suggesting that theatricality is characteristic of avant-gardist work. Thus, my suggestion amounts to the claim that avant-gardism is one shape modernism assumes when it fails.

Modernism and Legal Theory

It is time, finally, to say a bit more explicitly what the significance is of modernism, and of the distinction I have drawn between neo-Kantianism and avant-gardism, for law and social theory.

Let me make one point clear: My criticisms of avant-gardism are not intended as criticisms of radical leftist politics, only of an interpretation of such politics. It should be evident, in fact, that I have been assuming throughout this chapter that modernism is roughly correct: that the social contexts in which we organize our activities (and now we may think of legal and social systems) are no longer able to sustain the conviction of their own legitimacy and hence that they demand a more-or-less drastic criticism and revision. Many people will disagree with this; and though this chapter is surely not the occasion for undertaking a defense of this critical stance, a few remarks may be appropriate.

Let us follow the procedure of this chapter and break the modernist thesis down into two components: the moral criticism of premodernism's dissembling conventions and the exile motif. The exile motif is itself a conjunction of two ideas, which I have labeled *homelessness* (i.e., in any given context) and *isolation* (i.e., from each other). I will treat these three concepts in reverse order.

Isolation. The isolation thesis in social theory is familiar as an avant-gardist claim—raised by a variety of social critics, including perhaps its most drastic formulation in Debord's Situationist tract *La société du spectacle*—that we are a "lonely crowd," leading lives of quiet desperation, irretrievably alienated from each other. In legal theory, it may be found in Gabel's argument that when we understand our mutual relationships legalistically (e.g., as an interplay of rights), we become "withdrawn selves" engaged in a desperate prevarication.[86]

But many of us are inclined to protest this avant-gardist diagnosis of our condition: rumors of our demise are, we think, exaggerated. Our encounters may appear alienated, after all, only because we now have a richer variety of them; and we may seem like bad-faith role-players, Sartrian café waiters, only because the social theorist doesn't really get to know us. We play a variety of roles, after all, and it is small wonder that to the superficial observer—particularly one determined to find

---

86. Gabel, *supra* note 63.

something wrong—no one of them seems more than a caricature of a person.[87] (Consider this example from Marcuse: "The subway during evening rush hour. What I see of the people are tired faces and limbs, hatred and anger. . . . [M]ost of them will probably have some awful togetherness or aloneness at home."[88] How the hell does *he* know?)

I propose a more plausible neo-Kantian version of the isolation thesis. The great variety of our roles and encounters is in itself neither a cause nor a symptom of alienation. Rather, as our field of awareness and communication widens, we become more conscious of social conflict, because we become more aware of people who are different from us; and this heightened awareness of conflict may itself estrange us from each other. Disillusionment about the existence of consensus can actually accelerate the unraveling of whatever consensus there is. The problem is not alienation but strife.[89]

This is one aspect of the problem that Unger describes as our heightened awareness of "contextuality." By that he means that we are more conscious of other people's membership in interest groups or social classes in conflict with ours; we see these contexts as conditioning their behavior. And to that extent we mistrust them. ("They only say that because they are X.") The avant-gardist's alienation thesis may be only a conjecture, but I take it as a plain fact that ours is a wary age.

And wariness, mistrust, is a form of isolation. Those we do not trust we hold at arm's length, and an arm's-length society makes everything difficult for itself. In fact, as Luhmann has written, "a complete absence of trust would prevent [one] even from getting up in the morning."[90]

Noticing the social centrality of trust leads us directly to consider one way that the theme of isolation can be raised in legal theory. Recently, in a pair of suggestive and important essays, the philosopher Annette Baier has argued that *trust*, not *obligation*, is the root phenomenon upon which moral theory should focus.[91] The legal surrogate for trust—enforceable obligation—itself amounts, after all, simply to trusting enforcement authorities more than one trusts one's obligor, and so

---

87. These replies come from Niklas Luhmann, *Grundrechte als Institution: Ein Beitrag zur Politischen Soziologie* 50–51 (1965).

88. Marcuse, *supra* note 51, at 227.

89. For an enlightening CLS discussion of the loss of consensus in modern liberal society, see Unger, *Law in Modern Society: Toward a Criticism of Social Theory* 166–70 (1976).

90. Luhmann, "Trust: A Mechanism for the Reduction of Social Complexity," in *Trust and Power* 1, 4 (1979).

91. Annette Baier, "Trust and Antitrust," 96 *Ethics* 231 (1986); Baier, "What Do Women Want in a Moral Theory?" 19 *Nous* 53, 56–61 (1985). For an excellent CLS treatment of this subject, see William Simon, "The Invention and Reinvention of Welfare Rights," 44 *Maryland Law Review* 1 (1985).

enforceable obligation itself is nothing but a special case of trust. (A society of Holmesian Bad Men is an impossibility because the enforcement authorities, and those who monitor them in turn, would also be Bad Men; Holmes inconsistently presupposed that, somewhere in the governmental apparatus, there would be Good Men, that is, trustworthy men.)

Baier speculates that obligation, contract, and voluntary agreement came to be seen as paradigms of liberal morality because the (male!) moralist took as his paradigm of social intercourse

> cool, distanced relations between more or less free and equal adult strangers, say, the members of an all male club, with membership rules and rules for dealing with rule breakers and where the form of cooperation was restricted to ensuring that each member could read his *Times* in peace and have no one step on his gouty toes.[92]

This emphasis on "cool, distanced relations between free and equal adult strangers" may or may not correctly characterize moral theory, but it surely characterizes classical liberal legal theory; and so, if Baier is right, to understand ourselves in the terms of classical liberal legal theory is to understand ourselves in a way that ignores and undermines the trust that actually makes the world go 'round. Legal theory partakes of isolation, in short, because its central concepts are based on a paradigm of arm's-length relationships between adults—a paradigm of isolation.

My emphasis on mistrust and strife as the components of modernist isolation is neo-Kantian because, unlike the avant-gardist's focus on desperation and metaphysical estrangement, it builds its radical vision on a determinate content: trust and agreeableness, after all, are ideals that we understand and live with every day. The avant-gardist, by contrast, must hold out to us as an ideal the end of alienation, a messianic and contentless vision of communality.

Homelessness. By "homelessness," remember, I am referring to the modernist understanding of contexts—the modernist skepticism that any fixed context, set of roles, or station in life is a natural home for us. In legal theory, the experience of homelessness appears as skepticism that any set of rules, procedures, or reforms will actually achieve justice. Unger describes this eloquently as "a basic, common experience in modern society . . . : the sense of being surrounded by injustice without knowing where justice lies."[93]

---

92. Baier, "Trust and Antitrust," *supra* note 91, at 248.
93. Unger, *supra* note 89, at 175.

Unlike the case of the isolation motif, here I do not really find a difference between neo-Kantian and avant-gardist interpretations of this experience, unless the avant-gardist interpretation is to be a wholesale skepticism about the concept of justice that I do not see anyone, in or out of CLS, espousing. I will without further discussion maintain that the experience Unger describes is a precise expression in legal theory of the modernist theme of homelessness. And I will assume with Unger that the experience is one that many or most people share.

There is a kind of poetic justice here. The most famous of all modernist novels is Kafka's *The Trial*, which hit upon involvement in a modern legal process as a perfect metaphor for expressing the exile motif. If anything is to count as a political theme of *The Trial*—as opposed to the obvious theological and existential themes—it is the "basic, common experience in modern society . . . of being surrounded by injustice without knowing where justice lies." It is hard to forget such images as Joseph K., indicted but unable to discover the crime of which he is accused, or the gatekeeper at the court closing forever the door to justice that existed only for him. Now we find that the circle has closed. Modernist art such as *The Trial* offers us the truly illuminating metaphors with which to understand the legal system.[94]

The critique of premodernism. Modernist art, I have argued, is defined in part by its impulse to subject premodernist work to searing criticism, laying bare its constitutive conventions and displaying the way in which these dissemble about the relationship between art and its beholder.

I find the analogue in the CLS criticism of what are taken to be organizing principles in the various departments of legal doctrine—property, criminal law, etc.

CLS's best-known work has consisted of an attempt to show that liberal legalism has masked the arbitrary character of law by insisting that the acts of will that make it up are themselves responding to principles of neutral public policy. Typically, a CLS "deconstruction" of an area of law shows that these principles could as easily have led to a different, opposing result. And the conclusion of such a critique is the claim that law is indeterminate and thus open to extralegal determination, such as determination by class or gender interest. This fact undercuts law's claim to universality.

I am skeptical of such arguments. The fact that the result of a case does not follow from legal principles as a theorem follows from axioms

---

94. *See, e.g.*, Robin West, "Authority, Autonomy, and Choice: The Role of Consent in the Moral and Political Visions of Franz Kafka and Richard Posner," 99 *Harvard Law Review* 184 (1985).

does not show the absence of determinacy. It shows only the absence of mechanical determinacy. But that is a pretty weak result. It is scarcely surprising to learn that judgments involve judgment calls, and it is clear that judgment calls cannot themselves be carried out by mechanically applying rules, on pain of infinite regress. We would need rules telling us how to apply the rules of judgment, and further rules telling us how to apply those, and so on.[95]

The ability to make judgment calls arises from immersion in a culture, a set of social practices of rule application. The indeterminacy thesis, then, amounts to a mistrust of any such contextually formed capacity. Thus, Joseph William Singer dismisses determination if it arises (merely) from "legal culture, conventions, 'common sense,' and politics. Custom, rather than reason, narrows the choices and suggests the result."[96] Apparently, legal rules cannot be determinate if their application depends in any way on custom or convention.

In fact, however, the regress argument described above shows that *no* rules are determinate under such an austere constraint.[97] That includes rules of language use. So if Singer's argument is correct, it undermines not only the possibility of legal discourse, but of discourse of any sort. A contrast between reason and custom that has such consequences cannot be sustained.

Unger similarly argues that legal formalism depends upon the view that words have "plain meanings." This view, Unger believes, presupposes a doctrine of "intelligible essences" and is thus incompatible with a "conventionalist" view of language (i.e., a view that makes the plain meaning of words rest on conventions or shared practices). But conventionalism is the modern (i.e., postmedieval) view of nature and science, so formalism is incompatible with a belief in modern science.[98]

---

95. Both Kant and Wittgenstein emphasize this point. I have discussed their arguments in Luban, "Epistemology and Moral Education," 33 *Journal of Legal Education* 636 (1983).

96. Joseph William Singer, "The Player and the Cards: Nihilism and Legal Theory," 94 *Yale Law Journal* 1, 25 (1984). My understanding of these issues has been greatly assisted by John Stick, "Can Nihilism Be Pragmatic?" 100 *Harvard Law Review* 332 (1986). For a discussion of judgment, see Ronald Beiner, *Political Judgment* (1983); Hannah Arendt, *Lectures on Kant's Political Philosophy* (1982); Anthony T. Kronman, *The Lost Lawyer* (1993).

97. Another, related, line of argument leading to the same conclusion is Wittgenstein's "rule-skepticism" in the *Investigations*. For a contemporary discussion, see Saul Kripke, *Wittgenstein on Rules and Private Language* (1982), an elaboration of arguments first presented in Robert Fogelin, *Wittgenstein* 138–71 (1976). A criticism of rule-skepticism that is quite germane to the indeterminacy thesis is G. P. Baker & P. M. S. Hacker, *Scepticism, Rules and Language* (1984).

98. Unger, *Knowledge and Politics* 92–94 (1975).

Much is wrong in this argument—indeed, everything is wrong in it. First, there is no reason to believe that a scientific worldview is incompatible with a suitably sophisticated essentialism.[99] Second, it is untrue that giving up on intelligible essences means giving up on the ability to "subsume situations under rules,"[100] as Unger claims. To deny that a judgment subsuming a situation under a rule is *essentially* true is not to deny that it is true, and no classical essentialist ever said otherwise.[101] Third, even intelligible essences—nonconventional linguistic rules—would not help us make such subsumptions unless they too were buttressed by conventions, for our regress argument shows that we would need rules about how to apply those rules, rules about how to apply those, and so on.

Unger may wish to reply that to call an essence *intelligible* is to assert that it can be applied to its instances without appeal to conventions or further essences, so the regress problem is avoided. But that was not how any of its classical exponents understood the doctrine of intelligible essences. Indeed, the regress problem was known to the first philosopher to formulate a doctrine of intelligible essences: it is a version of the so-called Third Man Argument in Plato's *Parmenides* (132a–b). Parmenides asks Socrates this question: You believe that large things are large in virtue of a form [i.e., an intelligible essence] of Largeness; in virtue of what, then, will large things and the Form of Largeness all be large? If it is in virtue of another Form of Largeness, we will be confronted with an infinite regress of Forms.

We may understand Parmenides's argument as a variant of a different question—You believe in Forms; how can we know that a Form "applies to" a given object (i.e., that a given object participates in that Form)?—and a different answer—Not by virtue of another Form, on pain of infinite regress! And this is just the regress argument I have been discussing.[102]

Even leaving all that aside, however, the basic objection that I raised against Singer remains. Unger's attack on the plain meaning of language clearly does not rule out only legal formalism. It rules out all

---

99. The best-known contemporary defense of scientific essentialism is Kripke, *Naming and Necessity* (1972).

100. Unger, *supra* note 98, at 93.

101. I owe this point to an unpublished review of Unger's *Knowledge and Politics* by Mark Sagoff.

102. On the interpretation of the Third Man Argument, see the classic Vlastos-Sellars debate: Gregory Vlastos, "The Third Man Argument in the Parmenides," 63 *Philosophical Review* 319 (1954); Wilfrid Sellars, "Vlastos and the 'Third Man,'" 64 *Philosophical Review* 405 (1955); Vlastos, "Addenda to the Third Man Argument: A Reply to Professor Sellars," 64 *Philosophical Review* 438 (1955); Sellars, "Vlastos and 'The Third Man': A Rejoinder," in *Philosophical Perspectives* 55 (1959).

discourse. I take this to be a straightforward reductio ad absurdum of the argument.

The CLS indeterminacy critique is, in fact, a version of Unger's "heretical" modernist thesis, which I have termed avant-gardist: "skepticism about the possibility of . . . gaining access to another mind." (For what is discourse if not our normal means of gaining access to another mind?) Such skepticism carries with it the mistrust of judgment, since judgments can only be shared, not discursively justified "all the way down." Undercut the ground for sharing another's judgment, and you eliminate the possibility of judgment altogether; no wonder indeterminacy follows. Unger's arguments for indeterminacy violate his own warning against this heresy.

The neo-Kantian version of the critique of doctrine, on the other hand, does not suppose that all doctrinal principles are arid. Instead, it takes as a starting point the ethical ideals supposedly incorporated in the organizing principles of doctrine, demonstrates how they have been distorted in practice to suppress legitimate interests, and tries to show how they are to be worked up to empower, rather than suppress, those interests. This program is what Unger has called "deviationist doctrine,"[103] and it perfectly exemplifies neo-Kantian modernism.

Indeed, Unger's views about indeterminacy seem to me to be in flat contradiction to his neo-Kantian claim on behalf of deviationist doctrine, which substitutes counterprinciples for dominant legal principles. If doctrine is always and in principle indeterminate, how would substituting counterprinciples in doctrine do anyone any good? Doctrine would still be completely indeterminate.

The Bit Where I Take It Back

J. L. Austin once remarked that in philosophy there is always the bit where you say it and then the bit where you take it back. This is the bit where I take it back—or, less provocatively, where I make explicit the qualifications that must attach to my analogy of CLS to artistic modernism.

It would in fact be possible to write a counteressay to this one, stressing the dissimilarities between CLS and artistic modernism. These could be traced in part to the dissimilarities between law and art, and the latter are important. Without in any way attempting to diminish the human significance of art, we should observe that revolutions in art do not have consequences for the character of life in the way that revolu-

---

103. Unger, "The Critical Legal Studies Movement," *supra* note 1, at 576. For examples, see *id*. at 602–48.

tions in law do. Thus, a complete overthrow of traditional art may be disorienting and uncomfortable; a complete overthrow of traditional society could be accomplished only with enormous physical violence. That is why political revolutions are episodic responses to extreme provocations. Permanent revolution in art vacillates between being exciting and tiresome; permanent revolution in society, such as Unger calls for in his avant-gardist moments,[104] might well end civilization. These facts may explain why modernist theory is more important to the practice of art than CLS theory is to the practice of law; legal institutions have greater incentives to insulate themselves from radical theory. The message of the present chapter could then be restated as follows: if the radical theory is neo-Kantian, so much the worse for legal institutions; if the radical theory is avant-gardist, so much the worse for the theory.[105]

It may be objected, moreover, that in associating CLS writers with avant-gardism I am simply setting up a straw adversary. I am sympathetic to this objection, and I would like to stress that no CLS writer I have read is simply or flat-footedly avant-gardist. The situation is more complicated than that.

What I find is writings that have an avant-gardist sound though they do not make avant-gardist arguments, or that make avant-gardist arguments with neo-Kantian qualifications or reservations, or that back their arguments with citations to avant-gardist works, or (as in Unger) that contain both avant-gardist and neo-Kantian passages.

Thus, in a neo-Kantian vein, Unger argues that radicals should be interested in developing, rather than eliminating or trashing, legal doctrine.[106] Unger also forcefully criticizes the "existentialist" version of modernism—his term for what I have called the avant-gardist version.[107] From the avant-gardist side, on the other hand, Unger calls on CLS to thin or eliminate the contrast between reform and revolution[108] and demands

> an institutional structure . . . that would provide constant occasions to disrupt any fixed structure of power *and coordination* in social life. Any such emergent structure would be broken up before having a chance to shield itself from the risks of ordinary conflict.[109]

---

104. *E.g., id.* at 592.

105. I would like to thank Michael Kelly for pressing on me the dissimilarity between CLS and artistic modernism.

106. Unger, "The Critical Legal Studies Movement," *supra* note 1, at 576–80.

107. *Id.* at 660–62.

108. *Id.* at 583–84.

109. *Id.* at 592 (emphasis added).

A vision of society in which any attempt to coordinate activities would be preemptively and prophylactically smashed, whether it was harmful or not, is avant-gardism with a vengeance. It is also incompatible with the society's continued existence.

In the end, it may be merely that some CLS writers have retained avant-gardist habits of the heart despite having arrived at neo-Kantian belief, or the other way around. In any case, we should not be surprised to find a certain amount of uncertainty and confusion between the two approaches: I have argued above that it is characteristic of modernism that even the artist is uncertain of when he or she has crossed the line from art to theater, from prophecy to quackery. In the midst of the staggering proliferation of CLS writing,[110] superheated by an unusual amount of media attention, it is inevitable that CLS authors will continue to hurl missiles without knowing until much later where they have landed.

At bottom, the contrast between avant-gardist and neo-Kantian visions of politics is the contrast between permanent revolution and transformation followed by reconstitution. The attraction of the former is exemplified in the attitude of Thomas Jefferson, described by Hannah Arendt as follows:

> His occasional, and sometimes violent, antagonism against the Constitution . . . was motivated by a feeling of outrage about the injustice that only his generation should have it in their power "to begin the world over again." . . . When the news of Shays' rebellion in Massachusetts reached him while he was in Paris, he was not in the least alarmed . . . but greeted it with enthusiasm: "God forbid we should ever be twenty years without such a rebellion."[111]

Jefferson's attitude arises from a desire to stop time at the revolutionary moment, the only moment in which one is truly and demonstrably free. But the desire to stop time is really no different from the desire to end time, to end history: it is the messianic urge I have discussed previously. Let us remember, though, that history is full of false messiahs. And somehow their followers have had to learn how to rebuild a livable world after the rainbow bridge they thought led to paradise had dissolved. The real task of modernist art is only in part to make us discontent with the past: it is also to make art.

110. Kennedy and Klare's CLS bibliography, already a decade out of date, contains approximately 600 entries. Duncan Kennedy & Karl Klare, "A Bibliography of Critical Legal Studies," 94 *Yale Law Journal* 461 (1984).
111. Arendt, *On Revolution* 235–36 (1963).

Chapter 2

Legal Traditionalism

One of the minor dislocations brought on by World War II was an interruption in the manufacture of goose quill pens, the official writing instrument of the U.S. Supreme Court since its first session in 1790. As a result, the Court ran out of pens in 1946. In April 1954, however, just one month before his opinion in *Brown v. Board of Education* signaled the beginning of the Court's most revolutionary era, Chief Justice Earl Warren was finally able to reorder a supply of goose quill pens, which continued in use until 1961. Nor were quill pens the Court's only anachronism, for it was not until 1963 that the Court permitted pages to wear long pants or skirts rather than the traditional knickers.[1]

Evidently, even Earl Warren was enamored of his Court's traditions. Indeed, many of the law's most distinguished observers regard it as a profession that lives in and through its traditions. Surveying the historical development of law, Oliver Wendell Holmes observed, "Everywhere the basis of principle is tradition,"[2] and, in a more poetic vein, likened law's "eternal procession" to "the black spearheads of the army that has been passing in unbroken line already for near a thousand years."[3] Karl Llewellyn dedicated his great study of the appellate process to "the undying succession of the great Commercial Judges whose work across the centuries has given living body, toughness and inspiration to the Grand Tradition of the Common Law." For emphasis, he appended to this dedication a genealogical chart that traced the "undying succession" for two centuries, from Sir John Holt to Learned Hand.[4] Somehow, the continuity of its Grand Tradition seems central to the legal enterprise; indeed, Felix Frankfurter, arguing in 1947 against a proposed procedural change in the Supreme Court, insisted that "tradition, particularly in this disordered world . . . should be adhered to as one of the great social forces of justice."[5] Law stands for orderly, evolu-

---

1. Bernard Schwartz & Stephen Lesher, *Inside the Warren Court* 68–69 (1983).

2. Oliver Wendell Holmes, "The Path of the Law," in *Collected Legal Papers* 167, 191 (1920).

3. Holmes, "Learning and Science," in *The Occasional Speeches of Justice Oliver Wendell Holmes* 84, 86 (Mark DeWolfe Howe ed. 1962).

4. Karl N. Llewellyn, *The Common Law Tradition: Deciding Appeals* v (1960).

5. Schwartz & Lesher, *supra* note 1, at 68. Presumably for this reason he implored his colleagues to "[t]hink twice and thrice . . . before disobeying the injunction 'Remove not the ancient landmarks of thy fathers.'" *Id.*

tionary, and piecemeal change, and legal traditions provide the fixed background against which this change gradually occurs. In Otto Neurath's familiar figure of the ship that must be rebuilt at sea, only a few planks at a time can be replaced;[6] only a few practices at a time, that is, can be questioned and reformed, while the rest must be withheld from scrutiny and accepted on reflex. *Tradition* is simply our name for the repository of accustomed practices that we withhold from scrutiny and accept on reflex. Lenin is supposed to have said that the revolution would not be made by lawyers. Trained in law himself, Lenin well understood the profession's instinctive propensity for looking backward as it inches forward.

To some, traditionalism is not merely a conservative instinct in lawyers but a defining characteristic of legal reasoning, what Edward Coke called "the artificial reason and judgment of law."[7] Legal reasoning proceeds according to "the doctrine of precedent in which a proposition descriptive of the first case is made into a rule of law and then applied to a next similar situation."[8] The appeal to tradition—understood as the stock of precedents accumulated over the centuries—is, according to this view, internal to the very enterprise of legal thinking, a hallmark of its distinctiveness.

Traditionalism does not reign undisputed over law's empire, however. Over the last century, the self-contained character of legal thinking has come under attack. Holmes, for example, argued that

> science is gradually drawing legal history into its sphere. The facts are being scrutinized by eyes microscopic in intensity and panoramic in scope. At the same time, under the influence of our revived interest in philosophical speculation, a thousand heads are analyzing and generalizing the rules of law and the grounds on which they stand. The law has got to be stated over again; and I venture to say that in fifty years we shall have it in a form of which no man could have dreamed fifty years ago.[9]

Seven years later, in one of his most famous passages, Holmes argued that "the black-letter man may be the man of the present, but the man of the future is the man of statistics and the master of economics."[10]

6. Otto Neurath, "Protokollsätze," 3 *Erkenntnis* 203, 206 (1932/33), *translated as* "Protocol Sentences," in *Logical Positivism* 199, 201 (A. J. Ayer ed. George Schick trans. 1959).

7. Prohibitions Del Roy, 12 Coke Rep. 63, 65 (1607), *reprinted in* 77 Eng. Rep. 1342, 1343 (1907).

8. Edward H. Levi, *An Introduction to Legal Reasoning* 1 (1949).

9. Holmes, "The Use of Law Schools," in *Collected Legal Papers, supra* note 2, at 35, 41–42.

10. Holmes, *supra* note 2, at 187.

Holmes was prescient. Fifteen years after Holmes wrote those words, Louis Brandeis submitted to the Supreme Court his famous brief in *Muller v. Oregon*,[11] basing his argument for the constitutionality of a state law limiting women's working hours largely upon statistics— hundreds of pages analyzing the effects of prolonged labor on women. The so-called Brandeis brief, a legal brief based on empirical data rather than precedent cases, soon became such an established form of argument that, when Benjamin Cardozo wrote *The Nature of the Judicial Process* in 1921, he placed "the method of sociology" on an equal footing with "the method of tradition." Indeed, he argued that the method of sociology "in our day and generation is becoming the greatest method of them all."[12]

Cardozo's prediction did not prove entirely accurate: Sociology has not come to dominate legal thinking. Nevertheless, the sense that the artificial reason and judgment of law cannot remain in hermetic self-sufficiency has continued to influence contemporary legal theory and, to a lesser degree, legal practice. Most obviously, the law and economics movement has insisted on asking whether common-law rules are economically efficient and has advocated reform when they are not. But that movement is not alone in its effort to rationalize the legal tradition. Almost twenty years ago, Ronald Dworkin called for "a fusion of constitutional law and moral theory, a connection that, incredibly, has yet to take place."[13] He continued:

> There is no need for lawyers to play a passive role in the development of a theory of moral rights against the state . . . any more than they have been passive in the development of legal sociology and legal economics. They must recognize that law is no more independent from philosophy than it is from these other disciplines.[14]

A glance through the tables of contents of major law reviews over the past decade reveals that Dworkin's plea has been heeded. Today, to an extent greater than Holmes could ever have imagined when he wrote the words, "under the influence of our revived interest in philosophical speculation, a thousand heads are analyzing and generalizing the rules of law and the grounds on which they stand."[15]

As Holmes anticipated, the interpenetration of sociology, economics, and philosophy into legal thinking has had a profound effect on

---

11. 208 U.S. 412 (1908).
12. Benjamin N. Cardozo, *The Nature of the Judicial Process* 64–66 (1921).
13. Ronald Dworkin, *Taking Rights Seriously* 149 (rev. ed. 1977).
14. *Id.*
15. Holmes, "The Use of Law Schools," in *Collected Legal Papers, supra* note 2, at 41–42.

"the path of the law," signifying not just new answers but new questions as well. Common-law reasoning presupposes the authority of precedent without subjecting it to question. By contrast, sociology, economics, and philosophy insist on examining the soundness of past decisions before what Kant called "the tribunal of reason."[16] Post-Holmesian legal theory pits rationalism against a more or less uncritical acquiescence to tradition. It engages in the Enlightenment endeavor of substituting critical inquiry for deference to external authority. As Kant put it,

> *Enlightenment is man's emergence from his self-incurred immaturity. Immaturity* is the inability to use one's own understanding without the guidance of another. . . . The motto of enlightenment is therefore: *Sapere aude!* [Dare to be wise!] Have courage to use your *own* understanding![17]

In this sense, the movement of contemporary legal theory amounts to the enormous saga of Enlightenment, of modernization and modernism, writ small.

Enlightenment has proven a mixed blessing, however. Frankfurter's argument for tradition refers rather plaintively to "this disordered world," and it is true that the world modernization has bequeathed us is in many ways a frighteningly disordered one—a world of moral uncertainty, fundamental dissension, and anomie. In confronting such a world, one persistent response has been a call for the return to tradition. After the Enlightenment came the Counter-Enlightenment backlash, with its insistence on the emptiness of any thought detached from unique national traditions.[18] To Counter-Enlightenment thinkers, many of whom were appalled by the French Revolution, Kant had it all backwards: Turning to the past for guidance is a sign of maturity, not immaturity, whereas trifling with the inherited wisdom of generations on the basis of fads in political theory is irresponsibly childish. Typical was Johann Herder's dismissal of Kant's cosmopolitan view of history: "Every nation has its own core of happiness just as every sphere has its center of gravity! . . . Philosopher in a northern valley, with the infant's scales of your century

---

16. Immanuel Kant, *Critique of Pure Reason* Axi–xii, at 9 (N. K. Smith trans. 1933).

17. Kant, "An Answer to the Question: 'What Is Enlightenment?,'" in *Kant's Political Writings* 54 (H. Reiss ed. H. B. Nisbet trans. 1970) (emphasis in original).

18. *See* Isaiah Berlin, "The Counter-Enlightenment," in *Against the Current: Essays in the History of Ideas* 1 (1980). *See generally* Berlin, *Vico and Herder: Two Studies in the History of Ideas* (1976).

in your hand, hand do you know better than Providence?"[19] In our
society, political conservatives wish us to return to the traditional
values from which they fear we have come unmoored, and conservative theorists decry an excess of rationalism and Enlightenment in politics.[20]
  Within the microcosm of the law, one detects a similar backlash
against the freewheeling innovation of Enlightenment. In his much
heralded plurality opinion in *Michael H. v. Gerald D.*,[21] Justice Antonin
Scalia argued in favor of the "practice of limiting the Due Process
Clause to traditionally protected interests," a practice that would "prevent future generations from lightly casting aside important traditional
values."[22] Justice Scalia proposed that the Court determine the limits of
due process protection by "refer[ring] to the most specific level at which
a relevant tradition . . . can be identified,"[23] an approach designed to
limit drastically the Court's authority to reinterpret tradition. This is the
voice of conservative traditionalism protesting contemporary Enlightenment's penchant for moral revision. But it is not only conservative
jurists who don the mantle of traditionalism; in fact, Justice Brennan's
dissent in *Michael H.* counters Justice Scalia's invocation of *societal* tradition by appealing to the *legal* traditions embodied in the Court's own
precedents.[24]

---

  19. Johann Gottfried Herder, "Auch eine Philosophie der Geschichte zur Bildung
der Menschheit," in 5 *Herders Werke* 489 (B. Suphan ed. 1880), *quoted in* Ernst Cassirer,
The Philosophy of the Enlightenment 232–33 (F. Koelln & J. Pettegrove transs. 1951).
  20. *See, e.g.,* Alexander M. Bickel, *The Morality of Consent* (1975); Michael
Oakeshott, *Rationalism in Politics and Other Essays* (1962).
  21. 491 U.S. 110 (1989).
  22. *Id.* at 123 n.2.
  23. *Id.* at 127 n.6. In a later opinion, Scalia linked tradition to due process of law
even more bluntly, writing, "I affirm that no procedure firmly rooted in the practices of
our people can be so 'fundamentally unfair' as to deny due process of law." Pacific
Mutual Life Insurance Co. v. Haslip, 499 U.S. 1, 61 (Scalia, J., concurring).
  24. *Id.* at 138, 139 (Brennan, J., dissenting) ("It is ironic that an approach so utterly
dependent on tradition is so indifferent to our precedents. . . . Today's plurality . . . does
not ask whether parenthood is an interest that historically has received our attention and
protection. . . . "). As Robin West notes, both Scalia's and Brennan's positions "define the
liberty protected by the due process clause by reference to some set of past historical
traditions. The traditions on which they depend are different: Scalia prefers to defer to
societal or communitarian tradition, whereas Brennan wants to rely on the traditions
identified in the judicial precedent from a particular era. Both, nevertheless, define
liberty in terms of past tradition rather than, for example, by reference to some understanding of the ideally free or autonomous individual life." Robin West, "The Ideal of
Liberty: A Comment on *Michael H. v. Gerald D.*," 139 *University of Pennsylvania Law
Review* 1373, 1377 (1991). Appealing to "the ideally free or autonomous individual life"
is, of course, a quintessentially Enlightenment procedure.

A kindred countermovement may be found in the legal academy. Professor Charles Fried, one of the most important contemporary legal philosophers, has confessed that he and other philosophically minded lawyers once "thought that by doing philosophy we would illuminate law; indeed, by doing moral philosophy we thought that we were in fact doing a certain kind of law. . . . Lately, however, I have begun to feel doubts about the moralizing of law. . . . "[25] Fried concludes that "the law is a distinct subject, a branch neither of economics nor of moral philosophy. . . . [Thus] rights will be best and most reasonably respected if reasoning about them goes forward within [the law's] special discipline."[26] That special discipline is "the method of analogy and precedent,"[27] and thus Fried's argument amounts to a defense of traditionalism.

More recently, Robert Bork has defended tradition against rationalism, which he dismisses with this sardonic observation:

> Leading legal academics are increasingly absorbed with what they call "legal theory." . . . One would suppose that we can decide nothing unless we first settle the ultimate questions of the basis of political obligation, the merits of contractarianism, rule or act utilitarianism, the nature of the just society and the like.[28]

Not surprisingly, Bork disagrees with these academics. He argues instead that in law, as in theology, "the main bulwark against heresy [is] only tradition."[29] In his 1990 book, *The Tempting of America*, Bork diagnoses the rationalist attack on traditional values as a *Kulturkampf* waged by the "knowledge class" against middle-class morality and defends what may be the ultimately traditionalist understanding of constitutional interpretation, the theory of original understanding.[30] About originalism I shall have more to say.

Nor are these the only such arguments to appear in the past few years. For example, in a recent paper, lawyer-philosopher M. B. E. Smith asks whether lawyers should listen to philosophers about legal ethics and answers (rather heatedly) that they should not, for philosophy involves a "relentless pursuit of the necessary, and concomitant

---

25. Charles Fried, "The Artificial Reason of the Law or: What Lawyers Know," 60 *Texas Law Review* 35, 37 (1981).
26. *Id.* at 38.
27. *Id.* at 57.
28. Robert H. Bork, *Tradition and Morality in Constitutional Law* 9–10 (1984).
29. *Id.* at 10.
30. Bork, *The Tempting of America: The Political Seduction of the Law* 1–11 (1990).

disdain for that which is merely accidentally or fortuitously true."[31] As a result, Smith continues, philosophers "have failed to appreciate the moral weight upon lawyers of the body of law that governs practice."[32] Quite apart from published articles and books, my (admittedly subjective) impression is that the pendulum among both legal academics and law students is swinging rapidly away from the past decade's infatuation with theory drawn from other disciplines, back in the direction of law's aboriginal grand tradition. If my argument so far is correct, the backlash against philosophy, and more generally against "fancy theory," is a predictable and symptomatic response to the dislocations of modernity.

Kronman's Defense of Traditionalism

Neither Fried nor Bork offers a sustained argument on behalf of legal traditionalism, understood as an abiding reverence both for tradition itself and for its embodiment in legal reasoning through the doctrine of precedent. In a recent essay, however, Anthony Kronman has offered just such an argument, and in my view it is an admirable and powerful one.[33] In the next four sections of this chapter, I examine legal traditionalism through the lens of Kronman's argument, returning to the general topic in my conclusion. Kronman, I believe, has provided as fine an argument on behalf of traditionalism as we are likely to get, and if it fails—as I believe it does—it does so because traditionalism itself cannot be sustained.[34]

The force of precedent, according to Kronman, is best understood through "the traditionalist idea that the past possesses an authority of its own" rather than through the various prudential and moral arguments typically offered by philosophers of law, who are "no more capable of granting the past such an authority in law than in any other sphere of human life."[35] Kronman explains this "traditionalist idea" through an account of human culture. "[H]uman beings," he argues,

---

31. M. B. E. Smith, "Should Lawyers Listen to Philosophers about Legal Ethics?" 9 *Law and Philosophy* 67, 71–72 (1990). See my response, "Smith against the Ethicists," 9 *Law and Philosophy* 417 (1991).

32. *Id.* at 85.

33. Anthony T. Kronman, "Precedent and Tradition," 99 *Yale Law Journal* 1029 (1990).

34. For a criticism of "neotraditionalism" along rather different lines—but one with which I am in considerable sympathy—see Richard A. Posner, *The Problems of Jurisprudence* 423–53 (1990).

35. Kronman, *supra* note 33, at 1046.

are cultural creatures as well as biological ones. Each generation of human beings is born into a cultured or cultivated world, a world of things that earlier generations have made and which, having outlasted their makers, still exist—physical things like buildings, tools, and gardens, and less tangible ones like laws.[36]

The fact that human culture is cumulative makes available to us a realm of value inaccessible to other creatures:

> [It] permits us . . . to participate in projects that it would be point-less to pursue were our goals limited to those that can be reached in the time before we die, and thereby enhances human freedom by allowing us to escape, if only in a qualified way, the tyranny of our biological fate. . . .[37]

Yet the artifacts of human culture require constant tending, without which they soon return to their natural state like an overgrown garden. (By the end of the eighteenth century, the Roman forum was completely buried, and its site had become a cow pasture.) The ever-present threat of decay accounts for "the responsibility of preservation that the world of culture imposes on us,"[38] and this responsibility is tantamount to the moral claim that the past exerts on us.

Kronman thus grounds the authority of precedent in a philosophi-cal account of human culture, an account that he associates with the thought of Edmund Burke.[39] It is nevertheless an important aim of Kronman's to shield the law from philosophical scrutiny, from the in-cessant demand of philosophy (particularly modern philosophy) that law's claims be justified before the "tribunal of reason." Philosophers pursue timeless truths, and thus the bare fact that something occurred in the past can never provide a philosophically acceptable reason for offering it deference or respect. The pastness of the past must always be accidental or arbitrary to philosophy. Yet according to Kronman, the vindication of precedent is, at the deepest level, simply that we ought to revere the past for its own sake or, more specifically, for the sake of the freedom inherent in human culture, which vanishes unless we revere the past.[40] The authority of precedent is rooted in respect for tradition,

---

36. *Id.* at 1051.
37. *Id.* at 1052.
38. *Id.* at 1054.
39. *Id.* at 1047.
40. *Id.* at 1039. To his credit, Kronman does admit that in revering the past, one is not obligated to do so uncritically or unconditionally. Nevertheless, Kronman forcefully

and this in turn is grounded in the claims that the past lays on us merely by virtue of its having come before. Thus, Kronman insists, instead of defending the moral authority of precedent through philosophical argument, lawyers should decline the invitation to engage in the philosophical enterprise in the first place, because law rests ultimately on radically time-bound commitments whose meaning will be destroyed by the effort to recast them as timeless truths. Traditionalism, not rationalism, is the attitude appropriate to law.

Kronman's defense of traditionalism is noteworthy for its depth and passion, as well as for the beauty of its argument and prose. I nevertheless find myself in disagreement with him at nearly every turn. Unlike Kronman, I believe that the authority of precedent has little to do with respect for tradition, and, moreover, that reverence for tradition is a phenomenon quite distinct from respect for the past as such. I also fear that Kronman has wrongly characterized the law by attributing its distinctiveness exclusively to the role of precedent: he has omitted the other hemisphere of law, the hemisphere of statute, and in so doing has distorted his analysis of precedent. More fundamentally, I disagree with his philosophical account of human culture, a disagreement that lies at the root of my other doubts. In the final section of this chapter, I return from Kronman's essay to the general topic of legal traditionalism. Although I agree wholeheartedly with Kronman's defense of historical or backward-looking thinking in law, I shall argue in this concluding section that we inhabit a culture (call it modernist culture) in which our stance toward tradition has necessarily become too complex to permit the straightforward reverence for the past that traditionalism enjoins.

The Force of Precedent and the Claims of Tradition

The problem that precedent poses for philosophy is this: Judicial decisions lay down rules that may be arbitrary, foolish, or unjust, and judicial opinions vindicate those rules with reasoning that is frequently specious, anachronistic, or simply absent. The principle of stare decisis nonetheless instructs us to defer to those rules; thus, stare decisis seems more than occasionally like an injunction to persevere in injustice. No matter how compelling a reasoned argument about justice may be, the law accords it less authority than the ill-considered pronouncements of narrow-minded judicial timeservers appointed to the bench through

---

defends the autonomy of law against the incursion of philosophy: "The world of culture must be protected . . . from the world of thought, from Socrates and all his followers, and the threat to culture on this side [Burke] rightly assumed to be as serious as the danger [that biological processes will overwhelm culture]." *Id.* at 1064.

cronyism in the Harding administration. Stare decisis seems an outrageous doctrine; as Holmes once wrote, "It is revolting to have no better reason for a rule of law than that so it was laid down in the time of Henry IV."[41]

Some philosophers have undertaken to defend stare decisis, but Kronman finds their cures little better than the disease. These philosophers employ deontological arguments that fairness requires us to treat like cases alike or consequentialist arguments that stare decisis imparts predictability and stability to the law. Kronman does not deny the soundness of these arguments. Rather, he complains that both defenses ignore what he takes to be the true imperative of stare decisis, namely that "we are bound, within whatever limits, to honor the past for its own sake, to respect it just because it is the past we happen to have." Thus the philosophical defense of precedent "is not . . . a victory, as it may appear to some. It is instead a kind of defeat, for it closes the way to a deeper understanding of the human meaning of the past."[42]

Whatever its other merits, however, Kronman's appeal to traditionalism—the doctrine that "we are bound, within whatever limits, to honor the past for its own sake"—fails to explain, or even misexplains, some of the elementary facts about precedent. For instance:

1. The force of tradition increases with the antiquity of the tradition, whereas a precedent is at its strongest the day it is decided. Unlike tradition, the force of precedent deteriorates with the passage of time. Of course, a precedent may be refreshed by reiteration and reuse, but subsequent decisions typically rely most heavily on the most recent reiteration of a precedent ("Only last year, in *A. v. B.*, we reaffirmed the rule of the old decision *C. v. D.* . . . "). A lawyer might well attempt to overturn a sixty-year-old decision, but a lawyer who asked a court to overturn yesterday's decision would most likely face judicial sanctions for frivolous litigation.

2. A decision that breaks radically with tradition often sets just as strong a precedent as a decision that faithfully follows tradition. Indeed, the very definition of a landmark case is one that effects a sharp departure from tradition and that judges subsequently rush to embrace. But an antitraditional case need not be landmark to exert full precedential force. If, for example, only one case on point exists within a jurisdiction, stare decisis accords it full weight even if it turns tradition on its ear and even if the court or the issue makes the case too minor to count as landmark.

---

41. Holmes, *supra* note 2, at 187.
42. Kronman, *supra* note 33, at 1037.

Admittedly, some decisions are outliers that exert no subsequent "gravitational force."[43] However, cases typically become outliers because of their stupidity, political extremism, or impracticality, not merely because they depart from tradition.[44] When a case is treated as an outlier because it departs from tradition, that is generally because the tradition is considered reasonable, vital, and worthy of preservation, on the principle that "if it ain't broke, don't fix it"—precisely the sort of consequentialist defense of tradition that Kronman wishes to replace by appealing to tradition as such.

3. Conversely, a precedent located squarely at the heart of a tradition loses much if not all of its force when an authoritative court explicitly overrules it. This is true even if the overruling decision is antitraditional and, indeed, even if the overruling decision subsequently comes to be regarded as an outlier.

These familiar facts about the mechanics of precedent demonstrate that precedent derives its force from sources other than tradition. What are those sources? First, Kronman's misgivings notwithstanding, I believe that the deontological appeal to fairness and the consequentialist appeal to predictability and stability are powerful arguments for according authority to stare decisis. Moreover, these are sources that judges and lawyers take quite seriously—more seriously, I would hazard to guess, than they take the appeal to traditionalism. This is not to say that we should endorse either argument wholeheartedly. If a precedent is itself unfair, then perpetuating its unfairness is often a greater deontological wrong than treating like cases differently. To put it another way, treating like cases alike is of little value if doing so requires that we decide them all badly. Similarly, stability and predictability cannot stand as highest-order legal values, allowed to trump even justice.[45] But these qualifications suggest only that stare decisis is not an absolute rule. That the deontological and consequentialist defenses of precedent are self-limiting does not mean that the arguments of fairness and predictability (whatever their force) do not underwrite stare decisis (whatever its force).

---

43. Ronald Dworkin employed this metaphor to explain the force that a judicial decision exerts on later decisions "even when these later decisions lie outside its particular orbit." Dworkin, *supra* note 13, at 111.

44. A. L. A. Schechter Poultry Corp. v. United States, 295 U.S. 495 (1935), which held on separation-of-powers grounds that Congress could not delegate the legislative power to an executive agency, is a case in point: Taken at face value, its antidelegation doctrine would annul much of the administrative state, and thus it has become an outlier. Yet its reading of the separation of powers fit squarely within the prevailing tradition.

45. On this point see chapter 6.

A second source for the authority of precedent lies in the very nature of legality. As John Finnis has observed, the basic technique by which law orders human affairs consists in "the treating of (usually datable) past acts . . . as giving, *now*, sufficient and exclusionary reason for acting in a way *then* 'provided for.' "[46] That is, law orders human affairs by (1) specifying that all and only the members of a certain class of political acts—let us call them juridical acts—possess present legal authority and (2) stipulating that the authority of a juridical act stands undiminished until another juridical act supersedes it. These two conditions distinguish juridical acts from all other forms of political action, which can be contested by anyone at any time and whose authority begins to dissipate amidst the shifting winds of politics as soon as it has been asserted. Law is a means of channeling and controlling the primordial energy of politics by insisting that some political actions can achieve victories that last over time, that count as resting points or new baselines (no matter how temporary or provisional) in the never-ending whirlwind of human affairs.

Judicial decisions number among these juridical acts, which implies that the rule of a case must stand until a subsequent juridical act alters it. Now it is a platitude of contemporary legal theory that all judicial decisions, whether they reverse precedents or mechanically apply them, are political acts. Nevertheless, judges and citizens alike typically regard reversals and overrulings as more political and more problematic than reaffirmations and applications of past decisions. Stare decisis therefore plays a role in preserving the perceived political neutrality and legitimacy of courts.

I should add that I do not write as a supporter of judicial self-restraint, which I regard as a confused and often dangerous doctrine.[47] My point is simply that the force of precedent derives not from traditionalism but from a particular political theory about the role of judges in politics—a theory that rightly or wrongly (1) regards judges as subordinate political actors and (2) regards reversals and overrulings as more problematically political than affirmations and applications.[48]

---

46. John Finnis, *Natural Law and Natural Rights* 269 (1980) (emphasis in original).

47. On this point see my "Justice Holmes and Judicial Virtue," *Nomos XXXIV: Virtue* 235 (John L. Chapman & William A. Galston eds. 1992).

48. I do not mean to exclude the possibility that proposition (2) is the result, rather than the source, of stare decisis. Even if that is true, however, the proposition provides a reason to persist in stare decisis. We need not speculate whether the chicken or the egg came first to remain confident that chickens come from eggs as well as that eggs come from chickens.

Finnis's characterization of legality reveals one sense in which Kronman is right in saying that the force of precedent derives from respect for the past: Law simply is a device whereby we stipulate the undiminished authority of past political decisions until new decisions take their place. Yet Kronman rejects this sense of traditionalism. He observes that in the deontological argument for stare decisis, past decisions set the baseline for treating like cases alike: The injunction to treat like cases alike must mean treating the later case like the earlier, and thus the past does play a normative role.[49] Kronman, however, correctly recognizes that this role is distinct from, indeed antithetical to, the traditionalist injunction to revere the past for its own sake. For, clearly, what propels the deontological argument is not reverence for a particular earlier case that sets the baseline, but rather the (timeless) principle of treating like cases alike and the (timeless) philosophical defense of fairness that underlies this principle.[50] In precisely the same way, Finnis's argument accords the past no reverence: past decisions bind us only because they have not yet been replaced or repealed. Plainly, that is not what Kronman has in mind. The traditionalism he espouses regards tradition as providing a powerful reason not to replace or repeal past decisions.

In truth, however, the unromantic linkage of law to the past that I have taken from Finnis straightforwardly explains all the phenomena about precedent that Kronman's traditionalism cannot. Under this unromantic view, the most recent rather than the most ancient judicial decision is the law simply because later juridical acts supersede earlier ones; antitraditional decisions exert the same gravitational force as tradition-respecting decisions because both are juridical acts of the relevant sort; and explicitly overruling an old and deeply-rooted decision annuls its value as precedent precisely because law is designed to change at the explicit decision of authoritative courts.

These arguments amount to an illustration of the more general point that "the past" and "the traditional" are two distinct things, which Kronman erroneously runs together.[51] The distinction becomes clearer if we consider three points, analogous to the three observations I made about precedent.

1. "The past" can be recent as well as ancient, whereas tradition must emerge from practices that by now have become relatively ancient. In an old stand-up comedy routine, Severn Darden delivered a

---

49. Kronman, *supra* note 33, at 1041.
50. *Id.* at 1042.
51. *See, e.g., id.* at 1048 (identifying "the claims of tradition" with "the inherent authority of the past").

lecture on metaphysics: "What is time? [Pause] That was time. That was all the time there was in the world at that time." He thereby called attention to the truism that the past is as recent as . . . just now. "Just now," however, has nothing to do with tradition and exerts no claim on our reverence, though someday it might. (Give it time.)

2. Events and customs in the distant past may be outliers from what were then traditions, and this can be true even if the events were momentous at the time. Therefore, not just the recent past but also (much of) the distant past must be distinguished from tradition. Genghis Khan's Mongol invasion was an immense event, but it exerted no lasting role on the cluster of traditions and institutions we call Western civilization. It forms no part of the Western tradition. Likewise, the history of each of the arts contains examples of misfits who have exerted no lasting influence even though they created works of substantial quality. Composers such as Soler, Alkan, Scriabin, Hovhaness, Orff, and Partch, and painters such as Bosch, Redon, and Balthus simply do not belong to "the tradition." Tradition is a heavily edited anthology of the past, and most of the past fails to participate in it at all.

3. Moreover, countless traditions have come to arbitrary ends, be it through conquest, catastrophe, imperial ukase, economic change, or whims of fashion. Defunct religions are an obvious example of such traditions. With their passing, mourned or unmourned, they have become merely past. They deserve no allegiance from us or anyone else—a good thing, since otherwise we ought still to be offering animal sacrifices to Apollo—and they could not be revived even if we wanted to revive them. If living tradition is like a shrine, then the past is more like the burial mound of a long-forgotten culture.

For this reason we ought to be cautious about accepting Burke's vision of an unbroken chain linking us to our remote ancestors and our distant descendants, which, as he puts it, forms "a partnership . . . between those who are living, those who are dead, and those who are to be born."[52] Of course, the biological chain linking each individual to his or her descendants will, by definition, go on unbroken (at least until that individual's descendants fail to reproduce), but the cultural chain linking "us" to "our" descendants will be interrupted and begun anew countless times, as it has already countless times in the past.

Having drawn the distinction between tradition and the past, we may rephrase our earlier arguments. The force of precedent indeed arises from the fact that it is past, but for the straightforward and untraditionalist reasons Finnis offers. It does not arise from the fact that

---

52. Edmund Burke, *Reflections on the Revolution in France* 85 (J. Pocock ed. 1987).

precedent is part of tradition, for, as we have seen, even recent and untraditional decisions bind future courts. Now it is true that Kronman speaks most often of the past rather than of tradition, but the title of his essay and his repeated description of his view as "traditionalism" make it clear that he means the latter. The focus on tradition is confirmed when he points to the importance of law as "a cultural endeavor in the sense that I have indicated, an enterprise requiring a collaboration of many generations."[53] Kronman's emphasis on multigenerational collaboration singles out tradition, rather than the past as such, as the object of his defense. Though Kronman defines traditionalism as respect for the past simply because it is past, it seems clear that he has in mind respect for the more-or-less distant past. For if the recent or immediate past is included, the very idea of respect for the past simply because it is past seems alien and wrongheaded. For instance, the typographical error that I made fifteen seconds ago belongs to the past. Surely I could have no reason to leave it uncorrected.

Some may respond that my objection to Kronman's argument, based on the observation that very recent decisions exert full precedential force even though they are too recent to count as tradition, misinterprets his point. Perhaps he meant to say that the force of a precedent arises not from *its* antiquity, but rather from the antiquity of the common-law tradition of stare decisis itself. Perhaps, that is, Kronman intends his appeal to tradition to be a vindication of the time-honored judicial practice of respecting precedent, not an argument that judges ought to respect a precedent because of its own tradition-based moral authority.

I do not believe, however, that this is what Kronman had in mind, for, if so, he had no reason to take precedent as his theme. If the argument is that respect for precedent is vindicated by respect for the long-standing judicial tradition of respect for precedent, then we could substitute *any* long-standing judicial tradition and the argument would be the same. (In addition, of course, the argument as stated teeters on the brink of infinite regress.) There is, for example, a long-standing judicial tradition of straightforward consequentialist argument, often flying in the teeth of precedent.[54] Indeed, there is a long-standing judicial tradition of establishing novel holdings by distinguishing away inconvenient precedents. The argument we are presently considering would

---

53. Kronman, *supra* note 33, at 1057.

54. As Richard Posner has observed, an argument Sir James Stephen quotes from a medieval nuisance case bases itself explicitly on utilitarian considerations: "*Le utility del chose excusera le noisomeness del stink.*" Sir James Fitzjames Stephen, *A General View of the Criminal Law of England* 106 (1890). *Quoted in* Posner, *The Economics of Justice* 50 n.10 (2d ed. 1983).

vindicate both of these practices just as surely as it vindicates stare decisis, but it would plainly be a perverse misreading of Kronman's essay to attribute any such arguments to him.

To summarize: the force of precedent has nothing obviously to do with the claims of tradition; and those claims, whatever their source and strength, do not derive from the claims of the past as such.

The Realm of Statute

In laying out his case for the centrality of traditionalism in the law, Kronman begins by observing that

> the sphere of law is characterized by an attitude that is . . . alien . . . to the spirit of philosophy. . . . I have in mind . . . the practice of following precedent.
> . . . Respect for past decisions, for precedent, is . . . a feature of law in general, and wherever there exists a set of practices and institutions that we believe are entitled to the name of law, the rule of precedent will be at work. . . . By contrast, the rule of precedent has no place in philosophy, and is indeed antithetical to its governing spirit.[55]

Is it really the case, however, that law is *characterized* by the practice of following precedent? To say that is to characterize law by reference only to judicial decisions. This is a common enough presupposition in American legal philosophy, which has been decisively influenced by the legal realists. The realists, after all, defined law as "prophecies of what the courts will do in fact"[56] or as "the actual behaviour of courts."[57] Moreover, as long as law continues to be taught by the case method, law students and legal academics will find it natural to identify law with judicial decisions. But this characterization is rooted very much in the idiosyncratic perspective of trial lawyers and litigants, and it neglects the entire hemisphere of law occupied by statutes. It has become a commonplace that statutes have largely supplanted common law, that we live today in an "age of statutes."[58] That being so, it is anachronistic to focus our attention so exclusively upon judicial decision making.

---

55. Kronman, *supra* note 33, at 1031–32.

56. Holmes, *supra* note 2, at 173.

57. Felix S. Cohen, "The Problems of a Functional Jurisprudence," 1 *Modern Law Review* 5, 16 (1937).

58. I take the phrase from the title of Guido Calabresi, *A Common Law for the Age of Statutes* (1982). *See also* Bruce A. Ackerman, *Reconstructing American Law* 6–19 (1984) (arguing that statutes and regulations, once making up mere "islands" within the sea of common law, have now become continents).

When we turn from the hemisphere of judicial decisions to the hemisphere of statutes, we find no counterpart to the puzzle of precedent. Statutes exert no precedential force on legislators whatsoever, and the attitude of respect for past decisions that Kronman takes as law's defining characteristic is wholly absent. No legislature is constrained in its lawmaking powers by principles contained in statutes passed by its predecessors, unless those earlier statutes explicitly regulate the legislative function. That is not to deny that as a practical matter legislatures build on previous legislation; it *is* to deny that they are under the slightest obligation to do so. Similarly, the canons of statutory construction impose no obligation to interpret the meaning of a statute by reference to its predecessors, except insofar as these provide evidence from which to draw inferences about legislative intent.

Most importantly, the fact that a statute exists never provides a reason in principle for legislatures to refrain from amending, replacing, or repealing it. There is at most a practical argument that, for the sake of stability, statutes should not be changed too frequently. To amend, replace, and repeal legislation as the need arises is precisely why legislatures are in business. Legislatures are vehicles of political action and political change, and the attitude of legislatures is properly forward-looking and consequentialist, not traditionalist.[59] To be sure, a prudent legislature will not attempt to eradicate entrenched traditions at the stroke of a pen, but this judgment is decidedly *not* based on a principled reverence for tradition as such. For a prudent legislature will likewise not attempt to revive a dying and unpopular tradition in the face of constituents' wishes, and the reason in both cases is the same: Political expediency (or fear) directs legislatures toward the path of least resistance. Traditionalism has nothing to do with it.

In short, the legislative hemisphere exhibits little of the attitude of respect for the past that Kronman takes to characterize the law. Having observed that, we may also observe that the legislative hemisphere possesses authority superior to the judicial hemisphere. A line of precedent, no matter how unchallenged, unbroken, and firmly established it may be, loses its authority the moment the legislature replaces it with a statute. Indeed, that is the way that Congress from the New Deal on has broken the resistance of common-law judges to economic regulation. We share with civil-law societies a political theory that accords

---

59. That is not to deny Ronald Dworkin's insistence that legislators should attend to the integrity of law: "Statutes should be read . . . to express a coherent scheme of conviction dominant within the legislature that enacted them." Dworkin, *Law's Empire* 330 (1986). The requirement that a statute cohere with the rest of law is no more an injunction to revere the past than is the deontologist's injunction to treat the later case like the earlier.

legislatures authority superior to that of judges, who are often (if erroneously) regarded as mere conduits of legislative will. I have suggested that this political theory, and not traditionalism, lies at the heart of stare decisis; ironically, the same political theory guarantees that stare decisis plays only a subordinate role in characterizing the "sphere of law."

Kronman argues that the rule of precedent obtains even in code-based legal systems,[60] and I do not disagree with this observation, for both common-law and civil-law systems are amalgams of statutes and lines of judicial decisions. However, the observation cuts in both directions. Just as the rule of precedent obtains even in civil-law systems, the supremacy of statute obtains even in common-law systems. This supremacy ensures that statute, which has little to do with traditionalism or with the rule of precedent, characterizes law more truly than does precedent.

It may be, however, that Kronman did not intend his assertion that law is animated by force of tradition to be a description of legal systems as we now find them. He may instead have intended his argument as prescription, as a plea for legislators to adopt a less rationalist and more traditionalist attitude, or perhaps even as a polemic against the ubiquity and preeminence of legislation.

If that is the case, however, then Kronman's argument has dramatically shifted ground. It is no longer an effort to explain the rule of stare decisis, an acknowledged yet puzzling feature of our existing jurisprudence. It is rather an argument that we should recast our jurisprudence, and indeed our entire constitutional scheme, either by subordinating statute to common law, by affixing a rule of legislative stare decisis to the canons of statutory construction, or even by asking legislators to abandon the problem-solving and forward-looking function of setting public policy. I doubt the wisdom, not to mention the practicality, of any of these changes, but, in any case, an argument of this sort is quite an odd one for a traditionalist to advance. It proposes that we abandon a tradition of separation of powers that dates from the framing of our own Constitution (and, indeed, from the time of Montesquieu). As Michael Oakeshott has observed, the American Revolution and Constitution were profoundly rationalist, rather than traditionalist, in character.[61] Ironically, to be truly a traditionalist in America, one must give the rationalism that infuses our political culture its due. And

---

60. Kronman, *supra* note 33, at 1031–32.
61. Oakeshott, *supra* note 19, at 26–28. Oakeshott is a political philosopher who is quite close in spirit to Kronman.

before adopting major reforms in the structure or self-understanding of our legislatures, one should heed this warning:

> To understand or successfully reform our system of government, one must . . . appreciate the details of its institutional arrangements and take account of the social complexities in which these arrangements are embedded. Any theory that fails to do so will be hopelessly obtuse and, however powerful its philosophic premises, a poor foundation for reform.

Figuring prominently among those "social complexities" must be the highly rationalized character of our contemporary economy, the power of modern technology, and the rapidity of social change. All of these call for legislative and administrative regulation that is actively intrusive, firmly consequentialist, and forward-looking in character. Thus the argument that legislatures should turn their gaze from the present and the future toward the past is precisely the sort of "hopelessly obtuse" argument that the passage quoted above rightly warns against. The point, ironically, is Kronman's, taken from his remarkable essay on the thought of Alexander Bickel.[62]

Culture and Human Freedom

Let us now consider Kronman's argument for traditionalism. It turns, as I said earlier, on a crucial distinction that Kronman draws between human beings and other animals, namely that human beings inhabit a cumulative world of culture in addition to the "metabolic world"[63] of nature. In the metabolic world, all is consumed by the "circular routines of life"[64]—acquiring and consuming food, giving birth, growing, and dying.

> In the [metabolic] world . . . the generations do not build upon one another's achievements, nor is there anything they must work to keep up, to save from the ruin of time. There is no progress in the world of life but only circularity and repetition, the endless return of the same, and because every generation begins and ends at the same place, there can be no projects in that world that require the participation of successive generations, as in the realm of culture.

---

62. Kronman, "Alexander Bickel's Philosophy of Prudence," 94 *Yale Law Journal* 1567, 1597–98 (1985).

63. Kronman, *supra* note 33, at 1054.

64. *Id.* at 1055.

The liberating power of culture is therefore absent from the world of metabolic routine.[65]

The world of culture, in contrast, opens up a new dimension of human value, the dimension offered by projects that require the cumulative efforts of many generations to execute, such as the great European cathedrals (an example that Kronman uses[66]) or the common law. This dimension of value is foreclosed, however, unless future generations take upon themselves the burden of tending and preserving the cultural legacies we bequeath them; thus, to treat tradition cavalierly is to shut ourselves off from the realm of value that is most characteristically human.

Readers of Hannah Arendt's *The Human Condition* will recognize in it the source of Kronman's distinction between life and culture, or as Arendt put it, between the spheres of *labor* and *work*. Arendt begins her book with definitions of these terms.

Labor is the activity which corresponds to the biological process of the human body. . . . The human condition of labor is life itself.

Work is the activity which corresponds to the unnaturalness of human existence. . . . Work provides an "artificial" world of things, distinctly different from all natural surroundings. Within its borders each individual life is housed, while this world itself is meant to outlast and transcend them all.[67]

Later, in a passage that could as easily have come from Kronman's essay, Arendt writes:

While nature manifests itself in human existence through the circular movement of our bodily functions, she makes her presence felt in the man-made world through the constant threat of overgrowing or decaying it. The common characteristic of both, the biological process in man and the process of growth and decay in the world, is that they are part of the cyclical movement of nature and therefore endlessly repetitive; all human activities which arise out of the necessity to cope with them are bound to the recurring cycles of nature and have in themselves no beginning and no end, properly speaking; unlike *working*, whose end has come when the object is finished, ready to be added to the common world of things,

---

65. *Id.* at 1054.
66. *Id.* at 1051–52.
67. Hannah Arendt, *The Human Condition* 7 (1958).

laboring always moves in the same circle, which is prescribed by the biological process of the living organism. . . .[68]

Working is precisely the cultural activity of which Kronman speaks: It is the creation of "the sheer unending variety of things whose sum total constitutes the human artifice. . . . [T]hey give the human artifice the stability and solidity without which it could not be relied upon to house the unstable and mortal creature which is man."[69]

The distinction that Arendt and Kronman draw is illuminating and important, and perhaps for this reason I find Kronman's defense of traditionalism compelling on its face. If I nevertheless disagree with it, it is because Kronman has omitted something vitally important from his survey of the human condition, something, moreover, that forms the linchpin of Arendt's own philosophy.

Arendt's topic in *The Human Condition* is the *vita activa*, the active life that philosophers traditionally contrasted with the *vita contemplativa*, the life of the mind.[70] Labor and work form two components of the *vita activa*, but there is a crucial third component as well, which she calls *action*.

> Action, the only activity that goes on directly between men without the intermediary of things or matter, corresponds to the human condition of plurality, to the fact that men, not Man, live on the earth and inhabit the world. While all aspects of the human condition are somehow related to politics, this plurality is specifically *the* condition . . . of all political life.[71]

Action for Arendt always meant political action (including political speech), and throughout her career it was action that formed Arendt's deepest concern. Her first major book, *The Origins of Totalitarianism*, argued that totalitarianism embarks on its program of lies, terror, and mass murder because it aims to extinguish the faculty of action. *On Revolution* focused on the "public happiness" that the American founders discovered in the life of action, and her essays turned again and again to the decimation that is wrought on politics and political thought when action loses its centrality among the things we value.

---

68. *Id.* at 98 (emphasis in original). Compare this with the passage quoted from Kronman, *supra* text accompanying note 65.

69. Arendt, *supra* note 67, at 136.

70. Arendt, *The Life of the Mind: Thinking* 80–193 (1978). Kronman acknowledges that his discussion of the *vita contemplativa* was inspired in large measure by Arendt. Kronman, *supra* note 33, at 1055 n.72, 1058–64.

71. Arendt, *supra* note 67, at 7 (emphasis in original).

Strikingly, Kronman omits action entirely from his survey of the human condition, and this omission carries profound consequences. Arendt characterizes action as "beginning something new on our own initiative." Action is an interruption in the inherited world of culture, a kind of "second birth."[72] As she explains, "Without the fact of birth we would not even know what novelty is, all 'action' would be either mere behavior or preservation."[73] Kronman's argument is that mere behavior—meaning animal or "metabolic" behavior—and preservation (of the inherited world) are indeed the only choices available to us.

Yet it is hard to see how that could be so, for surely someone had to begin the cultural traditions that we continue and preserve. To consider Kronman's own example, it was not enough that generations persevered in the work of cathedral building: someone, after all, had to initiate the work, and that inevitably involved a break with tradition. The Gothic style was invented in 1140 by the (anonymous) designer of the Abbey at St. Denis, working under the guidance of the powerful Abbot Suger, and its invention abruptly overthrew centuries of Romanesque tradition. As Nikolaus Pevsner observes, "There are few buildings in Europe so revolutionary in their conception and so rapid and unhesitating in their execution."[74] Virtually all the Gothic cathedrals that proliferated over the next two centuries were built on the sites of Romanesque churches whose old-fashioned circular arches and square bays were mercilessly razed by the Gothic builders, typically at the behest of ambitious bishops who were anxious to make their mark.

In the same way that multigenerational projects such as the cathedrals all have a beginning (which involves the overthrow of an

---

72. *Id.* at 176–77.

73. Arendt, *Crises of the Republic* 179 (1972).

74. Nikolaus Pevsner, *An Outline of European Architecture* 89 (7th ed. 1963). One might object that substituting pointed arches for circular arches was hardly significant enough to count as overthrowing a tradition, but this objection is quite mistaken. On engineering grounds, replacing the circular Romanesque arch with the pointed Gothic arch permitted the construction of rectangular as well as square bays and enhanced the building's weight-bearing capacity. *Id.* at 90–91. These changes made possible the more intense horizontal rhythms and greater height of Gothic cathedrals, which in turn give Gothic cathedrals a wholly different look, feel, and spirit from their Romanesque precursors. In Pevsner's words, Romanesque "conveys to us at once a feeling of certainty and stability," *id.* at 61, whereas Gothic, which is "far from reposeful . . . possesses the tension of two dominant directions or dimensions, a tension transformed by a supreme feat of creative energy into a precarious balance," *id.* at 110. Pevsner writes aptly of "the Gothic architect, far bolder constructionally [than the architects of Greek temples], with his Western soul of the eternal explorer and inventor, always lured by the untried. . . . " *Id.* at 114. These words hardly describe a traditionalist.

older tradition), most come to an eventual end. At that point, the world of cultural value would itself come to an end, were it not for each generation's irreverent innovators, who undertake new projects. Without the faculty of action, of novelty and initiation, the task of preservation that Kronman urges on us would amount to the unrelieved dreariness of Atlas supporting the globe. Initiation without preservation is pointless, perhaps, but preservation without initiation is unbearable. Action thus forms the necessary counterpoise to work.

Arendt was not content to distinguish among labor, work, and action. She argued that these activities form a hierarchy, and that action occupies the summit. Labor, which sustains us simply so that we can labor again, is by itself the most futile of activities. It is only through work that some durable monument can be created, a monument that outlasts the effort of producing it. Work, however, creates artifacts whose sole purpose lies in their being a means to some end (art objects are perhaps the sole exception). Thus we cannot make sense of cultural artifacts on their own terms without falling into an infinite regress, in which each end is simply a means to another end. Even the cathedrals were built as a means to an end: They were erected to facilitate worship and to thank God for the town's prosperity (and, incidentally, to outdo other towns in making that prosperity conspicuous). So too, the common-law rules developed as a means to adjudicate disputes and bring order to human affairs.

If the world of culture is a world composed of means to various ends, then the sense of futility lurking in this realization is only heightened when we interrupt the infinite regress of ends by invoking the paradoxical concept of an "end in itself."[75] In this way, a life devoted solely to augmenting the stock of cultural objects is menaced by the threat of meaninglessness and futility, just as surely as is a life devoted solely to laboring for its own subsistence.

This is where action comes in. The realm of action serves "to throw light on the affairs of men by providing a space of appearances in which they can show in deed and word, for better or worse, who they are and what they can do."[76] Throughout history, Arendt observes, storytelling has been the prototypical way we impart meaning to mortal experience.[77] Action is the stuff of stories, and that is why action is crucial to the possibility of meaningful human life: stories, unlike either the consumer goods provided by labor or the use objects fabricated by work,

75. Arendt, *supra* note 67, at 155–56.
76. Arendt, *Men in Dark Times* viii (1968).
77. Arendt, *supra* note 67, at 181–88. See chapter 4 for further discussion of Arendt's views on the importance of storytelling.

116

are inherently meaningful. And thus it is "only through the interrelated faculties of action and speech, which produce meaningful stories as naturally as fabrication produces use objects,"[78] that we may avoid the infinite regress of ends. Action assumes the form of stories that unfold rather than ends at which we aim. It is the primary meaning-giver in the *vita activa*, just as thinking, philosophical contemplation, is the primary meaning-giver in the life of the mind.

Arendt therefore locates human freedom in the capacity for action, not (as Kronman does) in the capacity for carrying out intergenerational cultural projects: "With the creation of man, the principle of beginning came into the world itself, which, of course, is only another way of saying that the principle of freedom was created when man was created but not before."[79]

We need not accept all of Arendt's arguments to recognize the central role the possibility of new beginnings plays in maintaining our sense that life has meaning. Kronman's account, which stresses the importance of preserving our cultural heritage but neglects our capacity for transforming it, has simply begged the question in favor of traditionalism and against political change.

Indeed, Kronman's underestimation of the importance of innovation in human affairs leads him to an excessively one-sided view of intergenerational obligation. In one of his most stirring paragraphs, Kronman writes

> We are indebted to those who came before us, for it is through their efforts that the world of culture we inhabit now exists. But by the same token, they are indebted to us, for it is only through our efforts that their achievements can be saved from ruin. Our relationship with our predecessors is therefore one of mutual indebtedness, and so, of course, is our relationship with our successors, though the debts in that case are reversed.[80]

This realization lends itself naturally to Burke's metaphor of "the great primeval contract of eternal society," the "partnership . . . between those who are living, those who are dead, and those who are to be born,"[81] and Kronman proceeds to elaborate this metaphor as part of his case for traditionalism.

I believe, however, that neither Kronman nor Burke has adequately characterized the intergenerational social contract. The pledge to pre-

---

78. Arendt, *supra* note 67, at 236.
79. *Id.* at 177.
80. Kronman, *supra* note 33, at 1067.
81. Burke, *supra* note 52, at 85.

serve and elaborate the work of our forebears, so that our descendants will do the same for our own achievements, comprises only one clause of the intergenerational social contract. The other clause, which Kronman (like Burke) neglects, cuts in the opposite direction. Our forebears were not prophets; they could not be expected to foresee the problems that we now confront or the political circumstances that constrain our efforts to address these problems. We must, therefore, be permitted to shake ourselves free of our heritage as the need arises, just as they shook themselves free of the traditions that their ancestors bequeathed to them. That being so, we must extend to our own children the permission to unmake what we have made, trusting that our legacy will survive in their freedom as well as in their conservatorship. Thus we pass on to them a world of culture along with a space of action, knowing that their freedom from us is no more avoidable than our freedom from our own parents.

Correctly understood, the "great primeval contract of eternal society" contains two clauses that pull in opposite directions. The first, upon which Kronman and Burke focus exclusively, is a *preservation* clause, in which we pledge to conserve our ancestral heritage and trust that our descendants will likewise preserve theirs. The second, which Kronman and Burke neglect altogether, is an *innovation* clause, in which we offer our descendants the same freedom to break with the past that we ourselves enjoy. Of course, our descendants will in any event avail themselves of this freedom whether we offer it or not, just as we detached ourselves from our ancestors' purposes, and they detached themselves from the purposes of their own ancestors.

This conception of the intergenerational contract sheds light, I believe, on the issue of originalism in legal interpretation. The Constitution and statutes exemplify the kind of durable objects that will disappear unless each generation self-consciously tends them. One of the attractions of interpreting law by appealing to the intentions of its makers has always been its claim to keep faith with our ancestors; clearly, the Burkean contract argument, focusing exclusively on the preservation clause, may be invoked on behalf of originalism. Each generation, so the argument goes, fights political fights, and the victors aim to consolidate and codify their achievement in law. Indeed, as we have seen earlier, legal pronouncements can be understood as attempts to bring closure (however temporary) to political battles. If future generations depart from our intentions by refashioning the law through unfamiliar interpretations, our efforts to consolidate political victories through codification will fail. Thus, precisely because we wish to be able to consolidate our own political achievements, we owe it to our ancestors to respect theirs. So goes the argument based on the preservation clause of the intergenerational social contract.

As I have indicated, however, the argument has another side, corresponding to the innovation clause of the intergenerational contract. The framers of past laws enacted them to put out their own fires, and their time horizons were not necessarily long enough to envision the fires that we now confront. We must therefore be permitted to press their tools into the service of our ends, by extending or elaborating their language in ways that may be inconsistent with their intentions. (It is for this reason that the fundamental technique of legal reasoning has always been extension through analogy and metaphor.) The justification is deceptively simple: They did the same to their ancestors' legal inheritance. The intergenerational social contract is not just an agreement to accept constraints imposed by the past but also one that grants the freedom to adapt the past flexibly to meet the needs of the present. Antioriginalist arguments about the interpretation of a "living Constitution" have just as much grounding in the "great primeval contract" as do originalist arguments. All this is just to say that the metaphor of intergenerational contract settles the issue in neither direction. The tension between preservation and innovation inheres in every problem of legal interpretation, and the interpretive act consists largely in resolving that tension through an argument about specifics. Appealing abstractly to one of the two values can never do more than beg the question.

One additional point bears some emphasis in our discussion of Kronman's philosophical case for traditionalism. Although Kronman claims several times to be defending reverence for the past for its own sake, that is not the argument he actually makes. He argues instead that we must revere the past because such reverence is the essential means for realizing the value unique to multigenerational cultural projects. That, however, presumes that multigenerational cultural projects are in fact valuable, a crucial assumption built into Kronman's repeated reference to them as "achievements" and "accomplishments."[82]

Yet surely this assumption is open to question. To take an obvious counterexample, racial segregation was a multigenerational project that depended for its survival on the next generation pitching in to preserve it; yet it had no value, or rather negative value. A traditionalist would be hard pressed to explain why anyone should regard Jim Crow as an achievement imposing on us "the burdens of a trust that cannot be

---

82. *E.g.*, Kronman, *supra* note 33, at 1051.

escaped."[83] In the end, of course, it falls to us (who else?) to pass judgment on the traditions into which we are born and to determine whether a multigenerational project should be tended and cultivated or abandoned without regret. Thus, in the end, rationalist inquiry into the justification of traditions is inescapably our lot.

Claiming Our Past

Traditional societies were not traditionalist; during the centuries following the sack of Rome, the city's unsentimental residents innocently burned the marble statues and facings from the imperial capitol to make chalk. It was only when the nineteenth century came to regard history as the fountainhead of value that the excavation and preservation of ancient Rome began. To adopt the self-conscious attitude of traditionalism requires historical distance from the traditional—a sense of loss, a sense that one has become cut off from the past. Thus, traditionalism waxes as tradition itself wanes; like Hegel's owl of Minerva, traditionalism always arrives on the scene too late. It is the political counterpart of what individuals experience as nostalgia for lost innocence.[84] In Jaroslav Pelikan's well-known aphorism, tradition is the living faith of the dead, whereas traditionalism is the dead faith of the living.

As such, traditionalism amounts to something like an optical illusion of the spirit. Literary critic Raymond Williams once read a book that lamented the passing of English country life during the previous fifty years. This intrigued him, for he recalled a book of fifty years earlier that had uttered a similar lament, gesturing still further back. Williams found that "what seemed like an escalator began to move" backward into literary history. At each stop, another author, from an earlier generation than the last, lamented the passing "of the rural England 'that is dying out now.'"[85] Nine or ten stops back, in 1516, he found Thomas More pointing to

the settled Middle Ages, an organic society if ever there was one. To the 1370s, for example, when Langland's Piers Plowman sees the dissatisfaction of the labourers, who will not eat yesterday's vegetables but must have fresh meat, who blame God and curse the King, but who used not to complain when Hunger made the Statutes.[86]

---

83. *Id.* at 1055.
84. *See* Stuart Hampshire, *Innocence and Experience* 146–53 (1989).
85. Raymond Williams, *The Country and the City* 9 (1973).
86. *Id.* at 11.

Williams delved further into literary history, back to the time of the
Magna Carta, then to the Doomsday Book, then to the Norman inva-
sion. At each stage, authors lamented the loss of traditional England.
How much further to go? Perhaps

> the timeless rhythm [lies] in a free Saxon world before what was
> later seen as the Norman rape and yoke? In a Celtic world, before
> the Saxons came up the rivers? In an Iberian world, before the Celts
> came, with their gilded barbarism? Where indeed shall we go,
> before the escalator stops?
>   One answer, of course, is Eden. . . .[87]

Each generation finds itself at a historical distance from its ancestors
and thereby discovers the possibility of adopting a traditionalist attitude toward ancestral traditions that have vanished. What made the
nineteenth century unique was that its historians and philosophers took
these phenomena as a theme for explicit reflection. In so doing, they
brought the sense of alienation from the past to a crisis point.

This crisis, in turn, marked the beginning of twentieth-century
modernism, Clement Greenberg's "intensification, almost the exacerba-
tion, of [the] self-critical tendency that began with the philosopher
Kant. . . . The essence of Modernism lies . . . in the use of the characteristic methods of a discipline to criticize the discipline itself. . . ."[88]
Modernist painters built the critique of the representational tradition
into their abstractions; modernist composers abandoned tonality in
part to criticize the tonal tradition.

Once an endeavor has entered the modernist predicament, it
proves impossible to recapture the lost innocence of the tradition. A
twentieth-century composer who writes like Mozart or a contemporary
artist who paints like Titian creates only pastiche. Hence, traditionalism—the attempt to participate in traditions in the same unprob-
lematic way that our ancestors did—is doomed to failure. It can
succeed in reviving a lost tradition only by caricaturing it. Traditionalism is a natural, perhaps an inevitable, response to the sense of spiritual
exile that marks the modernist predicament. Natural or not, however, it
is self-defeating. Traditionalism denies the modernist predicament instead of facing up to it.

I am not arguing for a rejection of the past—which is in any event
completely impossible—nor am I advocating a relentlessly forward-

<hr>

87. *Id.* at 11–12.
88. Clement Greenberg, "Modernist Painting," in *The New Art* 100, 101 (Gregory
Battcock ed. 1966). See chapter 1.

looking and consequentialist mode of legal thinking; indeed, I will argue in chapter 5 that legal thinking must be backward-looking and historical. But histori*cal* thinking differs greatly from histori*cist* thinking, and I believe that it is the latter that lies at the heart of traditionalism. Historicist thinking reveres the past for its own sake, whereas—in the words of Walter Benjamin—"[t]o articulate the past historically . . . means to seize hold of a memory as it flashes up at a moment of danger."[89] Benjamin's striking image calls to mind the mysterious functioning of memory during an emergency, when it serves to release the forgotten bit of information we so desperately need. Benjamin thus regards historical thinking as a function of two variables, the past image and the present danger. Historicists focus on the past for its own sake and insist that "historians who wish to relive an era . . . blot out everything they know about the later course of history,"[90] including the present need. This historicist imperative is quite impossible, however, for as Williams's discussion of literary history suggests, it is the present need that opens up our vista on the past.

Indeed, it is largely present circumstances that move us to decide which tradition, which past, is ours. I, for example, am a second-generation American Jew whose grandparents were born in Poland and Latvia. Is the current Latvian nation part of *my* heritage? Is the American nineteenth century? Must I accept some responsibility for human rights violations in modern Israel, where no one in my family resides? If, as I believe, the answer to the first question is "no," but to the second and third "yes," these are plainly not brute facts of history but ex post political judgments arising from choices that are in large measure mine to make. (The answers would be different were I to move "back" to Latvia to join the struggle to rebuild an independent nation—and different still if I moved "back" to Latvia to rebuild the historic Jewish community that vanished in the Holocaust.) Traditionalism, which argues that the past claims *us*, overlooks the fact that it claims us only when we have colluded by claiming *it*. In the dislocated situation that comprises modernist culture, belonging to a tradition has become partly a matter of personal commitment, and in that way we differ decisively from participants in the tradition as it existed in its prime.[91]

---

89. Walter Benjamin, "Theses on the Philosophy of History," in *Illuminations* 257 (Hannah Arendt ed. Harry Zohn trans. 1969).

90. *Id.* at 258.

91. In a recent study of Spinoza and his connection with Marrano culture, Yirmiyahu Yovel writes movingly of Jews (the Marranos) inhabiting Spain and Portugal

Kronman, in fact, acknowledges that tradition has become increasingly anachronistic in the modern age. Like Max Weber, he attributes this trend to the rationalization of society and the disenchantment of life.[92] His solution is to follow Burke in rejecting the rationalization of politics, and herein lies his critique of the insinuation of philosophy into law.

Weber, however, tells only half the story. Alongside the rationalization of society, the nineteenth and twentieth centuries have witnessed an equally striking irrationalist and Counter-Enlightenment backlash. This backlash has included the Romantic movement in the nineteenth century and, in our own century, the deeply irrationalist understanding of human life promoted by Freud, by artistic expressionists, by religious fundamentalists, and by political reactionaries.[93] The backlash has also encompassed such antimodernist intellectuals as Heidegger, whose antipathy to the rationalization and disenchantment of technological society drove him into the arms of National Socialism,[94] and led him to pronounce in 1949 that the essence of the Holocaust is no different from that of modern agriculture.[95] Our century can be accused of many

---

during the time of the Inquisition, who were forced by the circumstances of persecution and compulsory conversion to practice their own religion secretly. The psychological oddity of practicing one faith openly and another secretly drove a number of Marranos to become skeptical of both faiths. Yovel argues that, in this respect, Marrano culture prefigured modernity. Discussing the case of Dr. Juan de Prado, a Marrano emigré who was excommunicated from the Amsterdam Jewish community as a result of his skeptical beliefs, he writes, "Faced with an external tradition, the individual demands to be able to find the exercise and consent of his own intelligence and personal knowledge at the bottom of all his judgments, confused and devoid of depth as they may be. Thus in setting out to learn and appropriate the Torah of his forefathers, it is he, Prado, not the Torah as given, that must be the ultimate judge. Prado's pride consisted in confronting the Law and tradition with his personal judgment and appointing himself as judge over them. In that sense, his sin of pride is that of modern man in general; Prado is one of the minor figures who heralded modernism while being crushed by the burden of their message." Yirmiyahu Yovel, *Spinoza and Other Heretics: The Marrano of Reason* 65 (1989).

92. Kronman, *supra* note 33, at 1043–47.

93. *See* Carl E. Schorske, "Politics in a New Key: An Austrian Trio," in *Fin de Siècle Vienna* 116 (1979).

94. Heidegger (a quotation from whom Kronman uses as an epigraph) wrote that "the inner truth and greatness" of National Socialism lay in "the encounter between global technology and modern man." Martin Heidegger, *An Introduction to Metaphysics* 199 (R. Manheim trans. 1959). *See generally* Victor Farias, *Heidegger and Nazism* (P. Burrell & G. Ricci transs. 1989).

95. "Agriculture is now a motorized (*motorisierte*) food industry, in essence the same as the manufacturing of corpses in the gas chambers and extermination camps. . . ." Bremen Address by Martin Heidegger (1949), *quoted in* Farias, *supra* note 94,

offenses, but a surfeit of reason is not among them. And legality has suffered indignities at the hands of irrationalists far worse than the questions of philosophers.

---

at 287. On Heidegger's view as a response to Weberian disenchantment and rationalization, see David Kolb, *The Critique of Pure Modernity: Hegel, Heidegger, and After* 121 (1986).

Chapter 3

Doubts about the New Pragmatism

In the second volume of his autobiography, Bertrand Russell recalls that after World War I Ludwig Wittgenstein became an elementary school teacher in the Austrian country village of Trattenbach.

> He would write to me saying: "The people of Trattenbach are very wicked." I would reply: "Yes, all men are very wicked." He would reply: "True, but the men of Trattenbach are more wicked than the men of other places." I replied that my logical sense revolted against such a proposition. But he had some justification for his opinion. The peasants refused to supply him with milk because he taught their children sums that were not about money.[1]

Like good Trattenbachers, pragmatic philosophy regards truths as, in the words of William James, "having only this quality in common, that they *pay*."[2] For James, the important point even about God is "his cash-value when he is pragmatically interpreted,"[3] and beliefs are merely "so much experience *funded*."[4]

Pragmatism has become of late the newest wave in American legal theory. Legal pragmatists draw their inspiration from historical figures such as Wittgenstein, Holmes, and Dewey as well as from contemporaries such as Richard Rorty and Cornel West. Today's legal pragmatists include figures as diverse as Richard Posner, Thomas Grey, and several critical theorists and feminists (Mari Matsuda, Frank Michelman, Martha Minow, Dennis Patterson, Margaret Radin, Joseph Singer, Joan Williams), whose writings share little beyond the optimistic sense that the pragmatic turn offers a release from the mental prison of speculative conundrums.

---

1. Bertrand Russell, *The Autobiography of Bertrand Russell—The Middle Years: 1914–1944* 134–35 (1968).
2. William James, "Pragmatism," in *Pragmatism and Other Essays* 96 (1963).
3. *Id.* at 35.
4. *Id.* at 99.

And yet the thought must occur even to pragmatism's staunchest adherents that the attitude of the Trattenbachers toward the life of the mind is not wholly beyond reproach. Nor is that thought merely the disdain of those to the manor born, such as Russell and Wittgenstein, for peasants who worry too much about money. The problem is not that the Trattenbachers care about money but that they don't care about arithmetic, at any rate arithmetic for its own sake. The problem lies (by extension) in their suspicion of any kind of thinking for its own sake. They are, one might say, pragmatic to a fault.

The same goes for James's commercial metaphors. Here too I do not object to his invocation of the bottom line, only to the thought that it swallows up all other lines. For Plato and Aristotle, philosophy begins in wonder and ends in the rapt, silent, yet active contemplation of truths—regardless of whether they pay. This classical picture of the life of the mind is the target of James's polemic, and he means his metaphors to suggest that thought which does not issue in action is worthless.

Yet surely Plato and Aristotle are truer to the experience of thinking. The value of wonder does not lie in its payoff, be it in action or money. It is thought's journey, not thought's destination, that makes thinking worthwhile, and James was too inveterate a thinker not to know this, his slogans notwithstanding. In the same way, I do not mean to suggest that contemporary pragmatists are anti-intellectual: on the contrary, it would be hard to find more aggressively intellectual figures than, say, Rorty and Posner. But where, then, lies their attraction to the Trattenbachian reductionism exemplified in James's epigrams?

In the case of neo-Wittgensteinian philosophers such as Rorty, I suspect that the root is a kind of unrequited love of wisdom. Hoping initially for answers to philosophical questions, the student of the history of philosophy finds instead an eternal recurrence of standoffs—between materialism and dualism, realism and idealism, skeptical and antiskeptical epistemology, ethical objectivism and subjectivism, and so on. For every position there are standard arguments, and for each argument there are standard responses—what analytic philosophers annoyingly refer to as "moves"—in an endless ourobouran cycle.[5] Much of Rorty's writing exudes a sense of having seen it all before and thus of knowing in advance the futility of each new "move." When every answer can be punctured and deflated by a devastating rejoinder, the natural response is to deflate the question instead. That is what pragma-

5. For a related suggestion, see Michael Williams, *Unnatural Doubts: Epistemological Realism and the Basis of Scepticism* 365 n.51 (1991) (referring to Rorty's "unrequited hankering after truth").

tism offers to do: it is a polemic on behalf of lowered (or at any rate diverted) intellectual expectations. Pragmatic philosophers may be suffering from the affliction of Alberich, the romantically thwarted dwarf in *Das Rheingold:* first enticed, then excited, finally mocked and spurned by the Rhinemaidens, Alberich renounces love forever in return for practical mastery and the power of gold (experience *funded,* as James might have said approvingly).

For lawyers such as Richard Posner, I think, the motivation is rather different. Law employs a variety of philosophically loaded concepts, including those of intention, reasonableness, responsibility, interpretation, and a whole panoply of ethical values promoted in statutes and cases. Philosophers are apt to insist that deciding cases based on undefended assumptions about these concepts is irresponsible, and thus that jurists owe it to themselves as well as to the citizens of the legal regime to get their concepts right. And yet getting these concepts right lands us in the never-ending game of moves and countermoves. Pragmatism, with its wholesale deflation of philosophical pretensions, offers the prospect of cutting the Gordian knot. In its rejection of speculative distinctions and possibilities detached from practice and its insistence that workaday concepts do not require theoretical foundations, pragmatism offers a liberating prospect to legal theorists: the prospect of proceeding directly to the ordering of practical affairs without becoming enmired in the scholastic swamps of philosophy.

In addition, academic lawyers on the political left have found (improbably enough) a rich vein of radical ore in the overworked mines of American pragmatism. Thus, the editors of a law review symposium on pragmatism refer to "modern pragmatism's central concern: how does one listen to the voice of the oppressed?"[6] Pragmatism's hostility to the notion of ahistorical essential truths translates readily into the hopeful message that human nature is not fixed within its current depressing parameters. Likewise, the pragmatic insistence that ideas take on life only within context-specific problem situations seems close to the antiformalist, anti-rule-fetishistic sensibility of critical legal theory; it resonates as well with feminists' and critical theorists' general predilection for the concrete and richly textured over the abstract and bloodless. To such theorists pragmatism seems less likely than other philosophies to filter out the voice of the oppressed. Finally, the pragmatic attack on rationalism and foundationalism assimilates easily to the left's view that the diktats of reason have almost always been proclaimed by those

---

6. Symposium on the Renaissance of Pragmatism in American Legal Thought, "Foreword," 63 *Southern California Law Review* vii (1990).

in power to further oppressive ends. (It is at this point—the identification of reason with the blandishments of smooth-talking, malign
slickers—that the cultural left joins the peasants of Trattenbach.[7])

Admittedly, the left's born-again pragmatism arises from a terribly
forced reading of pragmatic philosophy. The reference to "modern
pragmatism's central concern: how does one listen to the voice of the
oppressed?" would have left pragmatists from Peirce to Quine blinking
in bafflement. Indeed, I shall be arguing that pragmatism actually exerts a powerful conservative undertow and that the left's concern for
hearing the voice of the oppressed has little to do with pragmatism.
Nevertheless, the association of ideas that attracts leftists to pragmatism is readily understandable.

Pragmatism thus exerts powerful attractions for philosophers, lawyers, and leftists. In my view, however, the impulse to pragmatism goes
deeper than these somewhat psychologistic diagnoses suggest. I believe that pragmatism, like the traditionalism and avant-gardism I have
criticized in the two preceding chapters, is at bottom a response to the
modernist experience of intellectual vertigo. Reason, Enlightenment,
undermines our confidence that we understand the mind's place in the
world, or the objectivity of interpretation, or the meaning of justice. Like
Nietzsche's good Copernicans, we find ourselves rolling from the center toward X. Reason has taken away the old answers, but it also takes
away new ones and leaves us with very little beyond the ruins of past
certitudes. We cannot (yet? ever?) escape the past, History with a capital
H, but neither can we rely upon it with premodernist confidence.

Avant-gardism copes with Enlightenment-induced Copernican exile by trashing the past—by savagely rejecting the idea that there was
anything in the past that deserved confidence or credence in the first
place. Neo-Burkean traditionalism copes by deliberately withholding
the past from rational criticism. Pragmatism copes by changing the
subject from the past to the future. Pragmatism aims to cut the Gordian
knots of modernist uncertainty by insisting that such problematic concepts as mind, language, and justice have no meaning apart from their
role in solving practical problems. Both traditionalism and pragmatism
mistrust rationalism and philosophical speculation, but for opposite
reasons: traditionalism retreats from the modernist present to the past,

7. I should state clearly at this point that my repeated references to Trattenbach in
this chapter refer to the literary Trattenbach of Russell's memoir, not the actual village,
about which I know nothing. I do not mean to malign or insult Trattenbach, its residents,
or their great-grandparents whose children Wittgenstein taught. I have no way of
knowing whether the milk incident ever happened. This point is in fact significant, and I
discuss it in the concluding section of this chapter.

while pragmatism retreats (I use the word advisedly) to the future. It is my aim in the present chapter to argue these conclusions.

Far too much goes by the name of pragmatism to bear sensible discussion. For present purposes, I shall be limiting my discussion to a few exemplary texts. My principal point of departure is Thomas Grey's admirable essay "Holmes and Legal Pragmatism,"[8] which provides a particularly clear statement of the contemporary pragmatist viewpoint and which explicitly raises the challenge with which I began this chapter: *what is the difference between pragmatism and Trattenbach?* My answer, I fear, unlike Grey's, will be, none, really. I shall argue that the pragmatist critique of traditional philosophy is necessarily, and fatally, too wide or too narrow. Either it fails to touch traditional philosophy or else it rules out all forms of pure intellectual activity—in science and mathematics as well as in philosophy. Take away Plato and you take away Euclid. Take away Euclid and you find yourself in Trattenbach. Athens or Trattenbach: there is no third way.

My second point of departure is the work of Richard Rorty. Rorty's neopragmatism has been particularly influential among legal theorists, for reasons both good and bad. Rorty updates the classical pragmatists in several important ways. He translates their doctrines from a vocabulary that to contemporary ears sounds imprecise and overearnest into a seductively ironic and sophisticated postmodern idiom. He expands the purview of pragmatism to encompass postwar philosophical developments on both sides of the Atlantic, charting the byways of the contemporary intellectual scene and showing how, in the end, all roads lead to pragmatism; in this colonialist vein, Rorty has claimed writers from Derrida to Davidson to Dworkin in the name of pragmatism's empire. He brings to the surface latent Wittgensteinian themes in Dewey, revealing pragmatism as an attractive prefiguration of contemporary antiphilosophy. His fundamental polemical point is that philosophy represents a dead end, to which the only proper response is simply to walk away. Rorty's extraordinary knowledge of intellectual history enables him to paint a Frederick Church landscape of ideas, at once panoramic in scope and overwhelming in detail, exhibiting plainly the wrong turns taken by the entire philosophical tradition.

Plainly, all these are virtues of Rorty's work. On the debit side, I will note that all too often legal theorists use Rorty as an intellectual talisman, enabling them to announce triumphantly the End of the Old Paradigm of Western Thought and the Dawn of the New, the announce-

---

8. Thomas Grey, "Holmes and Legal Pragmatism," 41 *Stanford Law Review* 787 (1989).

ment accompanied by the footnote "See Richard Rorty, *Philosophy and the Mirror of Nature* (1979)," further argument being unnecessary. Why, after all, work through a technical and rebarbative batch of articles in analytic philosophy when Rorty has already done the dirty job and concluded that there's nothing there? There's some point to that, since everybody can't read everything all the time, but the danger should be obvious. Rorty's knowledge of the history of philosophy may be extraordinary, but it's hardly uncontroversial, and in places—his "two worlds" cartoon of Kant at the beginning of *Contingency, Irony and Solidarity*, for example[9]—his history is badly and tendentiously inaccurate. Dewey would be unlikely to recognize himself in Rorty's pages, and Ronald Dworkin, who devoted a long chapter of *Law's Empire* to savaging pragmatism, has brusquely dismissed Rorty's announcement that Dworkin, too, is a pragmatist.[10]

In this chapter, I offer arguments against two of the principal neo-pragmatist theses associated with Rorty: the rejection of essentialism and the so-called contextualist account of justification. I argue that each of these hits on important truths but that both theses must be scaled back drastically, in a way that leaves traditional philosophy unscathed.

I then turn to a matter of Rorty's (and other neopragmatists') intellectual history that proves important to the substance of my argument. The thesis that philosophy, alone among the disciplines, consists of a tangle of disreputable pseudoproblems is most prominently associated with the later work of Wittgenstein. It was Wittgenstein who described philosophy as "language on a holiday" and who insisted that the sole proper task of philosophy is the therapeutic one of curing the understanding of philosophy itself.[11] Rorty and other contemporary neoprag-

---

9. "Kant wanted to consign science to the realm of second-rate truth—truth about a phenomenal world." Richard Rorty, *Contingency, Irony, and Solidarity* 4 (1989). For Kant, however, there is nothing in the slightest degree "second-rate" about the phenomenal world nor about the scientific truths we discover concerning it; moreover, it badly misrepresents Kant's views to treat phenomena and noumena as denizens of different "worlds." Things-as-they-appear—phenomena—and things-in-themselves—noumena—are the identical things.

10. "[T]hough Rorty is correct that pragmatism suddenly seems banal, he is wrong about how and why. Not because it has been accepted by everyone, but because it has become particularly clear, in the last several years, that there is nothing in it to accept." Ronald Dworkin, "Pragmatism, Right Answers, and True Banality," in *Pragmatism in Law and Society* 359, 369 (Michael Brint & William Weaver eds. 1991). Dworkin is commenting on a passage in which Rorty claims that Dworkin, Roberto Unger, and Richard Posner are all pragmatists. Rorty, "The Banality of Pragmatism and the Poetry of Justice," 63 *Southern California Law Review* 1811 (1990).

11. Ludwig Wittgenstein, *Philosophical Investigations* § 38, at 19, § 133, at 51 (3d ed. trans. G. E. M. Anscombe 1958).

matists regard Wittgenstein as one of their patron saints and draw sustenance from the Wittgensteinian philosophy.

In my view, however, the neopragmatists have drastically misunderstood Wittgenstein. Far from regarding pragmatism as an attractive alternative to traditional philosophy, Wittgenstein approached pragmatism as a kind of siren song—a tempting but ultimately disastrous effort to state the unstatable. In this respect, pragmatism was for Wittgenstein no different from the traditional philosophy it aims to supplant, for traditional philosophy is also a misfired attempt to state the unstatable. And what is this unstatable truth of pragmatism and traditional philosophy? In the *Tractatus*, Wittgenstein called it "solipsism," the realization that the world as given through my point of view (my language) is all the world that I shall ever have. Some might find this prospect liberating, concluding that "all the world I shall ever have" is by the same token all the world I shall ever need. These are the pragmatists. Others may find this prospect to be the principal torment of Descartes's Evil Deceiver: condemnation to solitary confinement within our own idiosyncratic perspectives. These are the traditional philosophers, who from Descartes on have regarded transcending the egocentric (or logocentric) predicament as the fundamental task of philosophy. (In the brief afterword to this chapter I show in more detail that pragmatists have not succeeded in evading this task.)

Wittgenstein's solipsism, in other words, amounts precisely to the thoroughgoing appreciation of the modernist predicament of exiled subjectivity. The special insight he brought to the modernist predicament was the claim that its truth could be *seen* but not *said* and thus that both the traditional philosopher and the pragmatist are engaged in a mistaken enterprise—an enterprise, moreover, that poses a grave moral danger by its threat to distract us with false certainties and glib yammer. Though he abandoned the name "solipsism" in his later philosophy, it is precisely this problem that preoccupied Wittgenstein, even in the last days of his life. Or so I shall argue.

I do not share Wittgenstein's mistrust of argumentation. Though I do not know the answers to the perennial philosophical questions, I see no reason to preclude the possibility of answering them. Nor do I believe that philosophical questions are solely the concerns of professionalized philosophers. In the closing section of this chapter, I argue that the problems of philosophy, like the taste for pure inquiry, are the common property of mankind.

Why am I so interested in defending the traditional problems of philosophy against pragmatism? No doubt the answer is at bottom personal and temperamental; and perhaps a lifelong fascination with the traditional problems of philosophy requires no apology and should offer none. In one way, after all, explaining your loves cheapens them. Nevertheless, the reader interested in legal modernism is entitled to know why this chapter deserves his or her attention, and that requires an impersonal explanation of the connection I discern between philosophical thinking and modernism. Both focus attention on the largely unnoticed presuppositions of our everyday thoughts and activities, and both demand a critical justification of those presuppositions. Both contemplate the possibility that those presuppositions are merely conventional or arbitrary. And both focus considerable attention on the problematic way in which *I*, the subject, fit into the world (what in chapter 1 I called the exile motif of modernism). In this respect, Wittgenstein was both a paradigmatic philosopher and a paradigmatic modernist.

Indeed, Thomas Nagel has argued with some justice that all of the main problems of philosophy—ethical, epistemological, and metaphysical—derive from the single root perplexity of how the subjective and objective perspectives fit together—precisely the problem that so preoccupied the modernists.[12] Now philosophy may not be quite the Johnny-one-note that Nagel makes it out to be, but he clearly has a point. It seems plain that the contrasts between subjective freedom and objective determination, between the subjective experience of consciousness and the objective teachings of brain biology, between subjective belief and objective knowledge, between subjective disapproval and objective wrongness lie at the basis of, respectively, the problem of free will, the mind-body problem, epistemological skepticism, and the debate over moral realism.

At the root lies a basic perplexity, observed by Wittgenstein and echoed by Nagel: Compile a gargantuan encyclopedia that enumerates every fact in the universe, including every fact about me, about DL, and one fact will appear nowhere in that encyclopedia: *that I am DL*. This observation signifies the profound incongruity between the subjective and objective viewpoints, and—speaking autobiographically—I am simply unable to regard the puzzles this incongruity engenders as merely a raft of pseudoproblems. The inexplicable and wholly contingent fact that my subjectivity is wedged into this time and place and person (Heidegger calls this fact my "thrownness") is simply not part of the objective world, and yet my subjectivity is not something I can seriously deny. I would not know how to begin trying to deny it, nor would I have any desire to.

---

12. Thomas Nagel, *The View from Nowhere* (1986).

Yet pragmatism rejects the entire distinction between subject and object as a legacy of obsolete metaphysics. Pragmatists have no use for a concept of objectivity divorced from practice and regard "the objective world" as little more than a philosophical scarecrow. It follows that subjectivity, which takes its meaning in contrast to objectivity, goes as well. Engaged practical activity, what Dewey called "experience," bridges the alleged gap between the alleged subject and the alleged object, eliminating the need to invoke them and abolishing the basic perplexity that my subjectivity poses, along with all the philosophical problems that flow from that perplexity.

As for the modernist's concern that the constitutive presuppositions of our activities are merely arbitrary or conventional, pragmatists—as we shall see—don't think that should bother us. If a set of conventions, what Rorty calls a "vocabulary," is useful in the conversation of mankind, it doesn't matter whether it is arbitrary, and nothing prevents us from switching vocabularies once they have outlived their usefulness. Vocabularies are not grounded in the objective world, but that is small cause for concern inasmuch as there is no objective world for them to be grounded in. Vocabularies are neither objectively better nor worse, neither true nor false.

Yet here as well pragmatists seem to me to deny a basic existential fact: that when we have come to regard our basic presuppositions as merely arbitrary, we are no longer able to repose the confidence in them that we need if we are to continue presupposing them. That is what makes the modernist predicament a *predicament*. At precisely the moment that we realize that our enabling conditions represent no more than our own contingent choices, that particular set of conditions has become our inaccessible history. It is for this reason that the modernists believed that we must think our way through our history, in an unpragmatic spirit of inquiry, rather than simply acceding to it or discarding it. Thinking through our history—our presuppositions—is one form that philosophy takes.

In the end, then, I am defending philosophical inquiry from pragmatism's deflation because, like the modernist predicament, philosophical perplexity is not something we can simply walk away from. It would be like trying to walk away from our selves.

What Is Pragmatism? A Catalogue Raisonné

In Cornel West's succinct characterization, pragmatism's "common denominator consists of a future-oriented instrumentalism that tries to

deploy thought as a weapon of more effective action."[13] Thus, for
James, the heart of the pragmatic method is "[t]he attitude of looking
away from first things, principles, 'categories,' supposed necessities;
and of looking towards last things, fruits, consequences, facts."[14] Pragmatism adopts "the 'instrumental' view of truth, . . . the view that truth
in our ideas means their power to 'work.'"[15] As James puts it elsewhere,
" 'The true,' to put it very briefly, is only the expedient in the way of our
thinking."[16] A "future-oriented instrumentalism" treats concepts, conceptualization, and reasoning as instruments for advancing practical
interests and solving practical problems, not as contemplative activities
undertaken for their own sake.

This is indeed the common denominator of pragmatism. More
specifically, pragmatism lies at the confluence of eight streams of
thought—eight "isms." With apologies for the jargon, these are antifoundationalism, contextualism, conceptual conservatism, antiessentialism, experimentalism, conventionalism, biologism, and historicism.
I shall briefly review the first six of these in the remainder of this
section, reserving biologism and historicism for the section that follows,
for they tie directly into my principal argument that the pragmatic
critique of philosophy can succeed only at the cost of eliminating all
pure inquiry. Later I shall return to the first six "isms." I shall criticize
some of these, suggest that others are true only in a highly qualified
way, and argue that still others are not distinctively pragmatic. Taken
together with my *argumentum ad Trattenbach*, the outcome is not highly
sympathetic to pragmatism.

Antifoundationalism.[17] By foundationalism, pragmatists mean the
idea that claims of a certain category—knowledge claims, moral claims,
political claims—rest on or require foundations that must be unearthed
by philosophical inquiry. In epistemology, for example, foundationalists maintain that all justification consists of inferences from a class of
foundational or basic beliefs—the deliverances of the senses, clear and
distinct ideas, primary intentional experiences, or noetic essential
truths, to mention the empiricist, rationalist, phenomenological, and

---

13. Cornel West, *The American Evasion of Philosophy: A Genealogy of Pragmatism* 5
(1989).

14. James, *supra* note 2, at 27.

15. *Id.* at 28–29.

16. *Id.* at 98.

17. My discussion of antifoundationalism, its relation to skepticism, and contextualism is drawn from Williams, *supra* note 5, the most illuminating discussion of these
matters of which I am aware. Williams, in my view, makes a persuasive case against
foundationalism; my disagreements with him appear subsequently in this chapter, when
I discuss contextualism.

classical alternatives. In ethics, foundationalists seek to ground moral judgments in theories of human nature or in a realm of objective moral facts; in politics, foundationalists likewise appeal to human nature or to theories of progress; in linguistics, to theories of reference; in ascriptions of responsibility, to free will.

Foundational programs confront a twofold challenge: they must explain why the putative foundations form a secure basis for knowledge (or ethics, or politics, or meaning), and they must explain what warrants the inferential steps up from the foundations. When rationality is understood along foundationalist lines, skeptical arguments threaten to undermine claims to rationality by attacking them at either or both of these points. It is hardly surprising that foundationalists inevitably find themselves wrestling with the demon of skepticism: the architecture of foundational theories invites skeptical challenges.[18]

The problem is not that anyone takes skepticism seriously—is able to take skepticism seriously—in a practical sense. As Hume freely acknowledged, skeptical doubts about empirical knowledge vanish the moment we remove ourselves from the study.[19] The point is rather that skeptics conclude that human belief and action, though inescapable, are in the end nonrational. Knowledge (or ethics, or politics, or whatever) rests not on reason but on what Santayana termed "animal faith."[20] Our nature is such that we cannot do otherwise than believe, judge, or act. As Oliver Wendell Holmes put it, from the point of view of the universe, I can't be sure "that my *can't helps* which I call . . . truth are cosmic *can't helps*"[21]—but they are *can't helps* nonetheless. The real threat that skepticism forces to the fore is thus not the loss of belief but the realization that believing is at bottom nonrational.

What makes this threat a painful one is that skeptical arguments are often so compelling that the effort to meet the skeptical challenge leaves us more suspicious than we were before; indeed, the more sophisticated the antiskeptical argument, the better skepticism begins to look. Thus, fideism and not reason begins to seem like the only way out of skepticism.

What pragmatists find most objectionable about foundationalism is this supposition that we have no alternatives besides finding philo-

18. For an extended discussion of this point, see Michael Williams, *Groundless Belief: An Essay on the Possibility of Epistemology* (1977).

19. *See, e.g.,* David Hume, *A Treatise of Human Nature* 269 (L. A. Selby-Bigge ed. 1888).

20. George Santayana, *Skepticism and Animal Faith* (1923).

21. Letter from Oliver Wendell Holmes to John Wu (June 16, 1923), *reprinted in Justice Holmes to Doctor Wu: An Intimate Correspondence, 1921–1932* 14 (n.d.).

sophical foundations for our enterprises or conceding their irrationality. Pragmatists understand reason and rationality in instrumental terms, so that the idea that all activity—all instrumentality—is nonrational amounts to little more than a contradiction in terms. Reason, on the pragmatic view, is calibrated to the necessities of practical activity; thus, any argument that these necessities are at bottom nonrational must tacitly smuggle in some more metaphysical, and unjustified, conception of reason and rationality. According to pragmatists, the metaphysical skunk in the works is precisely the foundational picture of rationality, which unnecessarily makes reason a patsy for skeptical undermining.

Pragmatists likewise deny that morality requires philosophical foundations (a theory of human nature or human dignity, for example, that would explain why others deserve decent treatment), or that politics requires philosophical foundations (a theory of history or of progress, for example), or that ascriptions of responsibility require philosophical foundations (a theory of free will, for example), and so on. "In the beginning was the deed!" Faust proclaims, and for pragmatists there is likewise no hidden foundation lurking in the philosophical depths underneath our deeds.

Contextualism. The alternative to foundationalism is contextualism, the view that justification and rationality are context specific (and thus that there is nothing illuminating to say about them at the level of philosophical generality). Contextualists reject the idea that every chain of justification ends in a class of basic beliefs that share some property beyond the trivial commonality that they are all termini of chains of justification.

Instead, contextualists remind us that in our actual practices, different justifications end at different places, depending on the topic and the context. In some contexts, "I read it in the newspaper" is an appropriate answer to "How do you know that?" In other contexts, corroboration by a rival newspaper may be required. Other contexts may require eyewitness testimony, or verification through photographs or instruments, or experimental confirmation, or appraisal by an expert, or mathematical proof, or citation of legal authority. Each of these counts as an appropriate justification in some contexts, but beyond that fact they share no interesting properties. In particular, not all of them are perceptual reports, or clear and distinct ideas, or noetic intuitions, or primary intentional experiences, or (in fact) anything remotely like the candidates philosophers have offered for the foundations of knowledge.

Analogously, those who reject foundationalism in ethics are apt to insist that moral judgments are extraordinarily context dependent.

Antifoundationalists insist that one can seldom ask for a better pedigree for a moral judgment than that it is the considered opinion of a decent, experienced, and astute person fully immersed in the facts of the context.

It is hard to tell whether contextualism is an alternative picture of rationality to foundationalism or simply the denial that any *general* picture of rationality exists. Pragmatism persistently trades on this ambiguity, at times seeming to offer an attractive new philosophy, at other times assuming the more radical posture of showing us the way out of philosophy altogether. Be that as it may, contextualism sidesteps skeptical challenges by resisting the invitation to answer the skeptic's root question: "Granted that some beliefs justify others, what justifies all our beliefs?" For the contextualist, justifying all our beliefs is simply not something that we ever need to do. Justification, like inquiry, is local and not global. It depends on the context.[22]

Conceptual conservatism. The move from a foundational picture to contextualism is a change fraught with surprising consequences. As I just observed, to insist that justification must be understood relative to a context of inquiry is to insist that inquiry is invariably localized. We inquire about some things but not about others. It is far different in a foundationalist inquiry, where one asks what justifies all our beliefs. In the foundational inquiry, one is entitled to assume nothing and must always seek a presuppositionless beginning, as Descartes, Hegel, and Husserl insisted.

In a localized inquiry, by contrast, the defining features of the context are presupposed; indeed, they must be presupposed, for otherwise there is nothing to inquire about. All the presuppositions of those defining features are likewise presupposed. In the end, we must take almost everything for granted; doing so is the precondition of isolating the questions that interest us at the moment.

Perhaps the most characteristic feature of pragmatic epistemology is this insistence that though anything may in principle be called into question, not everything can be questioned at once. It is customary to cite Otto Neurath's famous simile for inquiry: "We are like sailors who must rebuild their ship on the open sea, never able to dismantle it in dry-dock and to reconstruct it there out of the best materials."[23] The image of rebuilding a ship at sea suggests that almost everything must remain untouched, on pain of disaster. An important feature of prag-

22. For a good discussion of pragmatic contextualism, see Martha Minow and Elizabeth Spelman, "In Context," 63 *Southern California Law Review* 1597 (1990).

23. Otto Neurath, "Protokollsätze," 3 *Erkenntnis* 203, 206 (1932/33); *translated by* George Schick, "Protocol Sentences," in A. J. Ayer, *Logical Positivism* 199, 201 (1959).

matic contextualism is the reminder that doubt and questioning are minute ice-motes on a vast undersea glacier of beliefs that are, at least for purposes of local inquiry, beyond doubt and question. In Peirce's words,

> [T]here is but one state of mind from which you can "set out," namely, the very state of mind in which you actually find yourself at the time you do "set out"—a state in which you are laden with an immense mass of cognition already formed, of which you cannot divest yourself if you would; and who knows whether, if you could, you would not have made all knowledge impossible to yourself?[24]

A further implication of the localization of inquiry is that, in Gilbert Harman's words, "in changing one's view one should make minimal changes."[25] Local inquiry is motivated inquiry—motivated, that is, by some perceived inadequacy in our beliefs about the subject at issue. We undertake inquiry to remedy that inadequacy, and it would be pointless and self-defeating to remedy the inadequacy by changing more beliefs than necessary. "If it ain't broke, don't fix it" amounts in pragmatism to a basic epistemological principle. As James put it, "In this matter of belief we are all extreme conservatives."[26]

In two ways, then, pragmatism—notwithstanding its seeming radicalism—requires us to treat our concepts conservatively. At any time we must withhold the overwhelming preponderance of our beliefs and concepts from critical scrutiny; and whenever we revise our beliefs, we must revise them minimally. Pragmatism represents in the arena of conceptual change what Burke represents in that of political change: a cautionary voice protesting those who seek to overthrow the amassed wisdom of generations on no better basis than the trifling speculations of philosophers.

It is this conceptual Burkeanism that in my view makes pragmatic philosophy inhospitable to radical social thought, particularly feminism, critical race theory, or ecological radicalism. These movements argue that vast subcontinents of ordinary belief and response have been colonized by ideological impositions of power groups. They argue for massive conceptual revision, often in directions that remain inchoate precisely because dominant ideology prevents us from seeing clearly

---

24. Charles Sanders Peirce, "What Pragmatism Is," in 5 *Collected Papers of Charles Sanders Peirce* § 416, at 278 (Charles Hartshorne & Paul Weiss eds. 1934).
25. Gilbert Harman, *Change in View: Principles of Reasoning* 59 (1986).
26. James, *supra* note 2, at 29.

which beliefs should be retained and which discarded. This situation, of course, inevitably leads radicals to venture some ridiculous suggestions; it would be astonishing if they did not, given the extent to which they are shooting in the dark.

Precisely their effort to resist the enormous gravitational tug of dominant ideology leads radicals to abandon the basic rule of pragmatic concept-revision, namely that existing beliefs get the benefit of the doubt. Harman labels this the "Principle of Conservatism": "One is justified in continuing fully to accept something in the absence of a special reason not to."[27] Radical theories offer only a general reason not to accept beliefs, namely that the beliefs might be the product of ideological corruption. This reason puts radicals at odds with pragmatism.

Antiessentialism. Pragmatists doubt that philosophers have discovered some special method of a priori inquiry that reveals necessary or essential truths about the world, truths that exist on a different level of logical priority from the promptings of experience. No conceptual analyses, transcendental inquiries, dialectical *Aufhebungen*, ordinary language ipse dixits, eidetic reductions, or noetic transcendences are capable of lifting us out of Plato's Cave into a region of special illumination where the logical structure of the world finally stands revealed in full resplendence.

Pragmatic hostility to essential truth and to claims to have discovered it through arcane inquiry is really nothing more than the flip side of points we have already reviewed. Not everything can be questioned at once, and for purposes of local inquiry many things must be presupposed. These things are, one might say, a priori relative to the inquiry at hand. As Wittgenstein puts it,

> The questions that we raise and our doubts depend on the fact that some propositions are exempt from doubt, are as it were like hinges on which those turn.
>
> That is to say, it belongs to the logic of our scientific investigations that certain things are indeed not doubted.
>
> But it isn't that the situation is like this: We just can't investigate everything, and for that reason we are forced to rest content with assumptions. If I want the door to turn, the hinges must stay put.[28]

Michael Williams refers to such "hinge" propositions as "methodological necessities."[29] Discovering that certain factual commitments are

---

27. Harman, *supra* note 25, at 46.
28. Wittgenstein, *On Certainty* §§ 341–43 (G. E. M. Anscombe & G. H. von Wright eds. Denis Paul & G. E. M. Anscombe transs. 1969).
29. Williams, *supra* note 5, at 121–25.

methodological necessities for a particular local inquiry may appear to philosophers to lay bare the "logical structure of inquiry" or something equally grandiose. But methodological necessities are not logical necessities, and even "hinge" propositions may be questioned in some other context. Not everything can be questioned at once, but pragmatists insist that nothing is immunized from questioning. Quine's assaults on analytic truth and necessary truth are perhaps the most explicit statements of this theme: every proposition is contingent, every proposition is empirical, every proposition is on the same level as every other.

Experimentalism. From this follows one of the most attractive features of pragmatism: its commitment to an experimental, try-it-and-see approach to life that is highly congenial to progressive politics.[30] Legal pragmatists are impatient with a view of law as a straitjacket imposed by the past to stifle honest social experimentation. Brandeis's commitment to social experimentation, expressed in *New State Ice v. Liebmann*,[31] is a classic legal representation of this theme in progressive pragmatism.

Conventionalism. Another moral in addition to experimentalism may be drawn from the pragmatic hostility to essences and foundations. This is the suggestion that what seem to be necessary truths about the world, truths that provide foundations for our social practices, are in reality epiphenomena of those practices. Since nothing metaphysical or foundational lies underneath our practices, the practices themselves are decisive. In Susan Wolf's words, "From a pragmatic perspective, then, it appears that whatever facts are relevant to the justification of . . . activities . . . are relevant only because we choose to make them relevant, because, in other words, we set up roles that assign these facts a certain weight."[32] Wolf is discussing two approaches to our practices of assigning people moral responsibility for their actions. One, the metaphysical approach, locates the basis for those practices in free will; this approach, therefore, must solve the philosophical problem of free will. The other, pragmatic, approach views free will not as a metaphysical actuality but as a construct that falls out as a byproduct of our practices of assigning responsibility.[33] Clearly, this distinction can be generalized

---

30. For a clear statement of this theme in legal and political theory, see Robin L. West, "Liberalism Rediscovered: A Pragmatic Definition of the Liberal Vision," 46 *University of Pittsburgh Law Review* 673 (1985).

31. 258 U.S. 287 (1932).

32. Susan Wolf, *Freedom within Reason* 16 (1990).

33. *See* Richard Boldt, "The Construction of Responsibility in the Criminal Law," 140 *University of Pennsylvania Law Review* 2245 (1992).

to other problems as well, and one strain of pragmatism—best exemplified in the work of Nelson Goodman—regards our practices as "ways of worldmaking"[34]: conventions that are in actuality constitutive of the objects that seem through an optical illusion to undergird them.

The Road to Trattenbach

As Thomas Grey observes, two additional themes go into the pragmatic fugue, and it is these that tie in most directly with my argument that pragmatism is the road to Trattenbach.

The first of these I shall call *biologism*. The classical pragmatists (Peirce, James, Dewey) insisted on regarding human beings as, first and foremost, biological organisms, whose faculties and capacities should be understood functionally. In particular, the faculty of reason was to be understood primarily as a complex capacity of the human organism to cope with the various problems its environment posed.

This biologism was a revolutionary step in the history of philosophy. In Plato's *Phaedo*, Socrates argues that the body is nothing more than an impediment to reason: reason brings the soul into communion with eternal things, and it is dragged down by the body's unfortunate propensities to passion, need, and exhaustion. The soul is unfettered only by death, and Socrates praises philosophy as "the practice of death."[35]

Something akin to this drastic opposition of body to mind—to the detriment of body—recurs persistently in the philosophical tradition. Plotinus's pupil Porphyry described his master as a man who "seemed ashamed of being in the body."[36] Descartes labored to demonstrate that the mind can hold fast to truth despite the fact that "the nature of man, inasmuch as it is composed of mind and body, cannot be otherwise than sometimes a source of deception."[37] Even Spinoza, whose commitment to naturalism prefigured and influenced modernist thinking,[38] was not entirely comfortable with the body. Arguing that the emotions arise from affections of the body, he famously declared that "the impotence

---

34. Nelson Goodman, *Ways of Worldmaking* (1978).

35. Plato, *Phaedo* 64e–67e.

36. Porphyry, *On the Life of Plotinus and the Arrangement of His Work* 1 (Stephen MacKenna trans. 1984).

37. René Descartes, "Meditation VI," in 1 *The Philosophical Works of Descartes* 198 (Elizabeth S. Haldane & G. R. T. Ross trans. 1969).

38. *See* 2 Yermiahu Yovel, *Spinoza and Other Heretics: The Adventures of Immanence* (1989), for an extended discussion on Spinoza's influence on modernism.

of man to govern or restrain the emotions I call 'bondage.'"[39] The body is thus the source of human bondage, and only reason—what Spinoza called "intellectual love of God"—can free us from it.

To the classical pragmatists, Plato's outlook, and indeed the whole philosophical tradition of exalting reason as a kind of supernatural power, amounts to little more than anachronism and superstition. Cognition is simply a capacity the human organism uses to solve its practical problems; as Dewey writes, "To account for the distinctive, and unique, characters of logical subject-matter we shall not suddenly evoke a new power or faculty like Reason or Pure Intuition. . . . [I]t is possible for the traits that differentiate deliberate inquiry to develop out of biological activities not marked by those traits."[40]

Other pragmatists share a biologistic outlook. Peirce analyzes inquiry and belief as an organism's effort to quiet the "irritation of doubt";[41] Quine justifies induction in Darwinian terms: "Creatures inveterately wrong in their inductions have a pathetic but praiseworthy tendency to die before reproducing their kind."[42]

This is not to say that the pragmatists thought biology is destiny. Human organisms do not typically bump directly against nature the way that the birds and the bees do. Rather, our encounters with nature are mediated through-and-through by human culture and technology, by the accumulated residues of history (cultivated land, cities, machinery, customs), and, above all, by language. Dewey argued that "the existential matrix of inquiry" has a cultural as well as a biological dimension. As Grey writes, "This concern with cultural as well as biological evolution provided the pragmatists with an essential safeguard against materialist reductionism,"[43] and its historicism and focus on the

---

39. Spinoza, "Of Human Bondage," introduction to part 4, in *Ethics* 187 (James Gutmann ed. 1967).

40. John Dewey, *Logic: The Theory of Inquiry* 24 (1938). Spinoza, it is true, anticipated Dewey's naturalism by insisting that reason lay within nature; he nevertheless found reason's highest manifestation only in nature viewed mystically "under the aspect of eternity," not, as in Dewey, nature viewed practically. I have argued that significant tensions exist between Spinoza's mysticism and his naturalism: Luban, "A Dilemma in Spinoza's Theory of Knowledge," *Proceedings of the Ohio Philosophical Association 1979* 20 (1979).

41. Peirce, "How to Make Our Ideas Clear," in 5 *Collected Papers of Charles Sanders Peirce, supra* note 24, § 374, at 231. Peirce explains, "Doubt is an uneasy and dissatisfied state from which we struggle to free ourselves and pass into the state of belief; while the latter is a calm and satisfactory state which we do not wish to avoid, or to change to a belief in anything else." *Id.* § 372, at 230.

42. W. V. Quine, *Ontological Relativity and Other Essays* 126 (1969).

43. Grey, *supra* note 8, at 797.

cultural matrix of inquiry distinguish pragmatism from other scientifically oriented and antispiritualist philosophies.

Contemporary pragmatists lay particular stress on the cultural and historical side of pragmatism, and many display little interest in the natural sciences or, more drastically, in the nonhuman world. Rorty criticizes humility before the larger cosmos as "culturally undesirable," and praises the effort "to sublimate the desire to stand in suitably humble relations to nonhuman realities into a desire for free and open encounters between human beings."[44] No doubt the political philosophy expressed in this sentence is commendable; the metaphysical assumption, however, may give us pause. Kant wrote that his soul was filled with wonder at the starry skies above; Rorty's, apparently, is not. Man is the measure of all things, and problem solving is the measure of man: "great scientists," on his view, "invent descriptions of the world which are useful for predicting and controlling what happens," nothing more.[45]

Yet this seems to leave us in the Trattenbacher's position of mistrust and suspicion of intellectual inquiry undertaken with no practical payoff in view—pure mathematics, for example, or cosmology. The French mathematician Jean Dieudonné used to announce triumphantly at his lectures that not only did the theorem he was discussing have no practical applications but that he had a proof that the theorem *could* have no practical applications. This attitude seems fundamentally at odds with the pragmatic theory of inquiry, yet every mathematician will understand perfectly the aesthetic source of Dieudonné's pleasure. Felix Klein once objected to the bromide that mathematics is like music: "But I don't understand; mathematics is beautiful!"[46]

Pragmatists will object that their criticisms are directed not at theoretical activity in general but only at philosophical speculation. Even the purest science or mathematics has roots in practice and (Dieudonné to the contrary) may someday turn out to have practical consequences. Thus science and mathematics pass pragmatic muster; philosophy, however, trafficking as it does in distinctions without differences, is simply—to use Wittgenstein's familiar figure—language on a holiday.

Now this objection misses Dieudonné's point: that in an important sense it would actually be disappointing to learn that a theorem proven for its elegance and depth may also someday make a better microchip and crass to imply that potential profitability is the highest praise we

44. Richard Rorty, *Objectivity, Relativism, and Truth* 8 (1991).
45. Rorty, *supra* note 9, at 4.
46. Raymond Smullyan, *5000 B.C. and Other Philosophical Fantasies* 35 (1983).

have to bestow on a mathematical result. (It is like coveting a Vermeer because it would match one's wallpaper.)

Let us waive this aesthetic and moral point, however, since to the philosophical Trattenbacher it merely begs the question. The fact remains that the argument that mathematics always has a potential for usefulness that philosophy lacks fails on the merits. Consider a simple mathematical example. Euclid devotes a great deal of attention to problems of construction with a compass and straightedge alone. Euclid's rules are strict: the geometer is not permitted to mark off distances on the straightedge, use a second straightedge, or press into service implements themselves constructed with compass and straightedge. The subject is fascinating, as the numerous vain efforts over the centuries to trisect the angle by Euclid's rules testifies. It is also a subject that ties in with deep results in analysis, in particular the distinction between algebraic and transcendental numbers and the basic theorem that only algebraic numbers are constructible.

It should nevertheless be perfectly clear that the subject of Euclidean construction, with its arbitrary self-imposed limitations, has no practical consequences whatever. Of course, one could imagine a science-fiction scenario in which the hero must make do with a compass and straightedge and is barred by mysterious extra-terrestrial forces from marking off distances on the straightedge. One can likewise imagine science-fiction scenarios in which we are all victims of Cartesian Evil Deceivers. So what? What is the difference, pragmatically speaking, between asking how to rule out the Cartesian hypothesis and asking how to square the circle? Pragmatists insist that bare imaginability gives rise only to "paper doubt," not real doubt or grounded inquiry, and it is hard to see why Euclidean construction fares better on this test than Cartesian speculation.[47]

This challenge is fundamental. As Thomas Grey perceptively notes, pragmatist theory has always been "essentially banal";[48] pragmatism's greatest force and greatest attractiveness is critical rather than constructive. Pragmatists in many respects trade on a polemical distinction between their own perspective and so-called "traditional" philosophy; and many of their positions would amount to little more than truisms and slogan slinging were it not for the invidious comparison they draw between pragmatism and traditional philosophy. If this

47. According to Peirce, the "preliminary propositions" of pragmatism "might all be included under the vague maxim, 'Dismiss make-believes.' . . . Do you call it *doubting* to write down on a piece of paper that you doubt? If so, doubt has nothing to do with any serious business." Peirce, *supra* note 24, § 416, at 278.

48. Grey, *supra* note 8, at 814. Rorty agrees: *see* Rorty, *supra* note 10.

polemical contrast is unsustainable, much of pragmatism loses its point.

The pragmatists offered the promise of a reconstructed philosophical landscape, missing the traditional frustrating conundrums. Pragmatists suggest that by situating inquiry in practice and insisting that inquiry is meaningful only when it grapples with genuine experiential problems and aims at their solution, these conundrums disappear.[49]

The essential problem with this suggestion lies in its fundamentally question-begging notion of "problems" and "solutions." How do we tell when we have solved a problem? More pointedly, how do pragmatists justify their polemical dismissal of traditional philosophical inquiries as *not* practice based, *not* real solving of genuine problems? Pragmatists are likely to answer that inquiry is first and foremost a practical activity. But that just reformulates the question: what makes a problem "practical"?

This is clearly a difficult question in any culture advanced above the level of bare subsistence, in which (therefore) many inquiries will be undertaken for reasons that are not directly related to tangible needs. As Grey shows, Dewey devoted considerable thought to this problem, which he addressed through the notion of a dialectic of means and ends.[50] Inquiry undertaken for solidly pragmatic, instrumental reasons will initially treat concepts and discoveries as means to some practical end. Thereafter, however, the elaboration of these discoveries will itself come to be regarded as a worthwhile end. New concepts will evolve as means to satisfy this end; then their exploration will in turn become an end. In Dewey's words:

[M]an begins as a part of physical and animal nature. . . . As an animal, even upon the brute level, he manages to subordinate some physical things to his needs. . . . But . . . things that serve as material of satisfaction and the acts that procure and utilize them are not objects, or things-with-meanings. . . . When appetite is perceived in its meanings, in the consequences it induces, and these consequences are experimented with in reflective imagination . . . —

---

49. "The pragmatic method is primarily a method of settling metaphysical disputes that otherwise might be interminable. . . . The pragmatic method in such cases is to try to interpret each notion by tracing its respective practical consequences. . . . Whenever a dispute is serious, we ought to be able to show some practical difference that must follow from one side or the other's being right." James, *supra* note 2, at 23.

50. Grey, *supra* note 8, at 850–56. See the passages in Dewey cited by Grey, *id.* at 855 n.331.

when this estate is attained, we live on the human plane, responding to things in their meanings.[51]

The point emerges more clearly in a remarkable letter from Oliver
Wendell Holmes to Morris Cohen that Grey discusses. Holmes writes:

> Man is like a strawberry plant, the shoots that he throws out take
> root and become independent centers. And one illustration of the
> tendency is the transformation of means into ends. A man begins a
> pursuit as a means of keeping alive—he ends by following it at the
> cost of his life. A miser is an example—but so is the man who
> makes righteousness his end. Morality is simply another means of
> living but the saints make it an end in itself. Until just now it never
> occurred to me I think that the same is true of philosophy or art.
> Philosophy as a fellow once said to me is only thinking. Thinking is
> an instrument of adjustment to the conditions of life—but it be-
> comes an end in itself.[52]

This suggests a genetic account of what counts as experientially
grounded inquiry, along the following lines: Begin with an unques-
tionably material or even biological problem. Humans develop intelligent capacities for resolving it; these capacities are means to a practical
end. But by the process Dewey, Grey, and Holmes describe, the habit of
inquiry transmutes to an end in itself. Partaking of that habit requires
the development of additional intelligent capacities and "intellectual
tools," which appear originally as means; they too transmute into ends,
calling for further such capacities.

A good example lies in the growth of pure mathematics. Initially,
mathematical tools such as the calculus are means to the end of solving technological and physical problems. But the study of calculus,
understood as an end in itself, requires more abstract mathematical
tools, leading to theoretical analysis; this in turn generates highly
abstract areas of topology, which yield even more abstract inquiries
such as category theory. The point is that even demonstrably useless
areas of mathematics count as "applied mathematics" in an extended,
strawberry-plant sense: they have applications in areas that have

---

51. Dewey, *Experience and Nature* 300 (rev. ed. 1929).
52. Letter from Holmes to Morris R. Cohen (Sept. 6, 1920), *reprinted in* Felix S.
Cohen, "The Holmes-Cohen Correspondence," 9 *Journal of the History of Ideas* 3, 23 (1948).

applications in areas that have applications . . . (etc.) . . . in material life.[53]

It is here that the distinction between biologism and historicism becomes crucial. The biologistic strand of pragmatism leads us to identify "problems" ahistorically and acontextually as threats to survival or, mediated by the nervous system, as "irritations," as in Peirce's "irritation of doubt." And, biologistically, a solution to a problem may also be defined (again, ahistorically and acontextually) as *whatever enables organisms to propagate their genes before dying* or, alternatively, *whatever removes the nervous-system irritation.*

The biologistic view is false, tautological, or beside the point. It is false if it denies that we ever engage in inquiry disconnected from bare physical or genotypic survival or biological promptings in the narrowest terms of what Holmes derided as "Feed—F-outre [Fuck] and Finish."[54] It is tautological if it merely makes the point that being gripped by an unsolved problem spurs us to solve it. Saying that we are really motivated by the "irritation of doubt" is trivial in the same way that the undergraduate's insistence that we always do what we desire is trivial: in both cases the explanatory term (irritation or desire) has been inferred from the bare facts of inquiry and action. Hence the explanation in reality explains nothing. Finally, if the argument is just that inquiry has a neurophysical basis—taking the irritation of doubt as a neurological event rather than a conscious motivation—it confuses the *mechanism* of inquiry for its *subject matter.* Physicalism does not differentiate grounded from ungrounded inquiry. Thus, physicalism is beside the point.

Once we move from biologism to historicism, however, as Dewey does when he proposes the dialectic of means and ends, the pragmatist's polemic against the traditional philosopher unravels. Where the biologist insists on a culturally nonrelative characterization of what a "problem," a spur to inquiry, is—felt biological irritations or whatever—the historicist insists that what counts as a problem (and, for that matter, what counts as a solution to the problem) can be characterized only in terms of cultural history. History and culture set problems for us. (For example, the suppression of women, which our culture

---

53. For a view of mathematics along this line, see Philip Kitcher, *The Nature of Mathematical Knowledge* (1984). Particularly instructive is Kitcher's capsule history of the evolution of analysis from Newton to Dedekind. *Id.* at 229–71.

54. Letter from Holmes to Harold J. Laski (Apr. 8, 1919), *reprinted in* 1 *Holmes-Laski Letters: The Correspondence of Mr. Justice Holmes and Harold J. Laski, 1916–1935* 194 (Mark DeWolfe Howe ed. 1953).

is finally beginning to understand as a problem, was, in the dominant culture of Golden Age Athens, a solution rather than a problem.)

For just this reason, it makes no sense for pragmatists to insist that traditional philosophical problems, which are widely regarded within our culture as important and gripping, are really pseudoproblems. The strawberry plant analogy carries the following implication: *Any intellectual problem that can be traced back historically and genetically to the material concerns of a culture is a genuine problem, not a pseudoproblem.* For the only connection between strawberry plants and their offshoots is a historical-genetic one. Thus if the mind-body problem emerges naturally from reflection on material facts of our experience mediated by the cultural discourse systems we use to make sense of those facts, its pragmatic credentials are perfectly in order. The bare fact that these inquiries are in some biologistic or feed-and-*Foutre* sense useless doesn't matter. The search for black holes is useless in precisely the same way. A good Deweyan will recognize that the solution to these problems has become a cultural necessity by virtue of their arising from natural reflection on material concerns and empirical methods that have previously proven their worth as means. The dialectical transformation of means to ends, which generates inquiries "inductively" at greater and greater remove from the immediacy of practice, is capacious enough to incorporate "even" the ruminations of a Descartes as pragmatically warranted inquiry.

Once this is understood, we must still show how the problems of traditional philosophy arise from live concerns in our culture. I think this is not hard to do. One need not study very practical areas of law very long before bumping up against problems of free will (in criminal law, contract, tort law), the objectivity of values (in constitutional law), and so forth. If, as I am presuming, law counts as a practical concern in our culture, these traditional philosophical problems are equally practical. Similarly, a few hours' reflection about cognitive science raises the mind-body problem in acute form; work in artificial intelligence and the psychology of language-learning implicates philosophical inquiry into reference and meaning, and so on.

Someone may object that the bare fact that a question arises historically or genetically from the practical problems confronting a culture does not suffice to show that it is not a pseudoproblem. This may be seen from the example of Zeno's so-called paradoxes of motion. Zeno argued that in order for an arrow to reach its target, it must first traverse half the distance, then half the remaining distance, then half the remaining distance, and so on. Thus, no matter how close the target, it can never be reached. His argument arose quite naturally from key achievements of Greek mathematics—from the technique of bisecting any given distance coupled with the concept of infinity—and yet the "proof" is specious, and the problem unreal. Once mathematicians had formulated the concept of continuity and of the sum of an infinite series, proven that infinite series can converge, and developed techniques for calculating the sums of infinite convergent series, Zeno's fallacy could be explained by any sophomore mathematics major. Zeno's proof of the unreality of motion is no genuine paradox.[55]

Analogously, the fact that philosophical questions emerge quite naturally from reflection on the practices of our culture does not imply that they are any the less pseudoproblems. They may be latter-day Zeno's paradoxes—that is, no paradoxes at all, merely fallacies.

In fact, however, this argument offers no comfort whatever to the pragmatist; quite the contrary. Zeno's paradoxes could be unraveled only by formulating a theory powerful enough to analyze continuous motion. That is, Zeno's background theory had to be rooted out by a better theory. It would hardly suffice for a fifth-century Rorty to suggest that Zeno simply change the subject and stop talking about motion. The cure for bad philosophy is better philosophy, not no philosophy at all.

None of this is meant to suggest that philosophical problems "really" lie at the foundation of unphilosophical endeavors—that, for example, we "really" must solve the problem of free will before criminal law can make any sense. In my view it is an open question with no general answer whether a given area of practice has philosophical underpinnings. That must be determined by the exacting process of arguing out the particulars. But the Holmes strawberry plant test is much weaker: it does not require us to show a genuine logical connection between the philosophical theory and the area of practice to which it seems related. The relation is historical and genetic, not logical: as long as the problem of free will arises as a historical concomitant to practical inquiries, it passes the strawberry plant test, even if free will is not logically prior to the ascription of criminal responsibility.[56]

---

55. I am following the treatment of Quine, "The Ways of Paradox," in *The Ways of Paradox and Other Essays* 5–6 (1966).

56. Consider this astute remark of Wittgenstein: "The *mathematical* problems of what is called foundations are no more the foundation of mathematics for us than the painted rock is the support of a painted tower." Wittgenstein, *Remarks on the Foundations of Mathematics* 171 (G. H. von Wright, R. Rhees, G. E. M. Anscombe eds. G. E. M. Anscombe trans., 2d ed. 1967). This does *not*, however, mean or imply that studying the mathematical problems of what is called foundations—problems of computability, self-

For this reason I reject the pragmatist dismissal of traditional philosophy. In response to the charge that philosophical problems are uniquely disconnected from culture, I would urge the following trilemma:

1. abandon Holmes's genetic or strawberry plant test of "groundedness in culture" because it clearly *does* let in traditional philosophical problems. But then the pragmatist critic must come up with some other non-question-begging, nonbiologistic, and nonarbitrary characterization of what counts as a culturally grounded "problem." Otherwise,
2. accept the strawberry plant analogy and admit that whatever the culture thinks is a problem (because it emerges from reflection on reflection on reflection on practical problems) is indeed a problem, admitting further that that includes much of traditional philosophy. Otherwise,
3. give up on all pure intellectual inquiry; don't pay your local philosopher, or mathematician, or cosmologist, if she is teaching your children sums that aren't about money.

Obviously, I think that pragmatists ought to embrace the second horn of the trilemma.

A Pragmatic Critique of Anti-essentialism

At this point I wish to turn to two characteristic pragmatic theses: anti-essentialism and contextualism. I shall argue that both can be accepted only in a severely qualified form, one that cannot sustain the pragmatic critique of philosophy.

Perhaps the most provocative contemporary pragmatist is Richard Rorty. Rorty insists, repeatedly and polemically, that the perennial philosophical conundrums are as stale and outmoded as theological debates of yesteryear and that rather than engage in them one should

---

reference, the appropriate axiomatization of set theory, incompleteness proofs, etc.—is a pseudosubject. Rather, it means simply that it is itself a branch of mathematics, and the mistake lies not in pursuing it but in claiming that the remainder of mathematics "rests" on it. Wittgenstein observes elsewhere that the hard problems of the foundations of mathematics are just hard problems of mathematics. This is far different from saying that they are pseudoproblems. They are new strawberry plants arising from standard mathematical areas. And my point is that even if the problem of free will is no more the foundation of criminal responsibility than the painted rock is the support of a painted tower, the problem of free will remains as a genuine object of inquiry.

merely change the subject.[57] Philosophers believe that they practice a unique science of philosophical analysis that arrives at necessary truths by a priori argument. According to Rorty, the whole idea of such a science is misguided, and there are no necessary truths for philosophical analysis to discover. Yet to try to refute these philosophical mistakes is to get drawn into the game by returning the serve. Hence Rorty's injunction to walk away, to just say no.

Yet there is something curiously upside down about this way of criticizing traditional philosophy. A pragmatist above all others should be wary of a priori arguments for abandoning philosophical problems that are as alive in our culture as (e.g.) the problem of free will. A pragmatist above all others should enter the fray and engage these problems rather than dismiss traditional philosophy as a seamless whole.

One way to put this point is to draw an analogy with a familiar criticism of the positivists' principle that unverifiable propositions are meaningless, namely that it is itself unverifiable. A precisely analogous point should be raised with respect to pragmatic antipathy to a priori arguments. Is it a necessary truth that all truths are contingent? Have pragmatists offered anything more than a priori arguments that a priori arguments should be rejected? The answer is rather clearly no: one searches in vain for an argument on behalf of pragmatism that is not just some more philosophy.

Pragmatists must be committed to the proposition that it is at best a contingent truth that all truths are contingent. Maybe some truths are contingent and some are necessary; maybe there are some essences out there, even if a lot of things that philosophers thought were essential are merely accidental. (In the realm of mathematics, for example, the case for essences seems quite powerful: is it merely an accidental or contingent truth about the number 3 that it is odd?)

Within feminist debates, to take a particularly important example, the true pragmatist will treat the proposition that some traits of gender are essential rather than socially constructed as a hypothesis to be tested. The pragmatist will *not* dismiss the proposition a priori as an "essentialist" claim that is ipso facto false.

A consistent pragmatist ought to admit that antipragmatic investigations may be required in some intellectual and social contexts *on pragmatic grounds*. Rorty, by contrast, too often argues by drawing conclusory global comparisons between us and them: we dialecticians ver-

---

57. *See, e.g.,* Rorty, *Consequences of Pragmatism* xxxviii, xliii, 32–33 (1982), for the philosophy-theology comparison.

sus they Kantians,[58] we ironists versus they metaphysicians,[59] we anti-representationalists versus they representationalists,[60] we anti-anti-ethnocentrists versus they wet liberals,[61] we pragmatists versus they realists,[62] we postmodernists versus they Enlightenment thinkers,[63] we pragmatists versus they Platonists.[64] This seems like a curiously unpragmatic way to dismiss the concerns of "they" (Kantians, Platonists, representationalists). The classical pragmatists saw their project as one of blurring or bridging sharp dichotomies; Rorty's neopragmatism, which makes its case through a whiggish history of ideas, relies on such dichotomies to an extent that I believe is unparalleled in the history of philosophy.[65] That is because he has abandoned the central guiding idea of pragmatic opposition to a priori argument—that claims ought to be addressed piecemeal through local inquiry rather than by assimilating them to global worldviews to decide how one stands toward them. Rorty's description of the "post-Philosophical philosopher" is accurate and self-revealing:

> He is a name-dropper, who uses names . . . to refer to sets of descriptions, symbol-systems, ways of seeing. His specialty is seeing similarities and differences between great big pictures, between attempts to see how things hang together.[66]

Such a philosopher, Rorty tells us repeatedly, wins debates by ducking them, by rejecting the vocabulary in which they are formulated. His procedure—to reconstruct history into global good guy–bad guy dichotomies, placing the disfavored vocabulary in the enemy's camp—is a strategy based on erecting precisely the sorts of ideological divides that Dewey thought pragmatism would efface.

At times it seems as though Rorty objects not to the conclusions that traditional philosophers have defended but merely to their specious claims to necessity, a priori truth, or ahistorical validity. But that too poses a wrenching dilemma to pragmatists. Does Rorty doubt the contents of Kant's theory or merely its claim to be true a priori? Here one must get specific. Does Rorty deny Kant's publicity principle, for

---

58. *Id.* at 92–93.
59. Rorty, *supra* note 9, at 74–78.
60. Rorty, *supra* note 44, at 2–5.
61. *Id.* at 203–7.
62. *Id.* at 22.
63. *Id.* at 197–210.
64. Rorty, *supra* note 57, at xiii–xvii.
65. I am grateful to Charles Larmore for this point.
66. Rorty, *supra* note 57, at xl.

example, which says that political acts incapable of sustaining full publicity are unjust?[67] Or does he merely deny Kant's claim that the publicity principle is a "transcendental formula of public law"? Does he deny Kant's "anticipation of perception," which holds that "In all appearances, the real that is an object of sensation has intensive magnitude, that is, a degree"?[68] Or does he deny only that this principle may be known a priori? If the latter, then pragmatism turns out to be little more than carping at the metalevel, concerned only with the modal operator attached to a proposition and not with the proposition itself. If the former—if, that is, pragmatists must deny the publicity principle or the anticipation of perception—then it would be nice to know why.

The problem, of course, is that traditional philosophers may attribute modal necessity to conclusions that aren't modally necessary but are, for all that, contingently persuasive. That being the case, anti-essentialism, even if it is true, leaves philosophy by and large untouched: it casts doubt only on philosophical claims to necessity, not on the propositions thought to be necessary.

The Limits of Contextualism

I believe that contextualism, like anti-essentialism, can be true only in a form that leaves philosophical inquiry unscathed.

Contextualism, recall, consists in the claim that what counts as justification depends entirely on the context. There is simply nothing general to say about whether a proposition P, taken out of context, justifies a similarly decontextualized proposition Q. As Williams puts it:

> If I had to offer an aphoristic statement of the essential nature of justification, I should probably say that being justified consists in doing or saying what your conscience and your society let you get away with. This is a vacuous remark, but it is meant to be. I have serious doubts whether there is much interesting to say about justification at this level of generality.[69]

There is, presumably, something specific to say about whether, within a stated context, proposition P justifies proposition Q. After all, people do

---

67. "All actions relating to the right of other men are unjust if their maxim is not consistent with publicity." Immanuel Kant, "Perpetual Peace," in *On History* 129 (Lewis White Beck ed. 1957).

68. Kant, *Critique of Pure Reason* B207, at 201 (Norman Kemp Smith ed. and trans. 1968).

69. Williams, *supra* note 18, at 115.

challenge each other's assertions at times. Those who are challenged do try to back up their assertions, and their interlocutors do accept or reject those justifications. Contextualists don't mean to deny that people play language games of justification. What they do deny, however, is that those language games ever proceed according to rules that can be derived or stated in advance, apart from particular contexts.

The alternative, evidently, is that within a particular context, justifications and rules of justification arise together. Rules or procedures of justification are custom built for each context. Thus, instead of a single language game called "justifying our beliefs," contextualists argue that we play many language games of justification, one for each context, sharing nothing that can be distilled into general maxims or rules of justification.

This will not do. The paradigm of justification is an interpersonal exchange, a language game of assertion, challenge, and substantiation. The game presupposes shared standards. If the parties to the exchange simply customize their own burdens of proof as they go, it is hard to see how any such conversation is possible. Indeed, "you're using a double standard" or "you're holding me to a different burden of proof than you held yourself to" count as important objections in the justificatory games we play. Standards that are made up on the spot are not public standards.

The case is no different in one's attempts at justification to oneself, for justification to oneself simply transfers the interpersonal game of assertion and challenge to *foro interno*. If in a new context I am honestly uncertain whether I should believe some proposition P, it will only compound my uncertainty if I must invent the appropriate burden of proof as well as deciding whether P meets it. Nor will it help to say to myself, "Remember: being justified consists in doing or saying what your conscience and your society let you get away with." For the question I am asking myself is whether my conscience will let me get away with saying Q. Contextualism suits only those whose intellectual consciences are untroubled.

In the end, context-specific justification is no justification at all, for shared language games can arise only when there is some stability from one context to the next. Another way to put the point is that a practice that changes with every change in context, or a family of practices, each of which applies only within a single context, cannot be taught or learned. The number of contexts of justification is unlimited, potentially infinite; human capacity, on the other hand, is finite. To learn or teach practices of justification is thus to learn or teach practices that, in Humboldt's words, "make infinite use of finite means."[70] That would be impossible if each context gives rise to its own unique mode of justification, for then the infinitude of contexts would require us to learn an infinitude of discrete and irreducible pieces of information.

In the passage just quoted, Humboldt was talking about language, not justification, and his observation that linguistic capacity makes infinite use of finite means is familiar to linguists: it is the starting point for generative grammar. Possessing a finite capacity, we can nevertheless understand an endless number of new sentences. Generative grammar proceeds from the observation that this would be impossible unless syntax could be reduced to a finite number of rules. My argument that a practice of justification must be finite if it is to be learnable is simply an epistemological version of a similar argument in the philosophy of language. As Donald Davidson argues, any theory of meaning for natural language must reduce meaning to a finite number of semantic primitives; otherwise language would be unlearnable.[71]

I believe that the Davidsonian argument rules out the most characteristic pragmatic theory of language, which states that the meaning of a proposition consists in its applications: in Wittgenstein's famous aphorism, "[T]he meaning of a word is its use in the language."[72] To learn the meaning of an expression is simply to learn the language games we play with it. This implies that to learn an unlimited, potentially infinite number of expressions—to acquire a language—means learning an unlimited, potentially infinite number of language games, each of which is semantically primitive. Such a language is unlearnable.

This is important for the following reason: For pragmatists, meaning is tightly tied to justification. To know the meaning of an expression is to know how to apply it, that is, to know the range of contexts in which it is appropriately used. In the case of factual assertions, this is simply to know when it is justified. To the pragmatist, meaning-conditions and justification-conditions are the same. Both are assertability conditions.[73]

It is unsurprising, therefore, that the Davidsonian argument that shows that on a pragmatic theory language is unlearnable will also

---

70. Wilhelm von Humboldt, *Über die Verschiedenheit des Menschlichen Sprachbaues* (1836), *quoted* in Noam Chomsky, *Aspects of the Theory of Syntax* 8 (1965).

71. Donald Davidson, "Theories of Meaning and Learnable Languages," in *Inquiries into Truth and Interpretation* 3 (1984).

72. Wittgenstein, *supra* note 11, § 43, at 20e.

73. One qualification: the meaning of an expression is given by its assertability conditions under ordinary circumstances, whereas justification must occasionally be offered in unusual circumstances in which the assertability conditions deviate from the ordinary. On this point, see Williams, *supra* note 5, at 243.

show that on a pragmatic theory justification is unlearnable. For both theories are thoroughly contextualist: both require learning something different in each of an unlimited, potentially infinite, range of contexts. And, to reiterate my earlier point, an unteachable practice of justification is no justification at all.

It will help to distinguish two senses of contextualism that I remarked on earlier. In one sense, contextualism insists only that foundationalist approaches to epistemology are too pat, rigid, and oversimplified. Foundationalists do not recognize that justification adjusts to contexts and thus that any epistemological rules must treat context as a key variable. This is *weak* contextualism. *Strong* contextualism, on the other hand, claims that there is nothing philosophical to say about justification at all. Weak contextualism calls for better philosophy; strong contextualism calls for an end to philosophy. The following passage from Williams will illustrate the contrast:

> [T]he antidote to foundationalism . . . is a *contextualist* view of justification. To adopt contextualism, however, is not just to hold that the epistemic status of a given proposition is liable to shift with situational, disciplinary and other contextually variable factors: it is to hold that, independently of all such influences, a proposition has no epistemic status whatsoever. There is *no fact of the matter* as to what kind of justification it either admits of or requires.[74]

The first of Williams's alternatives is weak contextualism: it views epistemology as the study of justification viewed as a function of two variables, the proposition to be justified and the context. Williams's latter alternative, which denies that propositions correspond with justificational standards even in this partially indeterminate manner, is strong contextualism. It is this view, which Williams embraces, that I believe renders justification unteachable and therefore impossible.

Epistemology understood along weak-contextualist lines will comfortably reject the foundationalist dogma that, regardless of context, justification is always inference from basic beliefs. Instead, such an epistemology will seek to uncover context-sensitive rules of justification. Weak contextualism is an important philosophical advance; I have been arguing, however, that strong contextualism cannot be sustained. Contextualism must abandon the antiphilosophy stance, the claim that there is simply nothing general to say about justification. A systematic account of context-sensitive rules *is* a general epistemological theory. At this point we're only haggling about the price.

---

74. *Id.* at 119.

Putting Pragmatism in Its Place

When we combine these reflections with the point Grey makes—that the nonpolemical, constructive, side of pragmatism is a trifle thin, even "banal" or truistic[75]—the result is rather devastating. For I have been arguing that the polemical and critical side of pragmatism is unpersuasive and in fact leaves the traditional philosophical problems it hopes to replace pretty much untouched. What remains of pragmatism, then?

First, the modest anti-essentialist claim that fewer truths are necessary than philosophers have said. Second, weak contextualism remains. Third, epistemological antifoundationalism remains. It is important to keep in mind that while pragmatists are among the most characteristic antifoundationalists, they are not the only antifoundationalists. (Michael Williams, who in my view has most persuasively criticized foundationalism, rejects pragmatism for reasons very much like those I have offered in this chapter.)[76]

Fourth, there is pragmatism's experimentalism or "methodological anarchism" (to use Feyerabend's term): its impatience with people who wish to foreclose inquiries on a priori grounds. As one who finds discussions of methodology generally stultifying, the pragmatist insistence that we should simply see whether an inquiry is getting anywhere without first pausing to worry whether second base has been touched seems quite right to me, and in every sense progressive.

Fifth, I think that pragmatism's best-known positive theses—the definition of truth as warranted assertability or the ideal endpoint of inquiry, its epistemological holism, its historicism, and its conventionalist view of knowledge as socially constructed or "constituted" by practice—are highly significant. They may even be right in some contexts.[77] But they are not distinctively pragmatic. In point of fact, they are the familiar theses of left Hegelianism (including some strains of Marx-

---

75. Grey, *supra* note 8, at 814.

76. *See* Williams, *supra* note 5, at 173.

77. In particular, I would urge that pragmatic conventionalism—the insistence that certain putative metaphysical entities are "socially constructed"—may be true in some contexts but not in others. The ascription of free will to a drug addict's criminal activities may be a social construction rather than a metaphysical fact. *See* Boldt, *supra* note 33. Likewise, the ascription of personhood to a corporation may be a social construction. *See* Note, "Constitutional Rights of the Corporate Person," 91 *Yale Law Journal* 1641 (1982). But facts in general are not social constructions; neither, I believe, are such moral facts as the wrongness of gratuitous cruelty; nor, for that matter, are such metaphysical facts as the truth of determinism (though we do not yet know whether determinism is true). For a dissection of the confusions that conventionalism engenders, see Judith Lichtenberg, "Objectivity and Its Enemies," 2 *The Responsive Community* 59 (Winter 1991/92).

ism). Idealists, after all, insist that truth is the ideal end of Spirit's journey of discovery, that knowledge is judgmental rather than sensory, that judgments must be taken in blocks rather than individually, that knowledge has no foundations, that it is constituted by activity, and so on. My ironic conclusion is that, far from abjuring the traditional philosophical dichotomies, pragmatism's most important contribution has probably been the serious revival of the idealist side in the epistemological debate between idealism and realism.[78] Similarly, the pragmatist effort to bridge the gap between subject and object by focusing on a category of "experience" that ontologically precedes both is a familiar theme in phenomenology; Mark Okrent and Michael Sukale have called attention to the striking similarities between Dewey and Heidegger in this regard; Rorty himself traces several such similarities and dismisses Dewey's *Experience and Nature* as just another system of metaphysics.[79]

Sixth, in its late Wittgensteinian guise, I think that the neopragmatist suspicion about discourse at the metalevel—about trying to formulate truths that are "always already" there, to use the current newspeak—touches on issues that are truly profound. At the heart of modernism lies a heightened appreciation of the "logocentric predicament," including the issue of whether that predicament may be formulated within language at all. The later Wittgenstein represents perhaps the most consistent effort to think through the implications of a negative answer to this question.

Wittgenstein Not a Pragmatist

In fact, however, I think that one of the principal flaws in the neopragmatist argument arises from a mistaken attempt to assimilate Wittgenstein to pragmatism. From Wittgenstein neopragmatists borrow the idea that philosophy is uniquely ineligible for the Eden of grounded

---

78. I have argued this point in connection with Stanley Fish's version of neopragmatism in Luban, "Fish v. Fish, or, Some Realism about Idealism," 7 *Cardozo Law Review* 693 (1986). Fish's insistence that knowledge is "constituted" by communities of discourse offers a particularly clear example of the neopragmatist revival of idealism. Rorty acknowledges the idealist strain in Dewey and James, insisting that this is the metaphysical side of the classical pragmatists that he rejects (retaining only their critical side). Rorty, *supra* note 57, at 214. In my view, Rorty has it backward: what pragmatism contains of greatest interest is its revival of idealism; its antiphilosophical polemic fails.

79. Mark Okrent, *Heidegger's Pragmatism: Understanding, Being, and the Critique of Metaphysics* (1988); Rorty, *supra* note 55, chap. 3 (on Dewey and Heidegger), chap. 5 (on Dewey's metaphysics); Michael Sukale, "Heidegger and Dewey," in *Comparative Studies in Phenomenology* 121 (1976).

inquiry, as well as the idea that ongoing practices simply don't need theory. But both these views graft Wittgensteinian appendages to the pragmatist trunk that ultimately cannot take. What is distinctive about Wittgenstein, I think, are the following:

1. Unlike pragmatists, Wittgenstein thinks that the sharp boundary between grounded and ungrounded inquiry is to be drawn linguistically. Grounded inquiry occurs within our language ("language games," in the later philosophy); ungrounded inquiry goes beyond the legitimate bounds of language. The problem with philosophy is that philosophical inquiries occur outside the limits of language. I phrase this in Tractarian terms because Wittgenstein's views about the meaningful-inquiry/philosophical-inquiry distinction did not change from the *Tractatus* to the later philosophy. Only his views about the limits of language and the nature of logic changed. That change is recorded explicitly in *On Certainty:* "[E]verything descriptive of a language-game is part of logic."[80] Instead of a formal calculus, logic now consists in the description of contextualized linguistic practices. This places the later Wittgenstein in the general vicinity of pragmatism, to be sure, but the assimilation of practice to logic and language rather than to instrumental problem solving marks a decisive difference. That Wittgenstein was no pragmatist should be clear enough from this passage in the *Investigations:* "Does man think, then, because he has found that thinking pays?—Because he thinks it advantageous to think? (Does he bring his children up because he has found it pays?)"[81] (Perhaps Wittgenstein was recalling the Trattenbachers who wanted their children educated only if it was about money.)

2. For Wittgenstein there is a truth to what the traditional philosopher wishes to say; however—and this is the point where Wittgenstein most decisively leaves the pragmatists—the truth of philosophy cannot be said within language, hence cannot be said at all, hence is ineffable.

This ineffability thesis appears prominently in the *Tractatus*, propositions 6.5–7, in the image of the ladder—language—that we use to reach the mystical insight that is the truth of philosophical solipsism and then kick away. But Wittgenstein maintained the ineffability thesis throughout his writings; in § 501 of *On Certainty*, composed less than two weeks before his death, he says, "Am I not getting closer and closer to saying that in the end logic cannot be described? You must look at the practice of language, then you will see it." And in a parenthetical addition to § 532, he writes, "I do philosophy now like an old woman who is

80. Wittgenstein, *supra* note 28, § 56.
81. Wittgenstein, *supra* note 11, § 467, at 134e.

always mislaying something and having to look for it again: now her spectacles, now her keys." This is a carefully constructed simile. The spectacles enable the old woman to see the keyhole, the keys enable her to pass through the door; when she remembers one, she mislays the other. We can describe (see) the truth of logic or we can engage it (pass through the door), but not both.

3. For Wittgenstein, the danger of philosophy is not primarily social or intellectual. It's not that philosophy is a reactionary moment in the conversation of mankind, as in Dewey or Rorty. The danger is wholly to one's own sanity, one's own capacity to deal with the truth of solipsism (one's own existentialized version of the egocentric predicament) without committing nonsense within the world. "The philosopher is the man who has to cure himself of many sicknesses of the understanding before he can arrive at the notions of the sound human understanding. If in the midst of life we are in death, so in sanity we are surrounded by madness."[82] Of course, when many of our contemporaries are afflicted by philosophical madness, the social result may be devastating; but that is not Wittgenstein's chief concern.

Wittgenstein found philosophical problems threatening not because philosophical theses are false, or even nonsensical the way jabberwocky is nonsensical, but because, though true, they are misconceived attempts to state the unstatable. Skepticism about other minds is not a pseudoproblem; indeed, it is hard to imagine how anyone could think that Wittgenstein, who professes himself a solipsist in proposition 6.52 of the *Tractatus*, could have taken it for a pseudoproblem; what is pseudo is the attempt to solve it analytically rather than live its truth. Here I think that Stanley Cavell has it exactly right: the true Wittgensteinian insight is that the problems of traditional philosophy possess existential truth and must be wrestled with as Jacob wrestles with the angel.

4. Most important for the present topic, *Wittgenstein's views about pragmatist themes were no different from his views about traditional problems of philosophy: the pragmatists' theses were true but unstatable, ineffable, and thus the pragmatists undermined sense and sanity by trying to state them.*

The vital text for placing Wittgenstein in relation to pragmatism is *On Certainty*, where we find Wittgenstein advancing recognizably pragmatic views *but then taking them back because they should not be expressed as "theses."* Because *On Certainty* was written in the last months of Wittgenstein's life, it has the character of a journal as much as a book: the author changes his mind at various points. And on my reading, two voices contend in it, one Wittgenstein-the-pragmatist and the other

---

82. Wittgenstein, *supra* note 56, § 53, at 157.

Wittgenstein-the-antiphilosopher, the ineffabilist, the mystic, the solipsist: Wittgenstein-the-Wittgensteinian. Indeed, Wittgenstein says all this explicitly: "So I am trying to say something that sounds like pragmatism. Here I am being thwarted by a kind of *Weltanschauung*."[83] In context, this must take the reading, "The pragmatist *Weltanschauung* is thwarting what I'm trying to say by making it come out as pragmatism."

Thus, for example, we find Wittgenstein-the-pragmatist advancing a holistic theory of belief, a kind of coherence theory of the sort we find in pragmatists such as Quine and Harman.[84] As we saw earlier, moreover, Wittgenstein elaborates a contextualist, pragmatist, Neurath's-boat conception of belief-revision when he introduces the notion of "hinge" propositions—otherwise empirical propositions that must be withheld from question because they are methodological necessities of a local inquiry. In §§ 95–97 he develops the same idea through another important metaphor: some beliefs take on the role of logical supports for others; they form the riverbed for those others. But the movement of the river can itself recarve the riverbed, so the river's course is neither eternal nor necessary. That is, belief and inquiry are in one sense framework relative, but the framework is not of a different categorial character from what it frames; it too can be modified, though such modification is never compelled, because given holism nothing logically prevents us from abandoning something else and leaving a framework belief untouched.[85] Ultimately, we must acknowledge that wholly other conceptual frameworks are possible, a historicist and conventionalist idea that resonates with pragmatism. "For there is also something like *another* arithmetic."[86] "On the other hand a language game does change with time."[87] Wittgenstein hammers on this historicist nail in numerous passages.[88] He is at his most pragmatic when he joins such views with views about the primacy of practice and action and his occasional insistence that he wishes to treat human beings as animals (e.g., "I want to regard man here as an animal; as a primitive being to which one grants instinct but not ratiocination. (Etc.)").[89]

---

83. Wittgenstein, *supra* note 28, § 422.

84. *Id.* §§ 140–42, 410, 594.

85. *Id.* § 512. This is the Duhem-Quine thesis, central to pragmatic philosophy of science.

86. *Id.* § 375.

87. *Id.* § 265.

88. *Id.* §§ 83, 124, 149, 152, 211, 248, 253, 309, 318, 343, etc.

89. *Id.* § 475.

But then comes Wittgenstein-the-Wittgensteinian, throwing all
these marvelous pragmatic insights out. The key passage is his critique
of the picture of inquiry contained in the hinge and riverbed metaphors:

> Isn't what I am saying: any empirical proposition can be trans-
> formed into a postulate—and then becomes a norm of description.
> But I am suspicious even of this. The sentence is too general. One
> almost wants to say "any empirical proposition can, theoretically,
> be transformed . . .", but what does "theoretically" mean here? It
> sounds all too reminiscent of the *Tractatus*.[90]

It sounds like the *Tractatus* because it makes its contextualism into a
thesis about the logic of inquiry (inquiry works pragmatically, not
positivistically; inquiry converts empirical beliefs into framework or
hinge or riverbed beliefs). Once the pragmatist begins advancing such
theses, they become just as dubious as the foundationalist accounts they
attempted to supplant.

Taking pragmatism as his adversary, Wittgenstein insists, "No, experience is not the ground for our game of judging. Nor is its outstanding success."[91] Why? Because *the game has no ground*.[92] Moreover, it is
not hard to detect the irony in Wittgenstein's use of the phrase "outstanding success" to describe our game of judging. Is the game
outstandingly successful? Wittgenstein, on my reading, invites this
question, and with it the follow-up question: by what criterion? Are the
lives we lead an outstanding success? Are they happy? Are they spiritually fulfilling? Are they as decent as we might hope? The answer may
be yes, but a more pessimistic Schopenhauerian no is surely not out of
order, and I suppose that it is the answer Wittgenstein means to imply.
In any event, Wittgenstein rather clearly means to direct his irony
against the Panglossian pragmatist assurance that we understand
which problems we need to solve and how we would recognize a
solution if we found one.

Similarly, Wittgenstein-the-pragmatist voices suspicion of skepticism that bases itself solely on the abstract worry that our beliefs may
someday prove false. Pragmatic conceptual conservatism insists that
we stick with the justifications that we have at hand for our beliefs until
we confront some specific, not merely abstract, reason to suspect them.
Two sentences later, however, Wittgenstein-the-Wittgensteinian dismisses this pragmatic rejoinder that "in the end we can only adduce

90. *Id.* § 321.
91. *Id.* § 131.
92. *Id.* §§ 110, 253, 559 (and many others).

such grounds as *we* hold to be grounds," remarking that to say this "is to say nothing at all."[93] This statement can be read in two ways: as a critique of conceptual conservatism, claiming that it is an empty theory, and as an ineffabilist affirmation of it. Though conceptual conservatism says nothing at all, some ways of saying nothing at all nevertheless gesture in the direction of deep truth.

Most important to this reading are the many passages in the latter half of the book that express self-doubt or even despair, brought on—I suggest—by the realization that Wittgenstein is attempting to state ineffable pragmatic truths. "I believe it might interest a philosopher, one who can think himself, to read my notes. For even if I have hit the mark only rarely, he would recognize what targets I had been ceaselessly aiming at."[94] "Here I am inclined to fight windmills, because I cannot yet say the thing I really want to say."[95] "What is odd is that in such a case I always feel like saying (although I know it is wrong): 'I know that—so far as one can know such a thing.' That is incorrect, but something right is hidden behind it."[96] This latter passage is particularly significant, for it reveals explicitly that even at the end of his life Wittgenstein was preoccupied with the complexities of the egocentric predicament, with the truth of solipsism that animated the *Tractatus.* The skeptic argues that because we know the world only from within our own perspective—the egocentric predicament—we cannot truly be said to *know* at all. The pragmatist replies that knowledge from within our perspective is all that we mean by knowledge (and all that we need from knowledge). "I know that—so far as one can know such a thing" aims to express that pragmatic insight. Wittgenstein-the-pragmatist insists that "something right is hidden behind it," but Wittgenstein-the-Wittgensteinian gloomily concludes that "that is incorrect." It is a misfired attempt to state the truth of pragmatism—misfired, because it opens the pragmatist to the rejoinder that the pragmatist has merely conceded the skeptic's point. To say that one knows "so far as one can know such a thing" means that one knows *only* so far as one can know such a thing. One doesn't unqualifiedly know, and that is precisely what the skeptic has been arguing all along. "I know that—so far as one can know such a thing" perfectly expresses the half-full/half-empty ambiguity that divides pragmatists from skeptics. And Wittgenstein's remark perfectly illustrates the concerns that divide Wittgenstein-the-pragmatist from Wittgenstein-the-Wittgensteinian.

---

93. *Id.* § 599.
94. *Id.* § 387.
95. *Id.* § 400.
96. *Id.* § 623, *see also id.* §§ 358, 397, 402, 404–5, 418, 422, 470–71, 532, 549, 601.

5. If my understanding of Wittgenstein is not fundamentally faulty here, then the major flaw of the neopragmatist appropriation of Wittgenstein is twofold. First, they "rush in where angels fear to tread" by advancing what Wittgenstein understands to be ineffable theses as though these could be "effed." Second, they fail to understand that the ineffable truth of pragmatism is accompanied in a full human life by the ineffable truth of skeptical doubt and other worries of traditional philosophy.

By failing to appreciate these points, the neopragmatists misunderstand why Wittgenstein thought philosophy was unique among abstract inquiries—why philosophy alone diseases our understanding. It is not because philosophical discourse is "theory about things that need no theory," nor is it because philosophy is as outmoded as theology. For Wittgenstein, it was because philosophy is uniquely liable to outrunning the limits of language and thus burying its own mystical truth— and Wittgenstein was clearly a mystic—under a suffocating pile of verbiage. It is because of philosophy's centrality, not its irrelevance, that Wittgenstein was determined to purge the world of philosophical maunderings. The neoprags, by contrast, have abandoned the truth of philosophy but perpetuated the verbiage.

Now I do not claim that Wittgenstein is right about ineffability and the pragmatists wrong; my own inclination is quite the contrary— to treat the philosophical problems as eminently, and sensibly, discussable. I don't find them posing an immense danger to the soul. But if I here side with the neoprags, I also draw the conclusion that their quarrel with philosophy on Wittgensteinian grounds arises not from their pragmatism but from their misunderstanding of Wittgenstein.

An Elitist Argument?

One might object to the general tenor of my defense of philosophy on grounds of its elitism. Obviously, I am basing the argument on the assumption that pure inquiry, of which I take abstract mathematics, cosmology, and philosophy as central instances, is pretty hot stuff—too hot to abandon lightly. And I am contrasting the love of pure inquiry, a central piety of intellectuals and academics, with the peasant's suspicion of intellectualism exemplified in Russell's Trattenbach anecdote. Is the argument anything more than an expression of the intellectual's well-known contempt for the preoccupations of ordinary people—people, in Brecht's words, who "do not think without reason"?[97]

I trust that the answer is yes. That answer I base on the Aristotelian conviction that all people by nature desire to know—that disinterested curiosity is not simply a piety of the knowledge class. Granted that all people do not by nature desire to know the prime number theorem, or whether there are black holes, or the solution to the mind-body problem—these indeed presuppose an advanced education and a taste for abstraction. But to presume that ordinary people lack disinterested curiosity or philosophical inclination is a gigantic error—an error that is truly elitist, on a par with Holmes's cynical assessment that "the formula of life to great masses would be Feed—F-outre and Finish."[98]

That this assessment is erroneous may be seen by reflecting on two characteristic institutions of popular culture: religion and sports. Hegel and Cassirer argued persuasively that religious concerns are nothing but the central problems of philosophy addressed through symbol systems that are mythical and concrete rather than conceptual and abstract. These shared questions include concerns with how and why life should be lived, with the origin and end of things, with mortality and immortality, with the discrimination of right and wrong, and with the place of the self in the scheme of things—the modernist problem of homeless subjectivity. Nor should one condescend to the conceptual subtlety of religion in addressing these questions; the Gospels and the Gita contain lengthy passages that are philosophically demanding by any standards. To suggest that philosophical questions move only a select circle of scholars is simply to overlook the concerns of the billions of people for whom the Bible and the Koran, the Upanishads and the Four Noble Truths are central preoccupations of daily life.

None of this is to identify philosophy with religion. In important respects, philosophy, which requires rational arguments to back answers to questions, marks a break with religion, which answers questions by appeal to revelation and authority. In Plato's *Euthyphro,* Socrates asks the priest Euthyphro to define piety. When Euthyphro replies that a thing is pious if the gods love it, Socrates traps him in contradictions and gets him to concede that the gods will love a thing only if it is antecedently pious—presumably on other, rational, grounds. At this moment, Socrates in effect substitutes reason for au-

---

97. *Quoted in* Walter Benjamin, "What Is Epic Theater?" in *Illuminations* 148 (Hannah Arendt ed. Harry Zohn trans. 1969).

98. Holmes, *supra* note 54.

thority, philosophy for religion. Crucially, Euthyphro hurries away rather than pursue this uncomfortable conversation, and at that moment Socrates understands that his own forthcoming trial on charges of impiety is as good as lost. Religious traditionalists will stop their ears against philosophical arguments.

I am thus not denying the immense gap between dogmatic religion and philosophy when it comes to answering questions. My point is rather that religion and philosophy arise in response to very similar questions, which are the common cultural property of billions. What I *am* denying is therefore the claim that philosophical questions occur only to the few within the walls of the academy.

There is another reason as well for doubting that philosophy is merely scholastic and culturally retrograde stuff. As William Galston has argued, the quest for philosophical objectivity, which pragmatists reject as an error, arises quite naturally from reflection on the divergence of beliefs in a pluralistic society.[99] Galston writes:

> [R]eflective citizens cannot help becoming aware of other communities resting on very different principles and containing very different ways of life. . . . Acquaintance with other societies forces upon us an awareness of the partiality and cost of our own. Wherever it may lead, such reflection asks us to take seriously standards of social justification other than the ones we ordinarily employ. And even if we end up by reaffirming our point of departure, it can no longer be on the basis of simple habit or loyalty.[100]

Certainly this was true at the birth of philosophy. It is a curious fact that the Presocratic philosophers and the best-known sophists all came from colonies and outposts at the periphery of Greek civilization rather than from the heartland. The periphery was the point of contact between Greek civilization and the various "barbarian" cultures. I will hazard the guess that this was no accident. For it is precisely the contact of one civilization with another that raises the basic question animating early Greek philosophy: how can one distinguish the natural from the purely customary?

A similar concern with pluralism and multiculturalism lies at the heart of current postmodern and pragmatist reflection, but pragmatists such as Rorty insist that the Greeks were barking up the wrong tree. We must give up the quest for the natural, for *physis* rather than *nomos*. We

---

99. William Galston, *Liberal Purposes: Goods, Virtues, and Diversity in the Liberal State* 22–41 (1991).

100. *Id.* at 30.

need not worry that our deepest commitments are *nomoi*, for we are fully entitled to favor our own *nomoi* over those of others without bothering to protest the charge that they are merely cultural biases. "Anti-anti-ethnocentrists," Rorty's term for his good guys, "should simply drop the distinction between rational judgment and cultural bias."[101]

The problem is that dropping this distinction is easier said than done. Drawing a distinction between rational judgments and cultural biases, where we value the former and treat the latter with opprobrium, happens to *be* one of our cultural biases (or rational judgments). In our modernist culture, once we have acknowledged that our commitments have no basis beyond the fact that we have inherited them, we are no longer able to value them in the same way. Perhaps it is different in traditional cultures, where "the ancestral" and "the good" more or less coincide. In a culture that changes as rapidly as ours, we cannot maintain any such identification of the ancestral with the good and still keep a straight face (or a sane mind). Nor should we. Rorty's proposal—that we can simultaneously maintain our full-strength commitments and adopt an ironic stance toward them, a stance that comes from conceding that they are merely the commitments we happen to have found ourselves with—seems implausible. Commitment attaches; irony detaches.

Perhaps that is why the twentieth-century alternative to posing the philosophical question between nature and custom has not been an ironically double-negatived anti-anti-ethnocentrism but straightforward ethnocentrism: "the explosions of nationalism, racism and, in places, of religious bigotry, which, interestingly enough, not one among the most perceptive social thinkers of the nineteenth century ever predicted."[102] No doubt the explosive growth of nationalism shows that the philosophical question—custom or nature?—is not inevitable. It shows only that it is desirable. However, the fact that sizable numbers of people in all walks of life and in all countries recognize the insanity of nationalism and the importance of cosmopolitan coexistence suggests that the distinction between nature and custom is hardly the exclusive province of an estranged intelligentsia.

Next consider sports. The attitude of spectators at a sports event is a shallow overlay of partisan cheering resting on a deeper substratum of disinterested curiosity and expertise. Real fans know the plays and

---

101. Rorty, "On Ethnocentrism: A Reply to Clifford Geertz," in *Objectivity, Relativism and Truth, supra* note 44, at 207–8.

102. Isaiah Berlin, *The Crooked Timber of Humanity: Chapters in the History of Ideas* 1 (1991).

the players; they know the stats and the strategy; they appreciate the fine points and have little respect for those who don't. Every game calls to mind a dozen past contests, instructive for their similarities or contrasts, which are at once technical and moral.

The distance is surprisingly slight between the sports fan's connoisseurship and the scientist's study of nature or society. Both are expressions of disinterested curiosity—the sheer pleasure in knowing that illustrates the truth of Aristotle's maxim. The sports fan's awesome, pedantic amassing of useless statistics illustrates in a large-scale way a point that I believe is more general: that the Aristotelian pleasure in pure knowledge is a phenomenon that inheres in all of the world's work and play except for the most mindlessly repetitious and unpleasant labor. The point may be seen by considering the nature of aesthetic pleasure.

For Dewey, art and aesthetics posed a challenge, for the universal delight men and women take in artistic creation appears at first glance to have little to do with future-oriented instrumentalism. Art seems at first glance to constitute a counterexample to pragmatism. In *Art as Experience* and *Experience and Nature* Dewey appealed to the dialectic of means and ends to argue that art is in fact "peculiarly instrumental in quality . . . a device in experimentation . . . a new training of modes of perception."[103] What appears to be the enjoyment of art as an end in itself is in fact a means of strengthening modes of perception that are basically instrumental. In Grey's words, "Though art, like play, has its own immediate rewards, it is not pursued purely for its own sake; as with play, a thread of purpose, ulterior motive, gives unity to the process."[104]

Pragmatists have grasped the right stick by the wrong end. I would put Grey's point in precisely the opposite way: though exercising our modes of perception, like work, has its ulterior motives, it is not pursued purely for their sake. Every piece of work complex enough to involve problem solving generates rewards that are intrinsic and that are at bottom identical to the pure mathematician's pleasure in proofs for their depth and elegance. Dewey argues that pursuits that appear to be ends in themselves are in reality means to ulterior ends. I am suggesting that even means to ulterior ends are in reality pursued in part for their intrinsic rewards. Disinterested curiosity is a basic component of everyday life, everywhere and at all times—even in Trattenbach.

Indeed, it is high time to rectify my defamation of Trattenbach, if that is still possible.

103. Dewey, *supra* note 51, at 317–18.
104. Grey, *supra* note 8, at 855.

Russell's anecdote makes for a striking image, but it is perhaps not one to take at face value. Russell was not above embellishing a story to make it a better tale. Even if Wittgenstein in fact related the story as Russell repeats it, he may well have been speaking of the refusal of a single farmer to supply him with milk on one occasion as though it represented the attitude of all the Trattenbachers. Wittgenstein and the Trattenbachers detested each other. He attributed this to the stupidity of the Trattenbachers, but the trouble was at least partly his own doing. Wittgenstein's biographer reports that the villagers turned against him not because of the sums he taught but because of the brutal corporal punishment he inflicted when his pupils got them wrong, his violent hair-pulling and ear-boxing.[105]

I am inclined to doubt that all or even most of the Trattenbachers were "Trattenbachers," that is, denizens of the literary Trattenbach of Russell's memoir and Wittgenstein's loathing, the Trattenbach that I have been pillorying throughout this chapter. That is not to deny the existence of philistines or philistinism. Obviously, the world contains people who find the pursuit of knowledge incomprehensible unless they can see how to cash in on it. What I doubt is simply that this attitude is typical or that the distinction between philosophers and philistines coincides with the distinction between cultural elites and working stiffs. I know philosophy professors who will not give a paper without an honorarium; "Trattenbach" is a state of mind, not a social class. Fortunately, it is not a common state of mind.

Afterword: On Pragmatism and Skepticism

I have argued in this chapter that pragmatism provides no way out of the traditional problems of philosophy. Where pragmatists advise us simply to walk away from philosophy, I have countered by suggesting that that is easier said than done. The main problems of philosophy connect so intimately with our other intellectual concerns that they await us on every path we might take. They can be ignored only by closing our eyes as we flee. The argument I offered was a blanket response to a blanket complaint: nothing in it is specific to any particular philosophical problem. Indeed, I suggested that once we get down to particulars, some of the main problems of philosophy may in fact be vulnerable to specific pragmatist arguments, while others are not. Getting down to particulars, I further suggested, should be especially congenial to pragmatists, who are (or should be) philosophically opposed to argument by blanket assertion.

---

105. Roy Monk, *Ludwig Wittgenstein: The Duty of Genius* 196 (1990).

I suggested as well that the *ur*-problem of modern philosophy has not been invalidated by its pragmatist critics. I refer to the problem of radical epistemological skepticism. In this brief afterword, I want to demonstrate, rather than merely assert, that pragmatism cannot evade the problem of radical skepticism.

Radical skepticism is the claim that none of our beliefs is to the slightest degree justified. That does not imply that they are false, but it does imply that we have no way of telling which of them is false. Though skepticism is an ancient philosophy, the ancient skeptics treated it primarily as a moral doctrine: skeptical arguments were used to quiet belief and thus to achieve what they took to be a salutary intellectual and emotional state of detachment. In its modern guise, skepticism is an epistemological rather than a moral doctrine and—ironically—is a source of anxiety rather than detachment.

In the introduction to this book, I took the Copernican revolution as a kind of guiding metaphor for the modernist predicament. The same metaphor may be useful in illustrating the connection between skepticism and modernism. The Copernican revolution suggests skeptical consequences in several ways:

First, it suggests that things may be drastically different than we had naively believed them to be—the naked beginning of skeptical doubt.

Second, it suggests that the evidence of the senses may be unreliable. It seemed plain to the eye that the earth stands still and the heavenly bodies move, but Copernicus taught us to mistrust what seems plain to the eye. Descartes's optical studies taught him that visual images may not be accurate representations of their objects, and this realization formed the scientific and empirical basis for his hyperbolic doubts.

Third, Copernicanism undermined the belief in the teachings of authority. Geocentrism was backed by the weight of the Church and the learned, as the trial of Galileo made plain; the long-term outcome was the humiliation of authority.

Fourth, the Copernican doctrine leads us naturally to reflect on the importance of standpoint and perspective to the formation of belief, engendering Nietzschean worries about our "inability to look around our own corner."[106]

In part, the modernist predicament lies precisely in the heightened appreciation that we cannot escape the point of view of our own subjectivity, nor can we express truths unconditioned by our own language.

---

106. Friedrich Nietzsche, *The Gay Science* § 374 (Walter Kaufmann trans. 1974).

The modernist predicament rests on the egocentric and logocentric pre-dicaments.[107] Both pose an immense challenge to the possibility of anchoring legal authority in natural law.

The most typical pragmatic argument against skepticism begins by asserting that the skeptic has been misled by faulty philosophy into a "quest for certainty." Once we acknowledge that our beliefs are fallible, then the fact that we cannot definitively rule out skeptical hypotheses—Descartes's Evil Deceiver, brain-in-a-vat stories, and the like—need no longer trouble us. Why should they? These skeptical hypotheses are clearly improbable, and probability is all we need for practical pur-poses. Holmes often described himself as a "bettabilist," one who iden-tifies credibility with what we would be willing to bet on, and the falsehood of skeptical hypotheses is eminently bettable. We should in-deed be skeptics, for acknowledging that we are fallible is a form of skepticism, but we should not be *radical* skeptics. Richard Posner is perhaps the most prominent contemporary pragmatic legal theorist to take this route.[108]

But what is the basis for maintaining that the antiskeptical hypoth-esis is more likely than the skeptical hypotheses? Nothing within one's past or present experience entitles one to that claim, for the skeptic's whole point is that hypotheses like the Evil Deceiver or the brain-in-the-vat would fully explain all of our past and present experience. As Williams writes,

> [W]e will miss the significance of sceptical alternatives to our ordi-nary views if we think of them as remote possibilities that, while

---

107. These terms were coined by two Harvard philosophy professors in the era of early modernism. The *egocentric predicament* is the realization that "[i]t is impossible for me to discover anything which is, when I discover it, undiscovered by me." Ralph Barton Perry, "The Ego-centric Predicament," 7 *Journal of Philosophy* 5 (1910). Perry argued that idealists had wrongly concluded from this simple predicament that the universe must be mind's creation. Whether or not the idealists erred in this way, it is nonetheless clear that the egocentric predicament poses a difficult challenge to our claims to objectivity.

The term *logocentric predicament* was coined by Henry M. Sheffer: "Just as the proof of certain theories in metaphysics is made difficult, if not hopeless, because of the 'egocentric' predicament, so the attempt to formulate the foundations of logic is ren-dered arduous by a corresponding 'logocentric' predicament. *In order to give an account of logic, we must presuppose and employ logic.*" Henry M. Sheffer, "Review of Whitehead & Russell, Principia Mathematica, vol. 1, 2nd ed. 1925," 8 *Isis* 226, 227–28 (1926). It refers more generally to the impossibility of expressing truths extralinguistically, an impos-sibility that leads some theorists to the conclusion that we are "prisoners of language." I am grateful to Allen Hazen for the reference to Sheffer.

108. *See* Richard A. Posner, *The Problems of Jurisprudence* 114–15 (1990).

they deprive us of absolute certainty, leave us with plenty of justification for what we ordinarily believe. Sceptical alternatives are
remote possibilities only relative to our ordinary views about the
world: if all those views are in question, the standards for calling a
possibility "remote" are not so clear.[109]

Posner recognizes this: "Most efforts to defend against the brain-in-
a-vat attack founder on the absence of an external reference point with
which to compare the experience of being a brain in a vat with the
experience of inhabiting the 'real' world. The conundrum is cleverly
designed to eliminate any such point." In the next paragraph, however,
he mysteriously loses the point of his own argument, insisting, "In fact
it [the brain-in-a-vat hypothesis] is more probably false than true,"[110] a
proposition that Posner has just finished acknowledging has no objective basis. Once pragmatists concede the conceivability of skeptical
hypotheses, they must concede as well that bettabilism is a sheer article
of faith, a kind of whistling in the dark. This raises the worry that if
radical skepticism is even possible, it is true: the possibility of skeptical
hypotheses implies that the skeptical and antiskeptical stories are equi-
probable on the basis of experience, which implies in turn that none of
our beliefs is justified. There is thus no fallibilist middle ground between radical skepticism and antiskepticism.

Perhaps, however, Posner's use of the word "probably" should be
understood along the lines of subjective probability rather than relative
frequency. Perhaps, that is, he does not mean that past experience has
shown that we are seldom brains in vats; perhaps he means only that
we would be willing to bet the farm that we are not brains in vats.
"Bettabilism," after all, suggests a subjective interpretation of
probability.

If so, however, we are entitled to answers to a number of questions.
To begin with, what would it be to lose the antiskeptical bet, or to
discover that one had lost the bet? Perhaps it is this: suddenly I find
myself floating bodyless in a vat, with an Evil Deceiver explaining to
me with pitiless clarity how I have been duped. But this presumes the
Deceiver's cooperation, which, after all, I am not entitled to count on.
No procedure available to *me* can decide the bet: that is the whole point
of skeptical hypotheses. Without a method for deciding a bet, however,
we cannot be said to have wagered with the serious intent that bettabilism assumes. You and I cannot bet seriously over whether Cleopatra
had an even or odd number of hairs on her head when she died; in a

109. Williams, *supra* note 5, at 49–50.
110. Posner, *supra* note 108, at 164.

sense, there is no such thing as a bet about this proposition, only a mock bet. In the same way, the antiskeptical bet lacks decision criteria, and in this way fails to be a bet.

The pragmatist may reply that I have already indicated the decision criteria. If someday I wake up in a vat, or the equivalent for other skeptical hypotheses, I have lost the bet. If I don't, then—by stipulation—I have won. I call this reply "pragmatist" because it stipulates that the case in which I really am a brain in a vat but go through life without ever finding out counts as winning, not losing, the antiskeptical bet. The assumption that delusions that never fail me are not delusions at all but truth, "the expedient in our way of thinking," characterizes pragmatism. In a way, therefore, the reply begs the question; but even waiving this point, I do not believe that these rules suffice to make the bet genuine.

To see why, let us ask another question: What are the stakes in the antiskeptical bet, and to whom would they be forfeit? Does the Evil Deceiver accept personal checks or MasterCard from brains in vats? These questions may sound facetious, but a moment's reflection shows why they are not. Losing bets is supposed to matter to us, but the world of things that matter to us is the very world that skepticism calls into question. If a skeptical hypothesis is true, then the fact that I have lost a bet to the contrary is, quite literally, the least of my worries. A Wittgensteinian might put it thus: the concept of a wager grammatically presupposes real consequences of winning or losing. A bet with no consequences is not, in the relevant sense, a bet at all. "I bet my life that I'm immortal: if I ever die, you can kill me"—like the antiskeptical bet, this is a wager in form alone. You cannot refute skepticism by staking play money on the flip of an imaginary coin—but, notwithstanding its veneer of tough-mindedness, that is all the argument from bettabilism amounts to. It refutes paper doubt with a paper bet.

To avoid radical skepticism, then, pragmatists must insist that the skeptical stories are not merely unlikely but unthinkable.[111] The difficulty of avoiding the problem in this way may be illustrated by a paper in which Richard Rorty claims Donald Davidson for the pragma-

---

111. Alternatively, one might argue that despite their apparent simplicity and intuitive appeal, the skeptical hypotheses rest on unproven and implausible philosophical assumptions. Williams takes this route in *Unnatural Doubts, supra* note 5, which in my view comes closer to an adequate response to skepticism than any other treatment of which I am aware. My hesitations about accepting Williams's argument lie principally in the doubts expressed in this chapter that his contextualist alternative explains how practices of justification can be taught.

tist camp.[112] For a number of years, Davidson has made extensive and important use of the so-called principle of charity to address problems of radical translation from one language to another—and, more importantly, to attempt a head-on refutation of skepticism based on the incoherence of the skeptical hypotheses.

The Davidsonian argument, which Rorty appears to adopt by incorporation, is this: Suppose that a linguist constructs a provisional translation manual for a foreign language. To her astonishment, she discovers that—according to her manual—the natives with whom she is conversing are uttering mostly false, and indeed preposterously false, sentences ("there is no such thing as a cloud," "people are much bigger than elephants," etc.). As a point of linguistic method, her proper conclusion is surely that her translation manual is wrong, not that the natives in fact hold largely preposterous beliefs. The principle of charity is nothing more than a generalized statement of this point of method: it enjoins the linguist to interpret the natives' utterances charitably, construing those utterances to maximize their truth and coherence.

From the principle of charity Davidson derives the noteworthy corollary that the natives' views cannot be mostly false. This corollary is on his view merely an elliptical restatement of the principle of charity: for methodological reasons we cannot construct a satisfactory translation manual for the natives' language according to which most of their views are false. To know the natives' views at all is thus to know views that are mostly true.

To complete the Davidsonian argument against skepticism—the argument that belief is "in its nature veridical"[113]—we merely note that (in Rorty's words) "radical translation begins at home—that if we want an outside view of our own language-game, the only one available is that of the field linguist."[114] Let us spell out this argument in detail. To raise skeptical worries is to doubt that our beliefs are true when viewed from an objective standpoint—that is, from the standpoint of an omniscient outsider, one whose own beliefs we stipulate to be true. The skeptic challenges us with the question, "How would an omniscient observer assess the truth of our beliefs?"

Davidson approaches the skeptic's question in a novel way: he insists that before it can be addressed we must first know how an

---

112. Rorty, "Pragmatism, Davidson and Truth," in *Objectivity, Relativism, and Truth,* *supra* note 44, at 126–50.

113. Davidson, "A Coherence Theory of Truth and Knowledge," in *Truth and Interpretation* 314 (Ernest Lepore ed. 1986).

114. Rorty, "Pragmatism, Davidson and Truth," in *Objectivity, Relativism, and Truth,* *supra* note 44, at 135.

omniscient outsider would determine what our beliefs *are*, and that is tantamount to asking how an omniscient outsider would translate our utterances into his or her own language. By the principle of charity, that outsider could not help but translate our language in such a way that most of our beliefs turn out to be true. In Davidson's words:

> We do not need to be omniscient to interpret, but there is nothing absurd in the idea of an omniscient interpreter; he attributes beliefs to others, and interprets their speech on the basis of his own beliefs, just as the rest of us do. Since he does this as the rest of us do, he perforce finds as much agreement as is needed to make sense of his attributions and interpretations; and in this case, of course, what is agreed is by hypothesis true. But now it is plain why massive error about the world is simply unintelligible, for to suppose it intelligible is to suppose there could be an interpreter (the omniscient one) who correctly interpreted someone else as being massively mistaken, and this we have shown to be impossible.[115]

What shall we make of this argument? Waive for the moment any doubts about the justification and limits of the principle of charity; waive in addition any doubts about whether a truly omniscient interpreter would need to use it in translating our utterances.[116] Even then, I believe, the argument fails. Its principal claim to insight—that there is no outside standpoint for us to occupy, even as a thought experiment, from which most of our beliefs turn out to be false—curiously neglects the most important such thought experiment in the history of philosophy.

Make Davidson's omniscient interpreter omnipotent as well and add that he is relentlessly deceptive. The result is Descartes's Evil Deceiver. The Evil Deceiver knows that when we offer our confident opinions about our environment we are doing so in ignorance of its most important characteristic: the fact that he has manipulated us to hold these opinions even though they are false. Charity therefore leads him to translate our sentences not by maximizing their agreement with his own (true) beliefs but by maximizing their agreement with the (false) beliefs that he is manipulating us to hold. Thus, from his stand-

---

115. Davidson, "The Method of Truth in Metaphysics," in *Inquiries into Truth and Interpretation, supra* note 71, at 201.

116. The latter point is made by Williams, *supra* note 5 at 314, who points out that it may be only because we are not omniscient that we must fall back on the principle of charity to infer from the natives' behavior what they are saying.

point, most of our beliefs turn out to be false.[117] Hence, contrary to Davidson's claim, there is an outside standpoint—that of the Evil Deceiver—from which most of our beliefs turn out to be false.

It is perhaps open to Davidson to reply that hypothesizing the Evil Deceiver begs the question: it assumes the possibility of massive error about the world, where Davidson aims to show that "massive error about the world is simply unintelligible." The principle of charity shows that we cannot really make sense of the possibility of the Evil Deceiver.

But this reply gets nowhere, for Davidson has misdescribed the principle of charity. The Davidsonian argument assumes that the principle of charity requires any field linguist (including the omniscient interpreter) to translate our sentences in a way that maximizes their agreement with the linguist's beliefs ("the truth," so far as the linguist knows). Only by means of this assumption can the argument conclude that no outside standpoint exists from which our beliefs are mostly false.

As we have seen, however, the principle of charity does *not* require the field linguist to translate native utterances to maximize their agreement with *the linguist's beliefs,* true or not. It requires only that the linguist translate native utterances to maximize their agreement with *what the linguist takes the natives to have good reason to believe (or to assert).* Ordinarily these two modes of translation coincide, for in most circumstances the natives have the same reasons for their everyday beliefs that we have for ours. But in some situations—those that the skeptic uses to mount his or her challenges—the two modes will differ drastically.

Let me illustrate the difference. Surely it begs no questions to imagine a mad linguist who believes *falsely* that he is Descartes's Evil Deceiver.[118] Such a mad linguist takes us to have good reasons to believe many false things, for he is convinced that he has duped us. He believes, for example, that we are in reality nothing but brains in vats being stimulated by the electrodes he has hooked to us.

The mad linguist would emphatically *not* translate our sentences to maximize their agreement with what he takes to be the truth, namely

<hr/>

117. This point has been noted by other writers: *see, e.g.,* Williams, *supra* note 5, at 314. Robert Wachbroit, "Theories of Rationality and Principles of Charity," 38 *British Journal of the Philosophy of Science* 35, 41–42 (1987), makes a related point.

118. After his breakdown, Nietzsche appears to have believed that he was God and that he was about to embark on a new phase of his creation by filling the next eternity with bad jokes. *See* Nietzsche's letters to Burckhardt (Jan. 4 and Jan. 6, 1889), *Selected Letters of Friedrich Nietzsche* 345, 346–48 (Christopher Middleton ed. and trans. 1969). Let us set the prankish Nietzsche to work as a field linguist.

that we are brains in vats. Given the way he is stimulating us, we would have to be raving paranoiacs to believe we were brains in vats. The principle of charity precludes him from translating our sentences in a way that presupposes that we are raving paranoiacs. Ironically, then, it is the principle of charity that ensures that he must translate our sentences in such a way that they are from his point of view mostly false.

Rorty and Davidson flatly disagree with this conclusion, for no reason that I can fathom. They claim (rather, Rorty attributes the claim to oral remarks of Davidson and accepts it himself) that "the best way to translate the discourse of a brain which has always lived in a vat will be as referring to the vat-cum-computer environment the brain is actually in."[119] That is like saying that we best translate the utterances of someone known to be an animist, who believes that every rock and tree contains a spirit-being, as references to the spiritless world the animist actually lives in rather than the spirits the animist believes in. Isn't it plain that this would be a preposterous way to translate the animist's utterances?

Let me summarize. On my construal, the principle of charity says,

1. Translate native utterances to maximize their overall agreement with what I know the native has good reason to assert.

That is, translate native utterances so that they come out sounding largely reasonable.

Since in the field linguist's circumstances I (by hypothesis) have only the native's utterances to go on, simplicity dictates the additional heuristic principle:

2. What the native has good reason to assert about our surroundings is largely what I have good reason to assert about our surroundings, viz., the truth.

Putting together (1) and (2), the conclusion in standard circumstances will be:

3. Translate native utterances to maximize their overall agreement with the truth (or with what I know to be the truth).

Number (3), of course, is Davidson's version of the principle of charity. But if I am the mad linguist, (2) is false. Because the mad linguist

---

119. Rorty, "Pragmatism, Davidson, and Truth," in *Objectivity, Relativism, and Truth, supra* note 44, at 133.

"knows" that he is feeding a delusory tape of bogus experiences into the native's sensorium, he will substitute:

2'. What the native has good reason to assert consists largely of the comments appropriate to the delusory experience-tape I am feeding into her sensorium.

And the conclusion, based on (1) together with (2'), is

3'. Translate native utterances to maximize their overall agreement with the delusory experience-tape I am feeding into her sensorium.

Clearly, (3') offers no grounds for concluding that the skeptical hypothesis is "simply unintelligible." On the contrary, it provides a straightforward recipe for making sense of a native all of whose beliefs are delusory and false.

These considerations already suffice to block Davidson's refutation of skepticism. But there is another conclusion that we can also draw from the example of the mad linguist. If we can imagine such a mad linguist—and why can't we?—then I see no reason why we cannot imagine the same setup with polarities reversed: the last laugh is on us, for the linguist is right. And thus Davidson's rejoinder that Descartes's Evil Deceiver story is unintelligible proves to be an empty threat. Nor should that surprise us: whatever the other flaws in the Evil Deceiver argument, we never really believed that we didn't understand it.

Chapter 4

Hannah Arendt and the
Primacy of Narrative

When she died in 1975, Hannah Arendt was one of the respected political thinkers of her time. It is therefore surprising that, until very recently, her work has exercised so little influence on the practice of her
contemporaries in the mainstream of political science. I believe that
much more is involved in this fact than historical accident, or even the
glossing over of her work by "the customary academic suspicion of
anything that is not guaranteed to be mediocre."[1] For the gap that
separates her work from what has come to be the practice of political
science in America arises from a deep difference in methods and goals,
rooted in turn in Arendt's understanding of the plight of politics in
contemporary civilization.

My purpose in this chapter is first and foremost to expound the
procedures of political explanation as Arendt understands them. It is,
second, to defend and adopt Arendt's procedures, which stress the
centrality of narrative in political explanation. By *political explanation*, I
mean the attempt to explain past or present political events in an intellectually rigorous way. This encompasses aims common to political
science, social science, and history. For short, I will call this enterprise
political science or *social science*, but I mean to be talking across disciplin-
ary boundaries. One further point of terminology: in the academy, "political theory" names a discipline: it is the name political science
departments give to political philosophy. When I will speak of political
theories in this chapter, however, I don't mean philosophical political
theory. I am thinking rather of something like scientific theories—sets
of laws that explain particular events—whose subject matter is politics.

To put her case briefly, Arendt denies that theoretical explanation
always furthers our comprehension of political affairs. Under certain
historical circumstances, those she refers to as "dark times," even the
most ingenious and plausible political theories lose their role in human

---

1. Hannah Arendt, *Men in Dark Times* 160 (1968).

knowledge. Yet this does not mean that no understanding is possible to us; rather, the role of theories can be assumed, imperfectly to be sure, by "ever-recurrent narration,"[2] frequently the narration of the stories of individual human beings.[3] Eventually, narration can be reified *poetically* (and not scientifically), and this is the closest we can come to a true mastering of the past.[4]

The bizarreness of this account need hardly be remarked. However, it is worth calling attention to two features of it that are especially important in their remoteness from textbook accounts of scientific method. First is the radically time-bound character of explanation (if I may stay with this word): historical circumstances determine not so much the character of explanation as its very possibility. This feature assaults the deepest motivation of the scientific method expounded in textbooks, namely, to sever the umbilicus between a timelessly true theory and the circumstances of its origin.

Second, the activity of comprehension demands a different type of personal virtue than scientific detachment, which Arendt, following Droysen, calls "eunuchic objectivity," the "extinction of the self"; and comprehension requires abilities that have little to do with cleverness or intelligence. Rather, comprehension demands objectivity in the sense of honesty and impartiality, as "when Homer decided to sing the deeds of the Trojans no less than those of the Achaeans" or when Herodotus "set out to prevent 'the great and wonderful actions of the Greeks *and* barbarians' from losing their due meed of glory."[5] And the ability is more than anything else "a purity of soul, an unmirrored, unreflected innocence of heart"[6] that allows one to narrate a story as it happened.

Dark Times as an Epistemic Condition

All of Arendt's thinking arises from her perception that we live in "dark times." The word "perception," of course, sounds like an awfully pompous label with which to dignify such a banal bit of wisdom. But here, as so often in her writing, Arendt brings a cliché to life simply by reflecting on what it literally says. Let us see what she finds in the notion of "dark times."

2. *Id.* at 21.

3. "[I]t is rather as though the colorless light of historical time were forced through and refracted by the prism of a great character so that in the resulting spectrum a complete unity of life and world is achieved." *Id.* at 33.

4. *Id.* at 20–22.

5. Arendt, *Between Past and Future* 51 (rev. ed. 1968).

6. Arendt, *Eichmann in Jerusalem* 229 (rev. ed. 1964).

The phrase, she tells us, is borrowed from Brecht's poem "An die Nachgeborenen," which begins "Truly, I live in dark times!" In it the poet speaks of the present as a time in which wisdom and goodness have come fatally apart from each other: in which the moderate life that the "old books" commend signifies guilty indifference to horror and suffering, for "a smooth forehead suggests insensitivity";[7] while on the other hand the path of moral action makes the actor coarse and brutal himself. ("Anger, even against injustice, makes the voice hoarse.") The social conditions of the time set this dilemma, as Brecht tells us in the second stanza, social conditions he likens to a "flood in which we have gone under." Disorder, hunger, uprising, massacre—all come between us and the life we would wish to lead, pushing us steadily away from it. "So passed my time which had been given to me on earth."

This seems to say no more than what we would expect of a description of "dark times." And we would agree that our century, the most destructive in human history, amply deserves the title. But what has this to do with the method of political science?

The answer comes when we recognize that for Brecht dark times are not merely times of horror but times of confusion in which theory no longer helps us to act. That is the outcome of the dilemma set up between wisdom and goodness. "I would also like to be wise," Brecht tells us; but in dark times what passes for wisdom is in reality a kind of forgetfulness, while to act righteously is to act unwisely, perhaps even viciously. For Arendt as well, " 'Dark times' . . . are as such not identical with the monstrosities of this century which indeed are of a horrible novelty."[8] First, of course, dark times are nothing new. But second— and this is Brecht's theme—is the fact that the phrase *dark times* has an epistemological as well as a valuational meaning. Dark times for Arendt are times in which (in Tocqueville's words, which she cites on several occasions) "the mind of man wanders in obscurity." In dark times traditional forms of explanation no longer explain anything (although, she observes, they can still explain things *away*, that is, obfuscate). Political science becomes a charade, "denying the outrageous, deducing the unprecedented from precedents, . . . explaining phenomena by such analogies and generalities that the impact of reality and the shock of experience are no longer felt."[9] Explanation—the construction of lawlike generalities, or empirically testable hypotheses, or theoretical models—can go on undaunted, but dark times cut it loose from any genuine role within human knowledge. In her most striking formula-

---

7. Bertolt Brecht, *Poems 1913–1956* 318 (John Willett & Ralph Manheim eds. 1976).

8. Arendt, *supra* note 1, at 9.

9. Arendt, *The Origins of Totalitarianism* viii (rev. ed. 1968).

tion, "the human mind had ceased, for some mysterious reasons, to function properly."[10]

All this *might* show is Arendt's distaste for social science, which is easy to document.[11] There is more to it than that, however. For Arendt finds a deep connection between politics and knowledge, a connection discussed most clearly in her essay "The Concept of History" in *Between Past and Future;* let us examine this essay.

Four Ages of Immortality

As is often the case in her writings, Arendt finds a historical key to the problem at hand by examining the ancient Greeks. Here the key lies in the connection between great deeds and immortality. For the Greeks, the world into which we are born is eternal; even the plants and animals, whose reality lies in the species and not the individual, have a sort of immortality. In this way the natural cycles are in effect eternal recurrences—a fact Plato recognized when he wrote in the *Timaeus* that time in its circularity is "a moving image of eternity."[12] Thus only humans (and only insofar as we are *more* than animals) are mortal.

This is not only a Greek idea, of course; it appears beautifully in this old Dinka (Sudanese) song:

> In the time when Dendid created all things,
> He created the sun,
> And the sun is born, and dies, and comes again.
> He created the moon,
> And the moon is born, and dies, and comes again.
> He created the stars,
> And the stars are born, and die, and come again.
> He created man,
> And man is born, and dies, and does not come again.[13]

---

10. Arendt, *supra* note 5, at 9.

11. "Their vocabulary is repulsive and their hope to close the alleged gap between our scientific mastery of nature and our deplored impotence to 'manage' human affairs . . . sounds frightening." *Id.* at 59. At the base of her distaste lies the insight that the jargon of theories is peculiarly suited to ideology because it annihilates "sensible language." Arendt, *Crises of the Republic* 221 (1972). When Adelbert Reif asked her if the student protest movement is "a historically positive process," he received the reply, "I don't know what you mean by 'positive.' I assume you mean, am I for it or against it." *Id.* at 201.

12. Plato, *Timaeus* 37d.

13. Peter Matthiessen, *The Tree Where Man Was Born* 29 (1976) (quoting *The Unwritten Song* (Willard Trask ed. 1966)).

For the Greeks, the belief in natural immortality combined with human mortality implies that "immortality is what the mortals therefore must try to achieve if they want to live up to the world into which they were born."[14] This they do by performing great deeds. As Diotima says in the *Symposium*, "Every one of us, no matter what he does, is longing for the endless fame, the incomparable glory that is theirs [famous heroes'] . . . because he is in love with the eternal."[15] This theme pervades the Greek historians and poets.

And that should not surprise us, for such a project of "immortalizing" would be futile unless some sort of collective memory exists to preserve glorious deeds. This function was initially fulfilled by poetry, by Homer and Hesiod singing the deeds of the heroes and recollecting the races of gods and of humans. In the words of Pindar, nearly all of whose odes were written for this purpose alone: "A thing said walks in immortality if it has been said well; and over the fruitful earth and across the sea fare the light that dies never of splendid deeds."[16]

The poetic project inaugurates a remarkable sequence of historical transformations of human devices of collective memory. The second stage partly overlaps this first, which we may call the *Age of Poetry*, and is described explicitly, near its close, in the funeral oration of Pericles:

> The admiration of the present and succeeding ages will be ours, since we have not left our power without witness, but have shown it by mighty proofs; and far from needing a Homer for our pan-egyrist, or other of his craft . . . we have forced every sea and land to be the highway of our daring, and everywhere, whether for evil or for good, have left imperishable monuments behind us.[17]

Pretty clearly this passage has to do with the very same project of "immortalizing" of which we have spoken. It is not a question of propaganda or public relations, for Pericles speaks of monuments to Athens's evil as well as good; the point is not what the deeds were but that they last. And the fact is that Pericles believed the Athenians to have no need for poetry in order to immortalize. Why?

On a first reading, it seems the reason is that Athenian prowess has left its mark everywhere, so that the deeds speak louder than any song. But this offers no answer at all, for the simple reason that deeds do not preserve themselves. Surely Pericles could not have missed the whole

---

14. Arendt, *supra* note 5, at 48; *see also* Arendt, *The Human Condition* 232 (1958).
15. Plato, *Symposium* 208d.
16. Pindar, "Isthmia 4," in *The Odes* 137 (Richard Lattimore trans. 1947).
17. Thucydides, *The Complete Writings* 106 (John H. Finley, Jr. ed. 1951).

point of poetic immortality at the very moment he was speaking of why
it was no longer necessary!

A hint of the solution may be found further in Pericles's oration:
"[T]heir glory is laid up to be eternally remembered upon every occasion on which deed or story shall fall for its commemoration."[18] Now
we see the point: as long as the polis exists it will commemorate its
heroes, and that is why the poets are not necessary. The polis substitutes
for poetry.

Without inquiring further whether this is a correct interpretation of
Pericles's oration, let us note that it is Arendt's: "[T]he polis could
dispense with the service of 'others of his craft' because it offered each
of its citizens that public-political space that it assumed would confer
immortality upon his acts."[19] This statement simply underscores another of Diotima's claims in the *Symposium* (209a–e): in Arendt's words,
"that the drive toward immortality should lie at the foundation of political communities."[20]

This conception of politics can seem adolescent to us; it seems to
overlook that political actions are customarily undertaken for specific
practical purposes and not to satisfy a yen to do something great. But
Arendt recognizes this fact. She sharply distinguishes between the
meaning of an action and its *end* and attacks as monstrous the confusion
of the two—monstrous, because the confusion lies at the root of totalitarian ideology, which thinks of the "meaning of history" as something
we can consciously aim at as if it were an end. The end is the particular
goal of an action, while its meaning is general. But, she argues, we can
keep these sorted out by noticing the difference between the expressions "for the sake of . . . " and "in order to. . . ."[21] A carpenter performs his action *in order to* make a table, but "his whole life as a
carpenter is ruled by something quite different, namely an encompassing notion 'for the sake of' which he became a carpenter in the first
place."[22] Keeping this distinction in mind, it is no paradox to say that
political communities are founded for the sake of immortalizing their
inhabitants, not in order to fulfill certain specific purposes; or that men
and women undertake political action for the sake of glory. And this
seems to be Pericles's conception of the matter.

This *Age of Politics* (as we may call the second stage of the historical
transformation) is the most important stage of all: for just as it provided
a full-blooded substitute for poems that "might charm for the moment

18. *Id.* at 107.
19. Arendt, *supra* note 5, at 72; *see also* Arendt, *supra* note 14, at 197.
20. Arendt, *supra* note 5, at 71–72.
21. *Id.* at 78–79; *see also* Arendt, *supra* note 14, at 197.
22. Arendt, *supra* note 5, at 79.

only for the impression which they gave to melt at the touch of fact,"[23] the subsequent stages vainly attempt to replace the "lost treasure" (Arendt's phrase) of a political space for human deeds.

Indeed, the *Age of Historical Narrative* (the third stage) was already under way at the time of Pericles's oration. Historical narrative, which of course can be composed at any time, becomes essential when the political community cannot keep memory alive. Herodotus wrote his histories "in order that . . . the memory of the past may not be blotted out from among men by time, and that great and marvelous deeds done by Greeks and barbarians . . . may not lack renown"[24]—that is, he wrote history to immortalize these deeds.

There are many obvious differences between the histories of the ancients and those we write today. Arendt focuses on one in particular. For the ancients, the great deeds and works "are not seen as parts of either an encompassing whole or a process; on the contrary, the stress is always on single instances and single gestures."[25] That does not imply that these histories are mere catalogues of facts with no lesson, meaning, or causal relationships to other events. On the contrary—and this is the crucial point—"Everything that was done or happened contained and disclosed its share of 'general' meaning within the confines of its individual shape and did not need a developing and engulfing process to become significant."[26] To put it in Hegelian terms, each event was a "concrete universal" that demonstrated its larger meaning by being a perfect paradigm of it. The event and its meaning were transparent to each other, so there was no need to enunciate its meaning. For this reason, ancient historical writing could satisfy the most stringent intellectual demands for the comprehension of events while remaining from first to last a *narrative*.

All that has changed for us moderns. To us history is not a series of events but a *process*. The historical reasons for this change of attitude are manifold and complex. The most important factor, however, in bringing about the transformation to what we may call the *Age of Historical Process* (the fourth and final stage) is the rise of modern science. On Arendt's interpretation—a plausible reading of early modern philosophy of science[27]—the Scientific Revolution was achieved by treating

---

23. Thucydides, *supra* note 17, at 107.

24. Herodotus, 1 *History* 3 (A. D. Godley trans. 1920).

25. Arendt, *supra* note 5, at 43.

26. *Id.* at 64.

27. Very illuminating here is Paolo Rossi, *Philosophy, Technology and the Arts in the Early Modern Era* (1970). For a striking example of this point, see the beginning of Book 2 of Descartes's *Géometrie*, where mathematics is assimilated to mechanics, a basically practical art.

nature as if it were man made. This in turn creates the secret link between science and technology: science that treats nature as an artifact will be most successful in precisely those applications that involve man-made control of nature.

Now technology involves humanity acting *into* nature (to use Arendt's striking and accurate phrase), and action always initiates processes.[28] Putting all of this together, we find that modern science is committed to viewing nature as a process or a collection of processes. Research, then, will be an attempt to discover the laws—literally, the laws of movement—that govern processes.

History, or any history that aspires to the intellectual seriousness of natural science, will therefore emphasize the laws of movement rather than the particular events. "What the concept of process implies is that the concrete and the general, the single thing or event and the universal meaning, have parted company."[29] And thus the focus on laws woven into *theories* supplants the focus on events recounted in narratives. The Age of Historical Process is equally the Age of Historical Law.

Meaning, Comprehension, and Underdetermination

Arendt's criticism of political science begins where this background account ends: she attempts to show that on its own terms, Historical Process will not do.

To begin the argument, let us recapitulate what we have found so far. We see a remarkable sequence of linked substitutions, thus:

POETRY → POLIS → NARRATIVE → LAWS

The red thread running through these is that they give human life meaning, that they allow us to overcome the futility that comes of being cosmic nomads who are born into the world as strangers and who disappear without a trace. All four of these modes defy mortality, as we have seen. But in addition they make sense of things. Poetry did so by condensing the complexity of events into figures that "transparently displayed the inner truth of the event";[30] the polis allowed the person to appear in public before others and thus mean something to them (disclose himself or herself to them, in Arendt's language); narrative exhibited events as concrete universals; and historical laws meaningfully organize the particulars over which they range.

---

28. Arendt, *supra* note 14, at 230–36.
29. Arendt, *supra* note 5, at 64.
30. Arendt, *supra* note 1, at 20.

This last clause looks objectionable: we do not seek scientific laws, it might be said, in order to give *meaning* to the events they explain; rather, their human significance lies in that they allow us to predict and control phenomena.

Arendt finds such a view of social science silly, misguided, and dangerous. Misguided, because it misunderstands the nature of scientific "control," which does not really control phenomena but rather initiates processes that are in the long run totally unpredictable.[31] Dangerous for this reason but also because the closest thing to successful social control in actual history is totalitarianism. And the silliness is obvious when we look at the success record of social science. On the one hand, it is notorious that most predictions that emerge from social science research can be derived from simple common sense;[32] on the other, the truly important political events of our century (such as popular uprisings or the fall of communism) come as a surprise to everyone.[33]

To Arendt, the facts themselves demonstrate that "prediction and control" talk in political science is a black comedy, by turns foolish and frightening. For unless someone makes us predictable and controllable, human action cannot be predicted or controlled. Her conclusion is, quite simply, that the only sane reason for explaining society and politics is to understand the meaning of events. Anything less is no explanation at all.

And that is where trouble appears, because facts underdetermine the laws that explain them:

[T]he perplexity is that the particular incident, the observable fact or single occurrence of nature, or the reported deed and event of history, have ceased to make sense without a universal process in which they are supposedly embedded; yet the moment man approaches this process in order to escape the haphazard character of the particular, in order to find meaning—order and necessity—his effort is rebutted by the answer from all sides: any order, any necessity, any meaning you wish to impose will do.[34]

---

31. Arendt, *supra* note 5, at § 60; Arendt, *supra* note 14, at 300. *See generally* Arendt, *supra* note 14, § 34.

32. For examples, see Arendt, *supra* note 11, at 72, 156.

33. "Needless to say, this is not science but pseudo-science." *Id.rFS at 109. On this topic, see id.* at 109–10.

34. Arendt, *supra* note 5, at 88–89.

The search for historical laws, that is, is a machine that turns itself off. "This is the clearest possible demonstration that under these conditions there is neither necessity nor meaning."[35]

In the past three decades a large literature has arisen on the underdetermination of theory by facts, deploying arguments of extreme subtlety and sophistication, with inconclusive results. Arendt, writing before much of this literature existed, was aware of none of these arguments. Indeed, she hardly presents an argument at all for her result, leaning (here as in other places) far too much on the philosophical speculations of physicists to support her point.

Yet is there really a bone to pick with her in this matter? What the philosophical literature debates is the existence of underdetermination in the natural sciences; one would have to be blind to dispute its existence in the social sciences. Nowadays just as much as when Arendt wrote, theories "in the social and historical sciences cancel each other out" and this "because they can all be consistently proved."[36] We can even point to the reason: a scientific law tells us that under circumstances A, B will hold true; but because historical circumstances are never constant, we can never know that any given configuration is like A in the relevant respects. Historical situations are essentially multifaceted, so we can single out any aspect of a situation as the relevant one or claim that other aspects prevent the relevant factor from operating in a given instance. Thus no consistent historical laws are falsifiable. To put it another way, because history does not repeat itself, no controlled experiments are possible, which means that no control on the number of acceptable explanations is possible. They are all just-so stories.

It is not simply a question of the complexity of historical situations, for science has often dealt successfully with complex phenomena. Nor is it a question of the unrepeatability of history; sciences such as geology and cosmology deal successfully with unrepeatable phenomena. Rather, the difficulty lies in the human condition that Arendt calls "plurality."[37] There are many aspects to a historical situation because there are many people—and many peoples—in action at each moment in history. Complexity can be reduced, but plurality is irreducible. Similarly, we reflect that geology owes its success to the existence of a unique record of the past written in the earth itself and to experiments that can be performed in the laboratory. Plurality, however, means that there are many versions of historical truth and that to isolate experi-

---

35. *Id.* at 89.
36. *Id.* at 89.
37. On "plurality," see Arendt, *supra* note 14, at 175–76.

mental subjects is to change the subject, to study men and women precisely as they are *not* when they act.

Let us suppose a political group or faction swings into action. Each member sees a story unfolding and bases his or her action on that story. It includes first of all an assessment of what the faction can do, based on one's perception of the unity in the group (i.e., what one thinks the other members are thinking), of the attitude of the noninvolved public, of the capability of the opposition. The assessment of the attitude of the public is always based on insufficient information. And how does one size up the capability of the opposition? This depends on their unity, their inadequate information, their projections, and their estimate of your estimate of their strength—an endless chain of mutual opacity, intentional or unintentional bluff, and false evaluations.

Within the faction, moreover, there are differences in opinion about whose estimates are most accurate, compounded by the difficulty of making one's position plausible to others. One soon understands that every public statement serves two gods, one who looks to the accuracy of what one says and the other to its effect on one's fellows. Inevitably, each member of the group attempts to advance a plausible surface perspective while harboring a much more complex perspective within. And of course what others see is neither of these two perspectives but rather an appearance that, precisely because it forms the basis of others' assessment of one, and thus of others' ventures with one, is politically speaking identical with reality.[38] It follows that this reality is accessible only to others. Each individual views the unfolding story as a drama with himself or herself as its hero, but it is not a drama so much as a manifold of superimposed ironies invisible to each agent exactly at the moment when he or she is its subject. *Historical truth* is simply the name for the kaleidoscope that successively reveals and dissipates these patterns. All of which is to say, there is no fact of the matter in politics, only a plurality of perspectives.[39]

Nor should one suppose that this points to merely empirical difficulties that do not bear on the theoretical question of objectivity. It is not just that it is difficult in practice to ascertain the objective state of affairs. The problem is rather that the objective state of affairs is radically decentered: it offers us no Archimedean point from which it can be comprehended, because every point is Archimedean. As I argued in the introduction to this book, causal explanation depends on our ability to distinguish (foreground) causes from (background) conditions, and hu-

---

38. *Id.* at 199.
39. For related arguments, see Alasdair MacIntyre, *After Virtue* 84–102 (1981).

man plurality guarantees that this distinction will be contestable. Every participant in politics is potentially an initiator of action based on his or her perspective: thus perspectival facts are among the objective facts of the matter. Conversely, no fact bearing on a situation can be translated into action without passing through the eye of the needle that each individual perspective is. Thus *only* perspectival interpretations are politically meaningful. As we have seen, moreover, the basic concepts of practical politics—strength, unity, support—refer not to unequivocal facts but to coincidences of perspective. That is why controlled experiment is impossible; in politics to control the variables is to erase the data. Theories are underdetermined because historical events are overdetermined.[40]

As a remedy against this epistemological disease we are presented with an unhappy choice. We can (1) stick with one theoretical structure, come what may, exploiting the unfalsifiable character of laws of historical movement. Philosophers of science call this conventionalism, but it is more properly described as adhering to an ideology. Or, given that many theories are capable of explaining the empirical correlations, we can (2) stick with the correlations themselves, remaining empirical with a vengeance.

The problem with (1) is that it purchases logical consistency together with the plausibility that gives facts their meaning at the cost of faithfulness to the facts themselves. This "escape from reality" character of ideological explanations forms Arendt's chief polemical target; it is, among other things, the theoretical premise of totalitarianism.[41] The problem with (2) is in one sense the opposite, namely, that while ideol-

---

40. It would be interesting to know how much Arendt was influenced in these reflections by Nietzsche's epistemology. Nietzsche remarks in *The Gay Science* § 277 that in hindsight even the most random series of events in our life takes on an aura of necessity. This fact is explained in the epistemological reflections in *The Will to Power* and *Twilight of the Idols* by the double hypothesis that (1) we do not actually see facts-in-themselves but only facts-from-a-particular-perspective and (2) each perspective forces a coherency on its experience. The conclusion Nietzsche draws is a rather strong skepticism about real necessary connections in the world.

Both (1) and (2) are consequences of Nietzsche's metaphysical doctrine of will-to-power, a doctrine Arendt rightly rejects. But she could not help realize that (1) and (2) are valid in the political realm, where plurality indeed guarantees the truth of perspectivalism. And as we have seen, Arendt argues from this conclusion to the identical skeptical conclusion concerning necessity in history and politics.

41. Arendt, *supra* note 9, at 468–74. To see it at work in American affairs, Arendt's essay "Lying in Politics," in *Crises of the Republic, supra* note 11, is important. Her analysis of the Pentagon Papers is devoted to proving that America's Vietnam policy resulted in part from the decision makers using their theories to immunize themselves against all facts, so that they moved in a "defactualized" world.

ogy gives more meaning to the world than the facts warrant, uninterpreted data gives no meaning at all (though immersion in data can
have the salutary effect of demolishing lies and the meanings they
suggest). But in another sense the quest for statistical correlations im-
ports its own ideology, an ideology of method.[42] This ideology believes
for no good reason in the validity of mathematical extrapolation from
today's trends to long-term regularities—regularities that presuppose
the metaphysical belief that history forms a law-governed process. The
embarrassing track record of economic and demographic forecasters,
whose predictions routinely explode in the face of unanticipated inter-
vening events, corroborates at least the history side of Arendt's (overly
dogmatic) assertion that "The notion of process does not denote an
objective quality of either history or nature."[43]

In either case, a blindness to particular events results. This blindness
is most noticeable, of course, in the case of the unprecedented events of
twentieth-century history, of which Arendt's work extensively explores
two: the rise of totalitarianism and the Holocaust. For if events really are
unprecedented, then both logical and empirical consistency are bound
to be misleading. Arendt is at her best in her polemics against the
inanities and false profundities that have emerged to "explain" these
events on the basis of analogies and precedents that—if she is right—
can never do the job.[44] In this context she writes in the preface to *The
Origins of Totalitarianism*, "Comprehension does not mean . . . explaining phenomena by such analogies and generalities that the impact of
reality and the shock of experience are no longer felt."[45] In a similar
vein, she condemns the Vietnam-era U.S. decision makers: "They were
unable to confront reality on its own terms because they had always
some parallels in mind that 'helped' them to understand those terms."[46]

For Arendt, the facts of the twentieth century do not need explaining;
they need confronting.[47] It is not their causes that are baffling but rather
the "grotesque disparity between cause and effect."[48] The *impotence of
explanation*, a second-order fact, is a primary datum for any investigation of politics in our century.

---

42. "[T]hey believed in methods but not in 'world views.'" Arendt, *supra* note 11,
at 40.

43. Arendt, *supra* note 5, at 62.

44. *See, e.g.*, Arendt, "Epilogue," in *Eichmann in Jerusalem, supra* note 6.

45. Arendt, *supra* note 9, at viii.

46. Arendt, *supra* note 11, at 40.

47. Arendt, *supra* note 9, at viii; Arendt, *supra* note 1, at 20.

48. Arendt, *supra* note 9, at viii.

Dark Times as the Collapse of the Illusion of Immortality

Before these conclusions can become plausible to us, we need to know what makes our age differ so much from any other that explanations no longer explain, for this seems on the surface as outrageous as the claim that at some time the law of gravitation should suddenly cease to be true.[49]

The answer will come from an examination of politics, for, as we have seen, *explanation* now, like *narrative* in ancient historiography, exists as a surrogate or stand-in for the experience of politics eulogized by Pericles.

The polis, we saw earlier, "was to offer a remedy for the futility of action and speech."[50] It did that by creating "the space of appearance in the widest sense of the word, namely, the space where I appear to others as others appear to me, where men exist not merely like other living or inanimate things but make their appearance explicitly."[51] However, this space provides a remedy for futility only as long as it lasts, and therefore one of the chief characteristics of the ancient polis was that it created for itself the illusion of continuity and immortality. Although nothing human can withstand the passing of time, the polis existed to maintain the illusion of a permanent "in-between" space that could immortalize words and deeds that otherwise would last but a moment.[52] "Not historically, of course, but speaking metaphorically and theoretically, it is as though the men who returned from the Trojan War had wished to make permanent the space of action."[53]

Our present attitude to the political realm could scarcely be further from this. It is perfectly embodied in two famous verses of Brecht's quoted by Arendt:

> We have sat, an easy generation
> In houses held to be indestructible.
> Thus we built those tall boxes on the
>   island of Manhattan
> And those thin aerials that amuse the
>   Atlantic swell.

---

49. I owe the inspiration for this section to an unpublished essay by Jon Bordo.

50. Arendt, *supra* note 14, at 197.

51. *Id.* at 198–99.

52. It is this illusion of immortality that allows Aristotle in the *Nichomachean Ethics* to substitute the continuity of virtuous upbringing for substantive moral rules. Aristotle's ethical system presupposes the continuity of the polis.

53. Arendt, *supra* note 14, at 198.

Of those cities will remain what passed
   through them, the wind!
The house makes glad the eater: he
   clears it out.
We know that we're only tenants, provisional ones
And after us will come: nothing worth talking
   about.[54]

The image of the winds punching holes through the human artifice is one of Brecht's favorites;[55] surely these are the winds of time, and the artifice (*Städten, das Haus*) is the man-made "in-between," the public realm.

Brecht's perception is surely no idiosyncracy. To stay within poetry, we find similar images in Auden's "September 1, 1939":

Faces along the bar
Cling to their average day;
The lights must never go out,
The music must always play,
All the conventions conspire
To make this fort assume
The furniture of home;
Lest we should see where we are,
Lost in a haunted wood,
Children afraid of the night
Who have never been happy or good.[56]

Here only lying conventions "make this fort assume the furniture of home"; in reality it is the flimsiest of barricades against the "haunted wood."

Both poems speak of the tavern, the house that "makes glad the eater." It is the zone of escape, the zone of forgetfulness—the last desiccated remnant of the City, the phantom boundary that guards us from "*der durch sie hindurchging, der Wind.*"

The image is a striking one. Where the ancient city existed to create a fully human space—a home, in Auden's words, and not just a fortress—the statist-liberal government claims only to provide fortress-like protection of private interests (and, by so claiming, fails to provide

---

54. Brecht, "Of Poor B.B.," in *Poems 1913–1956, supra* note 7, at 108.
55. *See, e.g.*, Brecht, "Song on Black Saturday at the Eleventh Hour of Easter Eve," in *Poems 1913–1956, supra* note 7, at 97–98.
56. W. H. Auden, *The Collected Poetry* 57, 58 (1945).

even this). This illusion of a fully human space can be recaptured only in anesthesia or false euphoria, and thus the tavern becomes the remnant of the public forum.

> Towards evening it's men that I gather round me.
> And then we address one another as 'gentlemen'.
> They're resting their feet on my table tops
> And say: things will get better for us.
> And I don't ask when.[57]

Curiously, both poems end with the same prayer: Brecht's

> in the earthquakes to come, I very much hope
> I shall keep my cigar alight, embittered or no[58]

and Auden's

> Yet, dotted everywhere,
> Ironic points of light
> Flash out wherever the Just
> Exchange their messages:
> May I, composed like them
> Of Eros and dust,
> Beleaguered by the same
> Negation and despair,
> Show an affirming flame.[59]

I will return to this prayer.

These poems, written from the tense foreboding of catastrophe, are reconfirmed by the history of our century. Let us look at Brecht's "Rückkehr" ("Return"), which returns to the earlier poem as well as to what Brecht calls *die Vaterstadt*:

> My native city [*die Vaterstadt*], however shall
>   I find her?
> Following the swarms of bombers
> I come home.
> Well, where is she? Where the colossal
> Mountains of smoke stand.
> That thing there amongst the fires

57. Brecht, *supra* note 54, at 108.
58. *Id.*
59. Auden, *supra* note 56.

Is her. My native city, how will she receive me?
Before me go the bombers. Deadly swarms
Announce my homecoming to you. Conflagrations
Precede your son.[60]

The illusion of immortality has collapsed, for now we can no longer believe that *die Vaterstadt* will live on beyond our deaths to perpetuate our actions. With it collapses that "for the sake of" which politics exists, "the conviction that the greatest that man can achieve is his own appearance and actualization."[61] What remains are the various "in order to's" of politics, the goals of protection and administration that have seemed self-evidently to be the purpose of politics since at least the time of Hobbes.

Now, rather than seeing the *bios politikos* as the most human of lives, we despise and distrust politicians. In Arendt's paraphrase of Sartre, "everybody who is publicly recognized belongs among the *salauds*."[62] Naturally: the public space now is a mere tool of our practical ends. One does not find meaning among one's tools, nor feel any particular admiration for a person who, for purposes of his own, chooses to place himself among them. The public space can (in Arendt's terminology) no longer show *who* one is, only *what* one is. It reveals the person only as a tool or an opportunist. And this is Arendt's *definition* of dark times: "periods . . . in which the public realm has been obscured and the world become so dubious that people have ceased to ask any more of politics than that it show due consideration for their vital interests and personal liberty." She adds, "Those who have lived in such times and been formed by them have probably always been inclined to despise the world and the public realm. . . ."[63]

For *die Vaterstadt* was never merely a tool or a place. It was place and home and generationally transmitted remembrance: it was tradition and Mnemosyne. Now, as Auden and Brecht tell it, *die Vaterstadt* no longer has the power to illuminate, and this means that appearance in public can no longer touch the deepest realities concerning ourselves; these have retreated to darker and more private corners.[64]

Arendt's insight is that darker and more private corners will not do:

---

60. Brecht, *supra* note 7, at 392.

61. Arendt, *supra* note 14, at 208; *see also* Margaret Canovan, *The Political Thought of Hannah Arendt* 84 (1974).

62. Arendt, *supra* note 1, at viii.

63. *Id.* at 11.

64. Arendt quotes four lines of Rilke, translated by Denver Lindley as follows: "Mountains rest beneath a splendor of stars, but even in them time flickers. Ah, unsheltered in my wild, darkling heart lies immortality." Arendt, *supra* note 5, at 44, 285 n.5.

"for without a space of appearance and without trusting in action and speech as a mode of being together, neither the reality of one's self, of one's identity, nor the reality of the surrounding world can be established beyond doubt."[65] Arendt allies herself with the greater part of twentieth-century epistemology, especially that of the later Wittgenstein, in rejecting the Cartesian model of founding knowledge in subjective self-certainty.[66] Like Wittgenstein the self-proclaimed solipsist, she acknowledges that in the "dark times" of modernity this retreat to subjectivity has become inevitable. But she, like Wittgenstein, sees as well that reliance on a purely private court of appeals, whether of Cartesian or phenomenalist-empiricist or romantic variety, can have only one outcome: a withering skepticism concerning the world and a corrupting self-deception concerning our private stance.[67] When what is most important, our "appearance and actualization," is no longer illuminated by the public space—when, that is, it is left for the privacy of our own heart—it blurs and falls out of focus: it becomes our "lost treasure."[68]

At this point it becomes easy to see why, with the collapse of the illusion of immortality, we should seek comfort in the principle that "nothing is permanent except change" and look for our immortality in the immutable laws of process.[69] The difficulty here, however, is that

---

65. Arendt, *supra* note 14, at 108.

66. It would be a not ungrateful task to compare Arendt with Wittgenstein, whose later work is in a sense a depoliticized and "socialized" counterpart of hers in its critique of the tradition, its emphasis on practice and activity, its assault on the private as a foundation for the public, and the generally tragic vision of the human capacity to understand that underlies it. Wittgenstein writes, "The philosopher is the man who has to cure himself of many sicknesses of the understanding before he can arrive at the notions of the sound human understanding. If in the midst of life we are in death, so in sanity we are surrounded by madness." Wittgenstein, *Remarks on the Foundations of Mathematics* sec. iv, § 53 (1956). We even find our key Brechtian image in the preface to Wittgenstein's *Philosophical Investigations* (G. E. M. Anscombe trans. 3rd ed. 1958), at x. "It is not impossible that it should fall to the lot of this work, in its poverty and in the darkness of this time [*der Finsternis dieser Zeit*], to bring light into one brain or another— but, of course, it is not likely."

67. *See* Arendt, *supra* note 14, at 208–9, 283, and Arendt, *supra* note 5, at 56, for discussions of phenomenalism and empiricism; Arendt, *supra* note 1, at 17–23, for one of self-deception. In Wittgenstein, see *Philosophical Investigations*, §§ 243–79, the private-language argument.

68. For this term, see the preface to Arendt, *supra* note 5, and Arendt, *On Revolution* chap. 6 (1965).

69. "History in its modern version could come to terms with this experience; and though it failed to save politics itself from the old disgrace, though the single deeds and acts constituting the realm of politics, properly speaking, were left in limbo, it has at least bestowed upon the record of past events that share of earthly immortality to which the modern age necessarily aspired." Arendt, *supra* note 5, at 85–86.

"[t]he world becomes inhuman, inhospitable to human needs . . . when it is violently wrenched into a movement in which there is no longer any permanence."[70] Something further is needed. This sets the stage for the dilemmas we have noted previously. The "something further" cannot be private and subjective, for then "an atrophy of all the organs with which we respond to" the world results;[71] but if it is public, it is simply a collection of facts that "exists in an opaque, meaningless thereness which spreads obfuscation"[72] and in which human-made patterns can be found but meanings will never "disclose or reveal themselves."[73] And if we choose to identify meaning with a human-made pattern or ideology, we defeat ourselves in precisely the ways we saw in the last section. In Arendt's words, "reality has become opaque for the light of thought and . . . thought, no longer bound to incident as the circle remains bound to its focus, is liable either to become altogether meaningless or to rehash old verities which have lost all concrete relevance."[74]

This, then, is the true source of dark times: when politics is no longer able to sustain the illusion of immortality for human deeds, historical explanation, rung in as a substitute for it, is doomed to self-defeat.

Of course much remains to be said to fill in this schematic argument, particularly a detailed historical account of the collapse of the public space: obviously I cannot offer such an account here. Nor is there much point in attempting it here, for Arendt's own account is too elaborate to condense. It is essential, however, to see how far her conclusion reaches: it poses a demand for a different sort of intellectual activity than theory construction or the discovery of laws. For the defeat of the possibility of immortalizing history is equally the defeat of the project of finding timeless truths about history. A radically time-bound approach, grounded in the sempiternal needs of mortal life and in the specific demands of our historical time, has become essential.

The Storyteller

Die Vaterstadt was tradition and remembrance. With the loss of validity of traditional categories *die Vaterstadt* has become impossible: "re-

---

70. Arendt, *supra* note 1, at 11. It is this that leads her to find in Marx "flagrantly contradictory statements," Arendt, *supra* note 5, at 18, that have at their root the paradox that the meaning of history must at once lie in the "inhospitable" law of its motion—class struggle—and in the abolition of that motion, as though the culminating event of history would cancel the premise that alone gave it meaning.

71. Arendt, *supra* note 1, at 13.

72. *Id.* at viii.

73. Arendt, *supra* note 5, at 80–81.

74. *Id.* at 6.

membrance . . . is helpless outside a preestablished framework of reference."[75] Faced with the collapse of *die Vaterstadt*, we need a capacity for "entirely free thinking, which employs neither history nor coercive logic as crutches."[76]

And here we turn again to the prayer of Brecht and Auden. Brecht hopes that his cigar will not go out in bitterness: we may imagine the glowing tip of his cigar together with Auden's desire to "show an affirming flame," to become one of the ironic points of light flashing out wherever the Just exchange their messages. It is in this image of universal darkness pierced by points of light radiating from just individuals, without being reflections of any higher source of illumination, that we have Arendt's solution.

> [E]ven in the darkest of times we have the right to expect some illumination, and . . . such illumination may well come less from theories and concepts than from the uncertain, flickering and often weak light that some men and women, in their lives and their works, will kindle under almost all circumstances and shed over the time span that was given them on earth.[77]

Unhappily, former President George Bush's speechwriters turned Auden's and Arendt's image into a political cliché ("a thousand points of light"); as such, the image has lost much of its power to move us and make us think. The political cliché can also confuse our understanding of Arendt's argument, for the cliché gives Auden's image a meaning almost diametrically opposed to the significance Arendt finds in it. Mr. Bush's "thousand points of light" referred to official programs aiming to devolve governmental functions onto private initiatives—in Arendt's terms, to collapse the public realm into the realm of the social, the realm of the private. She would undoubtedly have regarded the ideology of privatization, reflected in the "thousand points of light" slogan, as one more symptom of the collapse of the public realm, not as a solution to it.

As her choice of adjectives suggests, "the uncertain, flickering and often weak light that some men and women, in their lives and their works, will kindle" is hardly an alternative she prefers to a robust public world. Plainly, Arendt's points of light represent a desperate and dangerous last chance in the face of encroaching darkness.

It is in lives and their works that Arendt finds this last chance. She gathers these together under the general heading of "stories," and the

---

75. *Id.*
76. Arendt, *supra* note 1, at 8.
77. *Id.* at ix–x.

story is both the form and content of explanation for her, as it is both the form and content of human action.[78]
The unfavorable comparison of conceptualization with storytelling is one of Arendt's recurrent themes, stated again and again in her books:

No philosophy, no analysis, no aphorism, be it ever so profound, can compare in intensity and richness of meaning with a properly narrated story.[79]

Events, past and present,—not social forces and historical trends, nor questionnaires and motivation research, nor any other gadgets in the arsenal of the social sciences—are the true, the only reliable teachers of political scientists, as they are the most trustworthy source of information for those engaged in politics.[80]

[M]y assumption is that thought itself arises out of incidents of living experience and must remain bound to them as the only guideposts by which to take its bearings.[81]

It seems that the words she wrote concerning Benjamin (in her most sympathetic essay) could be taken equally as a motto by Arendt herself:

[W]hat profoundly fascinated Benjamin from the beginning was never an idea, it was always a phenomenon. "What seems paradoxical about everything that is justly called beautiful is the fact that it appears" . . . and this paradox—or, more simply, the wonder of appearance—was always at the center of all his concerns.[82]

This is perhaps the best place to resume our analysis, for we have seen the notion of *appearance* before. The function of the public realm, recall, was "to throw light on the affairs of men by providing a space of appearances in which they can show in deed and word, for better or worse, who they are and what they can do."[83] This concept corresponds with her fundamental idea that action, though undertaken in order to

78. *See* Arendt, *supra* note 14, at 181–88.
79. Arendt, *supra* note 1, at 22.
80. Arendt, *supra* note 9, at 482.
81. Arendt, *supra* note 5, at 14.
82. Arendt, *supra* note 1, at 164. Indeed, Arendt describes her own procedures in terms identical to her description of Benjamin's, *id.* at 193–206, including the same motto from *The Tempest*. Arendt, *Thinking* 212 (1978).
83. Arendt, *supra* note 1, at viii. She uses almost the identical words in her study of

accomplish some particular goal, is done for the sake of the agent's appearance. Appearance and action are cognate concepts: an agent appears by acting and acts for the sake of appearing. And this is where the notion of "story" makes its crucial entry. Action "'produces' stories with or without intention as naturally as fabrication produces tangible things."[84] Actions are not unconnected gestures erupting haphazardly into nature: it is part of the concept of action that actions form themselves into stories. And this is why only the narration of stories can give meaning to history. "That every individual life between birth and death can eventually be told as a story with beginning and end is the pre-political and prehistoric condition of history, the great story without beginning and end."[85]

It will be objected that this is an unacceptably voluntaristic way of looking at history, but the objection misses her point. For it is central to Arendt's notion of "enacted stories" that the agent is *not* the "author" of the story that can be told about him or her. "Somebody began it and is its subject in the twofold sense of the word, namely, its actor and sufferer, but nobody is its author."[86] This fact allows history to be told objectively and makes it a history of events and not of intentions.

By now it should look as though Arendt has tried to solve the problems of what I have called the Age of Historical Laws by moving back to the Age of Historical Narrative. That is partly true—with, however, one crucial difference. Historical narratives as the ancients understood them presupposed that general meaning could be disclosed by particular events, that stories were "concrete universals." But, if we think about it for a moment, it will be apparent that with the collapse of *die Vaterstadt* narrative can no longer bear this burden. For the demand that a story disclose its general meaning in a specific shape is the same as the demand that the meaning of each event be capable (epistemologically) of appearing in public. Herodotus, however well aware he was of the inability of the actual polis of his day to give meaning to specific deeds, never questioned the ability of the ideal polis constituted by his readers to do so. But the collapse of *die Vaterstadt* is equivalent to the impotence of *any* public appearance, actual or ideal, to disclose meaning. The attempt to moralize about the deeds of the great comes off as mere

---

Rosa Luxemburg to commend renewed study of her works; the implication is that Arendt's own studies of individuals are instances of what she thinks narratives can and should do. *See id.* at 55–56.

84. Arendt, *supra* note 14, at 184.
85. *Id.*
86. *Id.*

hagiography, for in Heidegger's phrase, which Arendt cites, the light of the public obscures everything.[87]

Thus, when Arendt speaks of narration, she speaks of an activity of storytelling in which the stories carry with them no statable lesson. She nevertheless believes that these stories can have meaning for us (" . . . we have the right to expect some illumination . . . "). To see what she can mean, we may turn again to the philosophy of Wittgenstein, who expressed the problem with uncanny precision. Wittgenstein realized that under conditions of scientific clarity, the meaning of happenings in the world can be shown but not said:

> The sense of the world must lie outside the world. In the world everything is as it is, and everything happens as it does happen: *in it no value exists*. . . . For all that happens and is the case is accidental. What makes it nonaccidental cannot lie *within* the world, since if it did it would itself be accidental. It must lie outside the world.[88]

This emphatically does *not* say that meaning does not exist: "There are, indeed, things that cannot be put into words. They *make themselves manifest* [*zeigt sich.*]"[89] This is what Wittgenstein called "the mystical (*das Mystiche*)" and described in terms reminiscent of Arendt's "wonder of appearance,"[90] which is, as we have seen, the source of meaning in history for her. We narrate stories in order to make manifest whatever unsayable meaning resides in them.

There is one difference, however, between Wittgenstein and Arendt in this matter. Arendt believed we *can* achieve a "transparent display of the inner truth of the event"[91] beyond the "ever-recurrent narration" that "solves no problems and assuages no suffering."[92] That happens when the story becomes a "*formed* narrative"[93]—formed, that is, by art, by "'poetry' in the broadest sense."[94] Art, not mysticism, discloses the event's meaning. Arendt gives as an example Faulkner's *A Fable*, which

---

87. Arendt, *supra* note 1, at ix.

88. Wittgenstein, *Tractatus Logico-Philosophicus* proposition 6.41 (1955).

89. *Id.* proposition 6.522. As we saw in the preceding chapter, Wittgenstein never abandoned this central insight of his philosophy. For Arendt's statement of this "ineffability doctrine," see Arendt, *supra* note 14, at 181.

90. "It is not *how* things are in the world that is mystical, but *that* it exists" Wittgenstein, *supra* note 88, proposition 6.44.

91. Slightly paraphrased from Arendt, *supra* note 1, at 20.

92. *Id.* at 21.

93. *Id.* at 22 (my emphasis).

94. *Id.*

revealed the meaning of World War I in such a way "that it became possible to say: Yes, this is how it was."[95]

Poetry reveals meaning through metaphor—"provided that 'metaphor' is understood in its original, nonallegorical sense of *metapherein* (to transfer). For a metaphor establishes a connection which is sensually perceived in its immediacy and requires no interpretation."[96] She adds, "Since Homer the metaphor has borne that element of the poetic which conveys cognition. . . . Linguistic 'transference' enables us to give material form to the invisible . . . and thus to render it capable of being experienced."[97] Poetry, when soundly and honestly made, will provide us with metaphors for the ineffable meaning of events: the poetic story will in a sense perfect the historical story without falsifying it.

Arendt has indeed gone into the past for her version of explanation, but since *die Vaterstadt* has collapsed, she has gone into the Age of Poetry, the Homeric world preceding the polis, and not into the more recent past of historical narratives that depend, albeit indirectly, on the experience of the polis for their validity. Yet Arendt insists that "[n]o turning about of the tradition can . . . ever land us in the original Homeric 'position.'"[98] Her procedure cannot provide us with any certainty of "mastering" the past, of finding a Heroic Age in the midst of dark times. Her claim is only that we have no choice other than this.

Many of her critics misunderstand this point about Arendt. In a well-known paper, for example, Noel O'Sullivan accuses her of "Hellenic nostalgia,"[99] and she is frequently criticized for her Grecophile politics.[100] Goaded, perhaps, by such criticisms, Arendt responds in her final book by quoting Nietzsche's attack on German idealism as an impossible longing for the Greek world and adds: "I did not want to cross the 'rainbow-bridge of concepts,' perhaps because I am not home-

---

95. *Id.* at 20. On *A Fable,* see also Arendt, *supra* note 14, at 181. She gives other examples as well: Melville in *Billy Budd* and Dostoevski in "The Grand Inquisitor" "show openly and concretely, though of course poetically and metaphorically, upon what tragic and self-defeating enterprise the men of the French Revolution had embarked almost without knowing it." Arendt, *On Revolution, supra* note 68 at 77.

96. Arendt, *supra* note 1, at 166.

97. *Id.* She develops this thought elaborately in Arendt, *supra* note 82, at 98–124.

98. Arendt, *supra* note 5, at 37.

99. Noel O'Sullivan, "Hellenic Nostalgia and Industrial Society," in *Contemporary Political Philosophers* (Anthony de Crespigny and Kenneth Minogue eds. 1975).

100. A sophisticated example is Jürgen Habermas, "Hannah Arendt's Communications Concept of Power," 44 *Social Research* 3 (Spring 1977), to which I have replied in "On Habermas on Arendt on Power," 6 *Philosophy and Social Criticism* 81 (Winter 1979).

sick enough. . . ."[101] The subtlety of her own procedures can be seen by contrasting them with the positions of Leo Strauss and Eric Voegelin, illustrious contemporaries with whom she is often fallaciously grouped.

Strauss and Voegelin, it seems to me, do share a Hellenic or at any rate "Mediterranean" (Voegelin) nostalgia, a desire to revive an image of politics and its study that they find in Plato and Aristotle.[102] Arendt differs utterly in her evaluation of the Greek philosophers, who she believed were suspicious of action and of genuine politics. Plato and Aristotle were looking for "an escape from politics altogether. . . . The hallmark of all such escapes is the concept of rule, that is, the notion that men can lawfully and politically live together only when some are entitled to command and others forced to obey."[103] For Arendt, plurality, the ability of each human being to initiate action, implies that participatory democracy is the true form of the polis.[104] Philosophers' programs for society, by contrast, would establish "tyrannies of 'truth' which . . . are as tyrannical as other forms of despotism."[105] Strauss and Voegelin are interested in a revival of classical virtue.[106] Arendt, however, discovered in the Eichmann trial that the presupposition of ancient virtue, the correspondence between human character and human deeds, had disappeared.[107] The classical tradition as such has lost its validity.

All three, it is true, criticize positivist political science, Arendt in the ways we have been examining and Strauss and Voegelin by arguments exhibiting a self-contradiction in the Weberian separation of fact and value.[108] Strauss and Voegelin, however, argue from this criticism to a demand for Greek "noetic" political science, the quest for a metaphysical theory of politics. Arendt, in *Thinking*, joins "the ranks of those who . . . have been attempting to dismantle metaphysics, and philosophy

---

101. Arendt, *Willing* 158 (1978).

102. I do not mean to suggest that the positions of Strauss and Voegelin can be assimilated to each other *grosso modo*, an idea that followers of each are likely to reject.

103. Arendt, *supra* note 14, at 222.

104. Arendt's paradigm polis is Athens, while Strauss's is Sparta. *See* Leo Strauss, *The City and Man* 145–53 (1964).

105. Arendt, *supra* note 5, at 246.

106. For Strauss, it is the classical tradition of natural right. *See* Strauss, *Natural Right and History* (1953). For Voegelin, it is *sophia* and *prudentia*. *See* Eric Voegelin, *The New Science of Politics* (1952).

107. *See* Arendt, *supra* note 6, at 26, 150; Arendt, *supra* note 82, at 3–5; Arendt, "Thinking and Moral Considerations," 38 *Social Research* 417 (Autumn 1971).

108. Strauss, *supra* note 106, at 35–80; Voegelin, *supra* note 106, at 13–23.

with all its categories, . . . from . . . Greece until today." She adds, "Such dismantling is possible only on the assumption that the thread of tradition is broken and that we shall not be able to renew it."[109] Noesis rests on fallacious visual metaphors for thinking, which Arendt replaces by the imagery of public dialogue.[110]

Arendt's "dismantling" procedure in some ways resembles Derridean deconstruction; its inspiration is the later Heidegger, but her immediate model is Benjamin. "What you are then left with is still the past, but a *fragmented* past, which has lost its certainty of evaluation. . . . It is with such fragments from the past, after their sea-change, that I have dealt. . . ."[111] Only here can meaning be found, albeit meaning devoid of certainty.

To conclude, let me briefly indicate how these procedures operate in Arendt's own work. All of her works to some extent exemplify Arendt's methods. Clearly, however, the case in point is the difficult and brilliant *The Origins of Totalitarianism.* Here she combines straightforward historical material and conceptual analysis with a variety of less orthodox techniques. She uses the stories of individuals' careers (Varnhagen, Disraeli, Lord Cromer) to illustrate more widespread social and historical transformations. In crucial portions of the argument she describes the experience of certain historical episodes by reference to literature (Conrad, Kipling, Proust, T. E. Lawrence). In addition, she makes innumerable points by treating particular incidents or statements of historical figures as in some sense paradigmatic of vital stages of the emerging pattern.

Of course this combination of procedures makes perfect sense in the light of what we have been saying: the web of stories *is* the fabric of history,[112] and the use of "poetic" works assists in the excavation and analysis of "the subterranean stream of Western history."[113] Indeed, if my previous arguments have been correct, these will mark high points in the historical comprehension of the narrative; and nothing short of this sort of analysis will do. Only words born from and connected to the

---

109. Arendt, *supra* note 82, at 212.

110. In this, at any rate, Arendt does not differ from Richard Rorty, *Philosophy and the Mirror of Nature* (1979). *See also* Richard Norman, "Aristotle's Philosopher-God," 14 *Phronesis* 63, 66 (1969).

111. Arendt, *supra* note 82, at 212.

112. For the notion of "web," see Arendt, *supra* note 14, at 181–88.

113. Arendt, *supra* note 9, at ix.

immediate experience of the events, or poetically distilled from them, can reveal their meaning.[114]

From this standpoint it is interesting to see how a more orthodox political scientist assesses this method. A. James Gregor, in *Interpretations of Fascism*,[115] finds that Arendt has proceeded "without empirical research of any sort—other than a careful reading of history and some 'representative' literature."[116] The account provides "a great deal of literary and speculative fill"[117]—referring, presumably, to those portions that on Arendt's understanding of method are of the greatest value. That is, we have seen, because they employ metaphor, enabling us to "give material form to the invisible" and thus partially avoid the epistemic paradoxes of contemporary political explanation. But that would hardly appease Gregor, who tells us that "[m]etaphors generally conceal gaps in argument and the absence of supporting evidence."[118] As for narrative, which for Arendt constitutes the soul of understanding, Gregor says, "Narrative historical explanations can . . . in general legitimately be spoken of as elliptical and partial."[119] They can be spoken of this way because "[f]ew historians or political analysts [who employ such explanations] . . . pretend to be in a position to predict events."[120] Instead, they merely help us to—Gregor's scorn-quotes— "'understand'" them. A few sentences later, Gregor insinuates that one's sense of understanding frequently results from "simple stupidities."[121]

Gregor didn't like the book.

Obviously, Gregor could not be further from Arendt's notion of explanation were he trying consciously to reverse all her propositions. How can one even raise the issue of who is right? Never mind that the

---

114. An example will show to what extent Arendt takes seriously the idea that political action is more illuminating than any theories can be: "[T]he development and expansion of postwar Soviet totalitarianism must be seen in the flaming light of the Hungarian revolution . . . the only authentic light we have. The words spoken during the event by men acting in freedom . . . carry more weight . . . than theoretical reflections. . . . If these people said that what they were fighting against was imperialism, political science must accept the term, although we might have preferred, for conceptual as well as historical reasons, to reserve the word 'imperialism' for [other purposes]." *Id.* at 502–3.

115. A. James Gregor, *Interpretations of Fascism* (1974).

116. *Id.* at 104.

117. *Id.* at 102.

118. *Id.* at 12.

119. *Id.*

120. *Id.*

121. *Id.*

model of explanation Gregor himself invokes rests on a creaky and antiquated logical empiricism; the question is whether his approach and Arendt's share enough ground to generate an interesting debate. And that question I shall not try to answer.

Arendt's methods require a style of "attentiveness to reality" that is more the mark of a political actor than a scholar. My argument suggests a disquieting conclusion: that political understanding relates more closely to political action than to political science and demands qualities of mind that are political virtues. Arendt says as much in several of her writings, and that conviction permeates and tempers all of them. Small comfort for the political scientist, but dark times offer small comfort.

Part 2
Trials

Chapter 5

Difference Made Legal:
The Court and Dr. King

> No set of legal institutions or prescriptions exists apart from the
> narratives that locate it and give it meaning. For every constitution
> there is an epic, for each decalogue a scripture. Once understood in
> the context of the narratives that give it meaning, law becomes not
> merely a system of rules to be observed, but a world in which we
> live.
>
> —Robert Cover

> No fact that is a cause is for that very reason historical. It becomes
> historical posthumously, as it were, through events that may be
> separated from it by thousands of years. A historian who takes this
> as his point of departure stops telling the sequence of events like
> the beads of a rosary. Instead, he grasps the constellation which his
> own era has formed with a definite earlier one. Thus he establishes
> a conception of the present as the "time of the now" which is shot
> through with chips of Messianic time.
>
> —Walter Benjamin

Legal argument is a struggle for the privilege of recounting the past. To
the victor goes the right to infuse a constitutional clause, or a statute, or
a series of prior decisions with the meaning that it will henceforth bear
by recounting its circumstances of origin and assigning its place in
history. I shall call such a historical placement of legal materials a *political narrative*. A string of precedents, a legislative history, an examination
of framers' intent are all political narratives. To the victor goes also the

---

Robert Cover, "The Supreme Court, 1982 Term—Foreword: *Nomos* and Narrative," 97
Harvard Law Review 4, 4–5 (1983).
Walter Benjamin "Theses on the Philosophy of History," in *Illuminations*, 255, 265 (Hannah Arendt ed. Harry Zohn trans. 1969). The phrase "time of the now" translates *Jetztzeit*
and refers (Benjamin's editor tells us) to the mystical "standing now," the moment in
which (to quote *Henry IV Part I*, act v, sc. 4, ll. 82–83) "time, that takes survey of all the
world, must have a stop." *cf.* Benjamin, *supra*, at 263n.

right to recite what I shall call the *local narrative* constituting the facts of the case at hand and, following on these two rights, the additional right to pronounce the correspondence or mirroring of each narrative in the other that renders further argument unnecessary.

By "correspondence" and "mirroring" I mean that legal argument aims to show that *these facts* precisely exemplify the political problem that *this body of law* was intended to solve and, conversely, that the history of this body of law precisely prefigures the problem that led to the present litigation. To legitimize legal argument it is essential that the political and local narratives mirror each other closely. For if an advocate or a judge were to admit that the legislative history or the precedents in a case were ambiguous or that the facts before the court failed to square with past political narratives in important respects, the argument would lose its aura of authority and invite a self-proliferating skepticism rather than conviction. It is to avoid this deflationary loss of aura that political and local narratives must dovetail in an improbable mutual correspondence that legitimizes both the favored conclusion and the political narrative that embeds it.

Thus the framers of past law are endowed with a weak prophetic power of anticipating today's controversies, for a legal argument not only invokes and applies the political history but also sanctifies and canonizes their judgment. And the everyday business described in local narratives is charged with the meaningfulness of recurrence or even predestination, for the facts of a case are not merely recited but also brought under the jurisdiction of a political narrative that reveals the case as a reenactment of an archetypal piece of the community's history.

When you control the power of recounting history, you have therefore won a legal argument, for a legal argument is nothing but the confluence of a political narrative culminating in a proposition of law (which, as Cover suggests in my epigraph, attains meaning only when it is embedded in such a narrative) and a local narrative of events surrounding the lives of the litigants. Forcing these two narratives into alignment imparts whatever power of conviction legal argumentation possesses.

That accounts for an experience that most lawyers have had, namely reading a majority appellate opinion and at first blush finding it thoroughly convincing, its arguments flowing inevitably from the precedents and the facts, then reading a dissenting opinion and finding it equally compelling. When we closely compare the two, we find that the authors have recounted a carefully edited selection of the facts of the case—what I have called a local narrative—together with a precedential or constitutional or legislative history (a political narrative) contrived to exhibit an (illusory?) correspondence with the local narrative.

As Benjamin puts it in the passage I have taken as my second epigraph, the author of a legal argument "grasps the constellation which his own era has formed with a definite earlier one," and out of that constellation radiates the authority and conviction of the argument.[1]

Historical time, Benjamin tells us elsewhere, is neither homogeneous nor empty.[2] To recount a history is to align certain moments with each other so that the later moments reenact the earlier and recreate them as their precursors, in just the way that today's fashion suddenly and rather mysteriously attunes itself to the sensibility of an earlier time, using its styles as a trope through which we understand our own orientation to the world.[3] Historical time is a structure of such pairings, mirrorings, affinities, backward causations, "constellations" formed by distinct epochs and episodes. (Since Watergate, journalists invariably abbreviate political scandals by coinages ending with the -gate suffix. Koreagate, Billygate, and Contragate reenact Watergate and recreate it as their precursor.) Political narrative and local narrative, past and present, press into alignment and are cemented together, as the jurist-storyteller literally narrates them into equivalence. The legal doctrine of stare decisis is nothing more than a formalist expression of the more fundamental juristic act of narrative imagination by which distinct historical episodes are fused into political equivalence.

Holmes was therefore wrong: The life of the law is neither logic nor experience, but narrative and the only partially civilized struggle for the power it conveys. To put the point in slightly different terms, legal argument is at bottom neither analytic nor empirical but rather historical. The life of the law is not a vision of the future but a vision of the past; its passions are unleashed, to use Benjamin's words, "by the image of enslaved ancestors rather than that of liberated grandchildren."[4]

We are all familiar with the struggle for the privilege of recounting our large-scale political narratives. To take one example, liberals and Christian fundamentalists currently contend for the privilege of recounting the history of the establishment clause: was it, as the liberal would have it, a chapter in the effort to expunge the madness of religious war from civilization by expelling religion from politics; or was it, as some fundamentalists would have it, part of the saga of dissident Christian sects, consolidating their right to prevent any one sect from

---

1. Walter Benjamin, "Theses on the Philosophy of History," in *Illuminations* 265 (Hannah Arendt ed. Harry Zohn trans. 1969).
2. *Id.* at 263.
3. "The French Revolution viewed itself as Rome reincarnate. It evoked ancient Rome the way fashion evokes costumes of the past. Fashion has a flair for the topical, no matter where it stirs in the thickets of long ago; it is a tiger's leap into the past." *Id.*
4. *Id.*

triumphing over the others in what was nevertheless an officially God-fearing republic?[5] To the victor of the struggle goes the spoils: the right to (re)tell the history of the establishment clause, including the self-referential (indeed, viciously circular) right to (re)tell the history of that very struggle. And from that right will flow the further right to determine the future course of American institutions. The civil rights movement and the forces of segregation waged such a struggle over the narrative history of the equal protection clause. Similarly, antebellum abolitionists strove vainly for the historian's scepter that would have allowed them to tell an antislavery history of the Constitution itself.[6] There is nothing mysterious about such battles: they are the stuff of doctrinal legal history.

Equally important is the parallel power over local narratives, the power of the victor to build whatever facts he or she wishes into the fabric of legal decisions by (re)interpreting the record.[7] Just as in the case of political narratives, losers endure not only the material burdens of defeat but also the ignominy of helplessly witnessing their own past edited, their own voices silenced in the attempt to tell that past.[8] And thus the fight of those whose voices have been silenced by the law—

5. This is not merely a fundamentalist view. The idea that the establishment clause allows the government to support religion provided that it does so without preference among sects has been propounded by influential nonfundamentalist conservatives, including William Bennett, Edwin Meese, and Chief Justice Rehnquist. Leonard Levy, *The Establishment Clause: Religion and the First Amendment* xi–xiii (1986).

6. *See generally* Robert Cover, *Justice Accused* (1975). The reader may note that by recounting these three episodes—abolitionism, civil rights, and secularism—as though they form a series, I am myself offering a meaning-giving and hence controversial political narrative. To accept this narrative is to accept that the liberal view of the establishment clause is like the civil rights movement's view of the equal protection clause and the abolitionists' view of the Constitution as a whole: all of them manifest a repeated pattern according to which the meaning of the Constitution lies in its promotion of cosmopolitanism—Jeffersonian enlightenment—over a backward sectarianism and particularism or racism. Anyone who accepts my series has already taken a large step toward accepting the value judgment toward which it is tacking, namely that the fundamentalist view of the establishment clause is as unenlightened and uncivilized as race segregation and slavery. *Caveat lector!*—political narrative *is* moral argument.

7. As Judge Posner astutely remarks, the facts as recited in appellate opinions are usually too distorted for forensic purposes to ground sensible judgments of how the world really works. Richard A. Posner, *The Problems of Jurisprudence* 100 (1990).

8. In Nietzsche's words, "The text finally disappeared under the interpretation." Friedrich Nietzsche, *Beyond Good and Evil* § 49 (Walter Kaufmann trans. 1966). Benjamin cautions the historical materialist historian thus: "Whoever has emerged victorious participates to this day in the triumphal procession in which the present rulers step over those who are lying prostrate. According to traditional practice, the spoils are carried along in the procession. They are called cultural treasures, and a historical materialist views them with cautious detachment. For without exception the cultural treasures have an origin which he cannot contemplate without horror." Benjamin, *supra* note 1, at 258.

and those obviously include not only the voices of miscreants and justifiably unsuccessful litigants but also the voices of racial minorities, of women, of homosexuals, of the poor—is, as Benjamin put it, "the fight for the oppressed past."[9]

It is a fight that can be joined (though not won) by resuscitating those voices and coming to understand how they organize legal materials, how they embed these materials in narratives, how they mirror local narratives in political narratives. It is a fight that requires in addition some understanding of the forensic limitations of these narratives—ultimately, of whether they subvert their own power to convince.

My aim in this chapter is to contrast two legal retellings of the same event: a set of demonstrations sponsored by the Southern Christian Leadership Conference (SCLC) in Birmingham, Alabama, in 1963 that led to the arrest and incarceration of Martin Luther King, Jr. One is the Supreme Court's majority opinion in *Walker v. City of Birmingham*, sustaining King's conviction;[10] the other, King's own defense of his actions in his *Letter from Birmingham Jail*.[11] I wish to show how the self-same event entails radically different legal consequences when it appears in different narratives, one the Supreme Court's official voice, the other the excluded voice of one of the defendants whose condemnation the Supreme Court affirmed. In each, I shall be focusing on aspects usually thought of as literary or rhetorical: the structure of narrative, the voice, the range of allusion, the questions that the authors intended to invoke and—equally importantly—those they hoped or had to forestall. If "rhetorical" is meant to indicate conviction through narrative rather than logical procedures, I accept the label; if "rhetorical" is meant to contrast with legitimate argumentation, I reject it. For I have been claiming so far that legal argument gains legitimacy just to the extent that it is able to ground the authority of its own narratives. The criticisms I shall offer of both the Court's opinion and King's *Letter* are criticisms of narrative vision as much as logical coherence.

Walker and King's *Letter* explicitly raise the theme of the legitimacy of political authority and thus of disobedience to authority. The themes of narrative and authority are related in that the state's claim to its

---

9. Benjamin, *supra* note 1, at 265.

10. 388 U.S. 307 (1967) (criminal contempt conviction of King and other demonstrators for violating injunction not invalidated by likely unconstitutionality of injunction).

11. Martin Luther King, Jr., "Letter from Birmingham Jail," in *Why We Can't Wait* 77 (1963). Since much of the chapter consists of a close reading of the *Walker* opinion and King's *Letter*, a reader may be well advised to read through them first; neither is especially lengthy.

citizens' unconditional obedience presupposes that officials' narratives, local as well as political, occupy a privileged, canonical position. Why should that be?[12] Previously, I have spoken as though the winner of a legal argument gets to recount its central narratives. But of course that is not true, if by *winner* we mean *winning litigant*. In each and every case a government official, a judge, preempts the historian's scepter. Can this particular piece of victor's history provide its own validation? This is the deep question raised in *Walker*, and part of my project is to suggest that the answer is no.

Legal narrative and legal authority, then, form two of the themes I shall be exploring. These two themes together point us to a third, one that in any event arises directly from a reading of King's *Letter*. Throughout history, narrative and normative authority have been successfully fused in just one canonical case; it is the only one in which the bare recounting of events grounds its own authenticity and the normative authority of the narrator. I am speaking, of course, of holy scriptures, theogonies. As we shall see, Martin Luther King's *Letter* embeds the Birmingham demonstrations in a biblical narrative that adds immeasurably to the power of his argument by invoking scriptural history.

In addition to his numerous biblical allusions, King offers secular political narratives and arguments, and these form a more obvious point of comparison with the *Walker* opinion. But one of the conjectures I shall be exploring is that even purely secular arguments are able to connect normative authority with narrative only by adopting an essentially religious or theological stance toward their narrative materials, and I shall suggest that *Walker* parallels the biblical portions of King's *Letter* fully as much as it does the secular.

Let me illustrate what I mean by "secular arguments adopting an essentially theological stance." In his provocative book *Constitutional Faith*,[13] Sanford Levinson investigates some of the ways in which Americans—citizens and judges alike—invest the (secular) Constitution with religious or divine properties. Madison described constitutions as "political scriptures"; Jefferson referred to the Philadelphia Convention as "an assembly of demigods"; Washington asked that "the

---

12. This is the question that preoccupies Cover, "The Supreme Court, 1982 Term—Foreword: *Nomos* and Narrative," 97 *Harvard Law Review* 4 (1983). His answer is that it shouldn't be, that even the narrative interpretations of the law offered by the U.S. Supreme Court have no special claims to validity. *Id.* at 28; *see also* Sanford Levinson, *Constitutional Faith* 27–53 (1988). It will be obvious to readers of Cover's essay that it has decisively influenced my own argument throughout the present chapter.

13. Levinson, *supra* note 12.

Constitution be sacredly maintained"; Lincoln spoke of "reverence for the laws" as the "political religion of the nation."[14] These metaphors were not meant figuratively; they were grounded in Madison's insight that the "complicated form of [the American] political system . . . requires a more than common reverence for authority,"[15] a reverence that demands a transference of religious sentiments to the Constitution.

That, moreover, is not the only example of comprehending secular political institutions through religious categories, for Levinson convincingly demonstrates that major political debates about the Constitution involve positions that correspond directly with familiar religious controversies. Thus, for example, the contemporary debate between constitutional textualists, who claim that constitutional truth lies wholly within the document's "four corners," and constitutional common lawyers, who claim that judicial opinions interpreting the Constitution are just as much constitutional law as the document itself, corresponds to a familiar argument between Luther and the Catholic Church about whether Church commentary forms part of the meaning of Holy Writ.[16] If Levinson is correct, the existence of a protestant-catholic split in constitutional interpretation may be explained by the fact that the Constitution has become an essentially religious object.

I shall be exploring the thesis that authoritative narratives more generally—and specifically the *Walker* opinion and King's *Letter*, including its distinctively secular portions—are best understood through theological categories. Therein may lie their power, but also their danger: faith unites, but it also divides. It moves mountains, but a moving mountain can crush those who live on its slopes and in its path. (To make my own position clear from the outset: I am deeply dismayed and fearful of the incursions by organized religion into our national politics; at the same time, however, I am persuaded that politics may best be understood—and worthwhile political action furthered—when we realize that even in its secular guise political action is through-and-through theological in character. I turn to these questions explicitly in the concluding pages of this chapter.)

Thus a deep connection exists among three apparently disparate themes arising from *Walker* and King's *Letter:* the narration of history,

---

14. *Quoted in id.* at 10, 14.
15. *Quoted in id.* at 10.
16. *Id.* at 18–53. Levinson, following Thomas Grey, points out that similar controversies over the status of commentary on holy writ have occurred in Islam and Judaism as well as Christianity. *Id.* at 19; *see* Thomas Grey, "The Constitution as Scripture," 37 *Stanford Law Review* 1, 7 (1984).

the foundation of authority, and the treacherous confluence of religion and politics. There is a fourth theme as well, of course, and that is how we are best to understand the civil rights movement. It is a movement whose aims were at once secular and religious: it aimed to achieve equal rights but also to redeem America from its racism. The movement was in many ways utopian, and in many ways it failed in both of its tasks. Yet it undeniably achieved remarkable successes as well, and in a sense the civil rights movement has become an icon and exemplar of grass roots organizing for progressive social change. In the concluding sections of the chapter I shall explore the successes and failures of the movement by linking these to the other themes I have just catalogued (narrative, authority, and the nexus between religion and politics).

Why do I choose these events and these two retellings of them? All were famous in their day, but they go largely unnoticed now. Since I have borrowed so much already from Benjamin's "Theses on the Philosophy of History," I shall borrow once more. "To articulate the past historically," Benjamin writes, "means to seize hold of a memory as it flashes up at a moment of danger."[17] The image is striking: we are to think of the unconscious mind pitching in to save us from a sudden threat by reminding us of something we had otherwise forgotten (a name, a telephone number, where we mislaid the key, whatever). We do not traffic in history for its own sake, according to Benjamin, but because a particular moment of the past is of use in a particular present situation. (They are, to return to my earlier image, mirrored in each other.)

We live in terrible danger today. The danger, quite simply, is that we are on the verge of becoming an irredeemably racist society: a society in which the possibilities celebrated in Martin Luther King's "I have a dream" oration—"all of God's children—black men and white men, Jews and Gentiles, Protestants and Catholics—will be able to join hands and sing in the words of the old Negro spiritual, 'Free at last, free at last; thank God Almighty, we are free at last.'"—are finally foreclosed.[18] Today we are faced with statistical indicators of residential segregation almost as high as they were before mass desegregation began—residential segregation, moreover, that appears to be based on

---

17. Benjamin, *supra* note 1, at 257.
18. For the crucial passages of this speech, see David Garrow, *Bearing the Cross: Martin Luther King, Jr., and the Southern Christian Leadership Conference* 283–84 (1986).

race alone, rather than on income or class.[19] We confront a staggering degree of misery among poor African-Americans, including abbreviated life expectancies otherwise unheard of in so-called First World countries and mortality rates vastly greater than those among whites; and we find a terrifying lack of political interest in these problems among whites. Today we face an unremitting tide of white ill will toward African-Americans, and in recent terms the Supreme Court affirmatively allied itself with the politics of white resentment. As the Court metamorphoses into an enemy of King's dream, it is worth recollecting an earlier clash between that dream and the Court's authority. For we live, additionally, in a society in which challenges to what might be called "the authority of authority"—the self-justifying legitimacy of official action—seem (to me at least) remarkably tepid and increasingly fragile. Finally, ours is an epoch in which religion and religious frenzy have erupted furiously into politics nationally as well as internationally. For what it is worth, this chapter is the memory that flashes up to me at this moment of danger.

Apparently I am not alone in my recollection. Within the last few years, two Pulitzer Prize–winning biographies of Martin Luther King have been published and received with interest and acclaim, and PBS aired a six-hour series on the history of the civil rights movement.[20] It is hardly surprising that in a time of racial crisis the memory of King and the 1954–1968 civil rights movement resonates with renewed strength, for this movement, many of the accomplishments of which are threatened in our contemporary political climate, stands in need of redemption in just the way that it redeemed the failed promises of the civil rights amendments to the Constitution.

---

19. On the statistical indicators of segregation, see Reynolds Farley & Walter R. Allen, *The Color Line and the Quality of Life in America* 141 (1987) (on a 100 point scale, residential segregation in the twenty-five U.S. cities with the largest African-American population averaged 88 in 1960 and 81 in 1980). Denton and Massey have recently found that African-Americans (and African–Puerto Ricans) alone among American ethnic groups remain at extraordinarily high levels of residential segregation regardless of improvement in income. Nancy A. Denton & Douglas S. Massey, "Residential Segregation of Blacks, Hispanics, and Asians by Socioeconomic Status and Generation," 69 *Social Science Quarterly* 797, 813–14 (1988). *See also* Denton & Massey, *American Apartheid: Segregation and the Making of the Underclass* (1993).

20. The biographies are Garrow, *supra* note 18, and Taylor Branch, *Parting the Waters: America in the King Years 1954–63* (1988); the PBS series was *Eyes on the Prize* (PBS 1986).

Project Confrontation

In January 1963, the SCLC held a retreat in Georgia to discuss strategy for a concerted attack on segregation in Birmingham, Alabama.[21] Project C—for "confrontation"—would consist of demonstrations and boycotts of Birmingham's downtown businesses during the normally busy Easter shopping season.

Birmingham itself had recently begun to display some sentiment for change in its segregationist ways. A group of whites headed by the Chamber of Commerce president campaigned to alter Birmingham's municipal government by abolishing the offices of the three segregationist commissioners (including the notoriously racist commissioner of public safety, Theophilus Eugene "Bull" Connor) who then ran the city. The voters agreed to move to a mayoral system, and in a special election Connor was defeated by a more moderate segregationist named Albert Boutwell. Connor went to court to demand that he be allowed to finish his term of office as commissioner of public safety;[22] and while this matter was pending Birmingham was governed by what were in effect two city governments, each passing its own laws and conducting city business after its own fashion; municipal checks were signed by both Connor and Boutwell. Some Birmingham whites hoped that the SCLC would cancel the Easter demonstrations to give the new government a chance to show what it could do, but the SCLC leadership—which had previously cancelled demonstrations to allow the run-off election between Connor and Boutwell to proceed without the pressure of demonstrations—went ahead with Project C.

A Birmingham city ordinance required the demonstrators to obtain a parade permit from the city commission. On April 3, Mrs. Lola Hendricks, representing the demonstrators, approached Connor to request a permit; Connor replied, "No, you will not get a permit in Birmingham, Alabama to picket. I will picket you over to the City Jail." On April 5—one week before Good Friday—Connor replied to a second, telegraphic, request for a parade permit with another refusal. The demonstrators proceeded with their protests.

Project C included plans for the Reverend Martin Luther King, Jr., to place himself in a position to be arrested on Good Friday, April 12.

---

21. My account of these events is drawn from Branch, *supra* note 20, at 688–747; Garrow, *supra* note 18, at 225–67; King, *supra* note 11; Juan Williams, *Eyes on the Prize: America's Civil Rights Years 1954–65* 181–89 (1987); and especially Alan F. Westin & Barry Mahoney, *The Trial of Martin Luther King* (1974), as well as from the *Walker* opinion.

22. *See* Connor v. State, 153 So. 2d 787 (Ala. 1963); *see also* Reid v. City of Birmingham, 150 So. 2d 735 (Ala. 1963).

Late Wednesday evening, April 10, Connor obtained an ex parte injunction from Alabama Circuit Court Judge W. A. Jenkins, Jr., forbidding
civil rights leaders, including all the leaders of Project C, from taking
part in or encouraging demonstrations. The injunction was served at
1:00 A.M. on Thursday, and the SCLC leadership debated how to respond to it. King feared that complying with the injunction would
deflate the protest, as had happened the previous summer in Albany,
Georgia. He went ahead with the planned demonstration the following
day and was arrested; a second demonstration took place on Easter
Sunday, April 14. Subsequently Judge Jenkins found several of the
demonstrators guilty of criminal contempt and sentenced each of them
(including King) to five days in jail and a $50 fine.[23] It is this conviction
that the *Walker* Court upheld.

This ends the sequence of events recounted in *Walker* and King's
Letter. But the larger chronicle of the Birmingham campaign did not end
with King's arrest. The demonstrators subsequently embarked on a
strategy of marches by schoolchildren, leading to literally thousands of
arrests. As the demonstrations continued, Bull Connor upped the level
of official response, ordering that fire hoses and police dogs be turned
on the demonstrators. Television news horrified its audiences with the
spectacle of children bowled over by hoses that hit with enough force to
rip the bark off trees. White moderates and the SCLC leadership under-
took negotiations that led to a settlement announced on May 10. On
May 11, the Ku Klux Klan staged a rally; after the meeting, the motel
where King had been staying and the home of his brother were
bombed. Crowds of angry blacks rioted, and President Kennedy eventually sent in federal troops.[24] A month later, Alabama Governor
George Wallace personally blocked the entrance of a University of Alabama building to prevent the entrance of two black students whose
admission had been ordered by a federal court. Evidently this action
was the last straw. That same day, President Kennedy spoke on national
television to announce that he was seeking comprehensive civil rights
legislation that eventually became the Civil Rights Act of 1964. The
summer ended with the March on Washington at which King delivered
his "I have a dream" oration; in a sense, the Civil Rights Act and the
march were the culminating events of Project C.

But let us return to King's original April arrest. While King was in
jail, eight white clergymen—significantly, they were liberals who had
publicly opposed Governor George Wallace's "Segregation Forever!"

23. For an account of the trial, see Westin & Mahoney, *supra* note 21, at 95–126,
141–42.
24. Branch, *supra* note 20, at 756–802.

speech[25]—took out a full-page advertisement in the Birmingham *News* denouncing the demonstrations. King responded from his cell, writing in the newspaper's margins until he was able to obtain paper; after he was permitted visitors, King's manuscript was typed by his friends and returned to him in jail for revisions. His *Letter from Birmingham Jail* attracted little attention at first.[26] It was eventually printed by the American Friends Service Committee and reprinted in numerous periodicals; its fame and influence grew, and by now it is perhaps the most famous document to emerge from the civil rights movement.[27]

At their contempt hearing, the civil rights leaders averred that the parade permit ordinance and Judge Jenkins's ex parte injunction were unconstitutional; the judge, however, refused to consider the issue, since the demonstrators had never attempted to get the injunction dissolved. Two terms after *Walker* the U.S. Supreme Court agreed that the ordinance on which the injunction rested was unconstitutional.[28] Nevertheless, the Court in *Walker* declined to overturn the demonstrators' convictions for criminal contempt, holding that even a constitutionally questionable court order must be obeyed—the so-called *Mine Workers* rule derived from *United States v. United Mine Workers*.[29]

Point and counterpoint: King's *Letter* has become one of the great classics in the literature of civil disobedience, both for its philosophy and for the soul-stirring magnificence of its language. No one has called Potter Stewart's *Walker* opinion a classic (in what might be called the literature of civil obedience), but its status as a Supreme Court precedent makes it the functional equivalent of a classic.[30] Both *Walker* and the *Letter* address an ancient question, a question that more than any other defines the very subject of legal philosophy: that, of course, is the question whether we lie under an obligation to obey unjust legal directives, including directives ordering our punishment for disobeying other unjust directives. All political philosophy, from Plato's *Apology* and *Crito* on, is driven by this question; all our political hopes and aspirations are contained in the descriptive and argumentative materials we use to answer it. It is those materials that form our topic.[31]

---

25. *Id.* at 738.
26. *Id.* at 744.
27. For a detailed account of the letter's composition, see *id.* at 737–45.
28. Shuttlesworth v. City of Birmingham, 394 U.S. 147 (1969).
29. 330 U.S. 258 (1947).
30. Roughly, a classic is a piece you can't ignore when you write in the canon.
31. There is, to be sure, this difference between the questions raised by *Walker* and King's *Letter*. *Walker* is concerned with the obligation to obey unconstitutional directives (whether or not they are just), whereas King is concerned with the obligation to obey

The **Walker** *Decision*

The Narrative of Authority

How does one describe a legally significant event? There is, I hazard, no such thing as an absolutely neutral description of the facts—"writing degree zero"[32]—and one's choice of focus, of beginning and end, and of voice may already contain the answers to crucial questions.

The Court's *Walker* opinion adopts the voice and viewpoint of governmental authority and recites a simple story of authority vindicated. As we shall see, authority is the protagonist, the subject of the narrative, and the narrative itself is simple and straightforward. Authority takes prudent (if possibly excessive) precautions to protect the community against danger. Well-meaning but shortsighted demonstrators recklessly bypass those precautions. All of authority's worst fears are subsequently confirmed. Then the demonstrators attempt to avoid legal accountability for their actions. Needless to say—and after such a narrative, it is indeed needless to say—the Court declines to assist them in this enterprise.

Stewart's opinion begins (without introduction) with unnamed "city officials" going to court to obtain their injunction; in this narrative, therefore, an official act is the initiating event, and city officials are its protagonists. Stewart provides no background or context for the demonstrations or the demonstrators' motives; nor does he provide any clue to the segregationist history and predilections of Birmingham or of Bull Connor; nor does he allude to the fact that the lame duck commissioners were in their last three days of office after having been voted out in what amounted to a referendum on their racial policies. He merely quotes the allegations by "officials of Birmingham" that the demonstrations were " 'calculated to provoke breaches of the peace,' 'threaten[ed] the safety, peace and tranquility of the City,' and placed 'an undue burden and strain upon the manpower of the Police Department.' "[33]

---

unjust directives (whether or not they are constitutional). Yet clearly the inquiries are close to each other in spirit, and there may be significant substantive overlap as well: an unconstitutional directive is at least prima facie unjust since it amounts to an illegitimate exercise of authority, and an unjust directive may run afoul of the constitutional principles of due process and equal protection.

32. Writing degree zero: "a colourless writing. . . . The new neutral writing takes its place in the midst of all those ejaculations and judgments, without becoming involved in any of them; it consists precisely in their absence. . . . [I]t deliberately foregoes any elegance or ornament. . . ." Roland Barthes, *Writing Degree Zero and Elements of Semiology* 76–78 (A. Lavers & C. Smith transs. 1967).

33. Walker v. City of Birmingham, 388 U.S. 307, 309 (1967).

He then devotes three paragraphs to insinuations that as events subsequently unfolded these official fears were fully confirmed. In the first of these paragraphs, he quotes an angry complaint by one of the petitioners that in past demonstrations state courts had favored local law enforcement, and "if the police couldn't handle it, the mob would,"[34] thus suggesting that even the demonstrators understood the potential dangers of such confrontations. (As they surely did; less than two years before, the Freedom Riders were brutally beaten when their bus arrived at the Birmingham terminal, after the Birmingham police had agreed to give the Ku Klux Klan fifteen uninterrupted minutes to assault the riders.[35]) The next paragraph notes that on Good Friday "a large crowd gathered," the onlookers "'clapping, and hollering, and [w]hooping.'" Members of this crowd "spilled" out into the street.[36]

Stewart's third descriptive paragraph portrays the Easter Sunday demonstration in the following terms: "Some 300 or 400 people from among the onlookers followed in a crowd that occupied the entire width of the street and overflowed onto the sidewalks. Violence occurred. Members of the crowd threw rocks that injured a newspaperman and damaged a police motorcycle."[37] Note the construction "Violence occurred." By making "violence" the subject of the sentence, Stewart obviates the necessity of attributing the violence, though in the next sentence he explains that "members of the crowd," not the demonstrators, threw rocks. As Justice Brennan's dissenting opinion points out, there were only three rock throwers, and the rock throwing occurred after (in anger at?) the arrests of King, Shuttlesworth, and Walker.[38] The reference to a crowd overflowing onto the sidewalks, like the earlier reference to a crowd spilling out into the street, is intended to buttress the Court's subsequent argument validating "the strong interest of state and local governments in regulating the use of their streets

---

34. *Id.* at 310.

35. Branch, *supra* note 20, at 420. Such circumstances raise in a graphic way, however, the question why the demonstrations should be halted rather than protected. King raises this question explicitly: "In your statement you assert that our actions, even though peaceful, must be condemned because they precipitate violence. But is this a logical assertion? Isn't this like condemning a robbed man because his possession of money precipitated the evil act of robbery? Isn't this like condemning Socrates because his unswerving commitment to truth and his philosophical inquiries precipitated the act by the misguided populace in which they made him drink hemlock? Isn't this like condemning Jesus because his unique God-consciousness and never-ceasing devotion to God's will precipitated the evil act of crucifixion?" King, *supra* note 11, at 85.

36. *Walker,* 388 U.S. at 310–11.

37. *Id.* at 311.

38. *Id.* at 341 (Brennan, J., dissenting).

and other public places" since "the free passage of traffic and the pre-vention of public disorder and violence become important objects of legitimate state concern."[39]

The three paragraphs also introduce a second theme: the willful-ness of the demonstrators. The demonstrators distributed a statement "declaring their intention to disobey the injunction";[40] they "an-nounced that '[i]njunction or no injunction we are going to march to-morrow'";[41] "calls for volunteers to 'walk' and go to jail were made."[42] And the angry complaint that state courts favored antidemonstration local law enforcement suggests that the demonstrators had little respect for state courts.

Thus, the Court's exposition of facts has consisted so far of a theme—the city officials' justifiable concerns about the forthcoming demonstrations—a second theme—the demonstrators' defiant intentions—and a tragic climax, the vindication of authority as its fears were borne out in the event by whooping and hollering crowds spilling into the street and by violence. The Court immediately lays this sonata-form exposition next to the rule of law that an " 'injunction duly issuing out of a court of general jurisdiction with equity powers upon pleadings properly invoking its action, and served upon persons made parties therein and within the jurisdiction, must be obeyed by them however erroneous the action of the court may be. . . .' "[43] Noteworthy is the rhythmic concatenation of formulaic legalisms piled one on top of the other. Rhetorically, this serves the function of infusing the conclusion with a sense of syllogistic inevitability. (What are all those carefully catalogued legalisms doing there unless they are minor premises of a deductive application of some rule of law presumably known by the Court? Therefore the conclusion must be right.)

Only then does the Court frame its legal issue:

We are asked to say that the Constitution compelled Alabama to allow the petitioners to violate this injunction, to organize and engage in these mass street parades and demonstrations, without any previous effort on their part to have the injunction dissolved or modified, or any attempt to secure a parade permit in accordance with its terms.[44]

39. *Id.* at 315–16. As we shall see, the very fact that the Court found it necessary to make this argument points to a fundamental problem with the Court's opinion.

40. *Id.* at 310.

41. *Id.* at 310.

42. *Id.* at 311.

43. *Id.* at 314 (quoting Howat v. Kansas, 258 U.S. 181, 189–90 (1922)).

44. *Id.* at 315.

Framed this way, the legal question is of course self-answering; but it also provokes from the Court a further description of the facts of the case that is worthy of note. According to the Court, the petitioners had not made "any attempt to secure a parade permit in accordance with [the injunction's] terms"; they "did not apply for a permit either to the commission itself or to any commissioner after the injunction issued."[45] In fact, Mrs. Lola Hendricks, a member of the petitioners' organization, had attempted to obtain a parade permit *before* the injunction was issued and had been threatened with jail by Bull Connor (who also turned down a second request). Inasmuch as it was Connor and the other commissioners who obtained the injunction, it is plain enough that they were not about to issue the parade permit the next day, so the Court is clearly insisting on a formality for formality's sake alone. The Court mentions the Hendricks incident, but stresses that Mrs. Hendricks was "*not* a petitioner in this case."[46] That was literally true, but the Court is being a bit cute at this point by ignoring the fact that she represented the petitioners' organization and sought the permit on the organization's behalf. This fact evidently has no relevance, so it disappears from the narrative; it is of a piece with the remarkable absence of civil rights organizations and the civil rights movement from Stewart's dramatis personae. The very existence of political collectivities other than governmental authority is missing from the Court's narrative vocabulary; only government and individuals (sometimes acting alone, sometimes whooping it up in unstructured mobs) form a part of *Walker*'s ontology.

In any event, Connor "had . . . made clear that he was without power to grant the permit alone, since the issuance of such permits was the responsibility of the entire city commission."[47] Now Chief Justice Warren alluded in his dissenting opinion to claims made by the petitioners that "parade permits had uniformly been issued for all other groups by the city clerk on the request of the traffic bureau of the police department, which was under Commissioner Connor's direction. The requirement that the approval of the full Commission be obtained was applied only to this one group."[48] Nevertheless, Connor "had made clear" his incapacity to act; notice the success-verb construction, which carries with it the twin implications that what Connor said was true and

---

45. *Id.* at 315, 318.
46. *Id.* at 317 n.9 (emphasis in original).
47. *Id.* at 317–18.
48. *Id.* at 326 (Warren, C.J., dissenting); *see also* Westin & Mahoney, *supra* note 21, at 105–6, 121 (detailing the petitioners' arguments presented at trial).

that—because he had made it clear—the demonstrators were on notice of its truth.

The Court then turns to its legal arguments. First, it insists that although the Birmingham statute and the ex parte injunction both raise "substantial constitutional issues," neither "was transparently invalid or had only a frivolous pretense to validity."[49] That was because "the free passage of traffic and the prevention of public disorder and violence become important objects of legitimate state concern,"[50] and (as we have seen) problems of traffic and disorder actually arose during the Birmingham demonstrations.

Because the statute and injunction were not transparently invalid, the Court argues, the demonstrators should have immediately proceeded to court to test them.

> There was an interim of two days between the issuance of the injunction and the Good Friday march. The petitioners give absolutely no explanation of why they did not make some application to the state court during that period. . . . It cannot be presumed that the Alabama courts would have ignored the petitioners' constitutional claims.[51]

For, and this is both the Court's ultimate argument and final paragraph,

> in the fair administration of justice no man can be judge in his own case, however exalted his station, however righteous his motives, and irrespective of his race, color, politics, or religion. This Court cannot hold that the petitioners were constitutionally free to ignore all the procedures of the law and carry their battle to the streets. One may sympathize with the petitioners' impatient commitment to their cause. But respect for judicial process is a small price to pay for the civilizing hand of law, which alone can give abiding meaning to constitutional freedom.[52]

Here the Court echoes Felix Frankfurter's concurring opinion in *United Mine Workers:*

---

49. *Walker,* 388 U.S. at 315, 316.

50. *Id.* at 316.

51. *Id.* at 318–19. In fact, the petitioners did not have two days since the injunction was not served until the day before the scheduled demonstration. (Though they knew all day Wednesday that Connor was preparing to obtain an injunction. Branch, *supra* note 22, at 727.) Norman Amaker, one of the movement's lawyers, recollects that "there was never any serious discussion of counseling the leaders to go into court to seek relief prior to the Good Friday march. Going into court would have required foregoing the weekend marches. . . . " Westin & Mahoney, *supra* note 21, at 80.

52. *Walker,* 388 U.S. at 320–21 (footnote omitted).

Only when a court is so obviously traveling outside its orbit as to be merely usurping judicial forms and facilities, may an order issued by a court be disobeyed and treated as though it were a letter to a newspaper. Short of an indisputable want of authority on the part of a court, the very existence of a court presupposes its power to entertain a controversy, if only to decide, after deliberation, that it has no power over the particular controversy. Whether a defendant may be brought to the bar of justice is not for the defendant himself to decide.

. . . There can be no free society without law administered through an independent judiciary. If one man can be allowed to determine for himself what is law, every man can. That means first chaos, then tyranny.[53]

There was a certain irony in Frankfurter's argument, an irony that moves us from the local history of the Birmingham events recounted in *Walker* to the political history encapsulated in the *Mine Workers* rule. *Howat*,[54] the Court's principal precedent in *Walker*, was a labor injunction case (as was *United Mine Workers* itself), and it is clear from *Walker's* reliance on *Howat* that the Court's political history assimilates Judge Jenkins's injunction against the Birmingham march to past uses of injunctions in labor disputes.

The labor injunction was a tool of union busting in the late nineteenth and early twentieth centuries. The parallels with Project C are clear: labor unions, like the civil rights demonstrators, sought to launch coordinated demonstrations and actions against their employers. Like Bull Connor, the employers would turn to sympathetic judges to enjoin these demonstrations and thereby to defuse the movement. The classic study of the labor injunction, launching a devastating attack on it, was coauthored by none other than Frankfurter.[55] Though the *Walker* majority fails to mention the fact, Chief Justice Warren's dissenting opinion alludes to the unsavory political history encoded in *Howat* and *United Mine Workers* (and cites Frankfurter's book).[56] It is a political history of judicial power pressed or manipulated into service by entrenched interests in order to stifle social change. And indeed, it is a political history to

---

53. United States v. United Mine Workers, 330 U.S. 258, 309–10, 312 (1947) (Frankfurter, J., concurring).

54. Howat v. Kansas, 258 U.S. 181 (1922).

55. Felix Frankfurter & Nathan Greene, *The Labor Injunction* (1930). The injunction device would later be pressed into service by opponents of the Progressive movement to prevent the enforcement of Progressive legislation. *See* Owen Fiss, *The Civil Rights Injunction* 1–4 (1978).

56. *Walker*, 388 U.S. at 330–31 (Warren, C.J., dissenting).

which *Walker* subsequently contributed: in the year following the decision, university administrators employed at least fifty-four injunctions
against the student movement, and—in another ironic historical
twist—*Walker* was used to buttress labor injunctions in sectors not
covered by the federal antiinjunction laws that Frankfurter had been
instrumental in creating.[57] *Walker'*s political narrative conceals and extends a secret history of judicial authority (secret, of course, because the
Court elects to leave unmentioned the history of the use of injunctions
registered in *Howat*).[58] It is that history that we must now explore.

The Republic of Laws and "Transparent Invalidity"
The rhetorical structure of the Court's opinion suggests that it is making
something like the following argument:

1. The city officials' concerns about traffic and rowdiness were
   borne out in fact, and so, a fortiori, they were reasonable
   concerns.
2. Because their concerns were reasonable, the injunction (and the
   statute upon which it was based), though arguably unconstitutional, was not *transparently* unconstitutional (the Court was
   not, in Frankfurter's words, "*obviously* traveling outside its
   orbit").
3. Had the injunction been transparently unconstitutional, the
   demonstrators would perhaps have been within their rights to
   disobey.
4. However, on the assumption that its unconstitutionality was
   debatable, the only legitimate course for the demonstrators to
   follow was to test it in court.
5. The rule of law instructing them to this effect was clear, and they
   were on notice of it.

---

57. Westin & Mahoney, *supra* note 21, at 277–78. The statistic on university injunctions is from Note, "Equity on the Campus: The Limits of Injunctive Regulation of
University Protest," 80 *Yale Law Journal* 987 (1971).

58. Another political narrative the *Walker* Court buries by exercising its victor's
prerogative of assigning the meaning it chooses to past events lies in its use of previous
Court opinions. The Court describes the *Howat* rule, 258 U.S. at 189–90, quoted *supra* text
accompanying note 43, as "consistent with the rule of law followed by the federal
courts," and cites a string of cases in support of this claim. *Walker* 388 U.S. at 314 & n.5.
But in fact two of the cases cited—*Ex parte* Rowland, 104 U.S. 604 (1881), and *In re* Ayers,
123 U.S. 443 (1887)—stand for precisely the opposite proposition. *Howat* requires obedience to invalid orders on pain of contempt, whereas *Rowland* and *Ayers*, like the related
cases *In re* Sawyer, 124 U.S. 200 (1888), and *Ex parte* Fisk, 113 U.S. 713 (1885), hold that
disobedience of an invalid court order cannot be punished as contempt. (For clear
statements of this holding, see *Fisk*, 113 U.S. at 718, and *Rowland*, 104 U.S. at 612.)

6. Since the demonstrators did not attempt to test the injunction's constitutionality in court, they can be punished for disobeying it.

Even the various dissenters appear to accept the validity of this argument, disagreeing not with its jurisprudence but with steps (2) or (5). Thus, Chief Justice Warren believes that the statute "is patently unconstitutional on its face,"[59] Justice Douglas agrees that it is "unconstitutional on its face or patently unconstitutional as applied,"[60] and Justice Brennan, though he insists that his opinion does not deal with the merits of the constitutional claim, accepts the contention that "the ordinance and injunction are in fact facially unconstitutional."[61] Similarly, the various dissenters contest the applicability of *Howat*, though to different extents. Warren believes that it was weakened by subsequent decisions;[62] Douglas stresses that its rule makes an exception when "'the question of jurisdiction' is 'frivolous and not substantial,'"[63] hence, when the ordinance is "unconstitutional on its face or patently unconstitutional as applied"; and Brennan accepts *Howat* as a "premise," arguing that the interest it underwrites can be outweighed.[64]

Clearly, however, the heart of the Court's treatise on civil obedience lies in the jurisprudential premise of its argument, with which even the dissenters appear to agree. I repeat it for emphasis: (3) *Had the injunction been transparently unconstitutional, the demonstrators would perhaps have been within their rights to disobey. (4) However, on the assumption that its unconstitutionality was debatable, the only legitimate course for the demonstrators to follow was to test its constitutionality in court.*

Now the Court never actually *says* that if the injunction's unconstitutionality had been transparent the demonstrators would have been free to disobey it; as we shall see, the Court's rhetorical stance did not permit it to say such a thing. But Stewart devotes almost a third of his opinion to demonstrating that the statute and injunction were *not* "transparently invalid," none of which would be relevant unless transparent invalidity might affect the outcome of the case.

---

59. *Walker*, 388 U.S. at 328 (Warren, C.J., dissenting).

60. *Id.* at 338 (Douglas, J., dissenting).

61. *Id.* at 342 (Brennan, J., dissenting).

62. *Id.* at 332 & n.9 (Warren, C.J., dissenting) (citing *In re* Green, 369 U.S. 689 (1962)).

63. *Id.* at 337 (Douglas, J., dissenting) (quoting United States v. United Mine Workers, 330 U.S. 258, 293 (1947)).

64. *Id.* at 343–44 (Brennan, J., dissenting).

This is a point worth emphasizing, because it points to a remarkable incoherence in the opinion (as well as Frankfurter's *Mine Workers* concurrence). Remember that the Court's decisive argument rests on the familiar maxim that no one can be a judge in his own case. The statute and injunction may have been unconstitutional, but that is for a court to decide, not for the demonstrators to judge on their own.

If this argument holds at all, it holds regardless of whether the statute and injunction were "transparently invalid." For even then, if it is left to the demonstrators to determine transparent invalidity, they are acting as judges in their own case. Since the Court will not permit anyone to be judge in his own case, the Court had no need to insist that the statute and injunction were not transparently invalid; it had no need to recite a set of facts designed to underscore that the statute and injunction were not transparently invalid. In fact, it had no need for most of its opinion.

The opinion is a remarkable instance of protesting too much. The Court's fervent desire to prove a point (that the statute and injunction were not transparently invalid), even though the Court's argument renders that point irrelevant, points to an abiding and deeply buried anxiety—a kind of Banquo's ghost—that the Court dared not acknowledge but that it could not help addressing.

The anxiety arises from the political narratives that give meaning to American constitutionalism. The very notion of the rule of law and not of men, which goes back as far as Plato,[65] implies a limit to what authority can do, and thus contains within it the concept of ultra vires action. Moreover, the theory of popular sovereignty says that when governmental authority runs out the actual exercise of sovereignty devolves back to the people.[66] Finally, the idea that law must be public, and publicly comprehensible, implies that there must be some point at which ordinary citizens can know that an action is ultra vires and thus that the power to disobey has devolved upon them. That is the point of transparent unconstitutionality to which the Court refers. The concept of transparent unconstitutionality, and the right to disobey transparently unconstitutional injunctions, is thus a linchpin of the legitimacy of American government; take it away, and you must abandon the rule of law, or popular sovereignty, or the publicity of law.

The Court cannot quite bring itself to acknowledge this point, however, for a very good reason: an open acknowledgment that we are entitled to disobey transparently unconstitutional injunctions would

---

65. Plato, *Laws* 715d. But cf. Plato, *Statesman* 294a-297b, for his doubts about the efficacy of the rule of law.

66. Thus also the Ninth and Tenth Amendments to the Constitution.

invite us to judge constitutionality for ourselves, thereby undermining
the authority of the courts. Clearly it is this possibility that the *Walker*
Court is most concerned to foreclose. The political narratives underlying the authority of American courts vest ultimate power—including
the ultimate power of understanding the law—not in the courts but in
the citizenry, and insist that courts' authority is bounded. In *Walker*,
however, the Court confronted the question of who is to determine the
bounds of judicial authority.

Now it may be that the logic of self-reference compels the Supreme
Court to insist on its own ultimate authority to answer this question.
After all, the Court cannot deny its authority to determine the bounds
of judicial authority unless it possesses the very authority it is denying.
The Court would become enmeshed in a form of the Liar Paradox,
almost as though it had said, "Our own rulings about our authority,
including this one, lack authority." The Court can deny its jurisdiction
over many matters, but it cannot deny its jurisdiction over questions of
its own jurisdiction, particularly since no higher court exists to which it
can defer.

But neither logic nor law compelled the Court to insist that *Judge
Jenkins* possessed the authority to determine the bounds of his constitutional authority. He was wrong about the constitutionality of his injunction, and that was transparent to the demonstrators; they were willing
to gamble that the Supreme Court would back their judgment by affirming the political narratives underlying American constitutionalism.

To see why the Court nevertheless felt compelled to deny them the
opportunity to take that gamble, recall Levinson's distinction between a
"catholic" mode of interpretation, according to which the Church—or
here the Supreme Court[67]—is the dispenser of ultimate interpretation,
and a "protestant" mode, in which the individual, or at any rate the
community, is the ultimate interpreter. It would be gravely perilous for
the Supreme Court to accept a "protestant" popular judgment that
Judge Jenkins had exceeded the bounds of his constitutional authority.
That would highlight the uncomfortable fact that the Supreme Court
too can exceed the bounds of its constitutional authority, and to stress
this would invite a protestant reformation reaching all the way to Rome.
For although the logic of self-reference precludes the Court from denying its own authority to adjudicate its authority, nothing precludes
others from denying that authority, any more than the fact that on logical
grounds *I* cannot say, "I am an inveterate liar," precludes others from
saying that I am an inveterate liar. To put it another way, the fact that the

---

67. Both are meanings of the Latin *curia*.

Court must necessarily adopt the catholic mode of interpretation shows nothing more than that it is the Court; it is entitled to insist on the catholic mode of interpretation, however, only on the question-begging catholic assumption that the choice is the Court's to make.[68] Perhaps for this reason the Court clings desperately and tenaciously to the catholic mode "all the way down" to Judge Jenkins's court (a theological stance harkening back to institutionalized religion at its most authoritarian). And thus it must simultaneously invoke the right to disobey transparently unconstitutional injunctions and foreclose the possibility that citizens might exercise independent judgment of the right's predicate.

The *Walker* opinion fulfills this self-undermining twin need. Instead of the history of publicity, of popular sovereignty, and of limited official authority, the Court's political narrative yokes the Constitution to the history of the labor injunction, of union busting. Its fundamental effect is to convert the notion of a transparently unconstitutional injunction into a kind of half-chimerical ideal. It is not quite mythical, for we can imagine that even the Court would find transparently unconstitutional an injunction saying, "It is hereby ordered that the Constitution of the United States of America is suspended."[69] But in *Walker* the Court comes close to saying that anything less extreme—anything that authority takes the slightest care to disguise, thereby presenting a litigable issue—is not transparently unconstitutional.

After all, in *Walker* we are confronted with an injunction that could hardly have been more irregular: it was issued ex parte, with less than a day available for appeal, at the behest of commissioners who had lost

---

68. That is not to deny that eventually—at the subsequent contempt hearing—a court and not "the people" will decide whether "the people" were right in their judgment that the injunction was invalid, nor is it to deny that the validity or invalidity of the injunction will be determined by the court in the "catholic" manner, looking at prior cases as well as the constitutional text. Thus, had the *Walker* Court chosen to hold that one cannot be punished for violating an unconstitutional injunction, the courts would still retain the authority of adjudicating the injunction's constitutionality. The argument here indicates, however, that we may not be able to find a cogent reason to believe that the retention by the courts of this ultimate authority is consistent with the liberal and antiauthoritarian ("protestant") premises of American constitutionalism (the rule of law, popular sovereignty, the publicity of law). The Court itself has raised the possibility that Congress ("the people's" virtual representative) retains interpretive authority. *Katzenbach v. Morgan*, 384 U.S. 641 (1966) (see especially the dissent of Harlan, J.). (This footnote was added as a result of a conversation with Peter Quint.)

69. Nor is this a wholly fictitious scenario: *Cooper v. Aaron*, 358 U.S. 1 (1958), an opinion that every Justice signed individually for emphasis, was provoked by Arkansas Governor Orville Faubus's declaration that the Supreme Court's *Brown* decision was not binding.

their mandate.[70] It would irreparably damage the demonstrators—a standard legal reason for not granting an injunction—by causing their moment to pass,[71] and it was based on an extraordinarily broadly worded statute granting the commissioners virtually unfettered power of prior restraint, inasmuch as the statute included mere "convenience" as a ground for denying parade permits. Indeed, in *Shuttlesworth v. City of Birmingham*, decided two years after *Walker*, the Court held the self-same Birmingham ordinance to be unconstitutional.[72] Nevertheless, the *Walker* majority insists (what the dissenters deny) that this injunction is not transparently invalid. Strikingly, however, Justice Stewart in *Shuttlesworth* cited numerous decisions that "have made clear that a person faced with such an unconstitutional licensing law may ignore it and engage with impunity in the exercise of the right of free expression for which the law purports to require a license."[73]

Walker's message could hardly be made more plain: provided that authority exerts the slightest effort to trick out its injunction in the trappings of legality, the injunction is not transparently unconstitutional and the citizen's power to defy it with impunity evaporates. *Walker* virtually issues instructions to judges and other officials about how to

70. In other cases the Court recognized the validity of the first two of these reasons: in Carroll v. President & Commissioners of Princess Anne, 393 U.S. 175 (1968), the Court backed off from *Walker* by insisting that injunctions restraining the exercise of First Amendment rights cannot be issued ex parte unless it is impossible to notify the opposing parties in time to allow them to be heard; and in Freedman v. Maryland, 380 U.S. 51 (1965), the Court had recognized that a speedy hearing and appeal are constitutionally required in a different First Amendment context, namely censorship proceedings against a movie.

71. For three reasons: first, demonstrators gathered from around the country cannot tarry indefinitely in Birmingham while waiting for the courts to rule on the injunction's validity; second, the religious symbolism of holding the demonstrations on Good Friday and Easter Sunday was important, and those days come but once a year; third, the demonstrations were intended to target downtown businesses during the extra-busy Easter shopping season, and that season is relatively short. *See* Westin & Mahoney, *supra* note 21, at 76. Moreover, the Court itself later recognized that when complying with a court order would do irreparable damage because it would subsequently be impossible to "unring the bell," one could defy the order without facing conviction for contempt if the order was invalid. Maness v. Meyers, 419 U.S. 449, 460 (1975).

72. 394 U.S. 147 (1969). Oddly enough, this opinion too was authored by Justice Stewart, who noted that the ordinance conferred on the City Commission "virtually unbridled and absolute power to prohibit any 'parade,' 'procession,' or 'demonstration' on the city's streets or public ways," so that it "fell squarely within the ambit of the many decisions of this Court over the last 30 years, holding that a law subjecting the exercise of First Amendment freedoms to the prior restraint of a license, without narrow, objective, and definite standards to guide the licensing authority, is unconstitutional." *Id.* at 150.

73. *Id.* at 150–51 (footnotes omitted).

insulate an injunction from the possibility of being legitimately disobeyed. On the assumption that judges and other officials will follow these instructions in the future, the Court thus simultaneously presupposes and denies the jurisprudential premise of constitutionalism—that a citizen may disobey a transparently invalid injunction.

I will borrow some suggestive terminology from Jacques Derrida and describe the notion that citizens may legitimately disobey a transparently invalid injunction as a "dangerous supplement" to the Court's actual argument: though the argument presupposes that citizens may legitimately disobey a transparently invalid injunction, this presupposition must remain unstated, for its acknowledgment within the argument would undermine the argument's claims to authority (by undermining the Court's rhetorical strategy of taking only authority's word seriously).[74] The "dangerous supplement" props the argument up but cannot actually appear within it.

The Naked Assertion of Judicial Authority

I have spoken only of the transparent invalidity of Judge Jenkins's injunction, not of the underlying statute, though the Court and dissenters discuss both. That is because the *Walker* opinion really concerns only the former, and indeed a key legal issue revolves around its asymmetrical treatment of injunctions and statutes, hence of judges and legislatures.

As Chief Justice Warren emphasizes in his dissent, one cannot be punished for violating an unconstitutional statute, and indeed it may be impossible to gain standing to test the statute in court unless one disobeys it.[75] Yet the *Walker* decision holds that the demonstrators can be punished for contempt when they violate an unconstitutional injunction. Evidently the authority of courts matters in a way that the authority of legislatures does not. Why?

The answer cannot lie in any supposed constitutional superiority of the judicial process over the legislative process. For the issue in *Walker* is whether the petitioners can test an *unconstitutional* court order by disobeying it; the unconstitutionality of the order is one of the givens of the problem, and the difference in the processes by which an unconstitutional order issues therefore drops out of consideration. Unconstitutionality is unconstitutionality. The Court treats court orders as different in *kind* from legislative enactments, whereas the judicial and

---

74. Jacques Derrida, *Of Grammatology* 144–64 (G. Spivak trans. 1976); Derrida, "Plato's *Pharmakon*," in *Dissemination* 156–71 (B. Johnson trans. 1981).

75. Walker v. City of Birmingham, 388 U.S. 307, 327 (1967) (Warren, C.J., dissenting).

legislative processes differ only in degree (of accuracy, responsiveness, law-abidingness, whatever).

Indeed, the most striking feature in *Walker* is the Court's anxiety to uphold judicial authority as such, as though it were civilization's final, frail barrier against a lurking catastrophe.[76] Hence the Court's final sentence: "But respect for judicial process is a small price to pay for the civilizing hand of law, which alone can give abiding meaning to constitutional freedom."[77] If I am right, the Supreme Court wanted to preclude the very possibility of testing the validity of injunctions by disobeying them because it viewed injunctions as utterly different in kind from statutes, as final barriers against civil anarchy. Frankfurter says this explicitly in the passage we quoted above from *Mine Workers:* "the very existence of a court"—hence, its existence as such, regardless of its legitimacy—"presupposes its power to entertain a controversy. . . . There can be no free society without law administered through an independent judiciary. If one man can be allowed to determine for himself what is law, every man can. That means first chaos, then tyranny."[78] A restraining order is a last-ditch attempt to stop something from happening, to pull the plug on an impending event, and the Court apparently believed that there must be some device that enables the authorities to pull the plug on an impending event.

That, I am convinced, is the heart of the *Walker* decision. The Court saw itself confronting a challenge to the judiciary's ultimate authority, the authority to stop events from getting out of hand; the Court was willing to go to almost any length to uphold that authority. As we have seen, ample grounds existed for the Court to find for the petitioners in a decision narrowly tailored to the facts: the ex parte hearing, its timing, the fact that Bull Connor had been voted out of office, his treatment of Mrs. Hendricks, his history of racism (known to the Court from prior cases),[79] not to mention the well-known commitment of the SCLC to

---

76. Similar concerns emerge in cases about judicial tort immunity. The most notable is Stump v. Sparkman, 435 U.S. 349 (1978), in which the Court found that a trial judge who had ordered a teenager sterilized at the ex parte request of the teenager's mother was immune from tort liability. Indeed, it is only in the most bizarre of circumstances that judicial immunity dissolves. *See, e.g.,* Zarcone v. Perry, 572 F.2d 52 (2d Cir. 1978) (upholding punitive damages against a traffic judge who had ordered a street vendor brought into his courtroom in manacles because he had sold the judge a bad cup of coffee).

77. *Walker,* 388 U.S. at 321.

78. United States v. United Mine Workers, 330 U.S. 258, 312 (1947).

79. In his dissent, Chief Justice Warren cites five cases and two governmental reports that take official notice of "[t]he attitude of the city administration in general and of its Public Safety Commissioner in particular. . . . " *Walker,* 388 U.S. at 325 n.1 (Warren, C.J., dissenting).

nonviolence. Each could have provided a convenient hook for a favorable decision.[80] The fact that the Court did not rest content with allowing even a narrow exception to the inviolability of court orders shows that it feared even the slightest diminution of judicial ability to stop events.

This fear is particularly striking in view of the Supreme Court's general support for the civil rights movement and civil rights demonstrations in the years preceding *Walker*.[81] In hindsight, *Walker* (together with the *Adderley* decision handed down seven months before[82]) in fact marks a turning point in the Court's attitude, away from the civil rights movement and in the direction of greater emphasis on civil order. In his dissenting opinion, Justice Brennan lets us know why: "We cannot permit fears of 'riots' and 'civil disobedience' generated by slogans like 'Black Power' to divert our attention from what is here at stake."[83] *Walker* was decided in 1966, when the nonviolent civil rights movement was metamorphosing into greater militance and the country had witnessed riots in Watts and Harlem spread elsewhere; by 1966, the slogan "Burn, baby, burn!" had raised the fear of self-fueling riots. The Court saw itself confronting a very real possibility of losing its grip.[84]

This context perhaps makes the Court's response more comprehensible; it does nothing to render it justifiable. The entire question of the legitimacy of judicial authority remains begged, and begged to its depths. Authority "needs" to be able to stop social protest from getting out of hand. It "needs" to be able to freeze the status quo in emergency situations, even by unconstitutional means. Why is that? To be sure, violence is an intrinsically terrible thing; but the Supreme Court of the United States did not base the "need" to stop matters from getting out of hand on grounds of pacifism, for the U.S. government is in no respect pacifist.[85] The status quo is itself always maintained by violence, and

---

80. Westin and Mahoney argue that the Court should have found in favor of King in an opinion narrowly tailored to the exceptional facts. Westin & Mahoney, *supra* note 21, at 286–89.

81. *See, e.g., Cox v. Louisiana*, 379 U.S. 559 (1965) (protecting demonstrators from state suppression); *Fields v. South Carolina*, 375 U.S. 44 (1963) (same); *Edwards v. South Carolina*, 372 U.S. 229 (1963) (same).

82. *Adderley v. Florida*, 385 U.S. 39 (1966) was the first Supreme Court case in the 1960s upholding the convictions of nonviolent demonstrators. Westin & Mahoney, *supra* note 21, at 205.

83. *Walker*, 388 U.S. at 349 (Brennan, J., dissenting).

84. This is a major theme in Westin & Mahoney, *supra* note 21.

85. An important case prefiguring *Walker* that runs contrary to my general line of argument here is *United States v. Shipp*, 203 U.S. 563 (1906). In that case, the Supreme Court issued an order preventing the execution of Johnson, an African-American man convicted of raping a white woman, pending appeal. A lynch mob gathered at the jail

never more so than in the case of Jim Crow.[86] The ultimate question remains: Why should courts be permitted to maintain an unjust status quo of which they are a part, even for a single second, by means that exceed their authority?[87] (That, too, after all, is an example of being a judge in one's own case.)

To freeze the status quo does more than delay social protest. It destroys it. Social protest is always a miraculous phenomenon; it is irrational for an individual to participate in collective action for social change even when the collective action is itself rational; whether or not the action occurs will never turn on the participation of a single individual, so for each individual it makes more sense to leave the risks and

---

and Shipp, the sheriff guarding the prisoner, joined forces with the mob to carry out the lynching. Shipp was convicted of contempt of court. He argued that the Supreme Court had no jurisdiction for its order and therefore that he could not be punished for contemning it. The Court rejected this argument in a discussion that links the necessity of preventing violence with the question-begging assertion of the Court's "catholic" authority to determine the limits of its own authority: "Until its judgment declining jurisdiction should be announced, it [i.e., the Supreme Court] had authority from the necessity of the case to make orders to preserve the existing conditions and the subject of the petition. . . . " *Id.* at 573.

Shipp appears to illustrate the necessity of some social mechanism to "pull the plug" on events that threaten to get out of hand, leading to incidents as appalling as the lynching of Johnson. But why should it be judicial authority? Why not the sheriff? In *Shipp*, of course, the answer is that the sheriff was part of the mob. But must it therefore be a judge? We can imagine judges who also fail to do their job for the same reasons as the sheriff; we could imagine the Supreme Court, or any other authority, failing to do its job for racist reasons. The argument from the need for a social mechanism to freeze events in their tracks to the vindication of judicial authority is thus a complete non sequitur. To see this clearly, consider a case cognate to *Shipp:* Johnson is unjustly convicted, and the unjust conviction is upheld by the Supreme Court. Now events are threatening to get out of hand: Johnson is about to be executed. What is needed, clearly, is some social mechanism to "pull the plug" on these events. Since all the authorities are united in their determination to execute Johnson unjustly, the task falls to a mob of Johnson's supporters, who rescue him dramatically from jail. Here the need for a social mechanism to freeze events in their tracks, to stop unjust violence, vindicates mob rebellion against judicial authority, just as in *Shipp* it vindicates judicial authority itself.

86. The history of violence employed to maintain Jim Crow goes all the way back to the dissolution of Reconstruction. *See, e.g.,* United States v. Cruikshank, 92 U.S. 542 (1875) (denying federal authority to punish private individuals for forcibly breaking up an African-American political meeting and thereby hindering the exercise by African-Americans of the right to vote). For an eloquent reminder that law rests on violence, see Cover, "Violence and the Word," 95 *Yale Law Journal* 1601 (1986).

87. In his *Letter,* King writes, "I have almost reached the regrettable conclusion that the Negro's great stumbling block in his stride toward freedom is not the White Citizen's Counciler or Ku Klux Klanner, but the white moderate, who is more devoted to 'order' than to justice. . . . " King, *supra* note 11, at 87. The debate over whether the highest legal value is order or justice is an old one; for more on the issue, see chapter 6.

labor to others than to participate.[88] Since this principle is true for all individuals, social protest is almost always stillborn, suffocated by cords of inertia, mistrust, and self-interest. Moreover, because members of victimized groups typically live at the margins of economic security, it may be more rational for them to emphasize the short run over the long, and thus consent to a substantial level of oppression that nevertheless offers a livelihood, rather than choose the risky path of seeking structural change.[89]

Social protest can occur only when individuals are stirred in their souls, stirred to act in a way that is not individually rational. For years, or decades, even centuries, the routine of oppression proceeds uninterrupted. Then, inexplicably, at certain privileged moments the curtain lifts and political action flames into existence. At a rally in Manila, or a shipyard strike in Gdansk, or a public funeral in Beijing, or a segregated bus in Montgomery, something unpredictable happens to interrupt the timid calculations of individual rationality. In Benjamin's words,

Where thinking suddenly stops in a configuration pregnant with tensions, it gives that configuration a shock, by which it crystallizes into a monad. . . . In this structure [the historical materialist] recognizes the sign of a Messianic cessation of happening. . . . He takes cognizance of it in order to blast a specific era out of the homogeneous course of history. . . .[90]

---

88. This argument was explored initially in Mancur Olson, *The Logic of Collective Action: Public Goods and the Theory of Groups* (rev. ed. 1971). *See also* Russell Hardin, *Collective Action* (1982). This argument is applied to the analysis of revolutionary social change in Alan Buchanan, "Revolutionary Motivation and Rationality," 9 *Philosophy & Public Affairs* 59 (1979). But see Gregory Kavka, *Hobbesian Moral and Political Theory* 266–79 (1986), for an argument that revolutionary participation can be rational. On the relationship between collective action problems and the legal system, see David Luban, *Lawyers and Justice: An Ethical Study* 364–91 (1988).

89. *See* Joshua Cohen & Joel Rogers, *On Democracy: Toward a Transformation of American Society* 47–87 (1983); Cohen & Rogers, *Rules of the Game: American Politics and the Central America Movement* (1986) (a succinct statement of the obstacles facing social protest movements in America); Adam Przeworski, "Material Bases of Consent: Economics and Politics in a Hegemonic System," 1 *Political Power & Social Theory* 21 (1980); Przeworski, "Proletariat into a Class: The Process of Class Formation from Karl Kautsky's *The Class Struggle* to Recent Controversies," 7 *Politics & Society* 343 (1977); Przeworski, "Social Democracy as a Historical Phenomenon," *New Left Review*, July–Aug. 1980, at 27; Przeworski & Wallerstein, "The Structure of Class Conflict in Democratic Capitalist Societies," 76 *American Political Science Review* 215 (1982).

90. Benjamin, *supra* note 1, at 264–65.

But if that moment—"shot through," as Benjamin says, "with chips of Messianic time"[91]—passes, if the momentum of social protest is interrupted, the miracle will no longer occur. The protestors lose their faith, or they must return to their families and jobs, or the media go home, or the instant of dialectical sympathy between the protestors and the larger community, which would draw the larger community into the movement, evaporates. Wyatt Walker recollected,

> One option we eliminated was going to court to try to get the injunction dissolved. We knew this would tie us up in court at least ten days to two weeks, and even then we might not get it dissolved. We would have a lengthy lawsuit to appeal but no Birmingham campaign. All of our planning and organizing, a year's effort, would have been in vain, and that was exactly what the city was trying to accomplish by going to court.[92]

Bull Connor and Judge Jenkins understood that for a protest movement delay means death. Authority *always* understands that for a protest movement, delay means death. The Supreme Court of the United States understood it. In the *Walker* decision, the Court imposed, so far as it was able, a death sentence on social protest. By what right did the Court cast its vote for existent injustice over social change? Why is a court's claim to authority greater than that of the civil rights movement?

One answer, of course, is that judges are democratically elected or chosen by democratically elected representatives. But this is scarcely a decisive argument, for two reasons: first, in many cases (and notably the case of African-Americans in the South of 1963) the protest movement has had no part in the democratic process (and the process is itself stacked against oppressed people) and, second, the question turns on *unconstitutional* injunctions issued by democratically elected judges.

Ultimately, the *Walker* Court reserved for the judiciary the authority to stifle social protest by any means, constitutional or not. Its assertion of authority is naked, unsupported by anything other than the assertion itself.

And, to underscore the argument of the preceding section, let me repeat that the assertion is an incoherent one, undercutting the premises of liberal democracy—the narrative of American political history— on which judicial authority ostensibly rests: by granting courts the right

---

91. *Id.* at 265.
92. *Quoted in* Westin & Mahoney, *supra* note 21, at 76.

to exceed the limits of their own authority, the Court must abandon the rule of law, or popular sovereignty, or publicity.

It may be objected that I have misread the *Walker* Court's emphasis: its main focus is not the vexed issue of transparent unconstitutionality. Rather, the Court's point is a simpler and less controversial one, namely that the demonstrators wrongly made no effort to get the injunction dissolved even though they had enough time to attempt to do so. After all, the *Walker* Court writes that "[t]his case would arise in quite a different constitutional posture if the petitioners, before disobeying the injunction, had challenged it in the Alabama courts, and had been met with delay or frustration of their constitutional claims."[93] This statement suggests that had the demonstrators challenged the injunction, *Walker* might have been decided differently. That, at any rate, is how the Court subsequently understood *Walker*.[94] This latter reading of the case implies that the *Walker* Court was not concerned, as I have been arguing, to make it as difficult as possible for demonstrators to disobey injunctions, even unconstitutional injunctions; rather, the Court was concerned merely to ensure that before disobeying the injunction the demonstrators must first exhaust judicial remedies.

Now I do not wish to deny that this is a possible reading of *Walker*, even though it ignores the third of the opinion devoted to proving that the injunction was not transparently invalid; but it is a superficial reading, for the seemingly minimal, seemingly reasonable request to seek the dissolution of an unconstitutional court order before violating it is itself offensive or even immoral unless the larger questions we have been considering about the legitimacy of judicial authority can be answered.

This point may be seen clearly when we reflect on hypothetical cases in which a local court issues a degrading, debasing, and transparently unconstitutional order. Part of the humiliation such an order inflicts on its recipients lies precisely in the need to go to another court to obtain authorization to disobey; the lower court humiliates the recipients by compelling them to offer gestures of respect and obeisance to the judicial system. Suppose, for example, that a Jewish group wishes to

---

93. *Walker*, 388 U.S. 307, 318 (1967).

94. *See* United States v. Ryan, 402 U.S. 530, 532 n.4 (1971) ("Our holding [in *Walker*] that the claims there sought to be asserted were not open on review of petitioners' contempt convictions was based upon the availability of review of those claims at an earlier stage."); *see also* Maness v. Meyers, 419 U.S. 449 (1975); Donovan v. City of Dallas, 377 U.S. 408, 414 (1964). The lesson of these cases, according to Wright, is that "the validity of an order can be challenged in a contempt proceeding for violation of the order only if there was no opportunity for effective review of the order before it was violated." Charles A. Wright, *Law of Federal Courts* 88 (4th ed. 1983).

stage a protest march and is ordered by a judge to wear yellow Star of
David armbands, ostensibly for the purpose of identification to help
police keep the traffic orderly. Much of the offensiveness of the order
lies precisely in making the group go through a charade of deference—
by seeking to dissolve an order that is so obviously unconstitutional
and so obviously intended as a mere racial harassment—before violating it. Nor is the example much more outrageous than the actual
Birmingham injunction, which issued under circumstances in which
it could hardly have been clearer that it was a mere racial harassment.

Another hypothetical example will illustrate the point. Suppose
that the Birmingham Ku Klux Klan had publicly issued its own mock
"injunction" to prevent the Project C march, announcing, however, that
it would be willing to "dissolve" its "injunction" provided that the
demonstrators publicly applied to the Imperial Wizard in writing.
Plainly, the Klan's offer to "dissolve" the mock "injunction" heightens,
rather than diminishes, the outrageousness of the "injunction" itself.
And it is equally plain that that is because the Klan has no authority to
issue such morally debasing commands in the first place.

The only difference between this hypothetical example and the
Walker Court's insistence that the demonstrators apply to a court to
dissolve Judge Jenkins's unconstitutional injunction before disobeying
it must lie in the fact that the court system has the authority that the
Klan so obviously lacks. And thus, to explain why the demonstrators
should not simply adjudge Judge Jenkins's order transparently unconstitutional and disobey (intending to accept their punishment if their
judgment was wrong), we need to explain why Judge Jenkins had the
authority to compel them to jump through additional judicial hoops
merely by issuing an unconstitutional order. The seemingly minimal,
seemingly reasonable request to seek the dissolution of the injunction
before disobeying it is neither minimal nor reasonable unless it can be
grounded in an account of why judicial authority to issue unconstitutional injunctions deserves respect in the first place.[95]

Thus, the Court cannot evade the deeper questions of judicial authority, and its "dangerous supplement," that we have been exploring.
To conclude our examination of *Walker,* let us see how, finally, the Court
answers them.

---

95. Not only is the bare fact of acceding to a racially harassing order in and of itself
an injury to the demonstrators, it is also likely to destroy their effectiveness by undermining confidence in their own leaders' commitment and courage. Thus, even on the
Maness v. Meyers "unring the bell" test, *see supra* note 71, the request to seek the
dissolution of the injunction before disobeying it is far from minimal.

"The Civilizing Hand of Law, Which Alone Can Give . . ."

> But respect for judicial process is a small price to pay for the civilizing hand of law, which alone can give abiding meaning to constitutional freedom.[96]

This, the Court's final sentence, contains an ironic grammatical ambiguity introduced by its most important word: "alone." It can be read as the assertion that the civilizing hand of law is *necessary* to give abiding meaning to constitutional freedom—presumably what the Court intended—or that the civilizing hand of law is *sufficient* to give abiding meaning to constitutional freedom.

Double meanings like this—Freud called them "parapraxes"—are almost enough to make one believe in psychoanalysis. The Court probably did not intend to say that law can give abiding meaning to constitutional freedom all by itself: but in addition to being a grammatical reading of the sentence, it is a conclusion to which the Court is inevitably driven by the logic of its own argument. For if the civilizing hand of the law—judicial and governmental process—is not sufficient to give abiding meaning to constitutional freedom, the Court has no business insisting that long-suffering citizens defer their attempts at self-help. Government's claim to exclusive authority is grounded in part on its ability to do the job, to keep its promises. It is precisely the ability of government to fulfill the constitutional promise of equality that the civil rights movement doubted. As King wrote in the *Letter*, "For years now I have heard the word 'Wait!' It rings in the ear of every Negro with piercing familiarity. This 'Wait' has almost always meant 'Never.'"[97] The Court must do more than warn that if judicial processes are bypassed anarchy might result (which is probably false and in any event beside the point, inasmuch as the demonstrators were willing to accept the punishment for contempt had the injunction ultimately been found valid, and were therefore scarcely attempting to bypass judicial processes). In addition, the Court must reassure us that King is wrong, that "the civilizing hand of law" is in and of itself sufficient to produce abiding freedom.[98]

96. *Walker*, 388 U.S. at 321.
97. King, *supra* note 11, at 83.
98. That is the defining belief of legal centralism, the almost universally accepted dogma of legal professionals. Legal centralism has been defined as "a picture in which state agencies (and their learning) occupy the center of legal life and stand in a relation of 'hierarchic control' to other, lesser normative orderings such as the family, the corporation, the business network." Marc Galanter, "Justice in Many Rooms," in *Access to Justice and the Welfare State* 161 (Mauro Cappelletti ed. 1981) (footnotes deleted). *See also* David

The problem, of course, is that this is untrue, even monstrously untrue. Without the will and willingness of the people it governs, the judiciary, like any other governmental authority, is helpless. Segregation was a decisive case in point, for one hundred years of the "civilizing hand of law" had yielded African-Americans little beyond Jim Crow.[99] Alexander Bickel argues persuasively that the South might actually have resisted court-ordered integration successfully but for southern officials' tactical blunders of loosing extreme brutality on black children in front of news cameras, which mobilized northern support for the civil rights struggle.[100] Had the southern white leadership responded more coolly, the civilizing hand of law would have been helpless. Indeed, as late as 1969 President Nixon could still refer to those who wanted to see *Brown v. Board of Education* enforced as "extremists."[101] That such a statement could pass for sane political discourse testifies to the lack of progress in school integration even after sixteen years and thus to the Court's thoroughgoing inability to "give abiding meaning to constitutional freedom" on its own. And, as a more general point, the very idea that legal institutions by themselves—that is, regardless of extrainstitutional social behavior—can guarantee freedom, or anything else for that matter, is false to the point of insanity. It attributes a kind of omnipotence to legal institutions that nothing human possesses.

Yet the Court's rhetoric in *Walker* could offer no escape from the closed circle of authority. We have seen that the opinion's rhetorical aim was not ultimately to decide a disputed question; it was to reserve for authority the only possible voice through which disputed questions can even be posed. *Walker*'s narrative structure tars every unofficial voice as a "judge in its own case" and thereby silences that voice's claim to enunciate justice for itself.

I suggested earlier that legal narratives gain their authority by implicitly comprehending institutions in religious categories. The *Walker* Court, faced with the need to deny the authoritativeness of unofficial voices, solved the problem by implicitly attributing to legal institutions a superhuman efficacy and disinterest that demands uncon-

---

Trubek & Marc Galanter, "Scholars in Self-Estrangement: Some Reflections on the Crisis in Law and Development Studies in the United States," 1974 *Wisconsin Law Review* 1062, 1070–72. For an illuminating discussion, see Robert Gordon, "Without the Law II (Book Review)," 24 *Osgood Hall Law Review* 421 (1986). Cover, *supra* note 12, offers a telling critique of legal centralism.

99. *See generally* Richard Kluger, *Simple Justice* (1976).

100. Alexander Bickel, *The Least Dangerous Branch* 266–68 (1962).

101. That was Nixon's response to the oral argument of Alexander v. Holmes County Bd. of Educ., 396 U.S. 19 (1969), the decision ending "all deliberate speed" and ordering immediate school desegregation in Mississippi. Jack Bass, *Unlikely Heroes* 314 (1981).

ditional obedience and faith. Facing a choice between the anti-authoritarian consequences of liberal constitutionalism and the over-whelming desire to maintain reverence for authority, the *Walker* Court opted for the latter, staking out an extravagant claim on behalf of the legal system that only a supernatural power could fulfill and demand-ing allegiance that only a supernatural power deserves. Unable to toler-ate the consequences of a merely secular liberalism, the Court chose to invest the legal system with an essentially religious authority.

In Sophocles' *Antigone* it is Creon who, like the *Walker* Court, is incapable of recognizing any claim to allegiance other than that exerted by the state: "[H]e who counts another greater friend than his own fatherland, I put him nowhere."[102] To which Creon's own son later responds, "You'd rule a desert beautifully alone."[103] Like Creon, the *Walker* Court was locked in the solipsism of an authority that recognizes only itself. Like Creon, the *Walker* Court, which failed even to mention the crucial social actors in Birmingham, put every social force other than the law itself "nowhere." Like Creon, the *Walker* Court would rule a desert beautifully alone.[104]

When the guard first tells Creon that someone has disobeyed his command (Antigone, like King, disobeyed the command in the name of honoring a higher religious law), he flies into a rage; he suspects every-one of inciting community-destroying civil war. The chorus comments: "Many the wonders but nothing walks stranger than man. . . . When he honors the laws of the land and the gods' sworn right high indeed is his city; but stateless the man who dares to dwell with dishonor. Not by my fire, never to share my thoughts, who does these things."[105]

It is the moment of supreme irony in the drama. We hear it through Creon's ears as a denunciation of Antigone; but as the action unfolds, we come gradually to realize that the chorus is referring to Creon him-self, who has dishonored the gods' sworn right through his impious command and who ends as a familyless exile from his own state, a prisoner of his own community-destroying autism.[106]

---

102. Sophocles, *Antigone,* in 2 *The Complete Greek Tragedies* 159, 165, ll. 182–83 (Elizabeth Wyckoff trans. 1957).

103. *Id.* at 184, l. 739.

104. For a related thought about *Walker,* see Robert Burt, *Two Jewish Justices: Outcasts in the Promised Land* 103–13 (1988) (*Walker* commits the error of "confounding the law and the judges").

105. Sophocles, *supra* note 102, at 170, l. 335, 171, ll. 369–72.

106. Several readers of earlier drafts of this chapter have asked me what rule I would propose in place of *Walker*'s. Though answering this question—or even raising it—is tangential to my purposes in this chapter, I believe that an answer is implicit in my analysis. That being the case, it might as well be made explicit. As we have seen, existing doctrine already permits a party to contemn a constitutionally infirm court order if it is

King's Letter

King understood Creon's tragic error. Addressing the National Association for the Advancement of Colored People (NAACP) in Atlanta nine
months before the Birmingham march, King reminded his law-oriented
audience that "legislation and court orders can only declare rights.
They can never thoroughly deliver them. Only when the people themselves begin to act are rights on paper given life blood."[107] So apt is this
response to the final sentences of Stewart's *Walker* opinion that it is
almost as though King had peered into the future to read it. Where the
Court sought its panacea in "the civilizing hand of law" rather than "the
petitioners' impatient commitment to their cause,"[108] King found legal
rights only where "the people themselves begin to act." In the same
Atlanta speech King sounded some of the motifs that would later appear in his *Letter* and indeed employed several of the similes and com-

issued ex parte despite the possibility of notifying the opposing party, if ample opportunity to challenge the order does not exist, or if complying with the order would
irremediably damage a party. Assume that none of these problems arise in the case of an
injunction. Even then, except in one circumstance, demonstrators should be able to avoid
punishment for contemning a court order by showing after the fact that the order was
unconstitutional. The exception is this: when the act of disobedience itself consists of
irreversibly and wrongfully damaging someone—for example, by revealing legitimately
confidential information or committing a violent crime—then parties may be punished
for contemning the order whether or not it was constitutional. The exception is intended
to grant courts authority to issue enforceable unconstitutional orders to deter intentional, wrongful damage to other people in emergency circumstances like those in *Shipp* (the
lynching case discussed *supra* note 85). Now this exception seems to beg the same
questions of judicial authority I have been accusing the Court of begging, since it allows
courts to exceed their constitutional authority. But the reason for the exception has
nothing to do with courts in particular: rather, I believe that *anyone* should be able to stop
intentional, wrongful damage to other people by proportional means, even when those
means are illegal. I am thinking here of something like the German law of "justifying
emergency": "Whoever, in the face of an immediate and not otherwise preventable
danger to life, limb . . . or other rights performs an act in order to hinder the danger . . .
does not act illegally if, upon balancing the conflicting interests, particularly the rights
concerned and the degree of danger which threatens them, the protected interest outweighs the impaired interest significantly. . . . " *Strafgesetzbuch* [StGB] § 34. The issue is
not a grant of extraordinary political authority to courts; rather, it is a recognition of
extraordinary authority that vests in all of us in the face of an emergency. Note also that
the exception in the rule I am proposing applies only when the act of disobedience itself
wrongfully injures someone; it does not apply when the act itself is not wrongful or
injurious, even in situations in which as it happens injuries result. In Project C, even if
the nonviolent march provoked others to violence, the marchers could not be punished
for contemning Judge Jenkins's order under the rule I favor. Nor does the rule permit
anarchy; violators of court orders assume the risk that at their contempt hearings the
order will be upheld, in which case they will be punished.

107. *Quoted in* Branch, *supra* note 20, at 598.
108. *Walker*, 388 U.S. 307, 321 (1967).

parisons that we shall later examine; in part, the Atlanta speech amounts to a prototype of the *Letter*. It shows how deeply King was thinking about the basic tension between juridical institutions and community as the true source of legal authority.

King's *Letter* is a prophetic call to community; so much is obvious from the moment that he enunciates his basic thought: "We are caught in an inescapable network of mutuality, tied in a single garment of destiny."[109] And by its invocation of community—an entity or category so strikingly absent in the *Walker* opinion—King's is a voicing of the Birmingham events that is supplementary or dual to the *Walker* Court's. King repopulates the Creonic desert over which the Court has elected to preside. But King, like the Court, is unsure whether to issue his call in religious or secular terms. The *Letter* in fact has it both ways; therein lies its power but also its temptation. I shall explain this by looking closely at King's political narratives, his identifications of the actions of himself and his fellow demonstrators with episodes of a larger, more universal history—or, more precisely, with several such histories, some of which are religious in character, some secular. First, to orient the reader, I briefly summarize the *Letter*.

After an initial greeting to his "fellow clergymen,"[110] King addresses the various accusations that the eight clergymen had leveled in their newspaper advertisement. To the charge that he and his fellow organizers are outside agitators, King insists on the "interrelatedness of all communities and states," and likens himself to St. Paul answering the Macedonian call.[111] To the charge that the demonstrations are "unwise and untimely," King responds by reviewing Birmingham's history of racism and of broken promises to the civil rights movement and outlines the careful steps taken by the campaign to prepare itself for nonviolence.[112] To the charge that the demonstrators have substituted confrontation for negotiation, King responds that it is naive to believe that negotiation will ever take place unless the demonstrators have forced it by creating a "tension" in the community.[113] To the charge that the demonstrators are forcing the issue before giving the Boutwell administration time to do what it can in race relations, King answers that Boutwell, like Connor, is a segregationist, differing from the latter only in that Connor is more crude. In the most moving and urgent paragraph of the *Letter*, he meditates bitterly on the evils of segregation to illustrate one of his main themes: that "it is easy for those who have never felt the

109. King, *supra* note 11, at 79.
110. *Id.* at 77.
111. *Id.* at 78.
112. *Id.* at 79–81.
113. *Id.* at 81–82.

stinging darts of segregation to say, 'Wait,'"[114] but wholly unreasonable
to expect long-suffering blacks to remain patient in their suffering.

Next, King addresses a charge that comes close to the issue in
Walker. How can King ask whites to comply with *Brown v.
Board of Education* if he is himself prepared to disobey a court order that he
doesn't like? In response, King sketches an argument based on a series
of distinctions from the natural law tradition: One is obligated to obey
just law but to disobey unjust law. Just law is law that uplifts human
personality, whereas unjust law is law that degrades it. Segregation
laws, by giving whites a false sense of superiority and blacks a false
sense of inferiority, degrade human personality, whereas an integrationist decree such as *Brown* uplifts it and is consequently just. Alternatively, just law is law that applies evenhandedly to minorities and
majorities—it is "sameness made legal"—whereas unjust law is law
that does not—it is "difference made legal"; by this criterion as well,
segregation laws and *Brown* fundamentally differ. Finally, a just law,
such as an ordinance requiring marchers to obtain a parade permit, can
be enforced selectively (as in Judge Jenkins's injunction), in which case
it too is difference made legal and hence unjust. Ergo, *Brown*'s decree
must be obeyed and segregation laws (including Judge Jenkins's injunction) must be disobeyed.[115]

After answering the white clergymen's accusations, King launches
his own. He expresses dismay at white "moderates," who are "more
devoted to 'order' than to justice," who agree with the movement's
goals but characterize all of its methods as too extreme, and who believe
fallaciously that the passage of time will by itself end segregation without demonstrators forcing matters.[116] In response, he condemns "the
strangely irrational notion that there is something in the very flow of
time that will inevitably cure all ills";[117] he then reminds his readers
that it is not his nonviolent movement but black nationalist groups such
as the Muslims who stand at the extreme of the race issue.[118] King then
reflects that on second thought he should willingly accept the "extremist" label, for it puts him in very good company. Since it will concern us
later, I reproduce this vital paragraph here for convenience:

> But though I was initially disappointed at being categorized as an
> extremist, as I continued to think about the matter I gradually

114. *Id.* at 82–83.
115. *Id.* at 84–86.
116. *Id.* at 87–93.
117. *Id.* at 89.
118. *Id.* at 90–92.

gained a measure of satisfaction from the label. Was not Jesus an extremist for love: "Love your enemies, bless them that curse you, do good to them that hate you, and pray for them which despitefully use you, and persecute you." Was not Amos an extremist for justice: "Let justice roll down like waters and righteousness like an ever-flowing stream." Was not Paul an extremist for the Christian gospel: "I bear in my body the marks of the Lord Jesus." Was not Martin Luther an extremist: "Here I stand; I cannot do otherwise, so help me God." And John Bunyan: "I will stay in jail to the end of my days before I make a butchery of my conscience." And Abraham Lincoln: "This nation cannot survive half slave and half free." And Thomas Jefferson: "We hold these truths to be self-evident, that all men are created equal."[119]

For future reference, let me refer to this as the *extremism passage*. I shall return to it several times.

In the concluding pages of the *Letter*, King excoriates the white churches for their failure to embrace the cause of civil rights as a fundamental moral matter.[120] Adopting a prophetic voice, King castigates the churches for urging compliance with civil rights laws merely as a matter of prudence rather than welcoming blacks as brothers and sisters;[121] he thunders that the churches themselves will face a day of reckoning for their moral failings.[122] Finally, King rebukes the clergymen for congratulating the Birmingham police for "preventing violence"; King bitterly points out that this ignores the police dogs and the violence employed by the police out of sight of the cameras, not to mention that their veneer of public restraint was merely a tactic in service of segregation.[123] In the end, however, King offers a conciliatory closing salutation: "I hope this letter finds you strong in the faith. I also hope that circumstances will soon make it possible for me to meet each of you, not as an integrationist or a civil-rights leader but as a fellow clergyman and a Christian brother."[124]

This, however, is a bare summary. The true meaning of the *Letter* lies more in the detailed narratives King invokes than in the larger structure of his argument. I shall be focusing on King's identifications of himself and his fellow demonstrators with a variegated but carefully

---

119. *Id.* at 92.
120. *Id.* at 93–98.
121. *Id.* at 94.
122. *Id.* at 96.
123. *Id.* at 98–99.
124. *Id.* at 100.

chosen collection of other historical actors. In what I have labeled the extremism passage and elsewhere in the *Letter*, King identifies with biblical characters (Paul, Amos, Jesus, Shadrach, Meshach, and Abednego); with Christian dissidents (unnamed Christian martyrs, Luther, Bunyan); with theological thinkers (Augustine, Aquinas, Buber, Tillich); with American egalitarians (Jefferson, Lincoln); and with the patron saint of civil disobedience (Socrates). Together, these self-identifications generate a dense and, as we shall see, multiply ambiguous political narrative.

King's Local Narrative

My primary focus will be on King's political narratives, his efforts to make legal sense of a larger history of which the Birmingham campaign forms just one episode, rather than his local narrative of the Birmingham events. That is because King's local narrative—his description of the Birmingham campaign—tries not to be self-contained but rather points explicitly outside itself toward the larger political narrative. The local narrative is "theory laden" to a remarkable extent. King organizes his account of the Birmingham campaign around a theory of direct action rather than a chronological sequence of events. "In any nonviolent campaign there are four basic steps: collection of the facts to determine whether injustices exist; negotiation; self-purification; and direct action. We have gone through all these steps in Birmingham."[125] Having propounded this schema, King proceeds in ordered sequence to describe Birmingham's racist predilections ("to determine whether injustices exist"), the events leading up to the demonstrations, including prior attempts at negotiation ("negotiation"), and the planning of the demonstrations, including workshops in nonviolence ("self-purification"). The local narrative he develops in this way is richer and more inclusive than that of the *Walker* Court; instead of a reductionist recounting of the event as an encounter between authority and individuals, King's narrative vocabulary also includes the civil rights organization and the Birmingham white community itself.

What is noteworthy about King's local narrative, however—apart from the striking set of categories he uses to organize it—is that he says virtually nothing about the demonstrations themselves, the fourth step of his schema ("direct action"). Or rather, he says virtually nothing about the march, the crowds, the arrest, or the injunction.[126] Instead, he

---

125. *Id.* at 79.
126. He does, however, describe these events in his 1964 memoir of the

recounts the events by describing what he takes to be the political and
spiritual import of direct action:

> Nonviolent direct action seeks to create such a crisis and foster
> such a tension that a community which has constantly refused to
> negotiate is forced to confront the issue. It seeks so to dramatize the
> issue that it can no longer be ignored. . . . Just as Socrates felt that it
> was necessary to create a tension in the mind so that individuals
> could rise from the bondage of myths and half-truths to the unfet-
> tered realm of creative analysis and objective appraisal, so must we
> see the need for nonviolent gadflies to create the kind of tension in
> society that will help men rise from the dark depths of prejudice
> and racism to the majestic heights of understanding and
> brotherhood.
>
> The purpose of our direct-action program is to create a situation
> so crisis-packed that it will inevitably open the door to
> negotiation.[127]

King, I believe, purposely refuses to recount the events without subsuming them within an account of their purpose.[128] In his narrative
vocabulary, a march or a sit-in simply resists flat-footedly behavioral
narration. A sit-in aims to dramatize an issue and thus to refer beyond
itself. To describe it in behavioral terms without building that dramatic
function into the description would be as misleading as a description of
Othello choking Desdemona that omits the fact that the action is occur-
ring in a play. To take another example—one that is highly pertinent to
King's spiritualized understanding of a direct-action campaign—a religious revelation may well resist flat-footedly behavioral narration.
("St. So-and-So knelt in prayer. Two hours later she stood up. That's all,
folks!") The physical events that transpired on April 12, 1963, are, in
King's narrative apparatus, shadow events or husks whose bare
recitation—here we must think of Stewart's local narrative in *Walker*—

Birmingham campaign. King, "New Day in Birmingham," in *Why We Can't Wait, supra*
note 11, at 55–75.

127. King, *supra* note 11, at 81–82.

128. This, of course, is a strategy that runs the risk of self-deception or even
whitewash, of substituting an idealized picture of what one hoped to do for an accurate
rendition of what one in fact did. In my view, however, the Birmingham campaign
actually lived up to the description that King offers in the *Letter*, so no self-deception or
whitewash actually occurs.

misleads and misses the truth of what occurred: a local narrative of crisis and creative tension.[129]

King's Socratic allusion in the passage I have just quoted is surely intended as a conscious underscoring of this point. The allusion to "ris[ing] from the bondage of myths and half-truths" is a reference to the famous allegory of the Cave in book 6 of Plato's *Republic*, which likens us to spectators of a shadow drama projected on a wall. According to Socrates, we mistake the shadows for reality, completely overlooking the solid objects whose images we are contemplating.[130] Once we have grasped the appropriateness of this allusion, we understand why King substitutes a conceptual narrative of the Birmingham campaign for a journalistic account of the events: the journalistic account mistakes shadows for reality. For what occurred on April 12, 1963, was not a march followed by an arrest but a maieutic drama "bring[ing] to the surface the hidden tension that is already alive. We bring it out in the open, where it can be seen and dealt with."[131] The bulk of King's *Letter*, its philosophical arguments as well as its political narratives, is an attempt to make good this description.

The *Walker* opinion and King's *Letter* are in an odd way mirror images of each other. *Walker* devotes most of its attention to its local narrative, its recitation of the events of April 10–12, 1963. This is unsurprising: since the Court has presumed the position of authority, it need not concentrate its efforts on political narrative, since its authority very literally speaks for itself. By contrast, King devotes most of his attention to the political narrative that will confer legitimacy on the Birmingham campaign; his local narrative of the events is abbreviated, for that narrative will make sense only when King's political narrative has persuaded us that the marches and sit-ins are indeed mere husks of a more profound story. Let us turn then to King's political narratives.

---

129. That is not to deny that sometimes it is appropriate to insist on the behavioral narration. The terrorist group insists that it merely dramatized the plight of its people (by setting off a car-bomb in a crowded street); we rightly insist that what it did was set off a car-bomb in a crowded street. The administration claims that it is signaling support for democratic institutions in Central America; we rightly insist that it is aiding and abetting murders and tortures. When the dramatic act is *malum in se*, when it consists of support for violence or violation of human rights, that fact swamps the expressive character of the act and becomes the only appropriate description. In the case of the Birmingham campaign, however, this is not the circumstance, and it would be as misleading to describe the demonstration as an unauthorized parade as it would to describe it as a pleasant stroll down the street.

130. Plato, *Republic* 514a–18b. For a useful discussion of the myth of the Cave, see Robert Fogelin, "Three Platonic Analogies," 80 *Philosophical Review* 371 (1971).

131. King, *supra* note 11, at 88.

King's Biblical Allusions

The literary prototype of King's *Letter* is immediately apparent: the letter is modeled after the epistles of Paul. Consider, for example, King's closing salutation: "I hope this letter finds you strong in the faith. I also hope that circumstances will soon make it possible for me to meet each of you, not as an integrationist or a civil-rights leader but as a fellow clergyman and a Christian brother."[132] The contemporary references apart, the language resonates with Paul's various salutations (perhaps especially with Ephesians, composed when Paul like King was a prisoner). King confirms this reading when he writes, "[J]ust as the Apostle Paul left his little village of Tarsus and carried the gospel of Jesus Christ to the far corners of the Greco-Roman world, so am I compelled to carry the gospel of freedom beyond my own home town. Like Paul, I must constantly respond to the Macedonian call for aid."[133] The reference is to the Book of Acts. "And a vision appeared to Paul in the night: a man of Macedonia was standing beseeching him and saying, Come over to Macedonia, and help us."[134] As we shall see, it is highly significant that King likens himself to Paul of the Book of Acts, for this book is the portion of the Bible closest in its utopian and communitarian ecstasy to King's own basic thought: "We are caught in an inescapable network of mutuality, tied in a single garment of destiny. Whatever affects one directly, affects all indirectly."[135]

None of King's biblical guises—Paul, Amos, Jesus, or even Shadrach, Meshach, and Abednego—are accidental. But Paul's is the most evident, since his guise shapes the literary form of the *Letter*. Why does King assume the guise of Paul? The answer should be clear when we recollect his audience: eight white clergymen. For King, the fact that they were white and the fact that they were clergy combined irresistibly to suggest a parallel with Paul's evangelism, his efforts to weld the people of many nations into a City of God. Paul's epistles are directed to small, insular Christian communities amid larger unbelieving nations. The *Letter* is nothing short of a reminder to brethren in Christ that, black or white, they are, indeed, brethren in Christ, therefore bound together by a bond that knows no distinction of skin color.[136]

---

132. *Id.* at 100.

133. *Id.* at 78.

134. Acts 16:9. (I use the Revised Standard Version of the Bible except where noted.)

135. King, *supra* note 11, at 79.

136. King's rhetoric, however, did not sway Episcopal Bishop C. C. Jones Carpenter, the instigator of the clerical attack on King that provoked the *Letter*. "Bishop

The *Letter* is more particular than that, however, as we realize when we turn to the biblical passages to which King refers. These are the Book of Acts, the Book of Amos, Paul's Epistle to the Galatians, the Sermon on the Mount, and the Book of Daniel. I take these up in turn (in an order chosen for ease of exposition, though it is not King's own order).

In structure, recall, King's *Letter* proceeds from a justification of the Project C demonstrations and of nonviolent civil disobedience more generally to an Old Testament denunciation of contemporary iniquity, particularly the iniquity of pusillanimous white moderates and the Southern churches. King moves along a course from communitarian creed to prophetic menace: "But the judgment of God is upon the church as never before."[137] All that is on the surface; but it is also in the depths, contained in the biblical allusions that King deploys, knowing that the clergy who read it would inevitably embed it in the biblical narratives it invokes.

Thus, the prophetic stance of King's *Letter* appears clearly in the contrast between the early Christians described in the most explicitly communitarian—even communistic—passages of Acts, the Book to which King points us in his evocation of Paul's call from the Macedonians, and the corrupted Israelites whose religious offerings God angrily rejects in the denunciations of Amos to which King later alludes. Thus the Book of Acts: "And all who believed were together and had all things in common; and they sold their possessions and goods and distributed them to all, as any had need."[138] "Now the company of those who believed were of one heart and soul, and no one said that any of the things which he possessed was his own, but they had everything in common."[139] "There was not a needy person among them, for as many as were possessors of lands or houses sold them, and brought the proceeds of what was sold and laid it at the apostles' feet; and distribution was made to each as any had need."[140] It is noteworthy, and

---

Carpenter sat down in his study with a copy of King's mammoth reply. He read the letter through to the end, then turned to his bishop coadjutor, George Murray, with a sigh of resignation. "This is what you get when you try to do something," he said. "You get it from both sides. George, you just have to live with that." Carpenter felt abused and misunderstood for his efforts to act as a progressive force in race relations. The clash of emotion turned him, like his great-grandfather, into a more strident Confederate." Branch, *supra* note 20, at 745.

137. King, *supra* note 11, at 96.
138. Acts 2:44–45.
139. Acts 4:32.
140. Acts 4:34–35.

scarcely coincidental, that Marx remembered these passages when, in his most utopian writing, he attributed to the future communist society the principle "from each according to his ability, to each according to his needs!"[141] For these passages from Acts have inspired utopian communists for over a thousand years.[142] Moreover, they inspired the Social Gospel theologian Walter Rauschenbusch to draw parallels between the Bible and Marxism, in a book that impressed King deeply in his seminary days.[143]

This is the City of God as it should be. Compare this with King's reference to the Book of Amos, one of the Bible's most vituperative denunciations of the actual community's unrighteousness. The line he quotes from Amos is this: "Let justice roll down like waters and righteousness like an ever-flowing stream."[144] Amos' line appears in the context of a ghastly denunciation of a corrupted Israel:

Therefore because you trample upon the poor and take from him exactions of wheat, you have built houses of hewn stone, but you shall not dwell in them; you have planted pleasant vineyards, but you shall not drink their wine. For I know how many are your transgressions, and how great are your sins—you who afflict the righteous, who take a bribe, and turn aside the needy in the gate.[145]

The applicability of these charges to the segregated South need scarcely be remarked ("turning aside the needy in the gate" may well stand as a literal description of Bull Connor's action in arresting King and his fellow demonstrators as they marched to downtown Birmingham). And because of these sins, religious observances will avail the unrighteous not at all:

I hate, I despise your feasts, and I take no delight in your solemn assemblies. Even though you offer me your burnt offerings and cereal offerings, I will not accept them, and the peace offerings of your fatted beasts I will not look upon. Take away from me the noise of your songs; to the melody of your harps I will not listen.

141. Karl Marx, *Critique of the Gotha Programme* 10 (C. Dutt ed. 1938).
142. *See* Norman Cohn, *The Pursuit of the Millennium* 194, 197 (rev. ed. 1970).
143. *See* Branch, *supra* note 20, at 73.
144. King, *supra* note 11, at 92.
145. Amos 5:11–12.

But let justice roll down like waters, and righteousness like an ever-flowing stream.[146]

The line King quotes thus appears in a passage that would convey a stern, even terrifying, reminder to the clergymen to whom King's letter is addressed.

As I noted earlier, King likens himself (for the second time in the *Letter*) to Paul immediately following his reference to Amos in the extremism passage. This reference too directs us to a biblical passage fraught with significance, for it bears with startling directness on King's confrontation with the courts. The line King quotes, "I bear in my body the marks of the Lord Jesus,"[147] appears at the end of the Epistle to the Galatians, the most fervid of all New Testament declarations that love and community stand above the law. Paul could not be more blunt: "Christ redeemed us from the curse of the law. . . ."[148] And again, "Now before faith came, we were confined under the law, kept under restraint until faith should be revealed. So that the law was our custodian until Christ came, that we might be justified by faith. But now that faith has come, we are no longer under a custodian. . . . "[149] Paul evokes the mystical, translegal, character of egalitarian community in language that resonates with King's aspirations for the redeemed American polity: "There is neither Jew nor Greek, there is neither slave nor free, there is neither male nor female; for you are all one in Christ Jesus."[150] (Compare this with the finale of the "I have a dream" speech: "all of God's children—black men and white men, Jews and Gentiles, Protestants and Catholics—will be able to join hands. . . . "[151]) "For the whole law is fulfilled in one word, 'You shall love your neighbor as yourself.'"[152] Community and brotherhood in faith trump fidelity to established law. Indeed, the Book of Acts, which we have seen forms one of King's referential reservoirs, itself contains an explicit statement

---

146. Amos 5:21–24 (emphasis added). The line was evidently dear to King, for he repeated it in the "I have a dream" speech in the March on Washington a few months later; moreover, King had used it in the first political speech of his career, the address to the mass meeting called after the arrest of Rosa Parks for refusing to move to the back of the bus in Montgomery that propelled him to leadership of the Montgomery bus boycott. Branch, *supra* note 20, at 141.

147. King, *supra* note 11, at 92 (quoting Galatians 6:17).

148. Galatians 3:13.

149. Galatians 3:23–25.

150. Galatians 3:28.

151. *Quoted in* Garrow, *supra* note 18, at 284.

152. Galatians 5:14. See Leviticus 19:18, which places "You shall love your neighbor as yourself" as but one of the Mosaic commandments—though Hillel would later enunciate the Golden Rule as the entire teaching of the Torah.

of the same antinomian principle: "We must obey God rather than men."[153]

This carries us quite naturally to King's reference to Jesus. The "Love your enemies" verse that King quotes in the extremism passage appears, of course, in the Sermon on the Mount.[154] Significantly, it is the continuation of this verse: "You have heard that it was said, 'You shall love your neighbor and hate your enemy.' But I say to you, *Love your enemies and pray for those who persecute you.*"[155] Christ's allusion here is to Leviticus 19:18, "You shall not take vengeance or bear any grudge against the sons of your own people, but you shall love your neighbor as yourself: I am the Lord." He interprets the Levitican injunction to love your neighbor as a negative pregnant: an implicit restriction of the injunction to those who are like oneself; the Sermon on the Mount radicalizes the message of love by extending it to those unlike oneself. Small wonder that King would invoke this biblical passage, since extending the injunction of love from one's own people to all people is precisely the universalist and cosmopolitan theme of King's *Letter.*[156]

A more important point is this. We recall that in the Epistle to the Galatians, to which King alludes shortly after his reference to Jesus, Paul takes this passage from the Sermon on the Mount to reject the Mosaic law. ("Christ redeemed us from the curse of the law. . . . For the whole law is fulfilled in one word, 'You shall love your neighbor as yourself.'"[157]) Yet this is not how Christ himself characterized the Sermon's import. On the contrary, Christ cautions, "Think not that I have come to abolish the law and the prophets; I have come not to abolish them but to fulfil them. For truly, I say to you, till heaven and earth pass away, not an iota, not a dot, will pass from the law until all is accomplished."[158]

Now it is possible to reconcile Paul's and Christ's characterizations of what Christ has done to the law when he proclaims "Love your neighbor as yourself." Christ has proclaimed, "I am not come to abolish

---

153. Acts 5:29. Cover refers to this principle as "a religious rule of recognition," functionally equivalent and therefore directly contradictory to the supremacy clause of article VI, § 2 of the Constitution. Cover, *supra* note 12, at 30.

154. Matthew 5:44.

155. Matthew 5:43–44 (emphasis added).

156. It is worth pointing out that the traditional Jewish understanding of *Leviticus* 19:18 is not "Love your neighbor and hate your enemy" but rather is fully as universalist and cosmopolitan as Christ's own message. *See* Jacob Hertz, *The Pentateuch and Haftorahs* 501 nn.563–64 (2d ed. 1981); *see also* Abraham Cohen, *Everyman's Talmud* 212–16 (1949). This is one of the theological points that divides Jews from Christians.

157. Galatians 3:13, 5:14.

158. Matthew 5:20.

[the law] but to fulfill," and Paul satisfies the letter of this warning when he writes, "For the whole law is fulfilled in one word, You shall love your neighbor as yourself." Yet that is surely not what Christ preached in the Sermon, where "You shall love your neighbor as yourself" appears as but one of a dozen or more revaluations of the Mosaic law, occupying no privileged position. Paul's is a reinterpretation of Christ's own word, transforming the Sermon on the Mount into an antinomian religion of love.

There is, however, another way to reconcile the attitudes toward law expressed in these two biblical passages (if not their religious substance). Paul understands the Sermon on the Mount to be Christ's radicalization, or purposive revaluation, of the Mosaic law—a radicalization that amounts to its rejection. Christ demands the fulfillment of the law's underlying purpose, which indeed annihilates it as (mis)interpreted by the "scribes and Pharisees."[159] On this reading, Paul's antinomian dicta merely make explicit what was indeed implicit in the Sermon: that in the fulfillment of the law's spirit lies the destruction of its received juristic interpretation. And King, by juxtaposing the Sermon with Paul's Epistle to the Galatians, invites his readers to interpret the Sermon in just this way: as an authoritative unofficial reading of the law that in effect overthrows the official reading. As we shall see, King's own analysis of legality in the Letter takes just such a tack.

Notwithstanding this interpretive finesse, there is no denying that Paul's "Christ has redeemed us from the curse of the law" and the Sermon on the Mount's "Do not think that I have come to abolish the Law" are quite different in tenor and import—the latter assuming the mantle of legality, the former proclaiming what Kierkegaard might have deemed a "teleological suspension of the legal."[160] It will form part of my argument that King's Letter itself vacillates between these two stances, with important consequences.

That King evidently saw no inconsistency between the Sermon on the Mount and the Epistle to the Galatians is important, for Paul's equation of the law's end with the law's fulfillment readily transposes into a justification of King's civil rights activity: if there is any obvious legal theme to the Letter, it is that the end of the segregationist legal

---

159. Id.
160. Kierkegaard actually spoke of the teleological suspension of the ethical, not the legal. Søren Kierkegaard, Fear and Trembling 64–77 (Lowrie trans. 1954). He used the term to describe Abraham's murderous attempt to sacrifice Isaac, which could be justified teleologically by reference to the miraculous commandment of God, though viewed from the sphere of the ethical it could never be regarded as anything but a transgression.

order is the fulfillment, the purposive revaluation, of the constitutional promise of equal protection. (I return to this point below.) King's is an authoritative unofficial reading of the Constitution that overthrows Southern officials' readings.

The final biblical reference I shall discuss in the *Letter* appears when King likens the demonstrators' civil disobedience to "the refusal of Shadrach, Meshach, and Abednego to obey the laws of Nebuchadnezzar, on the ground that a higher moral law was at stake."[161] The reference, to Daniel 3:8–30, is straightforward and transparent, but it is worth noting one peculiarity in the story. After Shadrach, Meshach, and Abednego were thrown into the fiery furnace for disobeying Nebuchadnezzar's command in order to remain faithful to their God, the Book of Daniel relates,

> And these three men, Shadrach, Meshach, and Abednego, fell down bound into the midst of the burning fiery furnace. Then Nebuchadnezzar the king was astonished, and rose up in haste, and spake, and said unto his counselors, Did we not cast three men bound into the midst of the fire? They answered and said unto the king, True, O king. He answered and said, Lo, I see four men loose, walking in the midst of the fire, and they have no hurt; and the form of the fourth is like the Son of God.[162]

This passage is often taken by Christians to prefigure the New Testament, and thus the Christian *Aufhebung* (to use Hegel's term meaning at once cancellation and preservation) of the Old Testament and the Mosaic law. As in the other allusions we have examined, King evokes a biblical context that suggests the finitude and inadequacy of law before the experience of an egalitarian, loving community.

Let me summarize my reading of King's biblical allusions. The key points are these.

1. King underscores his own communitarianism by invoking the God-intoxicated, overtly communistic, egalitarian Christian community of the Book of Acts.

2. King places the cosmopolitan and universalist message of the civil rights movement side-by-side with cosmopolitan and universalist passages of the Bible such as, "There is neither Jew nor Greek, there is

---

161. King, *supra* note 11, at 86–87.

162. Daniel 3:23–25 (King James Version). The Hebrew *bar Elohim* is coupled with a verb form implying the indefinite article: "*a* Son of God"—which weakens the New Testament prefiguration that the King James Bible question-beggingly builds into its translation. (Thanks to Steve Winter for the translation.)

neither slave nor free, there is neither male nor female; for you are all one in Christ Jesus,"[163] and the Sermon on the Mount.

3. King echoes his denunciation of the existing church by alluding to Amos' denunciations of Israel for empty, impious observances of a law that has become merely formal.

4. Crucially, King singles out passages in which the formal legality of Israel is either fulfilled—*aufgehoben*, to use Hegel's word once again—by the Christian law of love or, in the important alternative, annihilated by it.[164] That is, King points ambiguously in the incompatible directions of a higher law of love or a divine antinomianism. And thus the earlier themes of communitarianism, cosmopolitanism, and denunciation waffle dangerously between natural law legalism—a theme capable of purely secular development—and mystical anarchism, a doctrine of love grounded in the revelation of divinity. Insofar as King identifies himself more closely with Paul than with Jesus, he seems to tilt a bit more toward the latter alternative.

5. This is in no way to deny that King speaks often and reverently of the law: the natural law and legalist strain in the *Letter* is totally authentic. Yet legalism, too, becomes a communitarian and universalist tool in King's hands. For it is clear that King advocates what Levinson calls the protestant mode of legal interpretation, in which the individual, or at any rate the nonhierarchical community, retains ultimate interpretive authority. As we have seen, the *Walker* Court has built its entire argument around the necessity of the catholic approach, in which the Court–Church—the *curia*—is the sole repository of interpretive authority. Levinson's eloquent argument for the coincidence of religious and constitutional hermeneutics is nowhere more telling than in the contrast between *Walker* and King's *Letter*. The contrast is simply Catholicism and Protestantism revisited. Indeed, in King's *Letter* protestant interpretation of the Constitution quite simply coincides with Protestantism itself, King's own religious commitment. That makes two of King's other self-identifications in the extremism passage fall immediately into place: "Was not Martin Luther an extremist: 'Here I stand; I cannot do otherwise, so help me God.' And John Bunyan: 'I will stay in jail to the end of my days before I make a butchery of my con-

---

163. Galatians 3:28.

164. In this respect, the New Testament allusions are fully consistent with Amos' denunciation of Israel's empty formalities and the King James Bible's version of Daniel 3:25 as a prefiguration of the New Testament. In all of them, Christians are likely to identify the *Aufhebung* of formal legality by love with the *Aufhebung* of the Old Testament by the New.

science.'"[165] Luther's "stand," of course, inaugurated the Protestant Reformation, and Bunyan was jailed for his Puritan preaching.[166]

6. Finally, it is clear that King's chain of religious self-identifications, his transposition of the Birmingham events into a biblical key, offers a political narrative that refigures and reconstitutes the legal meaning of those events. In the sense explicated in my opening discussion, King's biblicizing of the Birmingham campaign in the *Letter* is legal argumentation in the full and unqualified sense.

King's Natural Law Theory

The ambivalence I have described between King's natural law legalism and what I have called his mystical anarchism pervades the argumentative or conceptual portion of the *Letter* just as it does the chain of biblical self-identifications. King's argument arises, recall, as an attempt to explain why he is willing to disobey a court order while continuing to urge white obedience to the Supreme Court's desegregation orders: "[T]here are two types of law: just and unjust. . . . One has not only a legal but a moral responsibility to obey just laws. Conversely, one has a moral responsibility to disobey unjust laws. I would agree with St. Augustine that 'an unjust law is no law at all.' "[167] King then offers what I take to be two different accounts of the distinction between just and unjust laws. The first is a theological and mystical account:

A just law is a man-made code that squares with the moral law or the law of God. An unjust law is a code that is out of harmony with the moral law. To put it in the terms of St. Thomas Aquinas: An unjust law is a human law that is not rooted in eternal law and natural law. Any law that uplifts human personality is just. Any law that degrades human personality is unjust. All segregation statutes are unjust because segregation distorts the soul and damages the personality. It gives the segregator a false sense of

---

165. King, *supra* note 11, at 92. Note that this quotation is the continuation of the extremism passage we have been examining.

166. However, Luther's own stance toward secular authority is considerably more quiescent than King's. *See* Martin Luther, *Temporal Authority: To What Extent It Should Be Obeyed*, in *Luther: Selected Political Writings* 51 (J. M. Porter ed. 1974). Moreover, I find it disturbing that King should liken himself to a tormented, dismal, and half-mad fanatic such as Bunyan. For a delightfully opinionated but illuminating discussion, see Macaulay's article on Bunyan. 4 *Encyclopaedia Britannica* 389 (14th ed. 1937). For a more sympathetic account, see Christopher Hill, *A Tinker and a Poor Man: John Bunyan and His Church 1628–1688* (1989).

167. King, *supra* note 11, at 84.

superiority and the segregated a false sense of inferiority. Segregation, to use the terminology of the Jewish philosopher Martin Buber, substitutes an "I-it" relationship for an "I-thou" relationship
and ends up relegating persons to the status of things. Hence segregation is not only politically, economically and sociologically unsound, it is morally wrong and sinful. Paul Tillich has said that sin
is separation. Is not segregation an existential expression of man's
tragic separation, his awful estrangement, his terrible sinfulness?
Thus it is that I can urge men to obey the 1954 decision of the
Supreme Court, for it is morally right; and I can urge them to
disobey segregation ordinances, for they are morally wrong.[168]

The second is a secular and essentially liberal argument based on considerations of fairness:

An unjust law is a code that a numerical or power majority group
compels a minority group to obey but does not make binding on
itself. This is *difference* made legal. By the same token, a just law is a
code that a majority compels a minority to follow and that it is
willing to follow itself. This is *sameness* made legal.

Let me give another explanation. A law is unjust if it is inflicted
on a minority that, as a result of being denied the right to vote,
had no part in enacting or devising the law. . . . Can any law enacted under such circumstances be considered democratically
structured?

Sometimes a law is just on its face and unjust in its application.
For instance, I have been arrested on a charge of parading without
a permit. Now, there is nothing wrong in having an ordinance
which requires a permit for a parade. But such an ordinance becomes unjust when it is used to maintain segregation and to deny
citizens the First Amendment privilege of peaceful assembly and
protest.[169]

I take it that the difference between these two descriptions of natural
law theory is readily apparent even on the surface. The first implicitly
presumes that "eternal law and natural law" are fulfilled by the end of
separation between human beings, the effacement of boundary and
even of the very possibility of boundary signified by Buber's "basic
word I-thou." For Buber, indeed, it understates matters even to say that
"I-thou" entails a fusion of I and thou, for the very thought of two

---

168. *Id.* at 85.
169. *Id.* at 85–86.

distinct entities that fuse belongs itself to the sphere of I-it. Here King's thought is close to Paul's insistence in Galatians that divine law achieves its fulfillment in the single injunction to love, and that "you are all one in Christ Jesus." This is communitarianism as mystical union. By contrast, the second characterization of natural law as "sameness made legal" emphasizes values of process, participation, and democratic equality. In my view it is best understood in terms of the fair play argument of Hart and Rawls, according to which we are obligated to obey the law only insofar as the law is a cooperative enterprise requiring and receiving widespread compliance to achieve its beneficial aims.[170] Insofar as the law is unfair ("difference made legal"), it cannot be understood as such a generally beneficial cooperative scheme, and thus it loses its obligatory character.

To lay my cards on the table, I believe that this argument is largely right.[171] But make no mistake: it is an argument wholly secular in character. It rests on a premise of human political equality that presumes no theological revelation of human unity in Christ (or out of Christ, for that matter). This premise arises from a nonbiblical political narrative of the American Constitution; indeed, we shall see that King himself provides such a narrative in the extremism passage when he likens himself to Jefferson and Lincoln.

The fair play argument, moreover, is grounded in the characteristically liberal political relationship of mutual respect, not in the mystical and loving communitarianism implicit in King's invocation of Buber and Tillich.[172] Obviously, the two arguments parallel each other in important respects: both ground legal obligation in equality, both attack the monstrous premise of white superiority underlying racial segregation, and both vindicate disobedience to segregation-preserving laws as well as obedience to the Court's *Brown* decision. But the difference between love and respect as defining relationships for the egalitarian community decisively distinguishes the two arguments. The purpose of any community-defining relationship is to establish social

---

170. John Rawls, "Legal Obligation and the Duty of Fair Play," in *Law and Philosophy* 3, 9–10 (Sidney Hook ed. 1964); H. L. A. Hart, "Are There Any Natural Rights?," 64 *Philosophical Review* 175, 185 (1955).

171. *See* Luban, *supra* note 88, at 32–49; Luban, "Freedom and Constraint in Legal Ethics: Some Mid-Course Corrections to *Lawyers and Justice*," 49 *Maryland Law Review* 424, 453–62 (1990) (wherein I elaborate a solidarity-based theory of legal obligation understood as fair play, derived from King's *Letter*).

172. On the distinction between respect and love, see Luban, "The Quality of Justice," 66 *Denver University Law Review* 381, 413–16 (1989).

trust, but love and respect do so in quite different ways.[173] For the primary concern of love is to abolish the distance between people, while that of respect is to maintain it.

Love, moreover, is an essentially antinomian relationship: as Roberto Unger argues, love rejects the very tincture of formality, and a political order founded on love rejects ex ante limitations on the content of loving action.[174] Therein lies the promise, but also the danger, of founding a political order on love or mystical union. The promise is of political relationships of unimaginable richness. The danger is that, historically, love-based utopias—no matter how benign their origins— have so often been appropriated by totalitarian prophet-leaders capable of terrifying acts of violence, since there are no limitations on the content of ostensibly loving action. Consider the historical precursors of King's own Baptist Church, the Muenster Anabaptists of the sixteenth century:

> On the morning of 27 February [1534] armed bands, urged on by Matthys in prophetic frenzy, rushed through the streets calling: "Get out, you godless ones, and never come back, you enemies of the Father!" In bitter cold, in the midst of a wild snowstorm, multitudes of the "godless" were driven from the town by Anabaptists who rained blows upon them and laughed at their afflictions. These people included old people and invalids, small children and pregnant women and women who had just given birth. . . . By the morning of 3 March there were no "misbelievers" left in Muenster; the town was inhabited solely by the Children of God. *These people, who addressed one another as "Brother" and "Sister,"* believed that they would be able to live without sin, in a community bound together by love alone.[175]

Now it is obvious that Martin Luther King, one of the great apostles of nonviolence, had nothing in common with the Anabaptists or any of the other violent millennial movements. And, to repeat my basic point, King's antinomian communitarianism forms only one strand of the *Letter;* it is combined with a natural law legalism that fully honors the liberal amenities. I intend my invocation of the Anabaptists merely to

---

173. On trust as a defining relationship in moral and political theory, see the discussion in chapter 1, together with the works cited in notes 90 and 91 of chapter 1.

174. Roberto Mangabeira Unger, *Law in Modern Society* 206–9 (1976).

175. Cohn, *supra* note 142, at 262–63 (emphasis added). Many millennial movements founded themselves on the communistic passages of the Book of Acts; this included the Anabaptists. *Id.* at 259.

illustrate the instability and danger of founding political relationships on love rather than respect. I mean in this way to underscore the distinction between love-based and respect-based political orders (and thus the tension between King's religious and secular arguments).[176]

In short, the two versions of King's natural law argument in the *Letter* correspond to the ambiguity between viewing the Christian narrative as a perfection of the law and as the mystical *Aufhebung* of it implicit in King's earlier juxtaposition of the Sermon on the Mount with Galatians.

King's American Allusions

This ambiguity emerges as well in the difference between King's biblical and secular political narratives. Just as King's biblical allusions in the extremism passage point—ambiguously, to be sure—in the direction of antinomian mysticism, his secular allusions point toward liberal natural law egalitarianism. The secular argument, recall, derives egalitarianism from the notion of fairness incipient in natural law. This notion entails a particular political narrative of American constitutionalism, one that tells the story of constitutional progress as the drive toward emancipation and equality.

Thus we find, immediately after King likens himself to Jesus, Amos, Paul, Luther, and Bunyan in the extremism passage, the invocation of Lincoln and Jefferson: "Was not Martin Luther an extremist. . . . And John Bunyan. . . . And Abraham Lincoln: 'This nation cannot survive half slave and half free.' And Thomas Jefferson: 'We hold these truths to be self-evident, that all men are created equal.'"[177]

Jefferson and Lincoln are well coupled. After all, it was Lincoln who, in the Gettysburg Address, claimed that the true meaning of America lay in Jefferson's Declaration of Independence rather than in the Constitution: he characterized America as "a new nation . . . dedicated to the proposition that all men are created equal." Dulled by long familiarity, we are inclined to read this sentence without giving it a

---

176. It is in part for this reason that I take a very dim view of the critique of rights advocated by some contemporary writers (Unger, Tushnet, Gabel); the vocabulary of rights expresses the discourse of mutual respect, and to abandon the centrality of mutual respect is to move in an unacceptable direction: either toward disrespect (domination and subservience) or toward a communitarianism of love about which we may rightly be skeptical. *See* Patricia Williams, "Alchemical Notes: Reconstructing Ideals from Deconstructed Rights," 22 *Harvard Civil Rights–Civil Liberties Law Review* 401 (1987) (also expressing skepticism about the critique of rights). Recall our previous discussion of the critique of rights in chapter 1 *supra* at 76–78.

177. King, *supra* note 11, at 92.

second thought (or even a first thought), and thus without realizing that it is a powerfully heretical—because deconstitutionalized—interpretation of the meaning of American history.[178] King's political narrative draws a straight line from Jefferson and Lincoln, through the Civil War amendments that finally constitutionalized this interpretation, to the civil rights movement. His narrative indicates that egalitarianism is the imminent truth of America.

He also, if I read him aright, alludes in the most powerful passage of the *Letter* to another link in this political narrative, the Court's opinion in *Brown*. King bitterly meditates on his experience as a black parent,

> when you suddenly find your tongue twisted and your speech stammering as you seek to explain to your six-year-old daughter why she can't go to the public amusement park that has just been advertised on television, and see tears welling up in her eyes when she is told that Funtown is closed to colored children, and see ominous clouds of inferiority beginning to form in her little mental sky, and see her beginning to distort her personality by developing an unconscious bitterness toward white people. . . .[179]

Surely King is here alluding to Kenneth Clark's experiments on self-perceptions of inferiority among African-American children, which formed the sociological linchpin of the *Brown* opinion. Rhetorically, the allusion is strikingly well-suited to the white clergymen to whom the *Letter* was addressed; just as his biblical allusions attempted to preach Christian community to the clergymen, the allusion to *Brown* attempts to remind white Americans of their unkept promise of equality. As part of a political narrative, *Brown* is another point on the line from Jefferson through Lincoln and the Fourteenth Amendment to the civil rights movement—a narrative line that aims to recall the promise of egalitarian constitutionalism incipient in *Brown* as a continuation of Lincoln's and Jefferson's political vision.

To summarize my reading so far, I have been tracing two versions of communitarianism in King's *Letter:* a religious and antinomian communitarianism based on love, and a liberal natural law egalitarianism aiming at communities based on respect. King's biblical narratives, particularly his self-identification with Paul, point ambiguously toward the former, whereas his American political narrative clearly points in the latter direction.

---

178. *See* Levinson, *supra* note 12, at 140; Garry Wills, *Inventing America: Jefferson's Declaration of Independence* xiv–xxiv (1978).

179. King, *supra* note 11, at 81.

King's Socratic Allusion

King's *Letter* incorporates one final self-identification. At two points King likens his own actions in Birmingham and those of his fellow demonstrators to those of Socrates, who "felt that it was necessary to create a tension in the mind so that individuals could rise from the bondage of myths and half-truths to the unfettered realm of creative analysis and objective appraisal."[180] King goes on to analogize the Birmingham demonstrators to "nonviolent gadflies," Socrates's self-description in the *Apology*.[181] Later he alludes again to the condemnation of Socrates: "Isn't [condemning the Birmingham demonstrators for provoking violence] like condemning Socrates because his unswerving commitment to truth and his philosophical inquiries precipitated the act by the misguided populace in which they made him drink hemlock?"[182] Though I shall later have occasion to doubt the appropriateness of the Socratic analogy, there is indeed an uncanny parallel between the moral and legal problem posed by King's arrest and a perplexing dilemma posed by Plato's *Apology* and *Crito*.

The dilemma is easily seen. In the *Apology* Socrates boasts that he has always been unwilling to comply with unjust official orders, including court orders. Thus, when the Thirty Tyrants had ordered him to arrest Leon the Salaminian unjustly, so as "to implicate as many in their crimes as they could," Socrates merely went home; he reminds his jurors that he would have died for his disobedience had the government not fallen soon after.[183] And earlier in his defense Socrates provokes his jurors by telling them that if they were to order him, on pain of death, to abandon his philosophical activities, he would reply, "Men of Athens, I respect and love you, but I shall obey the god rather than you, and while I live and am able to continue, I shall never give up philosophy."[184]

The *Apology* is thus the protean text of conscientious disobedience, and King's appropriation of the figure of Socrates seems completely clear. In the *Crito*, however, the convicted Socrates refuses to flee his impending execution, offering a series of arguments that he is obligated to obey the laws, including his own unjust death sentence. These arguments, based on consent or the "social contract," on gratitude, on the

---

180. *Id.* at 81; *see also id.* at 87. As we have seen, the imagery of removing fetters binding us to myths and half-truths comes from Plato's *Republic*.
181. *See* Plato, *Apology* 30e.
182. King, *supra* note 11, at 88–89.
183. Plato, *supra* note 181, at 32c-e.
184. *Id.* at 39d.

citizen's tutelage under government, and on the dire consequences were everyone to disobey, have shaped all subsequent philosophical discussions of the subject.[185] The facial contradiction with the *Apology* could scarcely be more striking, and it has puzzled generations of commentators. If it is wrong to disobey even unjust laws and court orders, why did Socrates disobey the Thirty Tyrants? How could he boast that he would continue to practice philosophy in the face of a court order to desist? On the other hand, if it is right to disobey an unjust edict, why should Socrates have complied with his death sentence?

Recently, Richard Kraut has offered a remarkable interpretation of the *Crito* aiming to show that, far from being an encomium to absolute obedience and submission, it is actually a powerful argument on behalf of civil disobedience that is fully consistent with the *Apology*.[186] Kraut focuses on Socrates' careful phrasing of his arguments for obedience in the *Crito*. Rather than concluding categorically that one must obey the laws, Socrates three times phrases the injunction in the alternative: one must either persuade the state about the requirements of justice or else obey.[187] Now this interpretation may suggest that Socrates is offering the unhelpful thought that the citizen may try to get a law changed or repealed, but if he fails he must obey. Since in practice one will seldom be able to get a law repealed, this suggestion amounts precisely to the encomium to absolute obedience.

Kraut responds that the forum Socrates had in mind for persuasion is not the legislature but the court.[188] And persuasion is not an attempt to get the law changed *before* obeying it, but an attempt to argue against a criminal conviction *after* disobeying it. That is, Socrates's position amounts to permitting one to disobey an unjust law provided one is subsequently willing to offer a defense in court and accept the punishment if the jury rejects that defense.

Kraut's reading of the *Crito* makes a lot of the text fall into place and ingeniously resolves the facial contradiction between the *Apology* and the *Crito*. However, there is one situation that Kraut's reading fails to resolve. What if a court, unpersuaded by the disobedient citizen, does not punish him for disobedience but merely reiterates the order to obey? That, after all, is the hypothetical situation Socrates himself raises

---

185. They are, however, unsound, and their unsoundness has been remarked often in the history of philosophy. *See* Luban, *supra* note 88, at 36–37.

186. Richard Kraut, *Socrates and the State* 54–90 (1984). *But see id.* at 75–76 (concerning the difference between Socratic conscientious disobedience and civil disobedience for expressive and political purposes).

187. Plato, *Crito* 51c–52d.

188. *See* Kraut, *supra* note 186, at 55–56.

when at the conclusion of his trial the jury orders him to abandon philosophy. He tells the jurors that he will disobey; but since he has failed to persuade, must he not obey?

The problem is this. Kraut seems to assume that disobedience will precede persuasion: you are hailed into court because you have disobeyed. Then you attempt to persuade, and if you fail you take your punishment. But when the court responds not with punishment but with another order, persuasion has failed *before* the choice between obedience and disobedience to the new order must be made. Now, surely, Socrates' persuade-or-obey conclusion leaves you no option but obedience; for it is plainly no answer to suggest disobeying the new court order, being hailed into court again, attempting once again to persuade, failing, receiving another court order, disobeying, and so on ad infinitum. That is simply a ruse for making an end run around the "obey" horn of the dilemma. No: if Socrates fails at persuasion and is subsequently ordered to abandon philosophy, Kraut's version of the persuade-or-obey doctrine requires obedience. Yet Socrates has told us he will disobey. And so the contradiction has not, after all, been resolved.

The basic dilemma between conscience and obligation reappears, that is, when a citizen is faced with an unjust court order (rather than an unjust punishment). It is this problem, in almost precisely this form, that the Birmingham events raise. One political narrative, then—the narrative of conscientious disobedience, from Socrates on—stands ready to offer placement to the argument between the *Walker* Court and King.

I do not mean to suggest that when he alluded to Socrates in the *Letter* King had anything in mind as specific as the textual inconsistency between the *Apology* and the *Crito*, to say nothing of classicists' disputations about it. Significantly, however, King invoked both dialogues in his Atlanta NAACP address, which (I noted earlier) amounts to a preliminary version of portions of the *Letter*. "Come if you will to Plato's *Dialogues*. Open the *Cr[it]o* or the *Apology*. See Socrates practicing civil disobedience."[189] In the *Letter*, King clearly *did* have the *Apology* itself in mind, and the dilemma between conscience and obedience is the explicit subject matter of the *Letter*'s argumentative portion. And we have seen King's own resolution of the dilemma. He offers an argument for the moral obligation to obey the law that is distinct from the standard arguments of the *Crito*; all of those arguments attempt to explain the obligation to obey the law as an obligation to the state, whereas the fair-

189. *Quoted in* Branch, *supra* note 20, at 599.

play argument offered by King explains it as an obligation to one's fellow citizens. It is a communitarian, rather than a statist, argument for obedience to just laws. And it yields the conclusion that this obligation exists only when the law in question reflects "sameness made legal" rather than "difference made legal"—only, that is, when the law is fair. Thus, King maintains the tradition of the *Apology* by abandoning the statism implicit in the *Crito*.

Where does the Socratic narrative of civil disobedience fit into the tension between mystical anarchism and natural law legalism I have been stressing? At first Socrates seems to belong in the second camp: natural law is closely tied to the rationalist ethical vision that appears in numerous Socratic dialogues, particularly the *Euthyphro* (and, ambiguously, the *Phaedo*, where the rationalism assumes distinctly mystical overtones). Moreover, Plato has long been identified as a principal source for the natural law tradition.

Nevertheless, it is noteworthy that neither in the *Apology* nor elsewhere does Socrates claim to be responding to a "higher law." Rather, he repeatedly says that he is responding to a divine call. Socrates tells us that the god at Delphi originally launched his philosophical career,[190] and he reveals to the Athenians that he is guided in all his endeavors by a divine voice, his famous *daimon,* that warns him whenever he is about to do anything wrong. Socrates' *daimon* is instantly recognizable as what later ages would call "the voice of conscience"; and it is important to realize that Socrates identifies conscience, and therefore conscientious disobedience, with fidelity to a supernatural being. Viewed as the prototypical conscientious disobedient, as King clearly views him, Socrates is much more the religious saint than the natural law adherent. And so King's Socratic self-identification falls more plausibly on the side of his mystical anarchism than on the side of his natural law legalism.

The Tension between Religion and Politics

So far my examination has stayed reasonably close to the actual language and range of allusion within *Walker* and King's *Letter.* In this section, I wish to venture further afield and explore the consequences this examination carries for social change as well as legal argument. I shall be borrowing again from Benjamin's "Theses," but also from a remarkably interesting essay on civil disobedience written by Arendt during the height of the Black Power, student, and antiwar move-

---

190. Plato, *supra* note 187, at 20c–21e.

ments, an essay that trenchantly addresses some of the issues I have raised.[191]

Arendt on the Self-Misunderstanding of Civil Disobedience

It should be clear from our foregoing examination that King's *Letter* contains a narrative complexity and richness wholly absent from the *Walker* opinion.[192] It also, I fear, contains a fundamental self-*mis*understanding with serious consequences. King's Socratic allusion may serve us as a point of entry to the discussion of this self-misunderstanding.

In her extraordinary essay on civil disobedience, Hannah Arendt points out the falseness of identifying politically motivated civil disobedience with the figure of Socrates (and of Thoreau as well).[193] As we have seen, Socrates opposes his conscience, which we might think of as an organ attuned to the supernatural, to the demands of the state. Conscientious civil disobedients are essentially solitary figures in communion with divinity; they are essentially unpolitical. Thus, the tension between King's mystical anarchism and his natural law legalism points to a tension between conscience and politics in his thought—a tension that disguises the political character of the movement by comprehending it through supernatural political narratives. Arendt writes,

> Here, as elsewhere, conscience is unpolitical. It is not primarily interested in the world where the wrong is committed or in the consequences that the wrong will have for the future course of the world. It does not say, with Jefferson, "I tremble *for my country* when I reflect that God is just; that His justice cannot sleep forever," because it trembles for the individual self and its integrity.[194]

The point, once made, is obvious: there is an important sense in which Socrates, like Paul and Amos and Shadrach and Luther and Bunyan, does not belong in the same political narrative as the SCLC. The defining relationship of Socrates' public stance, like that of the figures in the biblical narratives, was a relationship with a divine voice.[195] This rela-

---

191. Hannah Arendt, "Civil Disobedience," in *Crises of the Republic* 51–102 (1972).
192. Not to mention that the argument concerning obedience to the law is better.
193. Arendt, *supra* note 191, at 58–68.
194. *Id.* at 60–61 (footnote omitted) (quoting Thomas Jefferson, *Notes on the State of Virginia* Query XVIII (1781–85).
195. That is not to deny that King, too, was guided by a divine voice. Consider his recollections in King, *Stride toward Freedom: The Montgomery Story* 134–35 (1958): "It seemed as though I could hear the quiet assurance of an inner voice saying: 'Martin

tionship, to be sure, manifested itself in a politically significant action, but in the case of Socrates that was happenstance. That is in no way to deny the obvious, namely that religiously inspired people can be canny politicians and publicists. Paul and Luther were. But, unless we take Paul and Luther to be lying at the core of their being, their political acumen accrued to them (to speak scholastically) *per accidens;* it was their God-consciousness that defined their public stance *per essens.* And so the theological narratives contained in King's *Letter* may actually suppress or displace an explicitly political self-understanding of political action by substituting relationships with the divinity for political relationships.[196]

Now of course churches have always been among the most successful organs of political action, and a black political movement without black churches is virtually unthinkable; the church has always been the most powerful and significant of African-American institutions.[197] Moreover, among our permanent political images of the civil rights movement are those of demonstrators bowed in prayer as the police assault them or groups of enthusiasts singing in churches. We cannot imagine the movement without the hymn "We Shall Overcome," and that is another way of saying that we cannot imagine the movement garbed in secular clothing.

But it is equally important to realize that, whereas in King's religious narrative nonviolent civil disobedience was a matter of divine principle, others in the movement viewed it primarily as a tactic, to be used when it could be effective but discarded when it was not; and eventually, the civil rights movement as a whole abandoned it.

Luther, stand up for righteousness. Stand up for justice. Stand up for truth. And I will be with you, even until the end of the world.' . . . I heard the voice of Jesus saying still to fight on. He promised never to leave me, never to leave me alone. No never alone. No never alone. He promised never to leave me, never to leave me alone." I mean to say only that King's revelation does not constitute the public meaning of his actions nor those of the civil rights movement more generally.

196. The Situationist theorist Guy Debord perceptively writes, "Modern revolutionary expectations are not irrational continuations of the religious passion of millenarianism, as Norman Cohn thought he had demonstrated in *The Pursuit of the Millennium.* On the contrary, millenarianism, revolutionary class struggle speaking the language of religion for the last time, is already a modern revolutionary tendency which as yet lacks the consciousness that it is historical. The millenarians had to lose because they could not recognize the revolution as their own operation." Guy Debord, *The Society of the Spectacle* § 138 (unauthorized ed. 1970). It is ironic that Debord, writing only five years after the Birmingham campaign, evidently believed that revolution spoke the language of religion for the last time in the sixteenth century.

197. *See* Aldon D. Morris, *The Origins of the Civil Rights Movement* 4–12 (1984). *See generally* Branch, *supra* note 20.

Discouragingly, perhaps, many of the successes we ascribe to the civil rights movement emerged from other tactics and other circumstances, not the least of which were urban rioting and the rise of Black Power. After the Birmingham settlement, recall, Klan bombings provoked African-American riots, and these as much as Project C were an integral part of the chain of events leading the reluctant Kennedy to introduce civil rights legislation.

My point is not to suggest that violence is "better" or "more effective" than nonviolence (whatever that might mean); rather, it is to suggest that the religious strands of King's narrative make historical sense of only a fragment of the actual African-American movement, and to that extent they fail as a political narrative.

Arendt points to another difficulty with attempting to embed a political movement in a narrative framework based on individual relationships with the supernatural:

No doubt even this kind of conscientious objection can become politically significant when a number of consciences happen to coincide, and the conscientious objectors decide to enter the market place and make their voices heard in public. But then we are no longer dealing with individuals, or with a phenomenon whose criteria can be derived from Socrates or Thoreau. . . . In the market place, the fate of conscience is not much different from the fate of the philosopher's truth: it becomes an opinion, indistinguishable from other opinions.[198]

Religious truth "in the market place"—less metaphorically, in a secular democracy containing several powerful religious denominations— becomes in the long run politically indistinguishable from dogmatic factionalism. It cannot inspire those who do not share the faith and may instead provoke or antagonize them. At the limit, religious factionalism threatens to deteriorate into the kind of convulsive doctrinal strife that drenched Europe in blood for centuries (and has drenched the Middle East in blood for over a decade)—precisely the kind of doctrinal strife that led Hobbes to urge the absolute supremacy of legal authority that survives in the *Walker* opinion.

Indeed, perhaps the only political narrative that might yield a sympathetic reading of *Walker* is one that begins with the violent messianic movements of the Middle Ages, proceeds to religious conflicts such as

---

198. Arendt, *supra* note 191, at 67–68.

the Thirty Years' War and the English revolution,[199] and concludes by reading the American Constitution primarily as a device to avoid such God-intoxicated bloodletting by insisting on the absolute supremacy of secularizing officials.[200] In this way, the Christian particularism of King's *Letter* ultimately reflects a deep weakness in the biblical narratives as a mode of organizing a universalist political movement. Religion eventually divides a community, whereas egalitarian liberalism aims to unite it.

Lest these suggestions create a misunderstanding, let me emphasize that I have chosen to analyze King's *Letter* not because of its narrative weaknesses but because of its overwhelming strength. More importantly, I have been concerned throughout this essay to stress that the *non*biblical strand of the *Letter* promotes a remarkably attractive— let me go so far as to say true—political and legal theory. It is my view that King has pointed the way to a truly liberal communitarianism (a political possibility that philosophers have often neglected or denied[201]); that his fair-play version of natural law resolves the Platonic problem of political obligation; and that his narrative of American political history from Jefferson to Lincoln to *Brown* to Project C displays the Fourteenth Amendment to our Constitution in what may well be the best light it can truthfully sustain.[202] These are virtues for which we may well be moved to abandon the antinomianism of the Epistle to the Galatians and the political narrative of supernaturally inspired conscientious disobedience from Socrates through Bunyan.

"The Myth Concerning Time"

Having argued that political action cannot be understood through assimilation to religious narratives, I shall now court paradox by insisting that an adequate conception of political action must recognize its essentially theological character. Theological, but not religious: what does

---

199. On the role of religious factionalism in the English Revolution, see generally Christopher Hill, *The World Turned Upside Down: Radical Ideas during the English Revolution* (1972); Thomas Hobbes, *Leviathan* (C. Macpherson ed. 1968) (1st ed. 1651); 5 David Hume, *The History of England* (1778); Michael Walzer, *The Revolution of the Saints: A Study in the Origins of Radical Politics* (1965).

200. *See, e.g.*, Thomas J. Curry, *The First Freedoms: Church and State in America to the Passage of the First Amendment* (1986); Levy, *supra* note 5.

201. *See, e.g.*, Alisdair MacIntyre, *After Virtue* (1981); Michael Sandel, *Liberalism and the Limits of Justice* (1982); Unger, *Knowledge and Politics* (1975); Unger, *supra* note 174.

202. I believe, moreover, that King's liberal communitarianism harmonizes with the three premises of American constitutionalism I identified in my discussion of *Walker*, namely the rule of law, popular sovereignty, and the publicity of law—precisely the premises that the Court found it necessary to finesse.

this mean? What I wish to suggest is that certain structures of religious experience and religious thought correspond with similar structures in political experience and thought. Perhaps it is more accurate to say that certain fundamental structures of experience and thought are capable of being articulated in either religious or political language, and the ready (mis)translation of politics into religious terms arises from this deep underlying similarity. Thus even when politics is translated back out of biblical and religious narratives—as I have suggested we must do with King's *Letter*—theological categories may offer the best description we have of the underlying structures of experience. We have seen, for example, that the authority of laws may be experienced in either protestant or catholic modes—a theological distinction used to encode a political structure. And I shall now suggest, returning to themes I sounded at the outset of this chapter, that historical time—the time in which political action and political narrative unfold—may best be understood in theological terms. Here I shall rely again on Benjamin's "Theses," but also on the *Letter*.

In his local narrative of the Birmingham events, recall that King describes the purpose of nonviolent direct action as follows: "Nonviolent direct action seeks to create such a crisis and foster such tension that a community that has refused to negotiate is forced to confront the issue."[203] On King's characterization, nonviolent direct action seeks a qualitative transformation of the community. This observation recalls Benjamin's remarks about revolutionary social change that I elaborated at the beginning of this chapter. Historical time cannot be regarded as a homogeneous progression. Rather, it consists of periods of routine punctuated or in a sense even stopped by moments of crisis or creative tension in which the continuum of history explodes. These latter are moments that Benjamin describes as "a present which is not a transition, but in which time stands still and has come to a stop,"[204] or, again, as "a Messianic cessation of happening [i.e., routine happening]."[205]

This, of course, is the language of a high, and highly mystical, metaphysics. Benjamin is analogizing political action to the coming of the Messiah in Jewish theology, and it is this use of a theological category to explain politics on which I wish to focus. The messianic moment is not a part of the continuum; rather, it marks a rupture in the linear progression of history, bringing the previous era to a stop while at the same time redeeming it and preserving its meaning in a nongradualist *Aufhebung*.

---

203. King, *supra* note 11, at 81.
204. Benjamin, *supra* note 1, at 264.
205. *Id.* at 265.

Benjamin offered this theory to criticize the ideology of the German Social Democratic Party, which held that society would inevitably evolve toward socialism; to illustrate the vapidity of this view, he sardonically quotes Wilhelm Dietzgen's book *The Religion of Social Democracy:* "Every day our cause becomes clearer and people get smarter."[206] Because of their dogmatic and insipid optimism, the Social Democrats failed to mount an effective opposition to the emergency of Nazism, since they discounted the Nazis as a mere way station on Germany's route to a rosy future. Benjamin wrote in despair, "Nothing has corrupted the German working class so much as the notion that it was moving with the current."[207] "Social Democratic theory, and even more its practice, have been formed by a conception of progress which did not adhere to reality but made dogmatic claims."[208]

Benjamin locates the fallacy of the Social Democrats' position in something very abstract, namely their conception of time itself. J. G. A. Pocock once wrote that "the understanding of time, and of human life as experienced in time, disseminated in a society, is an important part of that society's understanding of itself—of its structure and what legitimates it, of the modes of action which are possible to it and in it."[209] Benjamin's theory, including its critique of the ideology of inevitable progress, operates on this level of understanding. It is the insidiously corrupting concept of (inevitable) progress that provokes Benjamin's metaphysical intervention: "The concept of the historical progress of mankind cannot be sundered from the concept of its progression through a homogeneous, empty time. A critique of the concept of such a progression must be the basis of any criticism of the concept of progress itself."[210] Hence the theory that progress lies in a Messianic ending of the past rather than in gradual change, and that political action is essential to create the Messianic break that redeems the past.

Benjamin's debate with German Social Democracy is not a mere historical curio, for the view Benjamin ascribes to the Social Democrats is in fact the most pervasive myth of our time: it is the theory of inevitable historical progress, which King terms "the myth concerning time." King's view, in fact, corresponds with Benjamin's with uncanny exactitude. King writes in the *Letter:*

---

206. *Id.* at 262.
207. *Id.* at 260.
208. *Id.* at 262.
209. J. G. A. Pocock, "Time, Institutions and Action: An Essay on Traditions and Their Understanding," in *Politics, Language and Time: Essays on Political Thought and History* 233 (1973).
210. Benjamin, *supra* note 1, at 263.

I had also hoped that the white moderate would reject the myth concerning time in relation to the struggle for freedom. I have just received a letter this morning from a white brother in Texas. He writes: "All Christians know that the colored people will receive equal rights eventually, but it is possible that you are in too great a religious hurry. . . ." Such an attitude stems from a tragic misconception of time, from the strangely irrational notion that there is something in the very flow of time that will inevitably cure all ills. . . . Human progress never rolls in on wheels of inevitability; it comes through the tireless efforts of men willing to be co-workers with God, and without this hard work time itself becomes an ally of the forces of social stagnation.[211]

This discussion of time, so strangely congruent with Benjamin's, harmonizes completely with King's view that nonviolent direct action is meant to provoke moments of crisis and creative tension. These are precisely what Benjamin identifies as messianic moments.

This view explains a characteristic risk of nonviolent civil disobedience: the risk of being domesticated into a kind of permanent and hapless loyal-oppositionism. Protest institutionalized is protest routinized, protest co-opted, protest that loses whatever messianic power it may possess. Such protest is no longer capable of shocking and arousing the community. Thus it will yield only "a negative peace which is the absence of tension" rather than "a positive peace which is the presence of justice."[212]

And indeed, since the 1970s, civil disobedience has become a purely symbolic and almost senseless exercise in protest-politics-as-usual. Demonstration leaders and police meet beforehand to work out the rules of the game so that there are no surprises, no violence, no injuries, and—of course—no moments of crisis and creative tension forcing anyone to confront anything. A drastic illustration of the deflation of nonviolent direct action occurred in the 1987 civil disobedience of gay activists at the U. S. Supreme Court building, protesting the Court's decision in *Bowers v. Hardwick*.[213] A section of the building was cordoned off and reserved for civil disobedience; demonstrators lined up to enter the cordoned-off section to undergo arrest; police stood by to make sure that nobody skipped in line or tried to get arrested anywhere else. Gay activist and philosopher Richard Mohr writes,

The arrests themselves were a Foucauldian ballet of police power diffused and modulated and of citizens disciplined and molded. In

211. King, *supra* note 11, at 89.
212. *Id.* at 7.
213. 478 U.S. 186 (1986).

the face of advance negotiations with the police, affinity groups, plastic handcuffs, police controlled turnstiles to the arrest site, quizzes before actual arrest, and school buses doubling as paddy wagons and holding tanks, individual dignity did not stand a chance. . . . Bull Connor, where are you when we need you?[214]

Where indeed? The disturbing conclusion of these melancholy reflections is that dissent can hope to succeed only when it is unofficial and therefore most typically extra- or contralegal. An officially recognized, undisruptive Messiah who abides by the law loses the power to redeem. Thus the excluded voice can be included in authority's narrative only at the price of domesticating its redemptive force. In this sense, the clash between King and the *Walker* Court was inevitable: social protest that pays "proper respect for judicial process," that fails to outrage, offers only a shell or husk of redemption—a shadow on the wall of the Cave.

Conclusion: On Our Weak Messianic Power

My discussion of King's *Letter* has attempted to separate out two strains of his thinking, one essentially religious and one largely secular. I have urged the priority of the secular side, both as a more credible form of communitarian political association and as a more authentic basis for political action.

At the same time, however, I have suggested that political authority and political action are best understood in terms that are thoroughly theological. Benjamin's "Theses," upon which I have relied so extensively, speaks recurrently about the messianic nature of political upheaval. To speak of the Messiah is to speak of a miraculous intervention into human affairs inaugurating an epoch that has broken decisively with what has hitherto constituted our history. Benjamin thus implies that political action amounts to just such a miraculous intervention.

Benjamin evokes a specifically Jewish tradition of messianism. On this view the Messiah occupies a uniquely past-oriented and backward-looking position: the Messiah's purpose is not only, indeed not even primarily, to create a better future but rather to redeem the past and make meaningful the sufferings of the Jewish people. Benjamin speaks

---

214. Richard Mohr, "Text(ile): Reading the NAMES Project's AIDS Quilt," *Gay Ideas* 105, 124 (1992). I should note that Mohr understands the purpose of civil disobedience to be the expression of individuality rather than the projection of small-group politics, as I have been arguing.

in the final thesis about a rabbinic tradition that prohibits Jews from investigating the future,[215] and earlier he had emphasized that the spirit of sacrifice is "nourished by the image of enslaved ancestors rather than that of liberated grandchildren."[216] Political action is messianic not only because it blasts the present moment out of the continuum of history but because its aim is first and foremost to redeem the past.

This redemption is not meant figuratively; rather, Benjamin—like King—suggests that political action transforms the structure of history, interrupting the calendrical sequence ("homogeneous, empty time") and stitching together past and present, so that the present redeems the past by reenacting it—literally, by *becoming* it.

What can this reenactment mean? The notion of discrete moments in the calendrical sequence fusing is, of course, a highly mystical one, and, we may fear, it is for that very reason little more than nonsense. Indeed, the claim that discrete—numerically distinct—moments are numerically identical is simply a self-contradiction. What Benjamin had in mind, I believe, was not the numerical identity of past and present but rather bringing the past back to life through celebration and commemoration, particularly where these include not just retelling the past but reenacting it. "The initial day of a calendar serves as a historical time-lapse camera. And, basically, it is the same day that keeps recurring in the guise of holidays, which are days of remembrance. Thus the calendars do not measure time as clocks do. . . ."[217] Here Benjamin may have had in mind not only the theological notion of holidays—holy days—as interruptions of clock-time devoted to remembrance but also the thought that Nietzsche once described as the "high point of the meditation": "That *everything recurs* is the closest *approximation of a world of becoming to a world of being.*"[218] A series of reenactments is the closest mortal approximation to immortality; we resurrect and redeem enslaved ancestors by refighting their battles for freedom.

Here it is useful to draw an analogy to improvisatory musical pieces, such as jazz compositions, which are realized differently in each performance. No archetype exists, and we understand precisely what it means to say that the piece is brought to life, and indeed lives, only in its realizations, even though the realizations differ considerably from one another. In the same category as jazz compositions we may place many

---

215. Benjamin, *supra* note 1, at 266.

216. *Id.* at 262.

217. *Id.* at 261.

218. Friedrich Nietzsche, *The Will To Power* § 617, at 330 (W. Kornhauser ed. R. Hollingdale & W. Kaufmann transs. 1967).

folk arts: dances that have never been notated but are simply handed down from dancer to dancer, epic poems in preliterate societies, folk songs, and—most to the point—folktales and stories. Such stories exist only in the retelling, and their retelling, like all acts of collective memory, revives the past by commemorating it. The very etymology of the word *commemorate*—literally, com-memorate, to remember together— suggests the combining of two epochs in one memory and the collective character of that memory.

Benjamin understands political action as a device of collective memory in precisely this sense.[219] In Benjamin's words, "There is a secret agreement between past generations and the present one. Our coming was expected on earth. Like every generation that preceded us, we have been endowed with a *weak* Messianic power, a power to which the past has a claim."[220] It is a "weak" Messianic power, of course, because no generation is truly the Messiah. We will not end history, and believing that we can is merely a millenarian delusion. Our power to act is messianic nonetheless because our victorious struggle for the priv- ilege of recounting the past makes sense of past suffering. The success- ful outcome of the Birmingham campaign makes sense of the deaths incurred by the campaign and, to a certain ("weak") extent, the suffer- ings endured through 400 years of African-American experience.

I am laboring this point because I believe it is central not only for a theory of political action but also for a theory of legal argument. It is, indeed, the view of legal argument that I sketched at the outset of this chapter: legal argument succeeds when it demonstrates that a local narrative has reenacted an episode of a political narrative and thus that the two have become stitched together, paired in affinity. Legal argu- ment understood as persuasion, hence as political action, works in a medium of historical time that is backward-looking and redemptive in structure.

This account contrasts starkly with another influential view of legal argument: in this view, which Ronald Dworkin has called "pragma- tism," legal argument is entirely forward-looking, seeking only to

---

219. I discussed the relationship between narrative, poetry, political action, and collective memory in chapter 4. It is hardly surprising that Arendt's views are close to Benjamin's: Arendt closely studied Benjamin's "Theses" and in fact was responsible for their survival. Benjamin entrusted the manuscript of the "Theses" to Arendt, who smuggled it out of occupied France and brought it to New York; Benjamin himself committed suicide when he was turned back at the Spanish border as he attempted to flee the Nazis. *See* Elizabeth Young-Bruehl, *Hannah Arendt: For Love of the World* 160–63 (1982).

220. Benjamin, *supra* note 1, at 256.

create a better future and remaining generally oblivious to the past.[221] In this view—its similarity to the Social Democratic view that Benjamin excoriates should be clear—a legal argument consists largely of an attempt to predict and assess the likely future consequences of a judicial decision; it seeks to show that a certain outcome would yield the best consequences overall.

My quarrel is not with the notion that we should aim to achieve the best consequences overall but rather with the notion that the best consequences are to be sought by peering into the future—in Frankfurter's words, attempting "[t]o pierce the curtain of the future, to give shape and visage to mysteries still in the womb of time."[222] This quarrel is partly because I have little faith in our predictive powers; more fundamentally, however, I am arguing that the consequences we seek are in large measure to be sought in the past—as Benjamin says, "our image of happiness is indissolubly bound up with the image of redemption."[223] We achieve happiness in the thought that we have resurrected the memory of our dead ancestors, rescued their history from the defamations of their enemies, and therefore given ourselves a past that makes us comprehensible.[224] That is the true function of legal narrative.

Perhaps the most self-conscious example of an exclusively forward-looking view of the sort I am criticizing is found not in legal pragmatism but in Marx. At the beginning of his greatest historical work, *The Eighteenth Brumaire of Louis Bonaparte,* Marx writes, "Hegel remarks somewhere that all great, world-historical facts and personages occur, as it were, twice. He has forgotten to add: the first time as tragedy, the second as farce."[225] Marx understands full well that revolu-

---

221. Ronald Dworkin, *Law's Empire* 95, 151–75 (1986). Pragmatism is the view "that judges do and should make whatever decisions seem to them best for the community's future, not counting any form of consistency with the past as valuable for its own sake." Utilitarian theories of adjudication are obvious examples of pragmatism.

222. Felix Frankfurter, "The Judicial Process and the Supreme Court," in *Of Law and Men* 39 (P. Elman ed. 1956).

223. Benjamin, *supra* note 1, at 256.

224. In this sense, the sharp distinction I have drawn between forward-looking and backward-looking understandings of action and argument blurs: the redemption of the past is one of the consequences we hope for in the future, and, as Cover, *supra* note 12, insists, narratives of the past will include our ancestors' prophecies of their and our futures. Thus, the backward-looking gaze will see the future reflected in the mirror of ancestral prophecies, just as the forward-looking gaze will find future happiness indissolubly bound up with the redemption of past wrongs and sufferings. The difference in emphasis and valuation the two understandings place on the past nevertheless remains decisive. (My thanks to Paul Kahn for stressing to me the extent to which past and future are caught up with each other.)

225. Karl Marx, *The Eighteenth Brumaire of Louis Bonaparte* 13 (C. Dutt ed. 1957) (3d German ed. 1883).

tionary action is typically backward-looking, seeking to explain itself by assimilation to a political narrative of the past; but unlike Benjamin (and me), he finds the attempt to be farcical, grotesque superstition:

> The tradition of all the dead generations weighs like a nightmare on the brain of the living. And just when they seem engaged in revolutionizing themselves and things, in creating something entirely new, precisely in such epochs of revolutionary crisis they anxiously conjure up the spirits of the past to their service and borrow from them names, battle slogans and costumes in order to present the new scene of world history in this time-honoured disguise and this borrowed language. Thus Luther donned the mask of the Apostle Paul, the Revolution of 1789 to 1814 draped itself alternately as the Roman Republic and the Roman Empire, and the Revolution of 1848 knew nothing better to do than to parody, in turn, 1789, and the revolutionary tradition of 1793 to 1795. . . .
> Similarly, at another stage of development, . . . Cromwell and the English people had borrowed speech, passions and illusions from the Old Testament for their bourgeois revolution. When the real aim had been achieved, when the bourgeois transformation of English society had been accomplished, Locke supplanted Habakkuk.[226]

After heaping his considerable scorn on backward-looking, ghost-ridden, and superstitious revolutionaries, Marx arrives at this exhortation:

> The social revolution of the nineteenth century cannot draw its poetry from the past, but only from the future. It cannot begin with itself before it has stripped off all superstition in regard to the past. Earlier revolutions required world-historical recollections in order to drug themselves concerning their own content. In order to arrive at its own content, the revolution of the nineteenth century must let the dead bury their dead.[227]

It has been my argument that these brave and passionate words amount to a profound misunderstanding of our possibilities of action. Marx aims to eliminate superstition and theology, to disenchant us; similarly, legal pragmatists aim at a disenchanted view of legal argu-

---

226. *Id.* at 13–14 (footnote omitted).
227. *Id.* at 16.

ment. In my view, it cannot be done; let me turn for the last time to
Walter Benjamin, who offered the following parable in criticism of the
(pseudo)scientific and disenchanted vision offered by orthodox
Marxism:

> The story is told of an automaton constructed in such a way that it
> could play a winning game of chess, answering each move of an
> opponent with a countermove. A puppet in Turkish attire and with
> a hookah in its mouth sat before a chessboard placed on a large
> table. A system of mirrors created the illusion that this table was
> transparent from all sides. Actually, a little hunchback who was an
> expert chess player sat inside and guided the puppet's hand by
> means of strings. One can imagine a philosophical counterpart to
> this device. The puppet called "historical materialism" is to win all
> the time. It can easily be a match for anyone if it enlists the services
> of theology, which today, as we know, is wizened and has to keep
> out of sight.[228]

This parable returns us to King but also to *Walker*. In Benjamin's ingenious jest we may find not only a critique of Marx, who was forced to
smuggle in his theology in the form of a necessitarian theory of historical change, but a moral applicable to the *Walker* Court as well. Instead
of calling Benjamin's puppet "historical materialism," call it "the civilizing hand of law," which must win all the time if the judicial suppression
of social protest is to be justified. I have argued that the Court buttresses
its preposterous deification of law's efficacy by a theological reliance on
authority, and this authority may serve as the hunchback crouching
beneath the table. The mirrors that disguise the hunchback are the
unmentioned premises of constitutionalism and popular sovereignty,
which the Court seems to evoke when it speaks of "constitutional freedom" but which in reality serve only to deflect our attention from the
authoritarian hand that drives the opinion.

   Martin Luther King, on the other hand, found no need to hide
theology under the table. In King's case the critical portion of my argument has been different: it is that the real theology required by King is
not a biblical or even Socratic doctrine of conscience but rather an
understanding of the essentially redemptive character of political action itself. And just as the real political narrative underwriting the Supreme Court's authority ought to be the suppressed protestant
narrative of constitutionalism under popular sovereignty, the real political narrative that embeds and fulfills the Birmingham campaign ought

---

228. Benjamin, *supra* note 1, at 255.

to be the narrative of constitutional egalitarianism and natural law legalism in Jefferson, Lincoln, and *Brown.* The two halves of my argument converge: *our* history—the history of black and white Americans, of protesters and the Supreme Court, that would allow us to speak of any history as a common possession—is a narrative of communitarian liberalism that redeems our past oppressions and iniquities. It is the narrative of social protest and moments of "creative tension" that remind us of unkept promises and of the moral emergency in which we live. It is a narrative yet to be written.

Chapter 6

Some Greek Trials

The first trial in Greek literature occurs in the Homeric *Hymn to Hermes*.[1] The infant Hermes, on the night of his birth, steals the cattle of Apollo, who eventually tracks him down. Hermes in the meantime has climbed back into his crib and donned his swaddling clothes. He indignantly denies the theft and swears mighty oaths of innocence: "I will swear the great oath on my father's head. I vow that I myself am not the culprit and that I have seen no one else stealing your cows—whatever these cows are."[2] Apollo takes Hermes before Zeus for judgment. Zeus is more amused than angered at Hermes' prodigious theft; he commands the two gods "to come to an accord and search for the cattle." Hermes shows Apollo where he has hidden them, then he placates Apollo with the gift of a splendid tortoise shell lyre, together with the secret of playing it. The delighted Apollo reciprocates by granting Hermes "a beautiful staff of wealth and prosperity"; and the two gods become eternal allies.

This delightful comic poem inaugurates a theme of profound importance. It is noteworthy that Zeus is concerned above all with harmony and friendship among the Olympians, and not with punishment for Hermes' crime or for his perjury in a sacred oath. The dispute between Apollo and Hermes is resolved by an amicable settlement and not a judgment. If we pose the dilemma, peace or justice, then Zeus's answer is peace.

However, authors in the Homeric age would not have posed this dilemma, for *dike*, "justice," was accomplished through peaceful settlement and not legalism:

> *Dike* in its largest sense is the society's system for settling disputes peacefully. This system among the early Greeks differed in a fundamental way from our own legal system. The legal process in early

---

1. "Hymn to Hermes," in *The Homeric Hymns* 31–47 (A. N. Athanassakis trans. 1976). It should be noted that the Homeric hymns are not in fact by the poet of the Homeric epics, though they were long thought to be.
2. *Id.* ll. 274–77, at 38.

Greece was essentially a system of peaceful arbitration, whereby a settlement (*dike*) is made between two conflicting claims, each claim itself being a *dike*. The fairness (straightness) of the settlement is determined by its acceptability to both sides and to the public.[3]

For the Homeric authors, then, there was no term to mark out legal justice as distinct from mutually agreeable settlements. We may nevertheless frame the contrast in our terms and describe the position as one in which amity or social stability is more important than equity or justice.

My aim in this chapter is to trace this theme through some Greek literature that poses the contrast. But my interest in it is not purely historical, for the tension between law as an instrument of order (which may be achievable only at the expense of justice) and law as an upholder of justice (which may have to be purchased at the cost of social instability or dislocation) is of enormous contemporary importance. Let me cite three examples.

First, in the initial *Brown v. Board of Education* decision (*Brown I*),[4] the U. S. Supreme Court found that school segregation violated the equal protection clause of the Fourteenth Amendment. I will say: the Supreme Court found racial segregation and the subordination of African-Americans to be unjust. Yet to end racial segregation would arouse enormous resistance on the part of Jim Crow adherents in the South; it would lead to dislocation and disorder. For this reason the Court approved desegregation at a very gradual pace ("all deliberate speed") in the second *Brown* decision (*Brown II*).[5] The Court chose order over justice in *Brown II*, and the official desegregation of public schools was not realized for two decades. An entire generation of African-American students attended officially segregated public schools after *Brown I*. At least one distinguished legal scholar has defended this priority of order over justice on jurisprudential grounds resting primarily on "law's characteristic role as mediating between the ideal and

---

3. Michael Gagarin, *Aeschylean Drama* 13 (1976); *see also* Gagarin "*Dike* in Archaic Greek Thought," 69 *Classical Philology* 186 (1974); Gagarin, "*Dike* in the *Works and Days*," 68 *Classical Philology* 81 (1973). But the meaning of *dike* is by no means a settled issue. For a different view—that *dike* has to do with prudence (in the form of avoiding divine punishment) rather than justice or morality—see V. A. Rodgers, "Some Thoughts on ΔΙΚΗ," 21 *Classical Quarterly* 289 (1971). For a dissenting voice against both Gagarin and Rodgers, see Matthew W. Dickie, "*Dike* as a Moral Term in Homer and Hesiod," 73 *Classical Philology* 91 (1978).

4. 347 U.S. 483 (1954).

5. 349 U.S. 294, 301 (1955).

the real."[6] The unsegregated society of *Brown I*—the society of Martin Luther King's dream—was the ideal; white resistance, and the prospect of violence and civil unrest, was the reality that the Court had to accommodate in *Brown II*. *Brown I* stands for the priority of justice; *Brown II* stands for the priority of order.

Second, many trial judges admit that their eagerness to settle cases leads them to lean hard on the weaker party—no matter who is legally in the right—to force the settlement. Federal Rule of Civil Procedure 16 explicitly mandates the "facilitation of settlement" as an aim of the pretrial conference, and Rule 68 provides an incentive to settle by shifting a defendant's costs to a plaintiff who refuses a settlement offer that is more generous than what the plaintiff ultimately obtains at trial. This prosettlement policy remains popular despite the acknowledged possibility that unscrupulous defendants will use Rule 68 as a tactical weapon to bludgeon opponents into accepting inadequate settlement offers if their cases are at all shaky.[7] In part, the drive to settlement is a judicial reaction to overcrowded dockets, rather than a principled commitment to settlement over decision. But it is a mistake to think reaction to the half-mythical "litigation explosion" is all there is to judicial enthusiasm for settlement. Judges often see their role as that of mediator or healer; like Zeus in the *Hymn to Hermes*, they fulfill a divine mission by making their litigants settle.[8]

Professor Owen M. Fiss, by contrast, favors (in his words) justice over peace, and comments, "Although . . . peaceful coexistence may be a necessary precondition of justice, and itself a state of affairs to be valued, it is not justice itself. To settle for something less means to accept less than some ideal."[9] In response to this, Professors Andrew W. McThenia and Thomas L. Shaffer write, "[T]he religious tradition seeks not *resolution* (which connotes the sort of doctrinal integrity in the law that seems to us to be Fiss's highest priority) but *reconciliation* of brother to brother, sister to sister, sister to brother, child to parent, neighbor to neighbor, buyer to seller, defendant to plaintiff, *and judge to both*."[10]

---

6. Paul Gewirtz, "Remedies and Resistance," 92 *Yale Law Journal* 587, 680 (1983).

7. *See* Delta Airlines v. August, 450 U.S. 346 (1980) (which attempts to avoid this tactic, but only at the price of reading Rule 68 in a highly artificial way (as Justice Rehnquist's dissent makes clear)); Note, "The Impact of Proposed Rule 68 on Civil Rights Litigation," 84 *Columbia Law Review* 719 (1984).

8. I discuss the criteria of justice in settlements in David Luban, "The Quality of Justice," 66 *Denver University Law Review* 381 (1989).

9. Owen Fiss, "Against Settlement," 93 *Yale Law Journal* 1073, 1085–86 (1984).

10. Andrew McThenia & Thomas Shaffer, "For Reconciliation," 94 *Yale Law Journal* 1660, 1666 (1985).

Fiss opposes the alternative dispute resolution (ADR) movement, which seeks to provide extrajudicial modes of compromising disputes, while McThenia and Shaffer support it. But the ADR movement itself has divided over the question whether the ethical standards of mediators or arbitrators permit them to compensate for an imbalance of power between the parties that may lead to unjust outcomes. Those who say yes to this question stand for the priority of justice; those who say no stand for the priority of peace and amity.

Third, the Chief Justice of the U.S. Supreme Court raises this worry: "Adjudicatory review of the decisions of certain institutions, while perhaps ensuring a 'better' decision in some objective sense, can only disrupt ongoing relationships within the institution and thereby hamper the ability of the institution to serve its designated societal function."[11] He later clarifies this: "[M]y hypothesis is not that an individual's claim for redress of wrong would be better vindicated in a nonadversarial system, but that in some situations it is best not vindicated at all."[12] Paradigmatic of such situations is litigation that places parents and their children in an adversary posture. Mr. Rehnquist poses a hypothetical in which a child has a serious disease and the child's doctor recommends that a limb be amputated; the parents choose to follow the recommendation, but the child is bitterly opposed. It would be quite wrong, we may think, for a court to appoint an attorney for the child who would attempt to enjoin the amputation until additional medical opinion was obtained.[13] The Chief Justice generalizes his concerns in this way:

> [T]he adversary process . . . best serves its purpose when any continuing relationship between the contending parties is at an end. . . . To pit children against their parents in these same surroundings, in order to determine whether an operation recommended by a physician should or should not be authorized by a court, may make for a better informed decision as to the operation, but may leave the family unit in a shambles.[14]

From this conclusion, Rehnquist expands his argument to include other cases that should not be heard by courts. He cites, for example, a case in which parents sued a clinic for an improperly performed vasectomy,

---

11. William O. Rehnquist, "The Adversary Society," 33 *University of Miami Law Review* 1, 2 (1978).

12. *Id.* at 10.

13. *Id.* at 8; *see also id.* at 6.

14. *Id.* at 15.

after conceiving their seventh child despite the vasectomy.[15] Mr. Rehnquist worries that since the claim is predicated on counting the birth of the child as a damage, such a wrongful birth action may make the child feel like an "emotional bastard."[16]

Once again, the question revolves around the tension between justice, which Rehnquist concedes may best be served by the adversary process, and institutional order, which may be salvageable only when parties who must continue their relationships to each other are compelled to swallow their grievances. Mr. Rehnquist concludes by generalizing to the level of social philosophy: "There are times when the claims of the individual should be subordinated to those of the 'species,' even if the species is not government itself but a private institution which serves a useful purpose."[17]

The choice posed by these examples (and many others that will readily come to mind) is between two conceptions of the function of a legal system. It may be thought of primarily as a dispenser of justice, or primarily as an instrument of compromise, of "dispute resolution" or "social control." We may, of course, object to posing the contrast this way. We may want to insist that compromise is just, that the social process of negotiation and mutual accommodation is precisely the construction of justice.[18] But that objection can be at most half the truth, for we also recognize that bargains may be unfair and compromises may be sellouts. Our language itself registers the ambivalence we feel between the need for peace and the claims of justice: disputants compromise; ideals are compromised.

Both poles of this tension are too complex to characterize in a phrase. But since I am in need of a phrase, I shall call the view that sees legality as an instrument of dispute resolution or social control—of order even at the expense of justice—*legal instrumentalism*. My aim, then, is to sketch one chapter in a history of legal instrumentalism. On

15. *Id.* at 10–12. The case is Sherlock v. Stillwater Clinic, 260 N.W.2d 169 (Minn. 1977).

16. Rehnquist, *supra* note 11, at 12.

17. *Id.* at 18.

18. This theme, I take it, is one that is central to James Boyd White's work. *See* James Boyd White, *When Words Lose Their Meaning* (1984). White, however, is fully cognizant of the enormous problems lurking in such a conventionalist or constructive account of justice. These problems are precisely the source of controversy between Plato and the rhetoricians. I have characterized the tension between a constructive and a transcendent standard of justice as a "paradox of compromise" raised by the deceptively simple question how we tell whether a negotiation has led to a fair outcome. *See* Luban, "Bargaining and Compromise: Recent Work on Negotiation and Informal Justice," 14 *Philosophy & Public Affairs* 397, 407–10, 414–16 (1985).

my reconstruction, Homer, Aeschylus, and Plato successively elaborate upon the value of legal instrumentalism that first appears in the *Hymn to Hermes*, while Hesiod extols the law primarily as a dispenser of justice, which he views as a precondition of, rather than an alternative to, authentic community.

My aim is not only historical, however. I also wish to take sides in opposition to legal instrumentalism: to argue in favor of justice rather than order as the more central value realized by a good legal system. I shall be siding with Hesiod against Homer, Aeschylus, and Plato—and thus, implicitly, with *Brown I* against *Brown II;* with Fiss against McThenia and Shaffer; and with such aggrieved plaintiffs as the Sherlock family, who ask for a forum in which to air their wrongful birth grievance, against Chief Justice Rehnquist.

Friendship Over Justice: The Iliad

The theme of peace or stability over justice is treated lightly and even with slapstick in the *Hymn to Hermes*. (When Apollo picks up Hermes to take him to Zeus, the infant sneezes and breaks wind.) In the *Iliad* it forms an important strand of the loftiest work of Western literature.[19]

The rage of Achilles is a rage at injustice. Agamemnon has stolen the captive woman Briseis, who by right of war belongs to Achilles. That, to be sure, is not how Homer's characters understand the quarrel between Agamemnon and Achilles: for them it concerns an insult to Achilles' honor (*timē*) rather than an injustice.[20] Moreover, as I have suggested, *dike* is served by compromise or settlement (such as that proposed by Nestor in Book 1) rather than by the punitiveness of Achilles' wrath. As White has observed, "[t]he central value . . . is . . . a willingness to put in the past what belongs in the past and to be reconciled after all. This is the fundamental way in which this community is maintained, a way as central to it as we might say the rule of law is to our own."[21]

---

19. My interpretation of the *Iliad*—as at once a critical reflection on the heroic-warrior culture it depicts and a meditation on the conditions of human life—has been encouraged by reading chapter 2 of White's *When Words Lose Their Meaning, supra* note 18, entitled "Poetry and the World of Two: Cultural Criticism and the Ideal of Friendship in the *Iliad*," and Jasper Griffin's *Homer* (1980). Both White and Griffin are among those rare critics who make great works even greater by exhibiting aspects of the work that the reader has not noticed or reflected upon but that change the whole way one reads the work. Except where noted, I have not borrowed specifics from either White or Griffin. I have also benefited from Eric A. Havelock, *The Greek Concept of Justice: From Its Shadow in Homer to Its Substance in Plato* 123–38 (1978).
20. *See* Hugh Lloyd-Jones, *The Justice of Zeus* 11–17 (1971).
21. White, *supra* note 18, at 50.

But as the poem proceeds, Achilles moves along a trajectory that
leads him out of the honor-and-compromise culture of Book 1 and into
a moral universe with very different concerns, which are neither named
nor fully articulated but which (as I shall argue) are closely related to
what we call justice.[22] His initial challenge to Agamemnon is a distribu-
tive (justice) argument countering Agamemnon's demand for a new
prize to replace the captive Chryseis. Chryseis was Agamemnon's
prize, just as Briseis was Achilles'. But Chryseis is the daughter of a
priest of Apollo and the god requires that she be returned to her father.
Agamemnon demands a new prize and Achilles responds, "How shall
the great-hearted Achaeans give you a prize? We do not know of great
heaps of common goods piled up anywhere; the things we have plun-
dered from the cities are all distributed and it is not fitting for the people
to collect these things back again."[23] It is Agamemnon's displeasure
over this response that provokes his seizure of Briseis from Achilles.

Achilles makes this argument in an *agora*, a public meeting. It is
important for our purposes to realize that this *agora* is a kind of legal
proceeding.[24] It incorporates elements of the adjudicatory gathering
(*agora*) that Hephaistos depicts on Achilles' shield in Book 18,[25] including the use of the scepter to indicate which speaker has the floor and the
requirement that business be transacted in public.[26] Here in Book 1,

---

22. The insight that Achilles gradually moves from the center to the margin of his
cultural world is White's. *See id.* at 38–39.

23. Homer, *The Iliad* bk. 1, ll. 123–26. Here I use White's translation. *See* White,
supra note 18, at 34. The word translated as "fitting" is *epieike*, which Aristotle will later
analyze as "equity," "a correction of law where it is defective owing to its universality."
Aristotle, "Nicomachean Ethics" (W. D. Ross trans.), in *The Basic Works of Aristotle*
1137b27–28 (Richard McKeon ed. 1941). Equity, for Aristotle, is substantive justice,
which comes into play when formal or legal justice "fails us and has erred by over-
simplicity." *Id.* at 1137b21–22. Thus, Agamemnon may have the formal authority to call
back the prizes or, for that matter, to take Briseis from Achilles—the best evidence of this
is that Achilles does not resist the seizure of Briseis—but to do so is unfitting, unreasonable, and inequitable (all meanings of *epieike*). A. W. H. Adkins claims that Agamemnon
has the legal authority to take Briseis. *See* A. W. H. Adkins, *Merit and Responsibility: A
Study in Greek Values* 51 (1960). Richard Posner apparently agrees: "[T]here is no suggestion that in ignoring the wishes of the *agore* he is exceeding his legal authority." Richard
A. Posner, *The Economics of Justice* 128 (1981). But I agree with White that we are simply
never told the basis or scope of Agamemnon's authority. *See* White, *supra* note 18, at 32–
33.

24. This point is heavily stressed in Havelock, *supra* note 19, at 129ff. On the *agora*
of Book 1 "as a form of what we would call due process," "giving a sort of judicial status
to facts generally known," *see* White, *supra* note 18, at 33, 296 n.8. *See also* 1 R. J. Bonner &
G. Smith, *The Administration of Justice from Homer to Aristotle* 2–11 (1968).

25. Homer, *The Iliad* bk. 18, ll. 497–508, at 452 (R. Fitzgerald trans. 1974).

26. The *agora* in Book 1, however, is not precisely an adjudication, for its procedure

however, the *agora* is a failure. In the *agora* depicted on Achilles' shield, the elders are supposed to "speak justice straightly,"[27] but when Nestor attempts to do so in Book 1, the "litigants" (Achilles and Agamemnon) do not accept his pronouncement. More importantly, Agamemnon is simultaneously litigant and king, both disputant and guarantor of the process, so justice cannot be done.[28]

The breakdown of the legal process is signalled when Achilles swears vengeance on the scepter of justice and peaceful debate and hurls it down:

> "But here is what I say: my oath upon it by this great staff. . . . Akhaian officers in council take it in hand by turns, when they observe by the will of Zeus due order in debate: let this be what I swear by then: I swear a day will come when every Akhaian soldier will groan to have Akhilleus back. . . ." He hurled the staff, studded with golden nails, before him on the ground.[29]

Achilles' action is a rupture of the army's social order, an abandonment of commitment, of trust, of martial and civil friendship.

This breakdown is clearly symbolized in the description of Achilles' shield in Book 18. There, the poet juxtaposes two contrasting city scenes. In the first, weddings and dancing are depicted, and strife has been cabined to a single format: a litigation taking place in *agora*. (To this scene, which portrays the litigants arguing before a group of elders whose task it is to render judgment, we owe much of our knowledge of Homeric-age legal procedure.) The second scene depicts war, ambush, siege, and death. There is strife even among the besiegers, half of whom want to sack the city while half want to settle for ransom.[30] This latter

is different in important details from the agora on Achilles' shield. For a fascinating account of archaic civil procedure based on a detailed analysis of the trial depicted on the shield, see Hans Junius Wolff, "The Origin of Judicial Litigation among the Greeks," 4 *Traditio* 31, 34–49 (1945). Wolff, it should be noted, convincingly refutes the claim—repeated by Judge Posner in *The Economics of Justice, supra* note 23, at 124—that the adjudication depicted on the shield scene is a private arbitration that is not underwritten by governmental authority. *But cf.* Michael Gagarin, *Early Greek Law* 28 (1986) (I am grateful to Judge Posner for calling my attention to this passage). For a different analysis of the trial scene, see Bonner & Smith, *supra* note 24, at 31–41.

27. Homer, *supra* note 25, bk. 1, ll. 503–4, 508, at 29.

28. As one writer has observed, "Had Nestor and not one of the disputants been the king, they would have been obliged to follow his instructions. But the quarrel is one in which the king, whose duty it is to give justice to his subjects, is himself a party, so that the human machinery for securing justice cannot be set into motion." Hugh Lloyd-Jones, *The Justice of Zeus* 13 (1971).

29. Homer, *supra* note 25, bk. 1, ll. 233–45, at 19–20.

30. *Id.* bk. 18, ll. 490–540, at 451–52.

reference in the second scene to the story of the *Iliad* itself is transparent, and the symbolism of the two scenes together is this: When the legal process of *agora* breaks down, as it did in Book 1, disastrous war will be the result. The only choices are peace through law or else war and civil war.

Achilles, who is only half mortal, removes himself from the human order in the name of justice; he takes on the role of an onlooker, of a god. Indeed, the gods themselves choose sides in the Trojan War, and of those involved only Zeus remains dispassionate. Homer implies that Achilles in his quest for justice has appropriated the Olympian role of Zeus himself, to whom Achilles conveys his prayer through the entreaty of his mother. Achilles prays that his own army be defeated in his absence. Achilles' prayer is granted (Achilles' wish becomes Zeus's will, underscoring the parallel Homer draws between them) and his comrades are thrown back, defeated, killed.

That it is Achilles' quest for justice that accounts for the parallel between Zeus and himself may be seen from one other significant passage. Zeus, like Achilles, becomes angry; and his anger is aroused when he is confronted with injustice. Homer likens the wrath of Zeus to a cloudburst

> when Zeus pours down the rain in scudding gusts to punish men, annoyed because they will enforce their crooked judgments and banish justice from the market place [*agora*], thoughtless of the gods' vengeance. . . .[31]

The parallel between the anger of Zeus, which is aroused by injustice in the *agora*, and that of Achilles reinforces the claim that Achilles too is furious over injustice. In the wrath of Achilles the demand for justice prevails over the requirements of civil and martial friendship. The crucial climax of this theme occurs in Book 9, when Agamemnon sends emissaries to win back Achilles with gifts. Agamemnon offers a settlement. On the principle of *dike* in the *Hymn to Hermes*, Achilles should accept it, but he does not. Agamemnon

> would not look me in the eye, dog that he is! I will not share one word of counsel with him, nor will I act with him; he robbed me blind, broke faith with me: he gets no second chance to play me for a fool. Once is enough . . . Not if his gifts outnumbered the sea sands or all the dust grains in the world could Agamemnon ever

---

31. *Id.* bk. 16, ll. 386–88, at 389.

appease me—not till he pays me back full measure, pain for pain, dishonor for dishonor.[32]

This speech is of crucial importance for the poem as a whole. As James Boyd White convincingly argues, it signifies a breakdown of the moral universe encompassed in the honor-world of Book 1:

> Achilles is angry because of an impairment of his honor, yet he rejects the one way in this world in which such an injury can be appeased: submission, expressed by excessive gifts. Injury implies redress, but redress is here rejected. . . . The problem is that he has, as it were, no other place to go, no language other than his inherited one in which to establish himself and his motives. He lacks the resources with which to make a coherent and intelligible statement, one that will be adequate to his situation.[33]

If Achilles' language does not contain the resources to explain his continued fury in the face of the culturally mandated payment of compensation, we must supply the words. What is apparent is this:

When Achilles finally ends the quarrel in Book 19, Agamemnon will attribute his insult to Achilles to a "fierce blindness" (atē) that overcame him.[34] Agamemnon regards his action as (merely?) a kind of imprudence, a judgment that is consistent with the mode of valuation current in the competitive honor-culture. But although Achilles accepts this explanation in Book 19,[35] at the present juncture in the poem he is angry at something more than Agamemnon's *folly*. Furthermore, to Achilles something beyond a maldistribution of *timē*, an insult, has occurred. An insult is something for which compensation can be paid (as we pay damages for a broken contract), but Achilles rejects all compensation. Only Agamemnon's equivalent suffering will pay him back.

Thus, the honor- and compromise-culture's moral categories permit him to judge only that Agamemnon's seizure of Briseis was *insulting, imprudent*, or (consequently) *shameful*. But Achilles in his punitive rage seems to be searching unsuccessfully for the intellectual resources to say something more, something in a different moral universe. What flickers like lightning through his speech is the sense that Agamemnon has done something *wrong;* and this wrongness cannot be assuaged by

---

32. *Id.* bk. 9, ll. 372–87, at 215.
33. White, *supra* note 18, at 48–49.
34. Homer, *supra* note 25, bk. 19, ll. 86–89, at 460.
35. *Id.* bk. 19, ll. 270–74, at 465.

compensation alone, nor even compensation accompanied by a confession of folly. It demands retribution and equivalent suffering. Achilles, I want to say, has discovered injustice (a reading supported when Odysseus later tells Agamemnon to be "more just" (*dikaioteros*) in the future.)[36] His speech amounts to insisting that justice must be done in full meed: Achilles will not settle the quarrel.

The tragedy of the *Iliad* is engendered by this fateful and awesome decision. Achilles oversteps himself. He is more than mortal, but he is no god: he cannot assume the justice-enforcing role of Zeus. He is a man. Homer chooses to omit from his poem the legend that Achilles is vulnerable only in his heel but rather incorporates it by sublime and complex indirection. Achilles, who has abandoned his human tie with the rest of his comrades, retains it with his beloved friend Patroclus. Symbolically, but quite literally as well, Patroclus is Achilles' point of humanness, his point of vulnerability, which eventually kills him.[37] Patroclus is Achilles' human aspect. Because he has not, like Achilles, removed himself from the social world, he cannot bear to see his comrades slaughtered. He takes Achilles' place in the martial order: he dons Achilles' own armor and goes out to fight. And he is slain by Hector.

Only now will Achilles rejoin the fight. But he will not yet rejoin the world of men. Achilles is still hungry for justice, in this instance for the revenge of Patroclus's death. Although there was nothing unjust about the killing of Patroclus in combat, Achilles' retributive spirit cannot distinguish the situations. His "moral mood" is one of wanting to pay the Trojans back "full measure, pain for pain, dishonor for dishonor": his own pain is proof enough of injustice. And Homer once more emphasizes Achilles' divine aspect: in Book 21 Achilles routs the Trojan army single-handedly. Again we think of Zeus himself, who boasts in

---

36. *Id.* bk. 19, l. 181, at 465. My thanks to Daniel Blickman for calling this passage to my attention. Achilles has understood justice on admittedly primitive retributivist lines; as Nietzsche would have it, explaining the origin of the concept of guilt, "the idea that every injury has its *equivalent* and can actually be paid back, even if only through the *pain* of the culprit." Friedrich Nietzsche, *On the Genealogy of Morals* second essay, §4, 63 (W. Kaufmann ed. & trans. 1967); *see also id.* §§5–6, at 64–66. That is not to say that retributivism must inevitably be understood along the lines of vengeance as compensation; for an analysis of retributivism that distinguishes carefully between retribution and revenge and justifies retribution in cognitive rather than emotional terms, see Jean Hampton, "The Retributive Idea," in Jean Hampton & Jeffrie Murphie, *Forgiveness and Mercy* 111 (1988).

37. As White says, "Patroclus' death . . . operates as the death of a part of Achilles himself." White, *supra* note 18, at 53. White also cites C. H. Whitman, *Homer and the Heroic Tradition* 199 (1958): "Homer . . . has externalized the humane side of Achilles in Patroclus." *Id.* The love of Achilles and Patroclus parallels Hector's love of his family, displayed in the famous and beautiful scene in Book 6.

Book 8 that if all the Olympians pulled on one end of a golden chain and
he on the other, he would prevail. "That is how far I overwhelm you
all."[38] In Book 22 Achilles slays Hector.

Still he is not appeased. He rejects Hector's dying plea to ransom
his body for burial and instead drags it behind his chariot before the
walls of Troy. Achilles' refusal of the offer of ransom is a scene self-
consciously parallel to his refusal of Agamemnon's offer of settlement
in Book 9.

In the end, however, Zeus intervenes and orders, "Achilles is to
take fine gifts from Priam, and in return give back Prince Hector's
body." As in the *Hymn to Hermes*, Zeus commands reconciliation. At the
end of the poem Achilles reenters the world of men—sharing food and
drink with Priam and joining him in tears at the grief and suffering that
is man's lot.

Homer condenses the theme of the conflict between human sociability and divine justice in the famous bargain of Achilles: the choice
between a long and prosperous life of anonymous peace or a short life
of glorious heroism.[39] Put this way, the theme can sound shallow and
juvenile. But Homer deepens it by linking Achilles' actual choice—the
short life of glory, in which what is most godlike is juxtaposed to the
brutal fact of mortality[40]—with Achilles' quest for justice at the expense
of participation in the everyday human world:

> Letting a tear fall, Thetis said: "You'll be swift to meet your end,
> child, as you say: your doom comes close on the heels of Hektor's
> own." Akhilleus the great runner ground his teeth and said: . . .
> "Now I must go to look for the destroyer of my great friend. I shall
> confront the dark dreary spirit of death at any hour Zeus and the
> other gods may wish to make an end."[41]

Ultimately, I believe that Homer does not assent to Achilles' choice.
Eventually, as we have seen, Zeus intervenes to bring an end to the
wrath of the doomed Achilles and enforce his reconciliation with Priam,
his own comrades, and the human world itself. Justice is for Zeus alone
to apportion; man's proper aim is reconciliation. More broadly, the
story of the *Iliad* as a whole is one in which the wrath of Achilles—his
quest for justice—spreads disaster over friend and foe alike. In Books 3
and 4 the warring armies are on the verge of settling their conflict and

---

38. Homer, *supra* note 25, bk. 8, ll. 19–27, at 182.
39. *Id.* bk. 9, ll. 412–16, at 216.
40. *See* Griffin, *supra* note 19, at 34–39.
41. Homer, *supra* note 25, bk. 18, ll. 94–116, at 438–39.

ending the war. The settlement explodes only because Zeus at that point makes Achilles' will-to-vengeance his own.

At the same time, however, Homer is much more ambivalent than the author of the *Hymn to Hermes* about the choice of friendship over justice. The bargain of Achilles exalts him over all other characters in the poem; it opens him to a deeper, more valid, even more humane understanding of life than anyone else attains. Griffin puts it thus: "It is suffering which produces song, and by song we understand suffering. It is part of the greatness of Achilles that he sees this with a clarity beyond the reach of Agamemnon or Hector."[42] If my interpretation is correct, this greatness of Achilles has at its root his quest for justice, his wrath. The poem begins,

> Anger be now your song, immortal one, Akhilleus' anger, doomed and ruinous, that caused the Akhaians loss on bitter loss and crowded brave souls into the undergloom, leaving so many dead men—carrion for dogs and birds; and the will of Zeus was done.[43]

If Homer finds the rage for justice a principle unsuited for the human world, he recognizes as well that without it the world is scarcely human, scarcely worth inhabiting. It is the willingness to sacrifice his life for justice, and not his skill at arms, that makes Achilles heroic. "For the poet, the greatness and the fragility of man go inseparably together, and it is their combination which makes up the nature of the hero."[44] Our fragility asks for peace; our greatness asks for justice.

The Primacy of Justice: Works and Days

Ultimately Homer, like the author of the *Hymn to Hermes,* opts for civic (or martial) friendship over justice—though he does so with a profound understanding of what is abandoned in that choice. The other alternative is the demand for justice: the thesis (since no one could sanely maintain *Fiat jus, pereat mundi!*) that social life is unlivable without justice. This we find in the second trial in Greek literature, described briefly in Hesiod's *Works and Days.* Hesiod, it seems, has lost an unjust suit against his wastrel brother Perses: "Our inheritance was divided; but there is so much you grabbed and carried away . . . a fat bribe for

---

42. Griffin, *supra* note 19, at 38.
43. Homer, *supra* note 25, bk. 1, ll. 1–6, at 11.
44. Griffin, *supra* note 19, at 35.

gift-devouring kings, fools who want to be judges in this trial. . . ."[45]
Now Perses has run into money troubles and wishes to mend the quarrel. Hesiod agrees, "Lose no time! Seize your only chance to let straight justice—Zeus's fairest—settle this quarrel."[46] But Hesiod will give him no money; instead, he offers advice. Perses is forced "to knock on doors in vain as a beggar. This is how you came to me but I have given enough and shall give no more. Work, foolish Perses."[47] The Homeric authors subsume justice under a mutually agreeable settlement of quarrels. For Hesiod, as we shall see, the settlement of his quarrel with Perses is a diatribe on the need for justice.

Hesiod's is a grim picture of our life. He tells the story of the gold, silver, bronze, heroic, and iron races of man and comments, "I wish I were not counted among the fifth race of men, but rather had died before, or been born after it. This is the race of iron. Neither day nor night will give them rest as they waste away with toil and pain."[48] In large part, the root of our condition lies in our injustice, and it is ever on the increase: "The man who keeps his oath, or is just and good, will not be favored, but the evil-doers and scoundrels will be honored, for might will make right and shame will vanish. Base men will harm their betters with words that are crooked and then swear they are fair."[49]

But such a society cannot endure:

> Justice is the winner in the race against insolent crime. Only fools need suffer to learn. The Oath Demon follows the trail of crooked decrees; Justice howls when she is dragged about by bribe-devouring men whose verdicts are crooked when they sit in judg-

---

45. Hesiod, *Works and Days*, in *Hesiod: Theogony, Works and Days, Shield* ll. 3–39, at 68 (A. N. Athanassakis trans. 1983). Michael Gagarin argues that Hesiod has *won* the suit against Perses and is now warning Perses against the folly of squandering his remaining resources by pursuing the litigation further. *See* Gagarin, "Hesiod's Dispute With Perses," 104 *Transactions of the American Philological Association* 103 (1974). But I am not convinced. Gagarin argues that the expression "gift-devourer" (*dorophagos*) refers to judges' fees, and does "not mean that Perses bribed the judges, and [it] impl[ies] neither the judges' dishonesty nor Perses' success." *Id.* at 110. According to Gagarin, "the 'crooked' rulings of which he [Hesiod] complains [e.g., at ll. 220–21, 263–64] are not necessarily the result of bribery. They may be 'unfair' because of the judges' stupidity or because of prejudice which they have acquired without corruption." *Id.* at 109 n.18. But these arguments, I think, miss the forest for the trees. It is simply too implausible that the victor in a just lawsuit would devote so many lines to bitter invective against crooked judges. Only losers complain about the judges' crooked rulings.
46. Hesiod, *supra* note 45, ll. 34–36, at 68.
47. *Id.* ll. 395–97, at 77.
48. *Id.* ll. 174–78, at 71.
49. *Id.* ll. 190–94, at 72.

ment. Weeping and clothed in mist, she follows through the cities and dwellings of men, and visits ruin on those who twist her straight ways and drive her out. But those who give straight verdicts and follow justice, both when fellow citizens and strangers are on trial, live in a city that blossoms, a city that prospers.[50]

For the gods will not suffer injustice forever:

[T]he immortals are ever present among men, and they see those who with crooked verdicts spurn divine retribution and grind down one another's lives. . . .
    [They] keep a watchful eye over verdicts and cruel acts as they rove the whole earth, clothed in mist . . . so that the people pay for the reckless deeds and evil plans of kings whose slanted words twist her straight path.[51]

Underlying Hesiod's spleen, and his reversal of the Homeric valuation of peace over justice, is a difference of basic social philosophy. The Homeric authors depict a society as a kind of friendship, which is undermined and unraveled by strict retributive justice. The wrath of Achilles, his spirit of justice, demolishes the settlement of the Trojan war, undermines his own army, and thus crowds brave souls into the undergloom.

Hesiod's vision is much different, and in many ways much more contemporary. For Hesiod, the basic contrast differentiating a good society from a bad one is not between friendship and strife, but between two sorts of strife:

There was never one kind of Strife. Indeed on this earth two kinds exist. The one is praised by her friends, the other found blameworthy. These two are not of one mind. The one—so harsh—fosters evil war and the fray of battle. . . .
    The other one . . . is much better, and she stirs even the shiftless on to work. A man will long for work when he sees a man of wealth who rushes with zeal to plow and plant and husband his homestead. One neighbor envies another who hastens to his riches. This Strife is good for mortals. The potters eye one another's success and craftsmen, too; the beggar's envy is a beggar, the singer's a singer.[52]

---

50. *Id.* ll. 217–27, at 72.
51. *Id.* ll. 249–62, at 73.
52. *Id.* ll. 11–26, at 67.

Hesiod's is a competitive, acquisitive society like our own not a martial or civil gemeinschaft. And the great problem of such a society is to transform the strife that "fosters evil war" into the strife that "stirs even the shiftless on to work" and is thus "good for mortals." This is the function of justice. Hesiod's astonishing insight is that in a competitive society, peace without justice is impossible, because of what we would now call a Prisoner's Dilemma or an assurance game. Even those who desire to be just cannot do so for fear of being double-crossed or put at a competitive disadvantage: "As matters stand, may neither I nor my son be just men in this world, because it is a bad thing to be just if wrong-doers win the court decisions."[53] For Hesiod, economic competition— the good strife—sets us to work. We prosper, however, only if we are prudent; and so most of his advice to Perses consists of detailed instruction on the practicalities of farming, sailing, and craft. The principle of prudence is that "each kind of work has its season."[54] The prudent person applies this overarching cosmic principle to advantage, but the advantage will disappear if we cannot count on the prudence of others. For the imprudent are ruined and must resort to injustice. Injustice, in turn, disrupts the plans of its victims, and thus they too are ruined and must resort to injustice. The principle of prudence, that "each kind of work has its season," thus incorporates the principle of justice at once as a special case ("to each his own") and as a necessary condition for its successful ordering of society. Stability without legal justice is quite literally impossible.

The Birth of Legal Instrumentalism: The Oresteia

In Homer and Hesiod we have Western civilization's first meditations on the role of legal justice in the social order. As I have analyzed them, they amount to thesis and antithesis—the Homeric valuation of sociability, of civic or martial friendship, over justice (though tempered with the recognition that the hero's quest for justice illuminates human life as a whole) and the Hesiodic counter that unless justice is primary, sociability will ultimately be unattainable.

Legality as such is touched on in only a few dozen lines of the *Hymn to Hermes*, the *Iliad*, and *Works and Days*. It first arises as a theme for explicit reflection centuries later, in a work purporting to explain the origin of the legal system. This is the trial of Orestes in Aeschylus's

---

53. *Id.* ll. 270–72, at 74.
54. *Id.* l. 641, at 83.

drama *Eumenides*.[55] Along with Plato's *Republic* and *Laws*, which I shall discuss later, it is the great and authoritative Greek treatment of the controversy between Homer and Hesiod. In the *Eumenides*, a form of culture and a system of justice are given articulation and defense. I will examine it at some length, partly as a courtroom drama. The trial scene warrants this treatment, for it depicts not only the mythical birth of the adversary system but also the first sophistical argument by the (mythical) first lawyer.

The Facts

The story, as it is expounded in *Agamemnon* and *Choephoroi* (the first two plays of the Oresteian trilogy), is horrible enough. As Agamemnon prepared to set sail against Troy, his fleet was becalmed at Aulis. A seer told him that the goddess Artemis was angry and could be appeased only by the sacrifice of Agamemnon's own daughter, Iphigenia. Agamemnon wrestled with the cruel dilemma—to betray his fleet or to kill his child—and finally performed the sacrifice.

Through the long years of the Trojan War, his queen Clytemnestra nursed her hatred of Agamemnon for murdering her child and plotted against him with her lover Aegisthus. When, at last, Agamemnon returned, she wrapped him after his bath in a purple robe skillfully woven as a sort of straitjacket, pulled it tight, and stabbed him. *Choephoroi* tells the story of Orestes and Electra, Agamemnon's and Clytemnestra's surviving children, who planned vengeance on their mother in their father's name. Orestes was impelled to this by the oracle of Apollo, at Delphi. At the god's behest, he drove his sword into Clytemnestra's throat. Almost immediately he was beset by the Erinyes, or Furies, ancient and terrible black goddesses with snakes for hair and eyes dripping blood, who hound blood-murderers to madness.

As the *Eumenides* narrates, Orestes sought asylum in the temple of Apollo, who cast the Erinyes into sleep long enough to enable Orestes to journey to Athens and seek the protection of its patroness Athena. When the Erinyes arrived in pursuit, Athena established a court and a jury—the first in Athenian history—to hear the case and render judg-

---

55. I use the Loeb Classical Library translation of the *Oresteia*, in 2 *Aeschylus* (H. W. Smyth trans. 1926), changing the language somewhat to eliminate archaisms. In some places I use David Grene's translation of *Eumenides*, in 3 *Greek Tragedies* (D. Grene & R. Lattimore eds. 1960), or Philip Vellacott's translation, *The Oresteian Trilogy* (1959), when Smyth's syntax becomes too tangled. The *Oresteia* consists of three plays: *Agamemnon*, *Choephoroi* or *Libation-Bearers*, and *Eumenides*. These three are cited by title and lines.

ment. Apollo himself represented Orestes, while the Erinyes went, so to speak, *pro se*.

The Holding and Aftermath

The issue before the court of Areopagus was not the factual question whether Orestes killed his mother, for he admitted that early in the trial.[56] As argued by the litigants, the question was whether Orestes' matricide was justifiable vengeance for the murder of his father or, more generally, *Which is worse, the murder of a father, or of a mother*? We shall examine the argument in some detail below. The jury divided evenly, and Athena cast the tie-breaking vote in favor of Orestes.[57]

The Erinyes were enraged at the "younger gods" who "have ridden down the ancient laws,"[58] and threatened to blight Athens. The final 250 lines of the play consist of Athena's attempt to placate the Erinyes by offering them an underground abode, where they would be honored as chthonic protectresses of the city. Eventually the Erinyes accepted, and the play ends with a choral procession escorting them to their grotto after their invocation of benign fate for Athens.

Procedure: The Origin of the Legal System

It is not entirely clear that Orestes' trial was the first in mythological history. Athena, in her instructions to the jury, refers to it only as "the first trial ever held for bloodshed,"[59] and Apollodorus describes it as the *second* homicide trial.[60]

---

56. See *Eumenides* l. 588.

57. There is some scholarly dispute about the number of jurors, and even about whether it was an even or odd number. Athena herself votes, then announces "Orestes, with equal ballots, wins." *Id.* ll. 740–41. This statement could indicate an odd number of jurors, with Athena tying the vote and a tie yielding acquittal; Euripides interpreted it thus in *Iphigenia in Tauris* ll. 1471–72 and *Elektra* ll. 1268–70. Or it could indicate an even number of jurors, tied, with Athena breaking the tie. Earlier, however, Athena has said "it is not lawful even for me to decide on cases of murder which involves swift wrath." *Eumenides* ll. 471–72. This statement suggests to me that she voted only to break the tie among what is therefore an even number of jurors. See Oliver Taplin, *The Stagecraft of Aeschylus: The Dramatic Use of Exits and Entrances in Greek Tragedy* 391–92 (1977); *but see* Michael Gagarin, "The Vote of Athena," 96 *American Journal of Philology* 121 (1975) (arguing the opposite view, that Athena's vote produces rather than breaks the tie).

58. *Eumenides* ll. 778–79.

59. *Id.* ll. 682–83.

60. *See* 2 Robert Graves, *The Greek Myths* 114, at 64 (1960). In fact, there were four mythical trials at the Areopagus—those of Ares (see Euripides, *Elektra* ll. 1260–63), Kephalos, Daidalos, and Orestes. Aeschylus innovated the last of the four, moving the

It is overwhelmingly likely, however, that Aeschylus means the
case to stand for the beginning of the system of justice. Athena, accepting jurisdiction, says that "since this cause has devolved on me, I will
. . . *establish* a tribunal, a tribunal to endure for all time."[61] And, in her
instructions to the jury, she says, "Henceforth, even as now, this court of
judges shall abide unto the people of Aegeus for evermore."[62]

The conception (or, if you will, philosophy) of law inherent in this
instauration is revealed in three speeches: Athena's acceptance of jurisdiction,[63] the Erinyes' choral poem as Athena assembles the jury,[64] and
Athena's instructions to the jury.[65] In summary, the features are these:

First, the purpose of the court is to resolve disputes peacefully. This
point is symbolically underlined by locating the court on the Hill of
Ares (the god of war), a hill on which the Amazons camped when they
warred against Theseus, the founder of Athens.[66] The point is clear.
Rather than private vengeance and violent contention, public justice is
established; the court replaces war. Athena's concern seems to be pragmatic: such procedures protect the city. That, in particular, is Athena's
motive for assuming jurisdiction. She claims that it is unlawful for her
or her citizens to pass judgment in such cases; furthermore, she asserts
that Orestes is "void of offense to my city."[67] Athena, however, worries
that if the Erinyes are denied, "the venom from their resentment will
. . . afflict the land."[68] It is for this reason that she changes the ancient
law by establishing the court.

Athena's proposal—an authoritative court to substitute for war
and private vengeance—is in a sense the solution to the moral and
political problem that drives the entire *Oresteia*. The setting for the
entire chain of events is the launching of the Trojan War, undertaken in
vengeance for Paris' theft of Helen in violation of the usages of host and
guest established by Zeus. Yet the war of vengeance, in which "Troy's

trial of Orestes from the Delphinion to the Areopagus and rejecting the story of the other
trials; he innovated as well by insisting that the Areopagus was only a homicide court.
See Felix Jacoby, 1 *Die Fragmente der Griechischen Historiker: Dritter Teil, Geschichte von
Städten und Völkern (Horographie und Ethnographie)* 22–25 (1954) (fragments of Hellanikos
of Lesbos).

61. *Eumenides* ll. 482–83 (emphasis added).
62. *Id.* ll. 683–84.
63. *See id.* ll. 470–89.
64. *See id.* ll. 490–565.
65. *See id.* ll. 683–706.
66. *See id.* ll. 685–90. Note that Aeschylus'sexplanation of the hill's name differs
from the traditional Athenian tale that Ares was tried there for murder. *See* Jacoby, *supra*
note 60, at 24.
67. *Eumenides* ll. 475–79.
68. *Id.* ll. 475–79.

violent doom shall swallow all,"[69] inevitably oversteps the requirements of just retribution—as symbolized by the gruesome portent of
Zeus' eagles tearing apart the body of a pregnant hare.[70] Artemis, who
"abominates the eagles' feast,"[71] reacts by laying a doom upon
Agamemnon. If he wishes to lead the expedition that destroys Troy, he
must sacrifice his own daughter.

Artemis' curse represents one of the most puzzling twists of the
story: if the goddess is so angered by the death of the hare, why does
she impose an infinitely more horrible command upon the king? Peter
Smith provides what I take to be the solution to this puzzle:

> The real cause of Artemis' wrath is of course not the single hare
> rent by Zeus' eagles but the excess of violence and the waste of life
> at Troy which the portent represents. . . . Artemis' response to the
> omen, taken beforehand, as befits a divinity, is to exact from
> Agamemnon an example of the blood-guilt his vengeance will in-
> volve, an example which sets in motion his inevitable
> punishment.[72]

Artemis compels Agamemnon to declare himself as a moral being—
either to abandon the war of vengeance or to doom himself by
demonstrating that he is ready for ruthless slaughter.

Yet Artemis' curse does more than provoke Agamemnon to commit a murder that draws down his inevitable punishment. In effect, the
curse brings the entire system of enforcing Zeus' justice by private
vengeance crashing down. The eagles, after all, came from Zeus, and
the expedition to Troy aimed merely to punish a transgression of Zeus'
own law. The intervention of Artemis turns a punitive expedition into
an endless chain of injustices committed in the name of justice: to punish Troy, Agamemnon must kill Iphigenia, whose death Clytemnestra
avenges by killing Agamemnon, whose death Orestes avenges by killing Clytemnestra, whose death the Erinyes propose to avenge in turn.
Artemis produces a bloody reductio ad absurdum of an entire system of
justice.

At the beginning of the *Agamemnon*, the chorus of Argive elders
recollects Zeus' portent and Artemis' curse in verses steeped in confusion and anxiety, each verse ending with the refrain "Cry 'sorrow,
sorrow'—yet let good prevail."[73] Smith observes that "[t]he eagle-

---

69. *Agamemnon* l. 131.
70. *Id.* ll. 113–19.
71. *Id.* l. 145.
72. Peter M. Smith, *On the Hymn to Zeus in Aeschylus' Agamemnon* 33 (1980).
73. *Agamemnon* l. 139.

omen prefigures victory for the agents of Zeus as inseparably linked with death for helpless innocents,"[74] and it seems that this is the moral dilemma that the refrain represents. The elders do not foresee how disastrously events will work out, but they fully understand that Agamemnon has transgressed divine law by killing Iphigenia, to fulfill his duty as commander and thus to carry out Zeus' doom on Troy. In traditional Greek procedure as represented in the shield scene of the *Iliad*, the role of the elders was to declare *dike* in legal conundrums; the *Oresteia*, however, begins with the tormented elders conceding defeat and bafflement in their ten-year-long meditation. The ancestral law with which they are familiar provides no way out of the disaster that is brewing.

That is why, in the *Eumenides*, Athena must root out the ancestral law completely and replace the institutions of private vengeance with a public court of justice.

Second, the Erinyes reply with a conservative argument that is Hobbesian in tenor. They argue that if the old ordinances are overthrown, all men will be ready to cast away restraint and no parent will be safe anymore. When the house of justice falls, fear of retribution will vanish and the impulses to anarchy as well as despotism will be unrestrained by moderation. The war of all against all will commence.

The ancient concept of justice represented by the Erinyes is private vengeance: when calamity strikes, we cry, "O Justice! O enthroned Spirits of Vengeance [*thronoi t'Erinyeon*]!"[75] It is precisely this conception of justice that Athena replaces by "witnesses, . . . proofs, [and] sworn evidence."[76] To rebut the Erinyes, she counsels against anarchy and despotism, for if it avoids these, Athens will "possess a bulwark to safeguard your country and your government."[77] Athena wins the Erinyes over to this conception, as evidenced by a portion of their final benediction:

This be my prayer: Civil War [or faction] fattening on men's ruin shall not thunder in our city. Let not the dry dust that drinks the black blood of citizens through passion for revenge and bloodshed for bloodshed be given our state to prey upon.[78]

---

74. Smith, *supra* note 72, at 32–33.
75. *Eumenides* ll. 511–12.
76. *Id.* ll. 485–86.
77. *Id.* ll. 700–702.
78. *Id.* ll. 976–83.

Third, the twin foundations of the new regime of law are Reverence (*sebas*) and Fear (*phobos*).[79] We obey it out of reverence for its
majesty but also out of fear of punishment.

Aeschylus' Allegorical Purposes

To understand the significance of this philosophy of law, it helps to
understand Aeschylus' intentions in composing the Oresteian trilogy.
The trilogy is an overwhelmingly potent literary achievement possessing multiple meanings and intentions. For our purposes we may isolate
three aspects of the allegory: political, religious, and sociosexual.

The first of these is displayed in the Erinyes' final benediction:
"This is my prayer: Civil War fattening on men's ruin may not thunder
in our city." Aeschylus represents civil war—municipal factional
struggle—by the horrific image of a family slaughtering itself. Atreus,
Agamemnon's father, kills his own nephews and feeds them to Thyestes, his brother, with whom he is struggling for control of the city of
Argos. Agamemnon kills his daughter and is killed in turn by his wife
and Thyestes' surviving son Aegisthus. Agamemnon's son and daughter kill Aegisthus and their own mother. This three-generation-long
slaughter mirrors the three-generation-long battle of the gods (Uranus
castrated by his son Kronos, and Kronos imprisoned by his son Zeus);
both are ended only when Zeus the Savior (Zeus Soter) brings them to a
halt in the *Eumenides* by Apollo and Athena calling off the Erinyes'
vengeance.[80] For otherwise the Erinyes will continue the chain, acting
on the ancient law of the vendetta. They work the *lex talionis*. And
Aeschylus puts in Apollo's mouth what this endless chain of vengeance
must mean. Apollo says to the Erinyes:

> Your place is where there are sentences to beheading, gouging out
> of eyes, and cutting of throats; where, by destruction of the seed,
> the manhood of youth is ruined; where men are mutilated, stoned
> to death, and where, impaled beneath their spine, they make
> moaning long and piteous.[81]

The founding of the Court of Areopagus resolves the problem of
civil war, of faction fighting and private vengeance, in three ways. First,

79. *Id.* ll. 976–83.
80. *See* Peter Burian, "Zeus Soter Tritos and Some Triads in Aeschylus' *Oresteia*,"
107 *American Journal of Philology* 332 (1986); Diskin Clay, "Aeschylus' Trigeron Mythos,"
97 *Hermes* 1 (1969).
81. *Eumenides* ll. 186–90.

it provides an alternative to the *lex talionis*. Second, that in the end the Erinyes succumb to persuasion and are thereby transformed from Furies to protectresses symbolically indicates that the battle of arguments (persuasion) on the Areopagus protects the city by taming the will to vengeance. Third, the Areopagus had itself become in Aeschylus's day the emblem of factional war. As Philip Vellacott explains:

> For the last 130 years, . . . the Areopagus had held a dominating position in the political life of Athens, . . . and as its members were life-members, its practice tended to become reactionary. Within a generation after the battle of Marathon the progressive democracy of the Athenian Assembly had decided to shake off this curb of freedom. In 462 B.C., four years before the production of the *Oresteia*, the Areopagus had been deprived of all its powers except that of jurisdiction in cases of homicide. This revolutionary change had aroused intense feelings among both supporters and opponents. . . . The Areopagites were recruited from the most wealthy Athenian classes. . . . A democratic leader named Ephialtes . . . carried the reform; he was murdered not long afterwards, and his murderer was never discovered. . . . Aeschylus . . . asserts that the Areopagus from its foundation was not a political executive, but a judicial court. He states its divine sanctions in the highest possible terms; . . . he pleads for a reasonable spirit of accommodation. When at the end of the play agreement is at last reached, those present on the stage . . . form a procession immediately recognizable as the great Panathenaic procession, the culminating event of the four-yearly Panathenaic Festival. . . . Thus the grand drama of justice is made to end in the glorification of Athens and her supreme judicial Court. . . .[82]

This is a fascinatingly contemporary motif: an activist right-wing court stripped of its powers by populist opponents and a writer recalling, or retelling, the tale of its origins to restore its legitimacy in a "reasonable spirit of accommodation." For our purposes, however, the key point of this story is that the battle over the Areopagus condensed a larger factional split within Athens, so the moral of its origin condenses a more potent message: that the court's authority is essential to civic peace.

---

82. Vellacott, "Translator's Introduction," in *The Oresteian Trilogy* 18–19 (1956). For discussion of the Areopagus and the Ephialtean reform, see 2 Bonner & Smith, *supra* note 24, at 251–78; J. K. Davies, *Democracy and Classical Greece* 63–75 (1983).

The religious reference of the trilogy is not so important for our purposes. The Erinyes frequently speak of themselves as older and the Olympians as younger gods. The trial between them marks an actual conflict between older and newer religions. It is overwhelmingly probable that the Olympian religion, the gods of which are almost identical to the Norse deities, was imported by Indo-European invaders, while the Erinyes were objects of devotion for older cults that were Mediterranean in origin.[83] Aeschylus's play thus symbolizes the triumph of the invaders' religion over an older, indigenous system of cults.

This fact is significant for our purposes only when we turn to the third, or sociosexual, signification. The older religion, it seems, was oriented toward women—goddesses and mothers—in a way that the Olympian religion was not.[84] And the trial scene is quite obviously a battle between the sexes.

This fact may be subsumed under the political interpretation of the plays. Just as Aeschylus symbolizes civil war by the self-slaughter of a family, he symbolizes factional or class strife within a society by a battle of the sexes. Note that the main line of slaughter is gender combat: Agamemnon (M) kills Iphigenia (F), Clytemnestra (F) kills Agamemnon (M), Orestes (M) kills Clytemnestra (F), the Furies (F) pursue Orestes (M), and Apollo (M) defeats the Furies (F). Even Aegisthus fits in, for he is belittled as a "woman."[85] The separate theme of gender combat, however, has an importance of its own.

"The World Historical Defeat of the Female Sex"

Which is worse, the murder of a father or of a mother? Early in the trial, the Erinyes give their answer. Orestes asks them why, after Agamemnon's murder, they did not pursue Clytemnestra into banishment as they have pursued him, and they reply, "She was not of one blood with the man she slew."[86]

Moments later, Apollo (representing Orestes) gives his answer to the question. He replies that he told Orestes to kill Clytemnestra, and he speaks nothing that has not been commanded by Zeus. The Erinyes are incredulous: Zeus had commanded that Orestes "avenge the slaying of his father, but of the honour due his mother take no account at all?"[87]

---

83. W. K. C. Guthrie, *The Greeks and Their Gods* 28–33 (1950).
84. *See* Robert Graves, "The White Goddess," in *On Poetry: Collected Talks and Essays* 238 (1969); J. E. Harrison, *Prolegomena to the Study of Greek Religion* (1903).
85. *Agamemnon* l. 625.
86. *Eumenides* l. 605.
87. *Id.* ll. 622–24.

And Apollo replies, "Aye, for it was in no wise the same thing—the murder of a high-born *man* . . . by a woman's hand."[88] And the Erinyes understand his point. "A father's death, according to your plea, is held by Zeus as of more account."[89]

The trial of Orestes must be read as a vindication of patriarchy. The *Eumenides* depicts a trial at law, the outcome of which legally justifies the dominance of masculine over feminine interests. It indexes what Frederick Engels called "the world historical defeat of the female sex."[90]

The play, not surprisingly, has been of great interest to contemporary feminists. This is particularly so because of an anthropological controversy which I must mention (though it does not form part of my own argument). In 1861 Johann Bachofen published a book entitled *Mutterrecht* (*Mother Right*), which argued that the battle between the old and new deities was in fact a mythification (or mystification) of a real battle in which a matriarchal or matrilineal society was overthrown by a patriarchal, patrilineal one.[91] The battle between the sexes, Bachofen believed, was a real historical event; and he skillfully used the *Oresteia* and other Greek works and myths to provide evidence for his theory.

Bachofen's theory was adopted by Frederick Engels, who combined it with other nineteenth-century anthropological theories and with his own and Karl Marx's historical materialism to provide an extremely coherent account of the origin of the family—an account, moreover, that became the more or less official anthropology of the socialist world. For obvious reasons, the theory of an original matriarchy has become popular among feminist writers as well; so it is predictably controversial. With near-unanimity, non-Marxist anthropologists dispute the theories on which it is based, and many question whether there have ever been genuinely matriarchal societies anywhere. Influential contemporary classicists have provided interpretations of the Greek sources alternative to Bachofen's. It is very difficult for the nonspecialist to tell who is right.[92]

---

88. *Id*. ll. 625–27.

89. *Id*. ll. 639–40.

90. This phrase comes from Frederick Engels, *The Origin of the Family, Private Property and the State* 120 (Eleanor Leacock ed. 1972).

91. *See* Johann Bachofen, *Myth, Religion, and Mother Right* (Ralph Manheim trans. 1967).

92. For the authoritative contemporary statement of the Marxist interpretation, see George Thomson, *Aeschylus and Athens: A Study in the Social Origins of Drama* (4th ed. 1973). The best (and most dispassionate) treatment of the controversy I have found is Marilyn Arthur, "Review Essay—Classics," 2 *Signs* 382 (1976). Arthur notes that "the cold-war attitude which has, until very recently, characterized American and British

Whether or not the *Oresteia* is a mythification of a historical matriarchy, it obviously legitimizes the position women occupied as an
underclass in Aeschylus' Athens.[93] Its misogyny is unmistakable.[94]
This fact will prove important to us later.

The Trial

Our question is simple: Did the Furies get a fair trial leading to a just
result?

Indictment and Answer

When Athena answers Orestes' call, she is confronted by the sight of the
Erinyes surrounding him as he clings to her image at the altar. The
Erinyes speak first, identifying their lineage and stating their office:
"We drive slayers of men from out of their homes."[95] Are they pursuing
Orestes for that reason?

Erinyes: Aye, for he held it his duty to be his mother's murderer.
Athena: Because of other constraint or through fear of someone's
wrath?
Erinyes: Where is there a spur so keen as to compel the murder of a
mother?[96]

This exchange is crucial, for part of Orestes' defense is that Apollo
"threatened me with cruel woes should I fail to do this deed upon the

classicists' evaluations of Marxist interpretations of antiquity has prevented a thorough
reevaluation of Thomson's evidence and conclusion." *Id.* at 384. However, Arthur
believes that "the concept of matriarchy as a historical stage or as a social reality should
be abandoned." *Id.* at 385. It should be noted, however, that the evidence against
Bachofen presented by Vidal-Naquet and Pembroke, upon which Arthur relies, is highly
indirect. *See id.* at 385 nn. 11–14; *see also* Jan Bremmer, "Avunculate and Fosterage,"
Journal of Indo-European Studies 74 (1976) (another piece of very indirect evidence against
Bachofen).

    93. *See* Eva C. Keuls, *The Reign of the Phallus: Sexual Politics in Ancient Athens* (1985);
Philip E. Slater, *The Glory of H ra: Greek Mythology and the Greek Family* 4–13 (1968) (the
point emerges throughout Slater's book); John Gould, "Law, Custom and Myth: Aspects
of the Social Position of Women in Classical Athens," 100 *Journal of Hellenic Studies* 38
(1980), *see also* A. W. Gomme, "The Position of Women in Athens in the Fifth and Fourth
Centuries," 20 *Classical Philology* 1 (1925) (providing a more upbeat interpretation of the
status of women).
    94. *See* Froma R. Zeitlin, "The Dynamics of Misogyny: Myth and Mythmaking in
the *Oresteia*," 11 *Arethusa* 149 (1978).
    95. *Eumenides* l. 421.
    96. *Id.* ll. 425–27.

guilty."[97] The Erinyes' rhetorical question amounts to a presupposition that the duty to a mother qualitatively outweighs any other duty or circumstance. Orestes has murdered his mother: *res ipsa loquitur.* No constraint could mitigate this.

The Erinyes claim that this is the ancient law, and nothing in the play suggests that they are not correct. As Athena later admits, however, "in all things, save wedlock, I am for the male with all my soul, and am entirely on the father's side."[98] It is for this reason, we may suspect, that she does not summarily find for the Erinyes. Neither does she respond to the Erinyes directly. Instead, Athena changes the subject to a procedural issue: "Two parties are here present; half only of the case is heard."[99] Strictly speaking, this is a dodge: first, because if the Erinyes' interpretation of the ancient law is correct, nothing the other side says could make a difference and, second, because the procedure of a bipartisan hearing has not yet been established. Athena, it appears, is groping for a legalism to save Orestes.

Orestes begins his defense by qualifying himself to testify. He has gone through ritual purification for the killing of his mother, and therefore "the law that he who is defiled by shedding blood shall be debarred all speech" does not apply in his case.[100] He next offers his defense, which rests on two grounds. First, the murder of his mother is justified because it avenged the murder of his father. Second, Apollo put him up to it. He then leaves it to Athena to "pronounce judgment" whether his act "was wrought in righteousness or not."[101]

Athena as Judge: A Fair Trial?

After the jurors have voted, Athena makes the statement quoted above that she is "for the male with all my soul" and then breaks the tie in Orestes' favor. Given her self-admitted bias, she was quite right in appointing a jury rather than deciding the case herself. For another reason as well, fairness favored an all-human jury. As we have seen, the case involved a conflict between the spheres of authority of the old and new (Olympian) deities, and it would have been quite improper for

---

97. *Id.* ll. 466–67.
98. *Id.* ll. 737–38.
99. *Id.* l. 428.
100. *Id.* ll. 448–50. Note, however, that the choruses in *Agamemnon* and *Choephoroi* have declared that such purification is impossible. *See Agamemnon* ll. 69–71, 381–84; *Choephoroi* ll. 66–74, 310–14, 400–404. In this and other points in my argument (which I note), I have depended upon Philip Vellacott, "Has Good Prevailed? A Further Study of the *Oresteia*," 81 *Harvard Studies in Classical Philology* 113 (1977).
101. *Eumenides* ll. 468–69.

Athena to render the decision, for precisely the same reason that the
Walker Court could not persuasively establish the basis of its own authority (as I argued in the preceding chapter). Symbolically, the human
jurors stand in for the Olympian gods.

In several respects, however, Aeschylus wants us to see that
Athena tilts the trial in favor of Orestes. The first is obvious: she ap-
points an all-male jury to hear the case. Perhaps, however, this should
not count, for it may not have seemed anomalous to Aeschylus's audience; even the U. S. Supreme Court found nothing untoward about
excluding women from juries until 1975.[102]

Athena's second error as a trial judge is more subtle but would at
any rate have been visible to Aeschylus's audience. In her instructions
to the jury Athena establishes the tribunal on the Hill of Ares, where the
Amazons camped in their war against Theseus. I have emphasized one
symbolic meaning of this location: the rule of law replaces war as the
just means of settling disputes. But the other symbolic meaning could
hardly have escaped the jurors (and audience): *Here is where women
made war against the man who founded our city, and here is where a new rule
of law must supersede war to "safeguard country and government."* The jury
instructions, that is, implant in the minds of the jurors the idea that

---

102. *See* Taylor v. Louisiana, 419 U.S. 522 (1975). For the earlier view that excluding
women was not unconstitutional, *see* Hoyt v. Florida, 368 U.S. 57 (1961); Strauder v. West
Virginia, 100 U.S. 303, 310 (1880).

In this paragraph and throughout this section, I am arguing that the Erinyes had
law (and perhaps justice as well) squarely on their side, and hence that Athena's
intervention, leading to the acquittal of Orestes, subverted the working of the law by
subordinating women to men for the sake of maintaining order. Let me note that there is
a plausible and important alternative reading. This is the view that before the establishment of the Areopagite court, the law was unclear—not because human affairs were
conducted in a lawless regime of private enforcement and vendetta but because there
was too much law, that is, too many plausible interpretations of the legal meaning of the
events. On this reading the function of the court was not to throw over one law for
another, as I have suggested, but rather to eliminate all but one of the conflicting
meanings. *See* James Boyd White, *Heracles' Bow* 176–80 (1985) ("In the world represented
here [in the *Oresteia*] no speaker can maintain any version of the story he has to tell, any
claim of its significance, against the pressure of other versions. . . . The law will thus
rescue us all from the unbearable incoherence of the world that has been presented to
us—an incoherence of story, of intellect, of action, of the very self."); Cover, "Foreword:
Nomos and Narrative," 97 *Harvard Law Review* 4, 40–41 (1983) ("Athena's establishment
of the institutionalized law of the polis is addressed to the dilemma of the moral and
legal indeterminacy created by two laws, one invoked by the Erinyes and the other by
Apollo."); Peter Euben, "Justice in the *Oresteia*," 76 *American Political Science Review* 22, 31
(1982) ("[T]he transparency of the *Eumenides* represents both a gain in clarity and a loss
of meaning (or at least a temptation to forgetfulness).").

warlike women (such as the Erinyes and Clytemnestra) are the enemy of civic order in general and of Athens in particular.

In yet another respect Athena's instructions to the jury bias the case. Initially, she had stated a procedural rule that it is the plaintiffs who define the matter at trial: "[T]he plaintiff at the commencement, speaking first, shall rightly inform us of the issue."[103] The Erinyes define the issue as one of matricide, for which no extenuating circumstances provide a defense.

Athena, however, redefines the crime (contrary to her prior rule) in her charge to the jury, describing the trial as the first "ever held for bloodshed."[104] She implicitly accepts Apollo's assimilation of Orestes' crime to Clytemnestra's—both are "bloodshed"—and thus denies the singularity of matricide. This, of course, begs the Erinyes' question.

I have already quoted Athena's frank statement of prejudice in favor of the male sex as she casts her ballot for acquittal. It is also worth mentioning her stated reason for this prejudice, namely that "mother have I none that gave me birth."[105] This suggests one final respect in which the trial was procedurally unfair. It is drastically unfair to put the deciding vote in the hands of one who is self-admittedly incapable of the moral sentiment underlying the Erinyes' position. Indeed, Athena offered this argument herself: "[I]t is not lawful . . . for me to decide on cases of murder which involves swift wrath."[106] Since the goddess cannot share the passion, she cannot judge the case; but surely the same principle holds here.

Orestes on His Own

When the court is assembled, the Erinyes question Orestes, and he defends himself. He admits that he killed Clytemnestra but claims that "she was attainted by a two-fold defilement."[107]

> *Erinyes:* Tell me how, and explain it to the judges here.
> *Orestes:* She murdered her husband, and thereby my father too.
> *Erinyes:* Of this stain, death has set her free. But you still live.[108]

This reply is far from persuasive. It is true that it suggests Orestes must be punished as Clytemnestra was. However, it also suggests that if his

---

103. *Eumenides* ll. 583–84.
104. *Id.* l. 682; *see* Vellacott, *supra* note 100, at 119.
105. *Eumenides* l. 736.
106. *Id.* ll. 471–72.
107. *Id.* l. 600.
108. *Id.* ll. 600–603.

punishment is justified, hers was as well, and Orestes has punished her. If he was barred from punishing her, who should have done it? That is the Erinyes' self-proclaimed office:

> *Orestes:* But why, while she lived, did you not pursue her into banishment?
> *Erinyes:* She was not of one blood with the man she slew.[109]

At this point, Orestes might reply that if the Erinyes would not punish Clytemnestra, and her punishment was nevertheless justifiable, then they had no complaint against his vigilantism. That would not settle the issue, for they could reply that the duty to preserve one's mother is greater than that to avenge one's father. Orestes, however, is simply lacking in the skill to cross-examine the Erinyes ably and promptly paints himself into a corner:

> *Orestes:* But am I blood-kin to my own mother?
> *Erinyes:* Murderer, yes. How else could she have nursed you beneath her heart?ˈ Do you forswear your mother's intimate blood?[110]

Orestes is stymied, for he has somehow gotten himself into the position of seeming to deny that he is a blood relative of his own mother. Orestes needs a lawyer, and he knows it. He calls on Apollo.

The Delphia Lawyer

Aeschylus' Apollo is depicted in a complex and highly ambivalent way. On the one hand he is a god, and the playwright does nothing to diminish his divinity. On the other, as Vellacott argues in the introduction to his translation of the *Oresteia*, Apollo is presented in a way designed to excite the suspicion of Aeschylus' audience. In *Agamemnon* the Herald reminds us that Apollo sided with the Trojans against the Greek army.[111] Cassandra laments that because she has spurned Apollo's love he has cruelly given her over to Clytemnestra's murderous hands.[112] Apollo indeed first opposed Agamemnon militarily, then assisted Clytemnestra in her murder of an innocent and sympathetic woman, and finally turned about and incited Orestes to murder

---

109. *Id.* ll. 604–5.
110. *Id.* ll. 606–8.
111. *See Agamemnon* ll. 509–13.
112. *See id.* ll. 1256–72.

Clytemnestra. Moreover, Apollo claims infallibility in his political ora-
cles,[113] and it was well known to Aeschylus's audience that Delphi was
pro-Persian at the time of the Persian invasion.[114]
    Remember also that Orestes was driven to kill his mother by
threats from Apollo. Specifically, Apollo told him that he would be
pursued by the Furies if he did not avenge his father's murder.[115] We
now learn that the Erinyes pursue blood-murderers, not those who
refrain from vengeance: "If a man can spread his hands and show they
are clean, no wrath of ours shall lurk for him."[116] Apollo was therefore
deceiving Orestes when he incited him to murder Clytemnestra and
again when he tells the court,

> *Apollo:* Unto you, this high tribunal created by Athena, I will speak
> as justice bids,—seer that I am, I cannot utter untruth. Never yet,
> on my oracular throne, have I spoken anything touching man or
> woman or polity but what has been commanded by Zeus. . . .[117]

---

113. *Eumenides* ll. 616–18.

114. *See* Vellacott, *supra* note 82, at 34–35.

115. *See Choephoroi* ll. 283–90.

116. *Eumenides* ll. 313–15; *see* Vellacott, *supra* note 100, at 115. Daniel Blickman has
objected that "this text is quite inadequate to indicate Apollo lied; *Choephorai* 283–90 [the
passage in which Apollo told Orestes that the Furies would pursue him if he did not
avenge Agamemnon's murder] is authoritative (and *living*) Greek belief" (private communication, March 1, 1991). I am not persuaded, however. Even though Apollo's oracle
may well have represented living Greek belief, the fact remains that the Furies describe
their own practice differently, in a passage where they have no conceivable reason to
lie—they are alone with Orestes before Athena has appeared on the scene. Moreover, the
best evidence that they would not have pursued Orestes had he refrained from murdering Clytemnestra lies in the fact that they *did not* pursue him in the interval between
Agamemnon's murder and Orestes' return to Argos. In at least two other passages
Aeschylus revises contemporary Greek belief: as we have seen, he moved the trial of
Orestes from the Delphinion to the Areopagus—*see supra* note 60; and, as we shall see
below, he altered the traditional Hesiodic account of the Erinyes' birth. These passages
indicate that Aeschylus was perfectly willing to deviate from contemporary Greek
beliefs when doing so would advance his literary theme.

117. *Eumenides* ll. 614–18. Here too Blickman objects: "I don't think that Apollo
could conceivably be portrayed by Aeschylus as the liar whom you describe—he is
closely associated with Zeus, as his mouthpiece, in the trilogy, and the *Oresteia* contains
the most exalted Greek poetry about Zeus" (private communication, March 1, 1991). But
Apollo's language is ambiguous. He states, to be sure, that he is incapable of uttering
untruth, but if Aeschylus means to portray him as a liar, then it hardly removes our
suspicions of him to find the god proclaiming his own veracity. Nor did the Greeks seem
to consider it sacrilegious to represent a god as a liar—consider the numerous intrigues
and deceits in which the gods engage in the *Iliad* or, for that matter, Hermes' lie in the
Homeric *Hymn to Hermes*. In the next sentence of his speech, Apollo says only that his
utterances represent the will of Zeus, which may mean only that to replace the old legal

Athena has convened a court "that they may decide this issue in accordance with the truth,"[118] "that their case may be decided on its just merits."[119] Aeschylus raises a doubt in his audience's mind, a question that has been raised ever since about the adversary trial: Is the truth obscured by that most extraneous of all factors, the personal credibility of a lawyer? This is simply one part of a larger question. Apollo wins the case. Does he do so through sound arguments? Or is he simply a Delphia lawyer?

Apollo's Arguments

The complaint is a timeless one. It concerns the lawyer's ability to prevail with weak arguments masked in eloquence; it is a complaint about the lawyer's sin against the truth. How good are Apollo's arguments? When he prevails, does truth prevail?

Near the beginning of the play Aeschylus intimates the answers to these questions. He tells us that Apollo's intentions are to win through eloquence rather than truth. For Apollo sends Orestes to Athens with these words: "There, with judges of your cause *and speech of persuasive charm*, we shall discover means to release you utterly from your distress."[120]

As we have noted, Apollo begins his arguments by claiming that Orestes' matricide was commanded by Zeus, speaking through Apollo's oracle. And, as we also have noted, Aeschylus presents Apollo in a light calculated to excite suspicion of his veracity. These suspicions are emphasized and confirmed in an angry exchange between the Erinyes and Apollo while the jury is voting. Apollo says, "I shall gain the victory," and they reply, "Such was your style of action also . . . when you moved the Fates to make mortals free from death."[121] They are referring to an incident in which Apollo plied the Fates with wine to get them to release his friend Admetus from death. Apollo replies, "Is it not

order represented by the Erinyes by the new order introduced by Athena, Zeus too finds a "noble lie" essential. Indeed, in the following lines Apollo says "I bid you, then, mark first the force of justice here;/But next, even more, regard my father's will. No oath/Can have more force than Zeus, whose name has sanctioned it." *Eumenides* ll. 619–21 (P. Vellacott trans., *supra* note 55, at 168). Though Apollo claims justice for his position, he implicitly distinguishes justice from the will of Zeus, and thus his close association with Zeus is perfectly consistent with a reading in which Aeschylus means his audience to acknowledge the necessity of an unjust trial as an instrument for creating a greater divine justice.

    118. *Id.* ll. 487–89.
    119. *Id.* ll. 572–73.
    120. *Id.* ll. 81–83 (emphasis added).
    121. *Id.* ll. 722–24.

then right to befriend a votary, above all in his hour of need?"[122] We thus see him as one who will freely use dishonest means to help out his votary. If he will swindle the Fates (the Erinyes' half-sisters) to assist Admetus, and if he will shamelessly defend this action on the grounds that Admetus was his votary, why will he not swindle the Erinyes themselves on behalf of his votary Orestes? Aeschylus could have had only one motive for including this exchange—to make his audience doubt Apollo's argument.

The Erinyes counterattack indirectly:

> *Erinyes:* Zeus . . . gave you this oracular command: to declare to Orestes here that he avenge the slaying of his father, but of the honor due his mother take no account at all?
> *Apollo:* Aye, for it was in no wise the same thing—the murder of a high-born *man* . . . by a woman's hand.
> *Erinyes:* A father's death, according to your plea, is held by Zeus as of more account; yet he himself cast into bonds his aged father Kronos. How does not this act belie your argument?
> *Apollo:* Oh, monsters utterly loathed and detested of the gods! Bonds Zeus might undo. . . . But when the dust has drained the blood of man, . . . there is no return to life.[123]

It is not clear whether the Erinyes' argument is meant to show that Zeus was unlikely to have given such a command or that, since Zeus did not show respect for his own father, his command cannot be exceptionless. In either case, their argument seems to be a telling one.

Apollo's response, on the other hand, is a diversion, a red herring. The Erinyes' point is that Zeus does not respect fathers as such, as Apollo asserted, for he did not respect his own father. Apollo replies that Zeus did not kill his father, while Clytemnestra killed Orestes'. Yet it seems absurd to suggest that casting a father into bondage shows no disrespect for him, that only murder shows disrespect. That, however, is precisely the implication of Apollo's reply. Apollo's attempt to distinguish murder from imprisonment on the basis of murder's finality has no relevance. Perhaps Zeus could release his father, but the fact remains that he didn't. If finality is the criterion of disrespect, Zeus is no more respectful of fathers than Clytemnestra.

The Erinyes do not pursue this point but turn to a different argument. Now that Orestes has killed his mother, what *phratry* (an ex-

---

122. *Id.* ll. 725–26.
123. *Id.* ll. 622–48 (emphasis added).

tended clan) will accept him? His acquittal would undermine the social order.[124] In reply to this Apollo unveils his final argument:

> *Apollo:* The mother of what is called her child is not its parent, but only the nurse of the newly implanted germ. The begetter is the parent, whereas she, as a stranger for a stranger, does nothing but preserve the sprout. . . . And I will offer you a sure proof of what I say: fatherhood there may be, when mother there is none. Here at hand is a witness, the child of Olympian Zeus.[125]

Athena, of course, was born by Zeus himself and had no mother.[126] It is a bold stroke: Apollo does not deny that the murder of blood kin is worse than the murder of one unrelated by blood—Orestes' initial claim. Instead he counters that the mother is not the child's blood kin at all; indeed, that she is not necessary for the child's birth.

This argument was apparently consistent with the embryology of the day.[127] Consider, for example, Aristotle's version (written, to be sure, 100 years after Aeschylus):

> That, then, the female does not contribute semen to generation, but does contribute something, and that this is the matter of the catamenia, . . . is clear. . . . For there must needs be that which generates and that from which it generates. . . . If, then, the male stands for the effective and active, and the female . . . for the passive, it follows that what the female would contribute to the semen of the male would not be semen but material for the semen to work upon.[128]

Apollo's theory, however, goes much further than Aristotle's by claiming that the mother contributes nothing, that she is totally unnecessary.

Leaving biology aside, Apollo's argument is sophistry on its own terms and Aeschylus'. The brilliant rhetorical stroke is his dramatic

---

124. *Id.* ll. 652–56.

125. *Id.* ll. 658–64.

126. *See* Hesiod, *Theogony,* in *Hesiod: Theogony, Works and Days, Shield, supra* note 45, ll. 886–900, at 35 [hereinafter *Theogony*].

127. So claims Zeitlin, *supra* note 94, at 168–69. However Hippocrates, writing just one generation after Aeschylus, argued (against this view) that reproduction requires both a male and female seed; Joseph Needham, *A History of Embryology* 35, 35 n.1 (rev. ed. 1959). *See* Keuls, *supra* note 93, at 146 (pointing out that "under Attic law paternal half-brothers and half-sisters could marry, maternal ones could not," thereby suggesting that Athenians understood the falsity of the theory of exclusive male parenthood).

128. Aristotle, *On the Generation of Animals,* in *The Basic Works of Aristotle* 728b22–729a32, at 675–76 (Richard McKeon ed. 1941).

invocation of Athena herself to prove that a mother is unnecessary. But Athena is a god, not a human being, while the question is whether a human child is its mother's blood kin. Gods can do things that humans cannot, so Apollo's argument proves absolutely nothing other than that Zeus and Athena are gods.

More importantly, Aeschylus finds a way to indicate in his text that Apollo's argument is not to be believed: *The Erinyes have a mother but no father!* They are the "daughters of Night"—a female, since they refer to her as "mother Night."[129] Aeschylus leaves no hint of a suggestion that they have a father, and the overwhelming gynocentrism of everything associated with the Furies (together with the fundamental male-female opposition pervading the play) suggests that they do not. If they had a father, Greek custom would dictate that they be referred to as daughters of that father, rather than daughters of Night. Aeschylus' genealogy of the Furies is his own innovation, moreover, deviating from the Hesiodic tradition according to which the Furies were born of Mother Earth when blood from the castrated genitals of Uranus fell on her.[130] Aeschylus, by revising their genealogy, underscores the fact that the Furies have a mother but no father. This fact annihilates Apollo's argument in a way that would be immediately apparent to Aeschylus' audience.

The Aftermath: Selling the Verdict, Co-opting the Furies (Athena as Negotiator)

Aeschylus has portrayed a trial bereft of fairness, and the Erinyes respond with a withering blast of wrath. It is now Athena's job to don the conciliator's mantle: she must negotiate with them to sell the verdict. She uses three argumentative tactics.

First, she redirects their attention from the question whether the verdict was fair to the question whether their honor has been maintained, which she realizes is the immediate source of their wrath:

> You have not been vanquished. Nay, the trial resulted fairly in ballots equally divided without disgrace to you; but from Zeus was offered clear testimony, and he that himself uttered the oracle himself bore witness that Orestes should not suffer harm for his deed.[131]

---

129. *Eumenides* ll. 844–45. Zeitlin, *supra* note 94 at 163, describes them as "parthenogenetic offspring," though I am unaware of any basis for this claim beyond the present passage.

130. *Theogony* ll. 178–85, at 17.

131. *Eumenides* ll. 795–99.

Second, she uses threats: "I, too, rely on Zeus—what need to speak of that?—and know, I alone of the gods, the keys of the armory wherein his thunderbolt is sealed. Yet of that there is no need."[132]

Third, she devises a low-cost settlement offer, taking advantage of their straitened circumstances. The Erinyes now perceive themselves as "bereft of honor and distressed,"[133] and Athena immediately exploits this fact to strike an advantageous settlement and co-opt them. They can become honored (but tamed) goddesses with their own underground grotto, provided only that henceforth they bend their powers to ensure Athens' continued prosperity. They accept the offer, and Athena says, "I am grateful to Persuasion that her glance kept ever watch over my tongue and lips when I encountered their fierce refusal. But Zeus, he that sways men's tongues, has triumphed."[134]

Contemporary feminists are likely to see this as an outcome at once symptomatic and typical. The Erinyes are divested of their ancient right, then of their freedom, and finally are talked into rejoicing in the outcome as their freely chosen good fortune.[135]

Aeschylus as Legal Theorist

We must now return to our original inquiry. Where does Aeschylus stand in the debate between Homer and Hesiod—the debate between stability over justice and justice as a precondition of stability? I have argued that Aeschylus means us to perceive the trial of Orestes as manifestly unfair. At the same time, however, the triumphal conclusion of the play leaves no doubt that Aeschylus endorses the outcome of the trial and expects that his audience will agree with this assessment. Nor can there be much doubt that the play portrays the outcome as the will and justice of Zeus. These facts should make it clear that Aeschylus cannot accede to the Hesiodic view, for according to that view a city with unjust judicial proceedings will be blighted by the gods. Here, however, Athens is blessed.

The paradox with which Aeschylus confronts us can be explained only when we understand that he adopts the Homeric valuation of legal justice. The dramatic climax of *Agamemnon* occurs when Clytemnestra

---

132. *Id.* ll. 826–28.
133. *Id.* l. 822.
134. *Id.* ll. 970–73.
135. *Id.* ll. 938–48. The widely publicized Berlin *Schaubühne* performance of 1980 ended with the jurors escorting the Erinyes to chairs on the floor below the stage, then tying them to the chairs with the same purple cloth in which Clytemnestra had wrapped Agamemnon. They were tied tighter and tighter until they were completely immobilized. After the play, women in the audience spontaneously rose to untie the Erinyes.

persuades her husband (against his better judgment) to enter his house, where she proceeds to murder him. In that play, persuasion is linked to murderous vengeance—it is a sinister principle. At the end of the *Eumenides*, Athena persuades the Erinyes to protect the city. The movement of the *Oresteia*, then, is a transformation of persuasion from a sinister to a benign force; a transformation effected by the institution of the Areopagite Court. The purpose of the court is not to administer legal justice in an absolute sense but to transform malignant persuasion into benign persuasion in the name of social peace. Only in this way can we explain why an unjust trial is supposed to result in a praiseworthy outcome.[136]

The parallel, and contrast, with Hesiod is clear. For Hesiod, legal justice transforms bad strife into good, resulting in prosperity. For Aeschylus, legal institutions that are not necessarily just transform bad persuasion into good. The result here also is prosperity. Part of the Erinyes' final blessing to Athens is this:

> May no hurtful wind blow to the destruction of the trees—'tis thus I declare my grace—and may no scorching heat, blasting the budding plants, pass the borders of its proper clime; may no deadly blight draw nigh to kill the fruit; may the earth foster the teeming flocks with twin increase at the appointed time, and ever may the rich produce of the earth pay the gods' gift of luck gain.[137]

And they conclude: "Fare ye well, fare ye well, amid the wealth vouchsafed by fate."[138]

Clearly, the Erinyes are invoking agricultural prosperity; but the scene has a deeper significance, for the Greek understanding of agriculture is quite different from ours. As Arendt writes,

> The Greeks tended to consider even agriculture as part and parcel of fabrication, as belonging to the cunning, skillful, "technical" devices with which man, more awe-inspiring than all that is, tames and rules nature. What we, still under the spell of the Roman heritage, consider to be the most natural and the most peaceful of

---

136. In Blickman's words, "for Aeschylus and his audience a fair and stable arrangement of either the divine government or a human πόλις is a fine achievement which, so far from excluding justice θέμις, δίκη), is synonymous with it." Daniel R. Blickman, "Styx and the Justice of Zeus in Hesiod's *Theogony*," 41 *Phoenix* 341, 349 n.28 (1987). I am arguing, however, that *stable*, not *fair*, is the operative term in this assessment.

137. *Eumenides* ll. 938–48.

138. *Id*. l. 996.

man's activities, the tilling of the soil, the Greeks understood as a daring, violent enterprise in which, year in year out, the earth, inexhaustible and indefatigable, is disturbed and violated.[139]

The clearest expression of this attitude is the famous chorus of *Antigone:*

> Many the wonders but nothing walks stranger than man. . . . And she, the greatest of gods, the earth—ageless she is, and unwearied—he wears her away as the ploughs go up and down from year to year and his mules turn up the soil.[140]

In the Olympian creation myth, Gaia, the Earth, is the mother of all things. Thus agricultural activity is, mythologically, an act of violence against the mother; it is the archetype of Orestes' crime, the ultimate affront to the Erinyes.[141] Their blessing, just before their interment as civic deities in the chthonic grotto, can mean only one thing: with the subordination of women, the earth is tamed, and prosperity is possible. The contrast with Hesiod is sharp and exact.

The *Eumenides* presents an instrumentalist conception of legal argument and legal institutions. Apollo, the first advocate, wins victory through sharp tactics and deceitful argument. Athena institutes a biased court for pragmatic reasons. Her persuasion pacifies the Erinyes for the sake of Athenian prosperity. Ancient right is overthrown to end factional slaughter and restore civil peace. And, in the name of prosperity and peace, an unfair verdict converts women into a permanent underclass of society. But Athena and Apollo are gods, speaking the will of Zeus, and we are intended to accept their instrumentalism as divine. That is the paradox.

A shallower playwright than Aeschylus would not have composed the trial scene as he did. The shallower playwright would have presented an exemplary, thoroughly fair trial, resulting in the same outcome. (This is how Euripides presents the trial in *Elektra.*) Aeschylus, however, like Homer before him, understood that the civil peace and stability that he implicitly elevated to the highest-ranked social value must be purchased at a high price. For Homer, that price was the loss of

---

139. Hannah Arendt, "The Crisis in Culture: Its Social and Its Political Significance," in *Between Past and Future* 212–13 (rev. ed. 1968).

140. Sophocles, *Antigone* (Elizabeth Wyckoff trans.), in *Sophocles I* ll. 323–43, at 170 (David Grene ed. 1954).

141. The image of women as agricultural animals, or earth to be sowed, was common in classical Athens. *See* Gould, *supra* note 93, at 53. According to the standard Athenian wedding formula, marriage was designed "for the ploughing of legitimate children." Keuls, *supra* note 93, at 100.

what is mostly fully and adequately human, the heroic quest for justice. For Aeschylus, the price of order is that we abandon legal justice in favor of social control.

The Triumph of Legal Instrumentalism: Plato's Republic and Laws

There is another price to pay for order as Aeschylus tells the story: the introduction of class hierarchy in society through the legal subordination of women. For Aeschylus, however, it is not clear that this counted as a problem or cost. The *Oresteia* contains no evidence that he found anything objectionable about class hierarchy and, if Zeitlin is right, a great deal of evidence that he considered the subordination of women a social good.

Plato, on the other hand, was profoundly aware of class hierarchy as a problem of political morality. In the *Republic* and *Laws* he explicitly connected the themes of (1) legal instrumentalism in the name of civic peace, (2) the consequent loss of justice as such, and (3) the introduction of class hierarchy. He introduced as well a fourth motif, to which I shall return in concluding this chapter and which is extraordinarily important in evaluating legal instrumentalism: as a psychological fact, people cannot believe that their legal institutions are not just if they are to abide by them. Thus, the instrumentalist doctrine of peace over justice must be an esoteric one, known to and believed by only a few in the society.

The *Republic* is often assumed to be the definitive statement of Plato's political philosophy, while the *Laws* is simply a puzzling, almost senescent, afterthought—in the words of J. N. Findlay, "a monumentally uninteresting work, . . . found so even in antiquity."[142] In fact, the works must be read together, for each without the other is incomplete. Their doctrines are consistent and complementary.

The *Republic* is a work explicitly about justice. It attempts to construct an ideally just state so that, seeing justice writ large, we can discover what justice is in a single human soul. This state is constructed in Book 4, and its features are famous. They include a "Guardian" class that is communistic in structure—the Guardians hold their property and their wives in common. Their children are educated in common, rather than by their parents, and philosopher-kings rule. In Book 8, however, Plato changes the description so that the whole state (and not just the Guardian class) is communistic:

This much has been agreed, Glaucon: for a city that is going to be governed on a high level, women must be in common, children

---

142. J. N. Findlay, *Plato and Platonism: An Introduction* 199 (1978).

and their entire education must be in common, and similarly the practices in war and peace must be in common, and their kings must be those among them who have proved best in philosophy and with respect to war.[143]

It is this latter description that Plato adopts in the *Laws;* and, as we shall see, this overlap explicitly connects the doctrines of the two dialogues.

The *Republic* is often assumed to recommend the city constructed in Book 4. In fact, the dialogue (beginning with Book 8) is pessimistic about it. Such a city will inevitably decay.[144] Factions will form within it because of imperfections in human nature—Plato explicitly alludes to Hesiod's myth of the races of gold, silver, bronze and iron[145]—and what began as blissful democracy ends as tyranny.[146] At the conclusion of the dialogue, Plato moves justice out of the state and into the individual, autonomous human soul.[147]

Ultimately, Plato believes that the best city—the just city—is a theoretical ideal that cannot be realized in practice. It is a city "that has its place in speeches."[148] That sets the problem for the *Laws,* which also attempts "to fashion the laws in speech,"[149] but with a pragmatic intent: "When we have looked over the territory and the neighbors we will decide these things in deed as well as in speech."[150]

For this reason, Plato asserts in the *Laws* that "a second-best city is to be constructed."[151] He continues by describing the best city in nearly the same communistic terms as in Book 8 of the *Republic:*

> That city and that regime are first, and the laws are best, where the old proverb holds as much as possible throughout the whole city: it is said that the things of friends really are common. If this situation exists somewhere now, or if it should ever exist someday—if women are common, and children are common, and every sort of property is common; if every device has been employed to exclude all of what is called the "private" from all aspects of life; . . . if with

143. Plato, *Republic,* in *The Republic of Plato* 543a, at 221 (Alan Bloom trans. 1968) [hereinafter *Republic*].
144. *See id.* 546a, at 224.
145. *See id.* 546e–547c, at 224–25.
146. *See id.* 569c, at 249.
147. *See id.* 608c–621d, at 292–303.
148. *Id.* 592a–b, at 274.
149. Plato, *Laws,* in *The Laws of Plato* 712b, at 124 (Thomas Pangle trans. 1980) [hereinafter Plato, *Laws*].
150. *Id.* 737d, at 124.
151. *Id.* 739a, at 125.

all their might they delight in laws that aim at making the city come as close as possible to unity—then no one will ever set down a more correct or better definition than this of what constitutes the extreme as regards virtue.[152]

The problem, however, is that such a city is not suitable for imperfect human beings: "Such a city is inhabited, presumably, by gods or children of gods,"[153] hence the need to choose the second best.

Plato makes it clear almost from the outset of the *Laws* that he is pursuing the problem noted in the *Republic*, which was Aeschylus's problem as well. The best city is destroyed by factions; thus, the second-best city must solve the problem of factionalism above all others. And, crucially, Plato believes that this solution requires a justice system that aims at reconciling the city's inhabitants with each other rather than doing strict legal justice (either by destroying the wicked or subordinating them):

> *Ath. Stranger:* Which [judge] would be better: the one who destroyed the wicked among them and set the better to ruling themselves, or the one who made the worthy men rule and allowed the worse to live while making them willing to be ruled? But I suppose we should also mention the judge who is third in respect to virtue—if there should ever be such a judge—one capable of taking over a single divided family and destroying no one, but rather reconciling them by laying down laws for them for the rest of time and thus securing their friendship for one another?
>
> *Kleinias:* Such a judge and lawgiver would be better by far.[154]

The second-best city, that is, will have the third-best judges, and the justice of the best city will be replaced by conciliation in the second best.

So far Plato's view has tracked Aeschylus's, though with an explicit acknowledgment of the lack of justice in a faction-free city that Aeschylus left implicit and a theory of the second best that is wholly absent from the *Oresteia*. In two other crucial respects Plato echoes the thought of Aeschylus. First, Plato insists on a rule-of-law regime:

> *Ath. Stranger:* I have now applied the terms "servants of the law" to the men usually said to be rulers, not for the sake of an innova-

---

152. *Id.* 739c–d, at 126.
153. *Id.* 739d–e, at 126.
154. *Id.* 627e–628a, at 6. The thought is reiterated at 628b and at 628c.

tion of names but because I hold that it is this above all that determines whether the city survives or undergoes the opposite. Where the law is itself ruled over and lacks sovereign authority, I see destruction at hand for such a place. But where it is despot over the rulers and the rulers are slaves of the law, there I foresee safety and all good things which the gods have given to cities.[155]

In the *Statesman*, Plato criticizes the rule of law because of the constraints it imposes on the wise ruler but argues that since in the world of the second best we cannot count on the wisdom of rulers, the rule of law is indispensable. Such appears to be the doctrine of the *Laws*.[156]

Second, since the classless city of friends is impossible, the second-best city will contain classes and class hierarchy. This is for the very contemporary-sounding reason that massive redistribution of wealth is inequitable.

> *Ath. Stranger:* It would surely have been a fine thing if each one could have entered the colony possessing an equal amount of everything . . . , but since that is impossible, and one will arrive with more money and another with less, it follows that for many reasons, and for the sake of equality of opportunities in the city, there must be unequal classes. . . . [157]

Plato then adds a proviso that Aeschylus mentions nowhere:

> *Ath. Stranger:* We assert that if (as we presume) the city must avoid the greatest illness, which has been more correctly termed "civil war" than "faction," then neither harsh poverty nor wealth should exist among any of the citizens. For both these conditions breed both civil war and faction. It follows, therefore, that the lawgiver must announce a limit for both conditions.[158]

It is striking that Plato anticipates doctrines that we associate with contemporary welfare liberalism: the theory of the second best, the emphasis on prudence and moderation (e.g., at 711e–712a), the tolerance of classes, and the idea that extremes of wealth and poverty are dangerous. In these respects, at any rate, Plato could as well be Louis

155. *Id.* 715d, at 102.
156. Plato, *Statesman*, 295c–297c; for similar criticisms of the rule of law, see Aristotle, *Politics* III, 14, 1286a12–16.
157. *Laws* 744b, at 131.
158. *Id.* 744d–e, at 132.

Brandeis.[159] Class war can be avoided only if class conflict is mitigated and contained—that is, only if the state effects a class compromise. This compromise will result in large part from third-best judges, who prefer "friendship and peace brought about through reconciliation" to "civil peace brought about by the destruction of some and the victory of others," even if the latter alternative is more just.[160]

We must not, however, mistake Plato for a protoliberal, for there is one other all-important fact about his second-best city: it is a theocracy, and a highly repressive one at that. It contains, for example, a special jail for the impious, called the "Moderation Tank" or, as Findlay translates it, the "Place of Softening Up." Here they undergo "admonishment and salvation of the soul" for at least five years at the hands of a sinister body known as the "Nocturnal Council." If, after such a period of "moderation" the prisoner still hasn't become moderate, he is to be killed.[161]

This idea may appear to be a mere idiosyncracy of Plato's argument, but in fact it returns us to the debate between Homer and Hesiod and by analogy raises general problems about legal instrumentalism, the doctrine of order over justice. This is what I now wish to argue.

The *Laws* begins by the Athenian Stranger asking, "Is it a god or some human being, strangers, who is given the credit for laying down your laws?"[162] By Book 4 the interlocutors reach the conclusion that "there can be no rest from evils and toils for those cities in which some mortal rules rather than a god."[163] It is from this idea that the Stranger draws both the conclusion that rulers must be "servants of the law" and the need for a civil religion; thus, theology appears to underwrite the rule of law (and not of men).

The Stranger mitigates this conclusion somewhat by explaining, "[W]e should obey whatever within us partakes of immortality, giving the name 'law' to the distribution ordained by intelligence."[164] This makes it seem that the theology underlying law is rational and not revealed, in other words, that we discover divine law by reasoning (a conclusion reinforced when we note that in the *Phaedo* Socrates identified philosophical reason with "whatever within us partakes of immor-

159. *See, e.g.*, Louis D. Brandeis, "The Opportunity in the Law," in *Business—A Profession* 313–27 (1914). Brandeis, it should be noted, possessed an enormous admiration for the Athenian polis. *See* Philippa Strum, *Louis D. Brandeis: Justice for the People* 237–39 (1984).
160. *Laws* 628b, at 7.
161. *Id.* 909a, at 309.
162. *Id.* 624a, at 3.
163. *Id.* 713e, at 100.
164. *Id.* 714a, at 100.

tality"[165]). Instead of religious law, then, we would have natural law in
the medieval sense of reasonable law. But this does not explain why the
city must have a civic religion. Rather, it almost contradicts the idea.
The puzzle is even more profound when we recall the argument
from the *Euthyphro:* the gods love a thing because it is (independently)
pious, it is not pious because the gods love it. This implies that the
authority of the laws must be independent of whether they are of divine
or human origin; their divinity is irrelevant and the civic religion unnecessary. A person could disbelieve in the religion and still recognize the
goodness of the laws and govern himself by them. This situation is
described in Book 10 of the *Laws*.[166] Yet Plato next says that such a
person is to be imprisoned for five years in the "Moderation Tank."[167]
   In the *Republic*, the rational philosopher will come to the brink of
recognizing the Form of the Good—the eternal principle of goodness—
without the need of theology. The Good is the harmony of all the eternal
principles (Forms) and is thus not itself a god or indeed anything substantive over and above the Forms themselves.[168] Then why the theology, which can be only a mythical expression of rational truth?
   The reason has to do with Plato's idea of the function of myth. Not
everyone is capable of comprehending rational truths, and for that
reason many people can understand them only if they are presented in
the form of concrete images. Such is the function of myth.[169] Indeed,
even the philosophical method of inquiry can be understood by the
uninitiated only through symbols or images.[170] In the *Laws*, the Athenian Stranger maintains that rational argument can prove the existence
of unchanging causes or "supervisors" of all things (he calls them
"gods"); but when it comes to fleshing out the details of the civic religion, and in particular to showing that these gods are just, he insists
that argument will not do: "[T]here are still needed, in addition, some
mythic incantations."[171] He then elaborates a myth almost identical

---

165. Plato, *Phaedo* 65e–67e.
166. *Laws* 908b–e, at 308–9. The description offered in this passage seems not
unlike that of Socrates himself.
167. *Id.* 908e, at 309.
168. I have defended this interpretation of the Form of the Good in Luban, "The
Form of the Good in the *Republic*," 12 *Journal of Value Inquiry* 161 (1978).
169. This view is one implication of the famous Divided Line and Cave metaphors
in the *Republic*. See *Republic* 509d–511e & 514a–518b, at 190–92 & 193–97.
170. *See id.* 533a, at 212.
171. *Laws* 903b, at 302. "The gods' justice, not mentioned in the *logoi* [arguments],
and especially their punitive justice is fully vindicated or at any rate powerfully asserted
in the *mythoi* [myths] in which the kosmic gods, with the help of a Homeric quotation,

with the final myth in the *Republic*, concerning divine punishment or reward of immortal souls.

This point is absolutely crucial, for Plato incorporates Hesiod's position, *but only as myth*. Hesiod, then, provides merely a distant image of the truth for popular consumption. In the *Republic*, Hesiod's myth of the gold, silver, bronze, and iron races[172] is described as a "noble lie" designed to make citizens believe that the different occupational classes they occupy are the work of "the earth, which is their mother" rather than of their rearing and education, which they must believe "were like dreams." The purpose of this is to make them defend their city "as though the land they are in was a mother."[173] Recall that Socrates repeats the same myth of the metals when he persuades his companions that the just city must collapse (though Socrates fails to remind them in the latter episode that the story is only a "noble lie").

This suggests that when Plato alludes to Hesiod it is for the poet's mythic, not his rational, value. And in the *Laws* this allusion occurs at a key point when the Stranger is trying to convince his hearers (who, as practical politicians and not statesmen, must be persuaded by myth and not philosophy) that the second-best city must be a theocracy with a rule-of-law regime:

> *Ath. Stranger:* Following [the god] always is Justice, avenger of those who forsake the divine law. He who is going to become happy follows Her, in humility and orderliness. But anyone whose soul burns with insolence and hence regards himself as needing neither ruler nor any leader but rather considers himself capable of leading others, is left behind, abandoned by the god. Once left behind . . . after no long while he undergoes the blameless vengeance of Justice, bringing complete ruin to himself and his household and city as well.[174]

The image is of a (female) Justice, following god to destroy wicked leaders and their cities. It comes directly from *Works and Days*:

> Justice is a maiden and a daughter of Zeus; the gods of Olympus respect her noble title, and whenever men mistreat her through

---

are identified with the Olympians. " Leo Strauss, *The Argument and the Action of Plato's Laws* 154 (1975).

172. Socrates described this as a Phoenician myth, but when he repeats it he attributes it to Hesiod. See *Republic* 546e–547c, at 224–25.

173. *Id.* 414c–e, at 94.

174. *Laws* 716a–b, at 102.

false charges she rushes to sit at the feet of Zeus Kronion and she denounces the design of men who are not just, so that the people pay for the reckless deeds and evil plans of kings whose slanted words twist her straight path.[175]

There is one difference between the two passages: Plato's Justice is herself the agent of retribution, while in Hesiod she brings her grievance to Zeus who effects retribution. Plato's Justice, we might say, combines qualities of Hesiod's Justice and Aeschylus's Erinyes. In Hesiod too, however, the Furies possess some of the features of Zeus avenging crooked verdicts and injustice: "[T]he Furies assisted at the birth of Oath, whom Strife bore as a scourge to perjurers."[176]

It is well known that the "Justice is a maiden . . . " passage in *Works and Days* adopts terms used originally by Homer to describe *Litai* (prayers or entreaties):

. . . The truth is,
prayers are daughters of almighty Zeus—
. . . If a man reveres the daughters of Zeus when they come near,
he is rewarded, and his prayers are heard;
but if he spurns them and dismisses them,
they make their way to Zeus again and ask
that Folly dog that man till suffering
has taken arrogance out of him.[177]

Hesiod juxtaposes this passage with Homer's characterization of Zeus's cloudburst we have examined earlier, in which "Zeus pours down the rain in scudding gusts to punish men, annoyed because they will enforce their crooked judgments and banish justice from the agora, thoughtless of the gods' vengeance. . . ."[178]

---

175. Hesiod, *supra* note 45, ll. 256–62, at 73.

176. *Id.* ll. 803–4, at 87. Compare *Theogony:* "Then loathsome Strife bore . . . the Quarrels and the Lies and Argument and Counter-Argument, Lawlessness and Ruin whose ways are all alike, and Oath, who more than any other, brings pains on mortals who of their own accord swear false oaths." Hesiod, *Theogony,* in *Hesiod: Theogony, Works and Days, Shield, supra* note 45, ll. 226–32, at 18–19.

177. Homer, *supra* note 25, bk. 9, ll. 502–14, at 219.

178. *Id.* bk. 16, ll. 386–89, at 389. For a magnificent detection of Hesiodic allusions to Homer, see Havelock, *supra* note 19, at 195–217; Havelock, "Thoughtful Hesiod," 22 *Yale Classical Studies* 61, 70–72 (1972). An interesting and important question is why Hesiod should substitute "justice" for "prayers" in the first passage. One conjecture: The *Iliad* begins with the prayer of Apollo's priest Chryses to Agamemnon to accept ransom for his daughter. Agamemnon's refusal engenders the rest of the action, which calls

We therefore find the Athenian Stranger borrowing a Hesiodic myth that in turn draws on (and reminds Plato's readers of) a similar Homeric myth concerning both justice and prayer. Remember also that the Stranger later says "mythic incantations" must be used to persuade us that our injustice will receive divine punishment. Hesiod is used only as a mythic incantation to identify justice with the civic religion.

Plato's final position, then, may be summarized approximately as follows. The best realizable city is one whose legal institutions aim at stability, achieved by effecting a class compromise, and are moderate and prudent but not necessarily just. The laws of such a city will be constructed by rational investigation. Most people, however, cannot follow the details of such an investigation and will therefore comply with the law only if they believe that it is divinely sanctioned. They must therefore be made to believe that Hesiod's view of justice is right (even though Plato in reality follows Homer and Aeschylus and rejects Hesiod). For this reason they must be indoctrinated in a civic religion, including a Hesiodic myth that the institutions are divinely sanctioned and just—a myth that in actuality is a noble lie. In the *Republic*, Hesiodic myths that are really noble lies are used to make people willing to defend their hierarchical society, and to convince Socrates's companions that a perfectly just city is unattainable because it will collapse into tyranny through faction fighting.

In effect, Plato has incorporated the Homeric thesis and Hesiodic antithesis into a single two-tiered structure. In this structure Hesiod's view of the primacy of justice appears as a public doctrine, promulgated to maintain a city secretly organized along the lines of the Homeric notion that stability and civic friendship are primary and justice merely secondary. The Platonic synthesis is the most sophisticated Greek version of legal instrumentalism. It attempts, finally, to resolve the tragedy of the *Iliad*—Homer's realization that we renounce something of infinite importance to us if we abandon the quest for justice. In Plato's synthesis, that quest is honored in myth even as it is denied in practice.

Conclusion

Plato, I believe, put his finger on an immensely important problem of political psychology. On the Aeschylean elaboration of Homer's view, institutions of justice exist (paradoxically) to stabilize a society rather than to do justice. But if people believe that these institutions do not do

---

punishment and disaster down on the Achaians. Perhaps Hesiod views the refusal of Chryses' proffered ransom as an injustice.

justice, if they believe the Aeschylean view, then they will not respect those institutions, and the institutions will break down—they (paradoxically) will not stabilize the society. Hence the Aeschylean view must remain esoteric, and most people must instead be made to believe in the justice of these institutions. That is why Plato incorporates the Hesiodic myth into his exoteric civil religion.

This is a very contemporary dilemma. The American Bar Association Code of Professional Responsibility requires that "a lawyer should avoid even the appearance of professional impropriety" and explains: "Continuation of the American concept that we are to be governed by rules of law requires that people have faith that justice can be obtained through our legal system. A lawyer should promote public confidence in our system and in the legal profession."[179] This is a troubling rule. Suppose a lawyer is convinced that the legal system does not deserve confidence, that it is profoundly corrupt. It sounds as though the lawyer could be disciplined for making these suspicions too public. The rule quotes a judicial opinion: "[C]onfidence in our law, our courts, and in the administration of justice is our supreme interest."[180] If confidence is the *supreme* interest, it follows that it is more important than our law, courts, and administration of justice really deserving this confidence. One may object that the court could not mean to be saying this, but it is in fact a logical consequence of legal instrumentalism, the view that stability is more important than justice. For stability comes from public confidence in our institutions, whether they deserve it or not; justice, by contrast, means that they deserve it. As Karl Llewellyn wrote, defending an instrumentalist view, "[A]n impressive ceremonial has a value in making people feel that something is being done; this holds, whether the result is right or wrong; and there is some value in an institution which makes men content with fate, whatever that fate may be."[181] The lawyer must therefore uphold the ceremonial "whether the result is right or wrong" and keep up public confidence in justice even if that confidence is misplaced. The lawyer must join in deceiving the public. Or, in the words of H. L. Mencken, "bosh is the right medicine for boobs."[182]

I earlier cited Professor Paul Gewirtz's defense of *Brown II* over

---

179. *Model Code of Professional Responsibility* Canon 9 and EC 9–1 (1979).

180. Erwin M. Jennings Co. v. DiGenova, 107 Conn. 491, 141 A. 866, 868 (1928), *quoted in Model Code of Professional Responsibility* Canon 9 n.2.

181. Karl Llewellyn, "On Reading and Using the Newer Jurisprudence," 40 *Columbia Law Review* 610 (1940).

182. H. L. Mencken, "Gamalielese Again," in *A Carnival of Buncombe* 43 (1956).

Brown I—of order over justice—based on the worry that speedy desegregation would be met by violent white resistance. Professor Gewirtz concludes his argument by reflecting on precisely the question we are addressing, of whether legal instrumentalism can be maintained only as an esoteric doctrine.[183] He raises the argument that concerned Plato—that candor about injustice would delegitimize governmental authority—but rejects it. Gewirtz vigorously criticizes courts that subordinate rights to resistance—justice to order—but are not candid about the fact that they are doing so.

Ironically, however, Gewirtz criticizes them only by accepting their crucial premise: that their credibility is of paramount importance.

> It might be thought . . . that the prestige and authority of courts would suffer if they were to admit candidly that the public sometimes resists their judgments and that they sometimes provide less than full remedies because of such resistance. . . . But dishonesty always creates the risk of its detection, and, with detection, harm to the courts' stature that may exceed any losses that result from candidly acknowledging limited power.[184]

However, this statement is hardly a principled argument for candor. It endorses truthfulness merely as the best way to avoid getting caught in a lie. Since Gewirtz accepts the instrumentalist premise that credibility is of supreme importance, it is quite open to legal instrumentalists to quarrel with Gewirtz's empirical assumptions. Courts may well be convinced that it is within their powers to dupe the public successfully, or that the damage to their authority resulting from detection is likely to be less than that resulting from confession. And I suspect that they would probably be right. Gewirtz remains enmeshed in the Platonic problem: precisely if legal instrumentalism is true, it must remain an esoteric doctrine.

The same problem appears for classical utilitarians, who realized that people are more likely to perform disagreeable but utility-enhancing actions if they are motivated by traditional, nonutilitarian moral values than if they actually believe in utilitarianism. For this reason Sidgwick declared that utilitarianism should remain an "esoteric morality" and indeed that the very doctrine of an esoteric morality must in turn remain esoteric (because "the moral consciousness of a

---

183. Gewirtz, *supra* note 6, at 665–74.
184. *Id.* at 671.

plain man broadly repudiates the general notion of an esoteric morality").[185]

Again, the same problem emerges for modern social engineers or technocrats who wish to make antidemocratic decisions in a democratic society. They must proceed under the guise of hypocritical disclaimers that that is what they are doing.[186]

In each case, the result is the same: a closed, stratified society, divided into Ins (who are privy to the esoteric morality) and Outs (who believe the exoteric). "The Ins," I have written elsewhere, "know the value of keeping up appearances. And the Outs must be fooled for their own good."[187] Surely the Moderation Tank and the Nocturnal Council are not inevitable consequences of such a society, but they are the logical conclusion of its underlying premise.

For this reason, I believe that the Platonic apotheosis of legal instrumentalism is its refutation. We have traced its gradual sophistication from the *Hymn to Hermes*, through the *Iliad* and the *Oresteia*, to Plato. Homer supplemented the *Hymn to Hermes* by noting the human cost of renouncing the quest for justice. Aeschylus added that abandoning justice for the sake of stability requires hierarchy, the continued dominance of dominant interests. And Plato showed that reconciling people in an instrumentalist system requires a society whose own workings are hidden from the majority of people. At the end, the bucolic idyll of friendship among the gods set to the enchanting music of Apollo's lyre has become, first, an unfair trial set to the enchanting music of Apollo's deceptions and, finally, a suffocating theocracy. The instrumentalist vision has died of oversophistication.

I believe, then, that we must renounce the Platonic method of treating Hesiod's plea for justice as myth. Instead, we should take our

---

185. Henry Sidgwick, *The Methods of Ethics* 489–90 (7th ed. 1907). Sen and Williams deride this view as "Government House utilitarianism." Amartya K. Sen & Bernard Williams, *Utilitarianism and Beyond* 16 (1982).

186. I discuss this problem in Luban, "The Twice-Told Tale of Mr. Fixit: Reflections on the Brandeis/Frankfurter Connection," 91 *Yale Law Journal* 1678, 1697–1706 (1982).

187. *Id.* at 1703. At stake in all these situations is the "publicity principle" originating in Kant and defended in contemporary philosophy by Rawls. Kant states the principle as follows: "All actions relating to the right of other men are unjust if their maxim is not compatible with publicity." Kant, *Perpetual Peace* 129, in Kant, *On History* (L.W. Beck ed. & trans. 1963) (translation slightly amended). See also John Rawls, *A Theory of Justice* 133 (1971). Of course, the question remains of whether we should regard the publicity principle as an indispensable piece of political morality. That is a large question, which I hope to treat in a book currently under way.

Hesiod neat. Two other reasons recommend Hesiod to us over Homer, Aeschylus, and Plato.

First, it is important to note that Hesiod's endless grumbling about unjust judges, "swallowers of bribes," originates from his own loss of an unjust suit. Hesiod, unlike Aeschylus or Plato, is writing from the standpoint of the victim. One can scarcely overstress the importance of this fact. The defining fact about legal institutions that do not do justice is that *they create innocent victims*. Aeschylus may end his drama with a triumphant procession of reconciliation, and Plato may speak of judges who create "friendship and peace brought about through reconciliation"; but reconciliation often means only that the victim has silently swallowed her injury. When you hear someone talking happily about a reconciliation between an injurer and the injured, it is often time to nod agreeably and head for the door.

Surely, however, the contemporary reader of the *Oresteia* does not need this reminder. I mentioned earlier that the sociosexual theme of the *Oresteia* has been of great interest to contemporary feminists. One need not be a student of Bachofen and Engels to bristle at Aeschylus' easy satisfaction at the subordination of women celebrated at the end of the *Eumenides*. For us it is no cause for celebration—and that is precisely because the modern audience has been made amply aware of the standpoint of the victim. Once we determine to make justice a genuine goal for an open society, rather than treating the yearning for justice as a tragic flaw or as "bosh for the boobs," the victim's is the standpoint we can no longer ignore.

Finally—I have already mentioned this point without stressing it—Hesiod's is a more realistic underlying social philosophy. The Homeric and Platonic view of social conciliation rests on an opposition between strife and friendship and models the good society after the relationship of friends or family members. This analogy of a properly working society to a loving family must have strained credulity even in fifth-century Athens, which was after all a large city with inhabitants of many nations, far too many for anyone to know all the others by name. The analogy is unintelligible in a nation of almost a quarter of a billion. For us, Hesiod's foundational distinction between two kinds of strife— economic competition and violence—rather than between strife and familial friendship, is self-evidently a more accurate idea of what the real social options are.

We need not, to be sure, rest content with economic competition as the highest principle of social solidarity. Certainly we can hope for a civilization less antagonistic and more friendly than that. Such a civilization, however, is not ours, or any that has hitherto existed. If it is to exist, it must be constructed on institutions different from our own. Civic friendship will be the result of an arduous pursuit of justice. It cannot be reached by instrumentalist shortcuts that base friendship on quiescence.

Chapter 7

The Legacies of Nuremberg

The past is never dead; it is not even past.
                              —William Faulkner

Almost fifty years ago, on November 20, 1945, the trial of the major war criminals of the Third Reich began in the ruined city of Nuremberg. It is a commonplace that the trial was a historic occasion, that it left a legacy for future generations. The men who conceived and conducted the trial understood it that way; they intended it to be epoch-making and viewed their own words and deeds from the perspective of a distant and more pacific age. They guessed boldly at the judgment history would pass upon the meaning of the trial.

They condensed that meaning to two focal points: (1) by enlarging the reach of law beyond conventional war crimes, the trial was supposed to move us closer to world order, placing previously unreachable conduct under the domain of international law; and (2) by replacing raw vengefulness with legal procedures, it was to provide a model of the rule of law to reeducate Germany and inspire the peoples of other nations.

Half a century after Nuremberg we are better able to judge what the framers of the trial could only guess about the legacy of Nuremberg. What are the enduring contributions of the Nuremberg trial to the moral life of mankind and to its legal embodiment? That is my question. And my answer is this: the achievements at which the trial was aiming were compromised, rendered equivocal, by the trial itself; but its very failure has much to teach us. The framers of Nuremberg were confronted with a new offense, the bureaucratic crime, and a novel political menace, the criminal state. Limiting themselves to traditional legal concepts—sovereignty, individual criminal liability, conspiracy—and unwilling to question either the political system of nation-states or the character of responsibility in bureaucratic settings, they came to the brink of recognizing the novelty of criminal states but ultimately failed to comprehend this major challenge of our century.

335

The First Legacy: Crimes against Peace and Crimes against Humanity

It is impossible for us to read accounts of the Nuremberg trial without realizing that it signifies something much different to us than it did to those who conceived it.[1] For us, Nuremberg is a judicial footnote to the Holocaust; it stands for the condemnation and punishment of genocide, and its central achievement lies in recognizing the category of *crimes against humanity*—

> murder, extermination, enslavement, deportation and other inhumane acts committed against any civilian population, before or during the war, or persecutions on political, racial or religious grounds in execution of or in connection with any crime within the jurisdiction of the Tribunal, whether or not in violation of the domestic law of the country where perpetrated.[2]

For those who conceived of the trial, on the other hand, its great accomplishment was to be the criminalization of aggressive war, inaugurating an age of world order. In the words of Robert H. Jackson, the chief prosecutor at Nuremberg, "This inquest represents the practical effort of four of the most mighty of nations, with the support of 17 more, to utilize international law to meet the greatest menace of our times— aggressive war."[3] For the trial's framers, then, its decisive legal achievement lay in recognizing the category of *crimes against peace*—"planning, preparation, initiation or waging of a war of aggression, or a war in violation of international treaties, agreements or assurances, or participation in a Common Plan or Conspiracy for the accomplishment of any of the foregoing."[4]

This idea that Nuremberg was to be the Trial to End All Wars seems fantastic and naive forty years (and 150 wars) later. It has also done much to vitiate the real achievements of the trial, in particular the condemnation of crimes against humanity. To end all war, the authors of the Nuremberg Charter were led to incorporate an intellectual confusion into it. The Charter criminalized aggression; and by criminalizing

---

1. For two such accounts, see Robert E. Conot, *Justice at Nuremberg* (1983), and Ann Tusa and John Tusa, *The Nuremberg Trial* (1984). The point I am making here is made as well in Judith Shklar, *Legalism* 165 (1964). Many points in this chapter were suggested to me by Shklar's oftentimes brilliant discussion.

2. Article 6(c), "Charter of the International Military Tribunal," 1 *Trial of the Major War Criminals before the International Military Tribunal* 11 [hereinafter *Trial*].

3. 2 *id.* 99.

4. Article 6(a), 1 *id.* 11.

aggression, the Charter erected a wall around state sovereignty and committed itself to an old-European model of unbreachable nation-states.

But crimes against humanity are often, even characteristically, carried out by states against their own subjects. The effect, and great moral and legal achievement, of criminalizing such acts (Article 6(c)) and assigning personal liability to those who order them and carry them out (Articles 7 and 8) is to pierce the veil of sovereignty. As a result, Article 6(a) pulls in the opposite direction from Articles 6(c), 7, and 8, leaving us, as we shall see, with a legacy that is at best equivocal and at worst immoral.

Aggression and Sovereignty

At neither the Nuremberg nor the Tokyo trials was the crime of aggression defined.[5] But in 1974 the United Nations offered the following definition: "Aggression is the use of armed force by a State against the sovereignty, territorial integrity or political independence of another State, or in any other manner inconsistent with the Charter of the United Nations."[6] Though not until 1974 was aggression explicitly linked with the violation of sovereignty, this definition is clearly in the spirit of Nuremberg—it belongs to the legacy. But what, then, is sovereignty?

The concept was formulated in the early modern era, when the nation-state began to emerge in Europe. It signified that there is only one ultimate source of law in a state, namely, the state's sovereign; sovereignty is thus the linchpin that holds the political theory of the nation-state together.

From it follows the notorious doctrine of *act of state*, which exempts sovereigns from legal liability for their depredations against other states, on the theory that the "prosecution of an individual by a court of the injured state for an act which, according to international law, is the act of another state, amounts to exercising jurisdiction over another state; and this is a violation of the rule of general international law that no state is subject to the jurisdiction of another state."[7]

Historically, the doctrine of sovereignty was formulated to secure the dominance of secular law over canon law and thus of secular authority (*imperium*) over the church (*sacerdotum*); however, the doctrine

---

5. Richard H. Minear, *Victors' Justice: The Tokyo War Crimes Trial* 55–60 (1971).
6. *Quoted in* Yehuda Melzer, *Concepts of Just War* 28–29 (1975).
7. Hans Kelsen, *Peace Through Law* 82 (1944).

had the additional consequence that so-called natural law—by which Aquinas meant constraints on the content of law ascertainable by reason alone—had no place in the theory. (Since in practice the church claimed the right to announce natural law—despite the fact that it was supposed to be a matter of reason and not of revelation—its elimination from the nation-state's political theory followed from the very practical struggle between *imperium* and *sacerdotum.*) Nothing constrained the sovereign: because he or she was the sole lawmaker, it followed that the sovereign was the highest lawmaker as well. Thus the classic doctrine of sovereignty eventually carried in its train the theory of legal positivism, which says that the sole criterion of a rule's legality is that it has been propounded by the sovereign according to his chosen procedures.

From this, in turn, it follows that, provided the sovereign follows his or her self-determined legislative procedures, anything the sovereign wishes to make law is law. There are no domestic legal standards according to which the sovereign can be held responsible, unless the sovereign chooses to impose them upon himself or herself. Conjoined with the act-of-state doctrine, this conclusion implies that sovereigns are liable under neither domestic nor international law, that "the king is above the law."[8]

It was this doctrine that Article 7 of the Nuremberg Charter assaulted: "The official position of defendants, whether as Heads of State or responsible officials in Government departments, shall not be considered as freeing them from responsibility or mitigating punishment."[9] By making even sovereigns legally liable for their deeds, Article 7 denies that the sovereign is the sole source of law in his or her state; it thus denies the doctrine of sovereignty itself.

Similarly with Article 8, "The fact that the defendant acted pursuant to an order of his Government or of a superior shall not free him from responsibility. . . . "[10] The law that obligates a citizen is an "order of his Government"; by criminalizing acts that are legal according to the positive law laid down by the sovereign, Article 8 thus denies that the sovereign is the sole source of law for his subjects—and this article, again, amounts to a denial of the theory of sovereignty itself.

Similarly, Article 6(c) outlaws crimes against humanity even when committed by a state against its own subjects and "whether or not in violation of the domestic law of the country where perpetrated." Article

---

8. For an interesting discussion of the role of positivism in the Nuremberg trial, see Stanley L. Paulson, "Classical Legal Positivism at Nuremberg," 4 *Philosophy & Public Affairs* 132 (1975).
9. 1 *Trial* 12.
10. *Id.*

6(c), the most enduring moral achievement of Nuremberg, is irreconcilable on its face with legal positivism and thus with the classic doctrine of sovereignty. Together with Articles 7 and 8, then, it perforates or even destroys the doctrine in the name of "humanity" and individual responsibility to it.

That is an important achievement, not anything to regret. As Jackson pointed out, the act-of-state and superior-orders doctrines taken together would imply that no one could be held responsible for the crimes the Tribunal was trying: the former would exempt those exercising sovereign authority while the latter would exempt their subjects.[11] Yet it would be a moral absurdity (and political impossibility) to punish nobody for Auschwitz. The plain fact of the matter is that the Third Reich was a criminal state in every moral sense that the word "criminal" possesses, and the law had to reach those who carried out its crimes.

Two Problems with Sovereignty: Criminal States
and Eurocentrism

It is an unhappy fact of human existence that we never forget how to commit a crime once we have been taught. The Third Reich may well be the first state whose criminality was virtually its defining feature; it will not be the last. (I drafted this chapter in 1985; as I revise it at New Year, 1993, the horrifying events in Bosnia vividly confirm this prediction.) In this regard, the framers of Nuremberg understood very well the importance of their endeavor. Since the Nazis had set dark precedent for criminal states, had invented new forms of evildoing, had made the unthinkable real (after which it is only a matter of time until it becomes routine), it was necessary to restructure our moral imaginations to fortify ourselves for a world of criminal states. If this meant exploding time-honored propositions and concepts, then so be it.

The trouble was that the propositions and concepts reflected a political reality—the system of nation-states—that no one was prepared to condemn. And so just at the moment Articles 6(c), 7, and 8 of the Nuremberg Charter undermined the doctrine of sovereignty in the ways we have just examined, Article 6(a) fortified it by making aggressive war—the violation of sovereignty—an international crime.

This proved in the event to be a moral problem even more than a conceptual one. If the law is to be anything humane it must guide our moral imaginations; and since it is now imperative that our moral imaginations include awareness of criminal states, the law must also include

---

11. 2 *id.* 150.

awareness of criminal states. For this reason alone, the doctrine of sovereignty, which acknowledges the authority of criminal states,[12] is no longer feasible. And so Article 6(a)—which protects the sovereignty of all states, even criminal states, as long as they do not launch wars—should be seen as a mistake.

In any case the doctrine of sovereignty bears little relevance to the modern world: it is an old-European concept meant for nation-states—literally, states whose boundaries correspond with those of homogeneous linguistic and cultural communities.[13] Outside of Western Europe, we find at best limited correspondence between states and homogeneous communities. For this reason statist politics implies perpetual ferment and instability as contending ethnic or tribal groups vie with each other for control of the apparatus of sovereignty.

Article 6(a) is Eurocentric in another way as well. The European nation-states (and the United States) exercised economic and often political dominion over much of Asia, Africa, and Latin America, and at Nuremberg this state of affairs was assumed by all to be fitting and uncontroversial. (It is startling to hear Jackson refer to the acquisition of colonies as a legitimate objective for Germany.)[14] By criminalizing any breaches of sovereignty, Article 6(a) criminalized anti-imperialist struggle as well. This was noted by Justice Pal in his famous dissenting opinion in the Tokyo trial:

> Certainly dominated nations of the present day *status quo* cannot be made to submit to eternal domination only in the name of peace. International law must be prepared to face the problem of bringing within juridical limits the politico-historical evolution of mankind which up to now has been accomplished chiefly through war. War and other methods of *self-help by force* can be effectively excluded only when this problem is solved, and it is only then that we can think of introducing criminal responsibility for efforts at adjust-

---

12. The recognition of a state as sovereign follows in international law from the bare fact that it exercises sovereign power: Ian Brownlie, *Principles of Public International Law* 89–108 (rev. ed. 1973).

13. It may not even be a useful theory for the modern nation-state. See Niklas Luhmann, *Politische Theorie im Wohlfahrtsstaat* 12–24, 42–49 (1981), arguing that the doctrine of sovereignty was one of a constellation of doctrines suitable for the formative stages of the nation-state but useless for the modern welfare state, since the doctrine presupposes that the political system knows and dominates society. In a complex and highly differentiated society, Luhmann argues, this presupposition fails—a society characterized as ours is by strong subsystem differentiation is a society "without summit and without center."

14. 2 *Trial* 105.

ment by means other than peaceful. Until then there can hardly be any justification for any direct and indirect attempt at maintaining, in the name of humanity and justice, the very *status quo* which might have been organized and hitherto maintained only by force by pure opportunist "Have and Holders". . . . The part of humanity which has been lucky enough to enjoy political freedom can now well afford to have the deterministic ascetic outlook of life, and may think of peace in terms of political *status quo*. But every part of humanity has not been equally lucky and a considerable part is still haunted by the wishful thinking about escape from political dominations. To them the present age is faced with not only the menace of totalitarianism but also the ACTUAL PLAGUE of imperialism.[15]

Pal is not attacking a straw man; his argument was directed to Jackson, who had stated in his opening address at Nuremberg, "Our position is that whatever grievances a nation may have, however objectionable it finds the *status quo*, aggressive warfare is an illegal means for settling those grievances or for altering those conditions."[16]

The Two Faces of Article 6: Statism versus Human Rights

These theoretical confusions and practical misfortunes are, unhappily, an enduring legacy of Nuremberg. I have said that we view Nuremberg in the light of the Holocaust, so that its greatest achievement is taking cognizance of crimes against humanity. Seen from this perspective, Nuremberg is one of the founding moments of the modern human rights movement and of that form of politics that favors intervention on behalf of human rights, even when violations occur within the boundaries of sovereign states. Articles 6(c), 7, and 8 are the main texts of Nuremberg for this form of world politics.

Seen from the perspective of its framers, however, Nuremberg was the Trial to End All War, and its main legal construct is Article 6(a). This article has in turn been a major moral enemy of the human rights movement, inasmuch as attempts at sanctions or interventions against human rights offenders are invariably denounced as violations of their sovereignty. It is the tension between statism and human rights that renders the legacy of Nuremberg equivocal; the human rights move-

---

15. Radha Binod Pal, *International Military Tribunal for the Far East: Dissentient Judgment of Justice R. B. Pal, M.A., LL.D.* 114–15 (1953).
16. 2 *Trial* 149.

ment and human rights violators are vying for the contested legacy of
Nuremberg.

Jackson saw this point all too clearly. When Gros, the French representative at the conference establishing the Nuremberg trial, argued
that humanitarian intervention in a country's internal affairs was a
traditional legal principle that would be contravened by Article 6(a),
Jackson countered that nonintervention was sacred to Americans, who
had no intention of letting other countries interfere in our own policies
of racial discrimination.[17] Jackson, in other words, argued for subven-
ing Article 6(c) to Article 6(a) in the Charter partly to enclose American
human rights violations within a wall of state sovereignty. By contrast,
the other horn of the Article 6 dilemma was seized by Thurgood Marshall and his colleagues in the NAACP in their brief in *Morgan v. Virginia*, a transportation-desegregation case: they argued that Americans
had not spilled their blood in a war against "the apostles of racism"
abroad only to permit its flourishing at home.[18] For the NAACP, the
moral message of World War II was the illegitimacy of racist human
rights violations (Nuremberg's crimes against humanity, though Marshall did not allude to Nuremberg in the brief). The Supreme Court
gave them a seven-to-one victory, striking down racial segregation on
interstate buses; Justice Jackson, ironically, could not participate in the
decision because he was in Nuremberg prosecuting the Nazis.

Let me be clear: I am not claiming that Articles 6(a) and 6(c) must
be logically or legally contradictory. They can be reconciled by carving
out an exception to the doctrine of sovereignty when crimes against
humanity are at issue: one allows humanitarian intervention in a sovereign state's affairs, but only when the humanitarian issue has risen to
the horrific level of crimes against humanity.[19]

17. Robert H. Jackson, *International Conference on Military Trials, London, 1945,*
Department of State Publication No. 3080 331, 333 (1945): "It has been a general principle
of foreign policy of our Government from time immemorial that the internal affairs of
another government are not ordinarily our business; that is to say, the way Germany
treats its inhabitants, or any other country treats its inhabitants, is not our affair any
more than it is the affair of some other government to interpose itself in our problems. . . . We have some regrettable circumstances at times in our own country in which
minorities are unfairly treated." Such also have been the concerns of American senators
who held up our ratification of the United Nations Genocide Convention for decades.
The stated reasons were always couched in terms of our "principled" attachment to
sovereignty (even at the expense of express concern for human rights); the unstated
reason has been fear that American racial policies might be condemned under the
Convention.
18. Morgan v. Virginia, 328 U.S. 373 (1946) (racial segregation prohibited on interstate public transportation); *brief quoted in* Richard Kluger, *Simple Justice* 238 (1975).
19. This line is followed by Michael Walzer in *Just and Unjust Wars* (1977), the best

Indeed, Article 6(c) reconciles the two clauses in precisely this fashion. It restricts its criminalization of "persecutions on political, racial or religious grounds" by adding the crucial phrase *"in execution of or in connection with any crime within the jurisdiction of the Tribunal."* The result is that persecutions on political, racial, or religious grounds are not crimes against humanity unless the perpetrator has also launched an aggressive war or committed war crimes. Persecutions do not, that is, cost a state its sovereignty until it has already forfeited it on other grounds.

The language of Article 6(c) suggests that a state can still lose its sovereignty for committing a crime against humanity without committing other crimes in addition, but only if it perpetrates "murder, extermination, enslavement, deportation, and other inhumane acts . . . against any civilian population." Thus Article 6(c) taken as a whole makes sovereignty fail only when domestic outrages reach population size or when other Nuremberg crimes have been committed. (However, the Nuremberg Tribunal elected to read Article 6(c) more narrowly still, holding that prewar persecutions within Nazi Germany fell outside the scope of the Tribunal's jurisdiction. The Tribunal thus insulated domestic persecutors even more strongly than the plain language of Article 6(c) suggests.)

In this way the logical consistency of Article 6 is maintained. But I am asking about the *legacy* of Nuremberg. That means the potential of its principles for growth and development, for extension and precedent-setting, for adaptability to changed political circumstances, for underlying moral commitments that are not so much the logical implications of the principles as they are their deep structure. Ronald Dworkin speaks of precedents exerting a "gravitational force,"[20] and we must ask what the gravitational force is of reconciling Articles 6(a) and 6(c) in the way just proposed.

As we have seen, Article 6(a) tells us we cannot intervene in the affairs of a sovereign state on behalf of human rights until—here Article 6(c) enters the picture—the violations are committed against an entire "civilian population." But when is that? We must indulge in each case in a grotesque and bloodcurdling calculus of murder, torture, and enslavement to determine which clause of Article 6 controls. We must ask questions like this: Is persecuted ethnic or religious minority M sufficiently distinct that it counts as a "civilian population"? Does an all-out assault on M's indigenous culture, or a brutal forced-relocation policy

---

defense I know of Article 6(a) and the doctrine of sovereignty.
   20. Ronald Dworkin, *Taking Rights Seriously* 111 (rev. ed. 1978).

with many casualties, amount to genocide? Do x deportations, y executions, and z tortures add up to enough that a state's sovereignty can be overridden? Or are such human rights violations a sovereign state's own business, twentieth-century business-as-usual? How many political prisoners writhing on the head of a pin does it take to make a crime against humanity?

This is the price we pay for making Article 6 consistent: its gravitational force pulls us in the direction of a kind of charnel house casuistry that offers to teach the human race little more than the equation of legalism with cynicism and indifference. If such is to be the legacy of Nuremberg, we are better off without it.

If, on the other hand, we abandon the attempt to reconcile Articles 6(a) and (c), we must choose one of them. The choice of 6(c) is a fecund one: when the condemnation of crimes against humanity is allowed to develop as a principle of law and morality, it flowers into the politics of human rights. For the condemnation of "inhumane acts committed against any civilian population" and "persecutions on political, racial or religious grounds" need not be restricted to Holocaust-size events in its gravitational force. It extends to human rights violations in general.

By contrast, Article 6(a), as Justice Pal predicted, flowers into a deification of the status quo and allows the notion of state criminality to slip through its conceptual net. The choice between the two should not be a difficult one.[21]

The Second Legacy: The Rule of Law

In September 1944, Secretary of State Henry Stimson wrote to President Roosevelt, "It is primarily by the thorough apprehension, investigation and trial of all the Nazi leaders and instruments of the Nazi system of

---

21. Abandoning Article 6(a) does not, I should note, mean abandoning the legal condemnation of unjust war. All we need do is change our criterion of unjust war from "war that violates state sovereignty" (aggressive war in the United Nations's sense) to "war that violates human rights." Such a criterion of unjust war, unlike Article 6(a), is fully in tune with Article 6(c) of the Nuremberg Charter. I have argued for this revised conception of unjust war: David Luban, "Just War and Human Rights," 9 *Philosophy & Public Affairs* 160 (1980). The conflict between statism and human rights is the underlying issue of my debate with Walzer over the theory of just war: Michael Walzer, "The Moral Standing of States: A Response to Four Critics," 9 *Philosophy & Public Affairs* 209 (1980); Luban, "The Romance of the Nation-State," 9 *Philosophy & Public Affairs* 392 (1980). These papers, together with selections from Walzer's *Just and Unjust Wars*, are collected in *International Ethics: A Philosophy & Public Affairs Reader* 165–243 (Charles Beitz, Marshall Cohen, Thomas Scanlon, and A. John Simmons eds. 1985). *See also* Luban, "Action and Reaction in International Law," *Proceedings of the American Society of International Law, 1987* 420 (1987).

terrorism such as the Gestapo, with punishment delivered as promptly, swiftly and severely as possible, that we can demonstrate the abhorrence which the world has for such a system and bring home to the German people our determination to extirpate it and its fruits forever."[22] This memorandum contains the root idea of the Nuremberg trial (which was in fact a brainchild of the Americans, who urged it on their more-or-less-unwilling allies). The trial was to serve an expressive and educative function.

As the thinking of the Americans who authored the trial idea developed, they became clearer about what the trial was to teach Germany. The German people would learn from it the foul deeds of their leaders and our abhorrence of such a system; but also—and it is upon this I wish to focus—it would teach the German people what the rule of law is all about by exemplifying it in the trial itself.

Alas, the German people at the time were too preoccupied with the sheer effort of surviving in "the ruin that lies from the Rhine to the Danube"[23] to care much about moral lessons. When cooking oil is scarce and needles and thread impossible to obtain, you do not pause to contemplate the law in its majesty. (Even the defense counsels were lured by the prospect of regular lunches in American cafeterias as much as by the legal and historic significance of the case.[24]) Whatever lessons the trial taught were therefore reserved for later assimilation; for this reason, the important question is not what effect the trial in fact had on the German sense of legality but whether, in hindsight, the trial did indeed exemplify the rule of law in action.

The Fullerian Concept of the Rule of Law

Before we can answer this question, we must review what the rule of law is. The notion of a "rule of law, not of men" dates back at least to Plato and Aristotle;[25] but the ideal of the rule of law has received its most thorough examination in the philosophy of Lon Fuller. For Fuller, law is a device for ordering society. To fulfill this function, law must be capable of structuring and guiding human action, and this capability in turn requires several necessary conditions for action-guiding; Fuller calls them "the morality that makes law possible." Fuller enumerates

---

22. *Quoted in* Tusa and Tusa, *supra* note 1, at 52.

23. Jackson, in 2 *Trial* 103.

24. Tusa and Tusa, *supra* note 1, at 124 (defense counsels' motives) and 221–24 (German public's indifference to the trial).

25. Plato, *The Laws* 715d; Aristotle, *Politics* bk. III, ch. 14, 1286a9–20. That Plato's support for the ideal was at best half-hearted may be seen from *Statesman* 294a–297e; Aristotle also expressed reservations: *Politics* bk. III, ch. 10, 1281a34–39.

eight such conditions; for our purposes, the important ones are these: (1) law must contain public rules; (2) these rules must not be retroactive or ex post facto (since you cannot follow today a rule that is not laid down until tomorrow); and (3) there must be "congruence between the rules as announced and their actual administration."[26] This last condition implies two important corollaries: (3a) like cases must be treated alike, and (3b) alternative enforcement of rules, such as lynch mobs, street violence, and vigilantism, which create noncongruence between announced legal rules and social reality, must be suppressed. To these I add a condition not found in Fuller, though it is fully consistent with his thinking, namely, (4) adjudication must respect the various elements of procedural fairness, publicity, and impartiality that constitute natural justice, due process of law conceived in its most general aspect. For if we are to guide our actions by reference to legal rules, as Fuller supposes, we must have reasonable confidence that the legal process will attempt with some degree of fairness and accuracy to find out what our actions really were and to apply the law to them in a reasonable and even-handed manner.

Fuller goes on to note that every legal system fails at some times and in some degree to satisfy these conditions; to the extent that it fails to do so, the rule of law is weakened. When the failure is egregious or systematic, the rule of law does not exist at all.

The Rule of Law in Germany between Versailles and Nuremberg

To see the point of the Nuremberg trial, it is important to realize that the rule of law had indeed vanished in Germany for over a quarter of a century. At the end of World War I Germany was on the verge of Marxist revolution, and indeed the Weimar Republic was hastily declared to preempt the declaration of a workers' republic. Gangs of demobilized soldiers, the *Freikorps*, joined with essentially lawless right-wing police to crush the German left. The early years of the Weimar Republic were punctuated by right-wing political murders: Kurt Eisner, the leader of the Bavarian socialist republic; Rosa Luxemburg and Karl Liebknecht, leaders of the Spartacists; Leo Jogiches, Luxemburg's lover, shot in the back in a Berlin police station; Matthias Erzberger, a centrist leader; Walter Rathenau, the Jewish foreign minister of Weimar.[27] Quite obviously, the violence on the streets and the lack

---

26. Lon Fuller, *The Morality of Law* 33–39 (rev. ed. 1964).
27. For an excellent brief discussion, see Peter Gay, *Weimar Culture* 9–22 (1968).

of congruence between law and administration continued in the Nazi era, becoming in fact the accepted way of doing things.

To maintain continuity and legitimacy, the founders of the Weimar Republic made a fatal error: they left the Kaiser's aristocratic-monarchist civil service in place, despite the fact that these men were enemies of the republic and of republicanism in general. That was true in particular of the judiciary, which engaged in what Thomas Mann called "the jurisprudence of political revenge"[28] to subvert the republic.

The statistics are startling. Right-wing political murders accounted for 354 deaths, as compared with 22 left-wing murders. None of the former murderers were sentenced to death, whereas ten of the latter were; sentences to right-wingers averaged four months, while those meted out to left-wingers averaged fifteen years. When a Communist republic was crushed in Bavaria in 1919, over 2,200 people were imprisoned; but after the rightist Kapp Putsch of 1920, "in the course of which the Reich Government was compelled to leave Berlin and which involved the entire Reich north of the Main and implicated many high-ranking army officers, only one single person, the former head of the Berlin police, was convicted and sentenced. Even he was allowed the benefit of honorable motives, and the courts held that the Prussian state was bound to pay him his pension both during and after serving his sentence."[29] Other stunning cases of rightist judicial unfairness involved the "black Reichswehr [army]" organizations,

> which under the cloak of training for the defense of the Eastern provinces against alleged Polish infiltrations organized terrorist activities for the nationalist parties and prepared the ground for National Socialism. The courts assisted the "black Reichswehr" by punishing journalists, who had discussed their activities in public, for treason. Members of the organizations, however, who had murdered disloyal fellow-members . . . were acquitted or received only nominal punishment, because they were held to have acted in self-defense or "for patriotic motives."[30]

Germans widely circulated Brecht's witty twist on Goethe's "land of poets and thinkers"—*Dichter und Denker:* Germany was now the land of *Dichter und Denker und Richter und Henker*—poets and thinkers and judges and hangmen. The German judiciary, according to Franz

---

28. *Quoted in* 1 E. J. Cohn, *Manual of German Law* § 43, at 29 (rev. ed. 1968).
29. *Id.* § 41, at 28.
30. *Id.*

Neumann, had "written the blackest page in the life of the German republic."[31]

All these actions offended against Fuller's third rule and its corollaries. Under Nazism, other rules fell as well; indeed, Nazi jurists denounced the very idea of the rule of law as "opposed and repellent to our own German world view."[32] Most obvious was the fact that under Nazi legal doctrine the Führer's *spoken word* (and not just written commandment) was law; in other words, the law was not public. The Nazis also made robust use of retroactive law. The day after the Röhm purge (the murder of the "left wing" of the Nazi party), Hitler retroactively legalized it; after *Kristallnacht*, the party- and Gestapo-organized anti-Jewish riots of November 1938, Göring imposed a one-billion-mark fine—on the Jews. More than twenty Nazi-era laws, including the Law on the Imposition and Implementation of the Death Penalty, contained provisions for imposing punishment retroactively.[33] The rule *nulla poena sine lege* (no punishment without law) was abolished, for section 2 of the revised criminal code provided that an act could be punished if "the spirit [*Grundgedank*] of a rule of criminal law and healthy folk-feeling" justified punishment.[34] Gürtner, the Reich minister of justice, wrote that "National Socialism replaces this concept of formal illegality with the concept of material illegality," which Edmund Mezger defined as "activity counter to the German National Socialist world view."[35]

During the war, the Ministry of Justice issued periodic letters to judges and defense lawyers. Thierack, the minister of justice, begins his judges' letters sanctimoniously enough: "I will, can, and must not tell the judge who is called to preside over a trial, how to decide an individual case."[36] Thus he will simply comment on and criticize decisions to give guidelines to judges. In one case, Jews went to court because they had been illegally denied their coffee rations, and the court found in their favor. Thierack: "The judge should have put himself the question: How will the Jews react to this 20-page-long ruling, which certifies that he and the 500 other Jews are right and that he won over a German

31. Franz L. Neumann, *Behemoth* 23 (1944).

32. Quoted in Ingo Müller, *Hitler's Justice: The Courts of the Third Reich* 72 (Deborah Lucas Schneider trans. 1991). Müller's book provides an enormous wealth of information about the travesty of Nazi justice; on Nazi rejection of the rule of law, see *id.* at 70–81. For a useful compilation of Nazi legislation, see Ingo von Münch & Uwe Broderson, *Gesetze des NS-Staates: Dokumente eines Unrechtssystems* (1982).

33. Müller, *supra* note 32, at 74.

34. "Gesetz zur Änderung des Strafgesetzbuchs vom 28. Juni 1935," 1 *Reichsgesetzblatt* at 839; *see* 6 BVerGE at 132–222 (1959); Müller, *supra* note 32, at 74.

35. Gürtner and Mezger *quoted in* Müller, *supra* note 32, at 76–77.

36. 3 *Trials of the War Criminals before the Nuremberg Military Tribunals* 524 (1951).

authority without losing one word about the reaction of our own people to this insolent and arrogant conduct of the Jews."[37]

In another case, a Jew pleaded mitigating circumstances after having been convicted of a foreign-exchange violation and received a light sentence. Thierack: "The court applies the same criteria for imposing punishment as it would if it were dealing with a German fellow citizen as defendant. This cannot be sanctioned. The Jew is the enemy of the German people, who has plotted, stirred up, and prolonged this war. In doing so, he has brought unspeakable misery upon our people. Not only is he of different but of inferior race. Justice, which must not measure different matters by the same standard, demands that just this racial aspect must be considered in the meting out of punishment."[38] In his letters to defense lawyers, Thierack appeals to the "healthy folk-feeling" section of the criminal code to argue that under present conditions the lawyer's duty to defend the state overrides his duty to defend his client.[39] This echoes a criminal law commentator's argument that a lawyer can reveal a client's confidences if healthy folk-feeling so commands.[40]

Such was the rule of law in post–World War I Germany. The Germans, evidently, had a lot to learn. The question is whether the Nuremberg trial had a lot to teach.

The Ex Post Facto Character of the Nuremberg Trial

The first, and obvious, objection to the Nuremberg trial on rule-of-law grounds is that it was itself based on ex post facto law, that it therefore violated *nullum crimen sine lege, nulla poena sine lege* (no crime without law, no punishment without law). The criminalization of aggressive war, the introduction of the category of crimes against humanity, and the abolition of the act-of-state and superior-orders defenses were legal novelties. Though some have claimed that none of these were unprecedented, the arguments are strained, having the character of what Jackson called "sterile legalisms" and Joseph Keenan, prosecutor at Tokyo, "legal sterilisms."[41]

37. *Id.* at 531.
38. *Id.* at 533. Thierack here seems to be endorsing "treat different cases differently." The question whether this letter violates Fuller's rule (3a) is left as an exercise to the reader.
39. *Id.* at 564.
40. Eduard Kohlrausch, *Strafgesetzbuch mit Erläuterungen und Nebengesetzen* 470–71 (33d. ed. 1937).
41. Minear, *supra* note 5, at 18. The best attempt I know to vindicate the legality of Nuremberg is Robert K. Woetzel, *The Nuremberg Trials in International Law* (1962).

Thus, for example, precedent was found for Article 6(a) (crimes against peace) in the Briand-Kellogg Pact of 1928, in which the signatories (including Germany) abjured the use of war. The pact indeed meant that Germarny had violated a treaty by starting the war; but treaty violation had not previously been treated as an individual criminal offense of a national leader, so the precedent is beside the point.

The twofold novelty—*individual, criminal* liability—is the key problem. There was no question that what Germany did was wrong, nor that many of her actions were violations of international law. The problem was showing that such violations of international law had been *crimes* and, moreover, crimes of individual persons. The trial's defenders simply glossed over this problem.

The Tribunal, to be sure, addressed the question, but it rested its case on the shakiest of grounds. To show that aggression was a crime, it cited two League of Nations documents that were never enacted and a Pan-American treaty; its only vaguely convincing precedent was a 1927 League of Nations declaration voted for by Germany, which declared aggressive war to be an international crime.[42] But this declaration was not a binding treaty—Germany had quit the League and the League was defunct—and in any event it did not suggest that individuals could be held liable for such a crime.

To demonstrate this latter proposition, the Tribunal could cite only a U.S. Supreme Court case, Article 7 of the Charter, and a provision of the Treaty of Versailles concerning the trial of war criminals.[43] The first obviously had little force in international law, and in any event the U.S. case was decided in 1942, long after the aggressive war had been launched. The second was a circular argument with a vengeance— Article 7 could not be based on Article 7. As for the third, it was irrelevant to the question whether crimes against peace and against humanity could be charged against individuals, for war crimes made up a separate category of offenses under the Nuremberg Charter (Article 6(b)); and, unlike the other two, it was a category that was not novel and whose offenses nobody denied could be tried as individual crimes.

The Tribunal evidently sensed that it was on shaky legalistic ground, for it also ventured an argument based on reason: "To assert that it is unjust to punish those who in defiance of treaties and assurances have attacked neighboring states without warning is obviously untrue, for in such circumstances the attacker must know that he is doing wrong, and so far from it being unjust to punish him, it would

---

42. 1 *Trial* 221–22.
43. *Id.* at 222–23.

be unjust if his wrong were allowed to go unpunished."[44] True enough, but the argument contains a double equivocation, on the words "punish" and "wrong." Though the invader knew he was doing "wrong," he did *not* know that he was committing a "crime"—the latter being a juridically precise subclass of the category of "wrongs." Similarly, he may have expected "punishment" of two sorts: (1) by starting a war, he would in turn be made war upon; and (2) if he went down in defeat, he would be burdened with ruthless terms and harsh reparations (as at Versailles). But he had no reason to expect (3) criminal trial and individualized punishment. Indeed, the World War I precedent to which the Nazis may have looked was the provision of the Versailles Treaty requiring Germany to try her own war criminals—a colossal farce in the event, for 888 out of 901 were acquitted or had their cases dismissed by the Leipzig court.[45] The Leipzig trials explain in part why Nuremberg was necessary, but they hardly provide a precedent showing it was possible.

Similarly, Jackson's claim that "[a]ny resort to war—to any kind of war—is a resort to means that are inherently criminal"[46] clearly begs the question. Nor does his famous argument-in-the-alternative that if this indeed be new law, the Nuremberg framers are entitled to make it—"Unless we are prepared to abandon every principle of growth for International Law, we cannot deny that our own day has the right to institute customs and to conclude agreements that will themselves become sources of a newer and strengthened International Law"[47]—save the point. Of course the Nuremberg framers are entitled to make new *prospective* law; what they are not entitled to do is apply it retroactively. The real consequence of Jackson's argument is, unfortunately, the dismissal of the cases requested in the defense counsels' motion of November 19, 1945:

> Wherever the Indictment charges acts which were not punishable at the time the Tribunal would have to confine itself to a thorough examination and findings as to what acts were committed, for which purposes the Defense would cooperate to the best of their ability as true assistants of the Court. Under the impact of these findings of the Tribunal the States of the international legal community would then create a new law under which those who in the

---

44. Jackson's opening statement, 1 *Trial* 219.
45. Tusa and Tusa, *supra* note 1, at 19.
46. 2 *Trial* 146.
47. *Id.* at 147.

future would be guilty of starting an unjust war would be threatened with punishment by an International Tribunal.[48]

Freeing the defendants is only half of what the rule of law demands, however. Many of them would consider freedom no favor, since their own compatriots were prepared to wreak private vengeance on them—Schacht, Papen, and Fritzsche, after all, had to be smuggled out of jail after they were acquitted at Nuremberg. Now of course the Allies might wink at such private vengeance ("we couldn't execute 'em, but at least they got dead anyway"), but to do so would violate condition (3b) of the rule of law—no alternative enforcement. Thus the Allies would truly honor the rule of law only by providing lifelong protection for Hermann Göring and Julius Streicher.

This idea is paradoxical to the point of obscenity. As Jackson argued, "The rule of law in the world, flouted by the lawlessness incited by these defendants, had to be restored at the cost to my country of over a million casualties, not to mention those of other nations [and not to mention 12 million gassed, shot, burned, and tortured victims of the camps]. I cannot subscribe to the perverted reasoning that society may advance and strengthen the rule of law by the expenditure of morally innocent lives but that progress in the rule of law may never be made at the price of morally guilty lives."[49]

The question, of course, is whether an ex post facto trial is "progress in the rule of law." I shall argue that Nuremberg was. In any event, the conclusion that the rule of law requires lifelong protection for the elite of a genocidal regime would imply that the rule of law is not an ideal worthy of respect. Fortunately, no such drastic conclusion is forced upon us.

The Nuremberg Trial as Progress in the Rule
of Law

On July 11, 1944, Churchill wrote to Anthony Eden, "There is no doubt that this [the Holocaust] is probably the greatest and most horrible crime ever committed in the whole history of the world. . . . It is quite clear that all concerned who may fall into our hands, including the people who only obeyed orders by carrying out the butcheries, should be put to death after their association with the murders has been proved."[50]

---

48. 1 *Trial* 169.
49. 2 *Trial* 147.
50. *Quoted in* Conot, *supra* note 1, at 11.

But "after their association with the murders has been proved" is ambiguous: does it mean a real trial before law? In fact, the British opposed such a trial; their idea was to round up the top Nazis and shoot them. As I have mentioned, it was the Americans who wanted a trial. The third paradigmatic view was that of Stalin, who said at Yalta that "the grand criminals should be tried before being shot."[51] First try them, then shoot them (a version of the rule of law that Stalin had perfected on his own Central Committee and military staff at the Moscow trials of the 1930s).

The British and Russian alternatives show us the clear sense in which the Nuremberg trial was "progress in the rule of law." It was progress, indeed, in four ways.

First, the association of the defendants with the deeds for which they were on trial had to be proved according to strict standards of evidence.

Second, the deeds for which they were held liable were specified in the Charter and their indictments. They knew in advance of the trial what the charges were and could prepare a defense.

Third, the notion of liability at work in the trial was the relatively tight legal notion of *direct causal involvement* and not the looser notion of moral liability. After all, even the three men who were acquitted bore a heavy burden of moral responsibility. Fritzsche had held a high post in Goebbels's Propaganda Ministry and had, in his weekly radio program, helped fan the flames of Jew-hating, jingoism, and war. Papen was a corrupt and conniving right-wing Weimar politician who had maneuvered to make Hitler chancellor and then accepted a diplomatic post in the Third Reich. And Schacht, the financial wizard who had ended the murderous inflation of the early 1920s, had used his influence to help cement the reactionary coalition that brought Hitler to power.[52] To be sure, both Papen and Schacht had assumed that they and their right-wing coalition partners would be able to control Hitler and had not counted on things turning out as they did (and Schacht had resigned from Hitler's government and ended the war in Dachau). But this hardly diminishes their moral responsibility: They had maneuvered to bring a man already known to be a raving, Jew-hating monster, whose private army of storm troopers was already the terror of the streets, into the government's chief executive position; they had hoped to treat him

---

51. Tusa and Tusa, *supra* note 1, at 77.

52. Schacht's prestige as a tycoon-hero made him the Lee Iacocca of the Weimar Republic, as witness the popular rhyme "*Wer hat die Mark stabil gemacht, das war allein der Doktor Schacht.*" [Who was it who made the mark stable? Doctor Schacht was the only one able.]

as their marionette; they had miscalculated, and because of their miscalculation, 35 million people had died violently. Morally, they deserved to hang if anyone did, as did Fritzsche and (for that matter) all the defendants who received only prison terms. The Nuremberg Tribunal, however, limited its inquiry to causal, legal liability and not moral responsibility. (The same cannot be said, however, of the Tokyo tribunal, which executed General Yamashita for crimes committed by his soldiers even though no evidence whatever contradicted his defense that the successful American invasion had disrupted his communication and command structure to such an extent that he was unable to control the troops who committed the crimes. Yamashita was not even morally responsible.)[53]

Fourth, and most important, the trial was fair—judges and prosecution abided by the rules set out in the Charter, and those rules did not bias the inquiry against the defense.[54] This fairness is evident from the record, but the simplest demonstration lies in the acquittals of Fritzsche, Papen, and Schacht.

These four features—the demand for proof, clear specification of offense, the restriction of liability to direct causal involvement, and fairness—clearly point to an advance in the rule of law over the alternatives of kangaroo court and summary execution; in this sense, Jackson was right to describe the defendants as "hard pressed but . . . not ill used"[55] as they would have been under the British or Russian plans.[56]

We may collect these features under the general rubric of natural justice. It is the first dimension along which we may assess the progress of the rule of law. A second major dimension is that of enforcement. It has always been the peculiarity of international law that it is sanctionless. Now it may be that, analytically speaking, law does not require sanctions;[57] nevertheless, it will be impossible to fulfill Fuller's condition of congruence between the law and its administration without them. The great advance of Nuremberg in this respect is the crude but attractive solution it offers to the problem of enforcement: to put it bluntly, Article 7 says, "if you transgress the law, we will catch your leaders and, if they prove to be responsible for the transgression, we

53. See Walzer, *supra* note 19, at 319–22.
54. On the fairness of the trial, see Tusa and Tusa, *supra* note 1, at 205–12.
55. 2 *Trial* 101.
56. These four features are not, of course, among those named by Fuller; his conditions are necessary, not jointly sufficient, for the rule of law. I have suggested, however, that these features, and natural justice more generally, are necessary to fulfill Fuller's condition of congruence between rules and their administration.
57. So argues John Finnis (to my mind persuasively) against Austin and Weber, *Natural Law and Natural Rights* 266–70 (1981).

will hang them." Nuremberg expands the reach of the rule of law by enhancing its grip.

In these obvious ways, Nuremberg is plainly an advance of the rule of law; to deny this on the ground that the trial was ex post facto seems hyperbolic or even deliberately paradoxical. I believe, however, that there is a natural explanation for the hyperbole.

For Fuller, recall, law is a device for ordering society and must therefore be capable of structuring and guiding human action: that is why a full-fledged rule-of-law regime must fulfill his eight conditions. The ideal type here is of a well-ordered domestic society. International society, however, is simply not well-ordered in this way: international law has evolved not as a device for ordering international society but as an improvisation for reconciling domestic legal systems when they are brought into contact (as in international trade). Most international interactions thus occur, as it were, in juridical outer space. For this reason, we should not measure the rule of law in international affairs against the Fullerian ideal but against a different ideal type: the so-called state of nature. This is implicit in Jackson's contrast between advancing the rule of law by the expenditure of morally innocent lives (i.e., by war) and morally guilty lives (i.e., by a fair albeit ex post facto trial): measured against the baseline of war, vengeance, and summary execution, the trial is a clear moral *and legal* advance. The hyperbolic denial that Nuremberg embodied the rule of law, on the other hand, results when we begin at the wrong end—with Fuller rather than Hobbes.

I can make this argument more precise by asking what is wrong with ex post facto law. The Fullerian argument, of course, is that agents cannot guide their actions by rules that do not exist until after the actions are completed. Agents who treat law as an action-guiding system are aggrieved by retroactive law because they were not expecting to be sanctioned for their acts. The premise here is that had they expected such sanction they would, or might, have refrained from the action. Thus ex post facto law is wrong because it violates the legitimate expectations of agents.

If Hobbes forms our baseline, however, the result is different. In the state of nature, and especially in the state of war, there are no such expectations to sacrifice, because agents do not try to guide their actions by corresponding them to rules. One expects violence in return for violence; one expects ill use if one is defeated. This principle is the force of Jackson's argument: "If these men are the first war leaders of a defeated nation to be prosecuted in the name of the law, they are also the first to be given a chance to plead for their lives in the name of the law. Realistically, the Charter of this Tribunal, which gives them a hearing, is also the source of their only hope."[58] Retroactive law violates no legitimate expectations when the alternative is no law at all.

It may be objected that the Nazi leaders did not expect to be held criminally liable for their deeds and that, since they did not believe that "resolving the Jewish question" was wrong, they did not expect retaliation in any form—perhaps they expected the world's gratitude, not its abhorrence.

But the latter objection is wholly implausible. If it were true, why did Himmler order all traces of the death camps to be removed? Why did Goebbels boast in September 1944 that he was number one on the Allied list of war criminals?[59] And once it is admitted that the Nazis knew that what they were doing would be supremely hateful to the Allies, the objection that they did not expect to be held criminally liable becomes unimportant. For their legitimate expectation was that they would be summarily shot. The plain conclusion is that Jackson was right: if the Nuremberg defendants' expectations were violated, it is because they received *better* treatment than they had any reason to expect. Since what is wrong with retroactive law is that it accords people worse treatment than they had reason to expect, it follows that the Nuremberg trial, though based on retroactive law, did not wrong its defendants.[60]

This does not mean, of course, that the Nuremberg trial was fully consistent with the rule-of-law ideal: retroactive law is retroactive law. It shows, however, that the moral wrong committed by violating the rule of law is at a minimum here; and since the trial constituted a clear advance of the rule of law in most other respects, we are right to remain sanguine in the face of the objection.

Nothing can illustrate more graphically the difference between the rule of law and its absence, between what the defendants actually got

---

58. 2 *Trial* 102.

59. Tusa and Tusa, *supra* note 1, at 61.

60. Richard Mohr has pointed out to me one way in which the trial may have given the Nazi leadership worse than it expected. The leaders may have seen themselves as world-historical heroes, for whom only the martyr's death of summary execution is appropriate. Instead, they found themselves in the humiliating position of being treated as criminals, as no different in kind from cutpurses and rapists. Though the trial offered a chance of acquittal, and therefore of life, it was an outrage, worse treatment than the Wagnerian *Götterdämmerung* suitable to conquered warriors.

Now it is likely that Göring thought this way, as perhaps did the military men Jodl and Keitel and romantics such as Baldur von Schirach. It is equally clear that the craven Ribbentrop would have done anything to save his life and that most of the defendants had no desire to end their lives before a firing squad, even in a glorious D-flat coda with Bayreuth tubas bellowing. In any event, we need not accept the leaders' *meschuggene* ideas about heroic death as legitimate expectations.

and what they had reason to expect, than this anecdote from Nuremberg. On December 11, 1945, the prosecution showed a four-hour film of German footage on the history of the Nazi party. As Tusa and Tusa report it,

> The defendants adored every moment of it. They gazed entranced at the newsreels of the Nazi Rallies in Nuremberg, tapped their feet to the marching songs, reveled in the sight of the flags and the sound of the 'Sieg Heils' and Hess crying 'The Party is the Führer and the Führer is Germany'. . . . When they got back to the prison several of the defendants were in tears—of pride and nostalgia this time.
>
> Not one of them commented on a sequence in the film that had particularly impressed others. It showed the trial before the People's Court in Berlin of the 1944 Bomb plotters. They had seen abject men, clutching at their trousers from which the belts had been taken, deprived of the dignity of their false teeth and the aid of their spectacles. There had been no defending counsel and the accused had been literally dragged by SS guards before Judge Freisler. As soon as they tried to speak he screeched at them a torrent of abuse. The contrast between Nazi justice and the tone of the Nuremberg trial and its Charter was vivid and telling—to those sensitive enough to see it.[61]

The Enforcement Problem

Despite the undeniable fact that it exemplified important features of the rule of law, the Nuremberg trial left us an equivocal legacy in this matter as it did in the matter of human rights. The problem begins, once again, with Article 6(a) of the Charter, which criminalizes aggressive war.

As we have seen, Nuremberg enforces the rule of law in international law in one fundamental way: it offers to punish the men and women who commit war crimes, crimes against peace, and crimes against humanity. By personalizing the punishment, it seems to make possible the first realistic deterrent in the history of international law.

Before there can be trial and punishment, however, the criminal must be apprehended, and we must ask how such apprehension is supposed to take place. Suppose, for instance, that members of some nation are guilty of crimes against humanity in peacetime rather than in war. To give ourselves concrete examples, we may think about the

---

61. Tusa and Tusa, *supra* note 1, at 169.

massacre of more than a half-million Communists in Indonesia in 1965—some put the number at a million—the current Indonesian depredations in East Timor, the persecution of Kurds and Shi'ites in Iraq or of blacks in South Africa, none of which is located in a war or civil war context at all. If we include crimes against humanity that take place in civil wars, we can readily add the "ethnic cleansing" of Bosnia and the warlord-sponsored starvation of Somalia, to take only the 1992 headline grabbers, to the list. There is, I take it, probable cause to believe that these are crimes against humanity, whether or not the charge could actually be proven at trial; in conjunction with Articles 7 and 8, therefore, Article 6(c) of the Charter allows the prosecution of national leaders, officials, and armed forces involved in the massacres and persecutions.

However, these persons cannot be taken to trial without violating the sovereignty of Indonesia and South Africa, Iraq or Serbia or Somalia, and Article 6(a) forbids such a violation. (Argentina, remember, protested on violation-of-sovereignty grounds the Israeli kidnapping of Adolf Eichmann—and Eichmann was not even a citizen of Argentina.) As a result, crimes against humanity can be punished as crimes under the Nuremberg Charter only when they occur in the course of a foreign war.[62]

The same is true of several of the crimes against peace detailed in Article 6(a), namely, the planning and preparation of aggressive war and conspiracy so to plan and prepare. For unless the plans and preparations are followed by actually initiating a war, it would be a criminal act of aggression to attempt to apprehend the planners and preparers. Nor is this an unimportant defect. Since it is clear that the chief threat to peace in the contemporary world is the destabilizing effect of military preparation, Article 6(a) is correct to note the criminality of planning and preparing for war even without actually initiating it; but by criminalizing any attempt to enforce itself, Article 6(a) cuts its own throat as an instrument of international peace.

In practice, then, crimes against humanity and most crimes against peace can be brought under the rule of law only if the criminal launches an aggressive war and meets with defeat. Even then arrest and punishment are far from inevitable, as demonstrated by the failure to deal with Saddam Hussein after the Persian Gulf war.[63] The same is true of war crimes, for that matter: think of war crimes (and crimes against peace)

62. As Jackson explicitly argued in *International Conference on Military Trials, supra* note 17, at 331, 333.

63. Theoretically, a victorious aggressor might try opponents for crimes against humanity; but it is more likely that, since the aggressor has itself violated Article 6, it will

committed by the United States in Vietnam and the Soviet Union in Afghanistan. Who is going to arrest Nixon?

Jackson said at Nuremberg, "Unfortunately, the nature of these crimes is such that both prosecution and judgment must be by victor nations over vanquished foes."[64] It is clear from the context that he was referring to the specific situation of the Nazis and not making a general point. If I am right, however, the general point follows from the Nuremberg Charter itself. Only victors' justice is possible.

Instead of actually arresting criminal leaders, one could introduce a different procedure, namely, trying them in absentia (as was done at Nuremberg in the case of Martin Bormann). I fear, however, that such a procedure would create a toothless court that would be so open to costless political manipulation that it would rapidly evolve into an arena for political grandstanding, that is, into an international joke.

A related alternative is an international criminal court with teeth that states voluntarily participate in. Signatories of the European Convention for the Protection of Human Rights and Fundamental Freedom yield jurisdiction in human-rights matters to the European Court of Human Rights in Strasbourg. It is not a criminal court; but on the lines of the Strasbourg model, states could establish an international criminal tribunal, whose jurisdiction they voluntarily accept and to which they grant extradition powers. This institution would amount to a self-imposed limitation on state sovereignty, and would thus circumvent the enforcement problem generated by Article 6(a). The problem with the idea, of course, is that precisely the most robust practitioners of crimes against humanity are least likely to enter into such an enforceable covenant. For this reason, I do not believe the suggestion addresses the enforcement problem in a practical way.[65]

It will be objected that the alternative to unenforceability is infinitely worse. It is difficult to imagine anything crazier and more destructive of world peace than allowing someone to go into countries such as Indonesia, South Africa, or Russia to apprehend national leaders for trial before an international court of law. The fact that we do not know who the police would be underlines the problem: somebody, from some nation, is to abduct P. W. Botha or former Soviet military commanders in the Afghan campaign. That is war, pure and simple, and the world will not long survive it.

---

not be moved to initiate trials based on the Nuremberg Charter.

64. 2 *Trial* 101.

65. On the European Court of Human Rights and proposals for an international criminal court, see the materials assembled in Richard B. Lillich and Frank C. Newman, *International Human Rights: Problems of Law and Policy* 560–627, 754–823 (1979).

The problem is that in a world of nation-states, the only method of enforcing the law of nations against an uncooperative violator is for one nation or group of nations to attack the culprit; the fact that the Nuremberg Charter is unenforceable, that only victors' justice is possible, is thus another artifact of the system of sovereign nation-states, which I have earlier criticized. I nevertheless accept the last paragraph's objection (as what sane person would not?): as long as we live in a world of nation-states, we must as a matter of political necessity regard the Nuremberg Charter mostly as unenforceable dead letter and its advance in the rule of law as (therefore) mostly symbolic. The symbolism is surely not to be denigrated, but it is undeniable that the legacy left by Nuremberg to the rule of law is compromised and equivocal.

That is so (we may summarize the foregoing discussion) for four reasons. First, the attempt to punish Charter crimes in peacetime is itself a crime; thus, second, the Nuremberg Charter labels as crimes deeds that can never be punished as crimes; third, its extension of the rule of law is therefore largely illusory; and fourth, proceedings under the Charter will always be victors' justice. That is an unavoidable fact of politics, written into the Charter itself in the criminalization of aggression.

The Nuremberg Trial as Victors' Justice

There is, however, one avoidable error committed by the Allies at Nuremberg that robbed the trial of much of its moral force and underscored the charge that it was merely victors' justice. I am referring to the fact that no members of the Allied forces were tried, though many were guilty of war crimes. Most notable among these were Churchill, who had ordered the bombing of specifically residential (working-class) areas of German cities to demoralize the enemy,[66] and Truman, who had ordered the atomic bombing of Hiroshima and Nagasaki. More in the bone-chilling spirit of Nazism, the Red Army had murdered 15,000 Polish officers and buried them in mass graves in the Katyn Forest. Indeed, Jackson wrote to Truman that the Allies "have done or are doing some of the very things we are prosecuting Germans for. The French are so violating the Geneva Convention in the treatment of prisoners of war that our command is taking back prisoners sent to them. . . . We are prosecuting plunder and our Allies are practicing it.

---

66. For an argument that this was a self-conscious and unjustifiable decision, see Walzer, *supra* note 19, at 255–63.

We say aggressive war is a crime and one of our allies asserts sovereignty over the Baltic States based on no title except conquest."[67] Now of course it is absurd to imagine that the victorious Allies would have tried their own heads of state, and an investigation into the Katyn Forest slaughter was impossible without Soviet cooperation, which did not come until the advent of *glasnost*. Moreover, it would have obscured the moral message of Nuremberg to treat the actions of Truman and Churchill on a par with those of the architects of the Holocaust. But there was at least one case in which there would have been no absurdity in putting an American officer on trial. This was the case of Admiral Chester Nimitz.

The background is simple. German Admiral Dönitz was accused at Nuremberg of criminally waging unrestricted submarine warfare. He countered that he had done nothing that the Allies had not done as well and introduced as evidence interrogatories posed to Nimitz. Nimitz candidly and honorably confirmed Dönitz's claim: the American Navy had itself waged unrestricted submarine warfare in the Pacific.

By itself, this was scarcely calculated to help Dönitz, because the Nuremberg court quite properly allowed no defense of tu quoque. However, Dönitz's attorney, Otto Kranzbühler, the ablest of the defense counsel, argued cleverly that he was not offering a tu quoque defense: rather, he was arguing that the fact that the Allies had engaged in the identical practices with which Dönitz was charged showed that the conventions of war had changed and that now submarine warfare was legal. (Remember Jackson: " . . . we cannot deny that our own day has the right to institute customs . . . that will themselves become sources of . . . International Law.") Neither Nimitz nor Dönitz, Kranzbühler argued, was a criminal. Dönitz was acquitted of the charge.[68]

He was acquitted as a result . . . of what? Not just of Kranzbühler's ingenuity; rather, Dönitz's acquittal followed from the fact that the Allies would not try Nimitz though he admitted doing just what Dönitz did. Nimitz's candor created an embarrassment: if the Allies were to convict Dönitz, the rule of law required that they try and convict Nimitz as well. Since they were unwilling to do this, they were compelled to accept Kranzbühler's argument that the law itself had changed.

The trouble lies in the precedential—"gravitational"—force that this argument creates: it legalizes any crime committed by the vanquished provided the victor committed it as well. The Allies' refusal to

---

67. *Quoted in* Conot, *supra* note 1, at 68. See Conot's discussion there of other offenses the Germans were tried for that were also committed by the Allies.

68. 1 *Trial* 313. On Kranzbühler's argument, see Conot, *supra* note 1, at 324–25; Tusa and Tusa, *supra* note 1, at 354–57.

extend the rule of law to their own troops and leaders initiates a kind of Gresham's law by which standards of conduct are driven down to whatever level of brutality the victors are willing to tolerate in themselves.

I am not concerned here with the details of Dönitz and Nimitz. Perhaps, in this case, the conventions of war really had changed, and Kranzbühler was right; in that case, Nimitz should still have been tried, and he would have been acquitted together with Dönitz. My concern is with the evil effects of allowing one's own criminals to go unpunished: either we are confronted with victors' justice pure and simple, or else Kranzbühler's argument will be accepted and the principles of international law will be shot onto the downward spiral.

If, on the other hand, the Allies had tried their own war criminals as well as the Germans', the moral force exercised by Nuremberg would have been immeasurably greater than it is. Though the problem of unenforceability in a world of nation-states could not be solved, the world would have at least one example of international justice that was not victors' justice.

The Third Legacy: The Threat of Bureaucracies

So far, I have considered the legacy of Nuremberg more or less in the terms in which the framers of the trial conceived it: as providing through its recognition of new crimes a new world order and as inspiring by its example a rededication to the rule of law. In both cases, I have argued that the legacy of Nuremberg is equivocal, that the rule of law and the politics of human rights are contending for its soul with the realpolitik of sovereign nation-states.

The third legacy of Nuremberg was recognized barely or not at all at the time of the trial, but we are gradually coming to the realization that it is the central moral challenge of our time. I refer to the problem of moral irresponsibility in bureaucratic settings.

"Rule by Nobody"

Evidence was introduced at Nuremberg concerning the Nazis' euthanasia program to remove so-called "useless eaters" and carriers of inferior genes from the world. Conot summarizes this part of the evidence as follows:

> The euthanasia program, serving as the prototype for the exter-
> mination of millions that was to follow, demonstrated how,

through fragmentation of authority and tasks, it was possible to fashion a murder machine. Hitler had enunciated an offhand, extralegal decree, and had not wanted to be bothered by it again. Brandt had ordered the "scientific" implementation of the program and, like Hitler, wished to hear no complaints. The directors and personnel of institutions rationalized that matters were out of their hands and that they were just filling out questionnaires for the "experts" in Berlin, though in reality each form was the equivalent of a death warrant. The specious "experts" perused the questionnaires only to cull out prominent persons that might have been accidentally included, then passed them on to Himmler's myrmidons, who transported the afflicted to the annihilation installations. The personnel at the end of the line excused themselves on the basis that they were under compulsion, had no power of decision, and were merely performing a function. Thousands of people were involved, but each considered himself nothing but a cog in the machine and reasoned that it was the machine, not he, that was responsible.[69]

The euthanasia program is not the prototype only for the Holocaust; it is the prototype as well for the moral plague of modern life, bureaucratic irresponsibility, which is in turn the precondition for state criminality. Hannah Arendt described

the latest and perhaps most formidable form of . . . dominion: bureaucracy or the rule of an intricate system of bureaus in which no men, neither one nor the best, neither the few nor the many, can be held responsible, and which could be properly called rule by Nobody. (If, in accord with traditional political thought, we identify tyranny as government that is not held to give account of itself, rule by Nobody is clearly the most tyrannical of all, since there is no one left who could even be asked to answer for what is being done. It is . . . impossible to localize responsibility and to identify the enemy.)[70]

The discovery, however, is not Arendt's; for as long ago as 1843 Marx had written, "The mind of the bureaucracy makes . . . the real mindlessness of the state a categorical imperative. . . . The bureaucracy is a circle from which no one can escape. Its hierarchy is a hierarchy of knowledge. The highest point entrusts the understanding of particulars to the

---

69. Conot, *supra* note 1, at 210–11.
70. Hannah Arendt, *On Violence* 38 (1969, 1970).

lower echelons, whereas these, on the other hand, credit the highest with an understanding in regard to the universal; and thus they deceive one another."[71]

Though they emphasize different aspects of bureaucracy—Arendt focusing on irresponsibility and Marx on self-deception—it is reasonably clear that both have the same picture of bureaucratic institutions in mind. The core idea is that actions that would be recognized immediately as destructive or even criminal if a single person performed them are fractured by bureaucratic division of labor into "action-shards" that lack the telltale signs of awfulness. A criminal action can be put together out of many action-shards that are not, or do not seem, criminal (e.g., filling out a form). A bureaucrat gives a general directive to eliminate a problem but does not know how it will be done and in any case is completely dependent on his or her subordinates for information about the problem. The subordinates assume that there are good reasons for what they are asked to do, reasons to which they are not privy; they substitute a superior's authorization for a reason. And those who pull the trigger at the end of the line proceed secure in the knowledge that their actions have been approved by everyone in the chain of command.

That is why Marx calls the bureaucracy "a circle from which no one can escape": the "real mindlessness of the state" arises because nobody in a bureaucracy acts unconditionally; every action is constrained by the actor's jurisdictional limits, and conditioned by the actor's beliefs, which are in turn conditioned by the conditioned actions and beliefs of other actors. Every interaction within the institutional framework assumes that the knowledge or authority is possessed by someone in another office; as Alexandra Kollontai is supposed to have said, in a bureaucracy every decision is made by a third party.[72]

Finally, every action-shard is motivated by the everyday incentives of job-holding: praise by a superior, a good performance report, a Christmas bonus. What could be more innocent? Bureaucracy masks the significance of one's job in everydayness. It divides the labor into bite-sized tasks, so that no bureaucrat has the sense of performing a complete action; and it links the mechanical performance of such tasks to career advancement, so that the less one thinks the better off one is. In Marx's words, "[a]t the very heart of the bureaucracy [lies] . . . the materialism of passive obedience, of trust in authority, the mechanism of an ossified and formalistic behavior. . . . As far as the individual

---

71. Karl Marx, *Critique of Hegel's 'Philosophy of Right'* 46–47 (Joseph O'Malley ed. and trans. 1970).

72. I have been unable to track down the source for this remark.

bureaucrat is concerned, the end of the state becomes his private end: a pursuit of higher posts, the building of a career."[73]

We must still see whether, as Conot suggests, such a model—of group criminal actions fragmented into action-shards that are not themselves criminal, or whose criminality is hidden—accurately characterizes the Nazi regime; or whether, on the contrary, the action-shards were themselves obviously criminal.

The question, in other words, is whether the action-shards are *morally opaque* or *morally transparent*. Before addressing this question, however, let us first look more closely at the model itself.

In these accounts of Conot, Arendt, and Marx we find three different problems, not always carefully distinguished. First is the psychological problem of a diminished or even nonexistent sense of individual responsibility in bureaucratic organizations. Second, most prominent in Arendt's account, is the political problem of (nonexistent?) organizational responsibility ("rule by Nobody," "the real mindlessness of the state," which Marx explicates thus: "The state, then, exists only as various bureau-minds whose connexion consists of subordination and dumb obedience"[74]). Third is the moral problem of fragmented knowledge, knowledge that is therefore inadequate for agents in a bureaucracy to base decisions upon (Marx's "hierarchy of knowledge" in which higher and lower echelons deceive one another).

Nuremberg and the Three Problems of Bureaucracy

The Nuremberg Tribunal, I wish to argue, attacked the first problem and grappled with the second and third with only partial success.

1. *The Problem of Diminished Individual Responsibility.* Its attack on the first was a full frontal assault through Articles 7 and 8. It responded to the claim that individuals in a bureaucracy do not feel responsible for what they do simply by declaring them responsible and holding them liable for their deeds regardless of their positions in the hierarchy. To induce responsibility, we must change the bureaucrat's incentives, and criminalizing his activity is the straightforward way to do this.

Implicit in this maneuver seems to be the idea that individuals in a bureaucratic setting may well have the subjective psychological experience of nonresponsibility (what Eichmann described as a kind of "Pontius Pilate feeling"[75]), but that sense of nonresponsibility is to be combatted by the law, not tolerated as an excuse. The sense of non-

---

73. Marx, *supra* note 71, at 47.
74. *Id.* at 47.
75. *Quoted in* Arendt, *Eichmann in Jerusalem: A Report on the Banality of Evil* 114 (rev. ed. 1964).

responsibility is created by the bureaucrat's need to rationalize com-
pliant performance of his or her duties, and this compliance is in its turn
motivated by the incentives of the job—pleasing superiors, enjoying
the modest pleasures of promotion, "the building of a career" (as Marx
puts it). The Pontius Pilate feeling emerges as a rationalization for giving in to a *resistible* temptation.

The famous experiments of Stanley Milgram, in which subjects
were ordered by an authority figure to administer what they believed
were dangerous or fatal electric shocks to another "subject" (really a
confederate of the experimenter), tend to confirm this view: an ap-
pallingly high percentage of the subjects shocked the "subject" to
"death," but between a third and a half refused to. It is possible to refuse
evil orders and thus culpable to comply.[76]

This assumption behind Articles 7 and 8—that the psychological
sense of diminished individual responsibility is self-deception and thus
no excuse—is beyond a doubt a morally worthy one, and any attempt
to deal with the problem of bureaucracy that denies it will have great
difficulty getting off the ground. So far, at any rate, it appears that the
Nuremberg solution is the most plausible one.

2. *The Problem of Organizational (Ir)responsibility.* Less successful is
the attempt at Nuremberg to address the problem of organizational
responsibility. This problem was addressed in two ways: by invoking
the concept of conspiracy in Article 6(a) and by indicting whole
organizations—the Party Leadership Corps, the Reich Cabinet, the
High Command, the SS and SA, the Gestapo—as criminals.

The conspiracy idea was the brainchild of Murray Bernays, an
American lawyer who initiated the framework of the Nuremberg trial.
With the conspiracy idea, Bernays hoped to show that the entire rise of
the Nazi party and Nazi state had been directed to criminal ends; he
hoped to put the history of Nazism on trial. Jackson's prosecution was
mostly faithful to this scheme; in the opening minutes of his great
oration he described the trial as an attempt "to bring within the scope of
a single litigation the developments of a decade, covering a whole

76. Stanley Milgram, *Obedience to Authority: An Experimental View* (1974). See also
Heinrich Böll, "Befehl und Verantwortung: Gedanken zum Eichmann-Prozess," in
Aufsätze Kritiken Reden 113 (1967), arguing that obedience to orders was the Nazi disease,
but that so many people disobeyed orders that the disease hardly amounted to an
irresistible malady. One might, of course, argue that Milgram's findings show that
normal people will comply with evil orders, and thus that it is not culpable to comply,
since "the reasonable person" would. I would reply that the notion of reasonableness is
normative, not statistical: even if 65 percent of us would shock someone to death because
a man in a white coat told us to, it is the 35 percent who would not that are "reasonable."

continent, and involving a score of nations, countless individuals, and innumerable events."[77]

It was an unfortunate plan. The problem was that the concept involved a shallow, Hollywood conception of history and politics— one, moreover, that missed the moral challenge of organizational responsibility.[78]

Conspiracy charges are primarily an Anglo-American device for attacking organized crime, gangsterism (though they were also used, in a less savory way, to attack labor organizers in the nineteenth century). The shock value and moral message of using a conspiracy charge at Nuremberg lay in the analogy it presented: it demystified and depoliticized World War II by suggesting that the Nazis were simply gangsters who had seized control of the German state in furtherance of their plan to launch a war. Bertolt Brecht had once allegorized Nazism in a play about Chicago gangsters, *The Resistible Rise of Arturo Ui;* Bernays's conspiracy charge elevated the Ui motif to official doctrine.

There were, to be sure, points of analogy: Especially in its early years the Nazi party had operated through street violence; the storm troopers were indeed little more than gangsters; and the party's unifying ideology, articulated in *Mein Kampf,* had always aimed explicitly at war-making and Jew-killing (the "criminal plan" that forms the essence of the conspiracy concept). Moreover, the Ui scenario of a mob seizing the state was useful to the Allies in that it allowed the convenient fiction that the German people were passive victims: in Jackson's words, "We . . . have no purpose to incriminate the whole German people. We know that the Nazi Party was not put in power by a majority of the German vote."[79]

But surely all this is a caricature of history! The Nazis did not *just* seize power, as in a coup d'état; their rise was the product of complicated, even profound, forces; as Arendt more accurately assesses it, "The subterranean stream of Western history ha[d] finally come to the surface. . . . "[80] Likewise, an ideology is not *just* a criminal plan; quoting Arendt once again,

It is the monstrous, yet seemingly unanswerable claim of totalitarian rule that, far from being "lawless," it goes to the sources of authority from which positive laws received their ultimate legit-

---

77. 2 *Trial* 100.
78. On Bernays's plan, see Conot, *supra* note 1, at 10–13, and especially the critical discussion of Tusa and Tusa, *supra* note 1, at 54–57.
79. 2 *Trial* 102.
80. Arendt, *The Origins of Totalitarianism* ix (rev. ed. 1958).

imation, that far from being arbitrary it is more obedient to these suprahuman forces than any government ever was before, and that far from wielding its power in the interest of one man, it is quite prepared to sacrifice everybody's vital immediate interests to the execution of what it assumes to be the law of History or the law of Nature.[81]

This is the antithesis of a gangland plot. Hitler, moreover, was not *just* Arturo Ui: he was one of the most effective populist politicians of our century, the acme of the new style of symbolic and mystical politics that characterized early modernism and continues to plague us today.[82] And, of course, the German people were not *just* innocent, passive victims. The Nazi regime enjoyed immense popular support from its inception until the war began to go badly.

Most importantly, however, the conspiracy concept ignores the fact that the Nazis did not act as a *gang* but as the *state*. Here again the Nuremberg trial came just short of recognizing the problem of organizational responsibility. Instead of a "criminal state," it saw only a "state run by criminals."[83]

For this reason, the concept of criminal organizations, with its "theory of 'group criminality,'"[84] was a more promising avenue to pursue than was the concept of conspiracy (though the Tribunal evidently did not see the crucial difference, writing in its judgment, "A criminal organization is analogous to a criminal conspiracy . . ."[85]). Sifting the evidence cautiously, the Tribunal separated out more culpable strata of the accused organizations from those less culpable, more culpable or-

---

81. *Id.* at 461–62.

82. *See* Carl Schorske, "Politics in a New Key: An Austrian Trio," in *Fin-de-Siècle Vienna: Politics and Culture* 116 (1980).

83. In the end, the Tribunal did not treat the conspiracy charge as an offense separate from the crime against peace itself. 1 *Trial* 226. If it had, it would have had to come to terms with a lurking problem in the very Anglo-American concept of conspiracy it had adopted. A common-law device known as Wharton's Rule holds that when a crime can be committed only by a group (e.g., adultery, duelling, gambling) and only after group deliberation, there is no conspiracy separate from the crime itself. It would be wrong to criminalize the group deliberation in addition to criminalizing the act itself when the act could not be committed without group deliberation: that would amount to double punishment. *See, e.g.,* Ianelli v. United States, 420 U.S. 770 (1975); "Comment: An Analysis of Wharton's Rule: *Ianelli v. United States* and One Step Beyond," 71 *Northwestern University Law Review* 547 (1976). But surely "planning, preparation, initiation or waging of a war" is an act that cannot be committed except by a state, that is, by a group of people; crimes against peace are undoubtedly Wharton's Rule offenses.

84. 1 *Trial* 256.

85. *Id.*

ganizations from those that were ineffectual, such as the Reich Cabinet, or merely technical, such as the High Command. It was one of the Tribunal's best-considered judgments.

Unfortunately, the concept of group criminality was not quite the concept of state criminality, which I have claimed as the key to Nazi crime. The indictment applied the concept to very specific subgroups in the state but not to the state as such. Nor, however, *could* the indictment apply it to the state as a whole, for a reason that carries profound implications for the rule of law.

It is important to realize that at Nuremberg group criminality meant collective rather than corporate criminality—it meant, that is, that every member of the criminalized group was liable to punishment rather than the more familiar idea that the organization, but not its members, was sanctioned. When a business corporation pleads guilty, the corporation (and not its officers) pays the penalty. Obviously, there is a reason this would not work at Nuremberg: you can fine a corporation, but what sanction could be levied against the Reich Cabinet as an organization? The only way to punish it is to punish its members as individuals.

Given this understanding of group criminality, it could not be charged against the state as a whole since it is completely unclear what individuals should be encompassed in the charge. (Which individuals are "the state"?) And this must be known: even though it is the state that was criminal, it is individuals who would be punished. As we have seen, legality dictates that one cannot punish individuals without demonstrating their causal responsibility in the crime. Did we really want to criminalize every highway construction foreman and railway conductor simply because they worked for "the state"?

But this just *is* the problem of irresponsibility in a bureaucratic setting. We may put it this way. In an era of criminal states, the rule of law must expand its grip to punish state crimes. But punishment is always individualized, and the rule of law also insists that it is wrong to punish an individual without localizing criminal agency to that individual. If criminal agency could be localized to individuals, however, we would not need the notion of group criminality. To the precise extent that the rule of law makes the group-criminality concept essential, therefore, it cannot be employed. Bureaucracy threatens the rule of law.

This is simply the legal working out of Arendt's "rule by Nobody" problem—the problem that "there is no one left who could . . . be asked to answer for what is being done [since i]t is . . . impossible to localize responsibility. . . ." In the end, the concept of group criminality runs up against the same problem as the concept of conspiracy. Both are

designed to catch planners who did not act, whereas "the real mindlessness of the state" means that a bureaucratic organization is more like a
collection of actors who did not plan.

How can such a thing be? The root of the difficulty lies in the third
great problem of bureaucracy, the problem of fragmented knowledge.

3. *The Problem of Fragmented Knowledge.* Early in the Nuremberg
trial, the prosecution showed an hour-long film on concentration
camps. "The screen filled with images of skeletal men and women,
crematoria and gas chambers, the scarred and disfigured bodies of
women who had survived medical experiments, mound upon mound
of cadavers whose sticklike arms and legs gave the appearance of
jumbled piles of driftwood, displays of human lampshades, Germans
holding their noses as they were compelled into sightseeing tours
through the camps and impressed into burying details, and tractors
pushing the dead into mass graves like contaminated jetsam."[86] The
reactions of the defendants to this film were astounding. Funk, Ribbentrop, and Fritzsche wept, and the latter lamented that evening, "No
power in heaven or earth will erase this shame from my country—not
in generations—not in centuries!"[87]

Didn't they know? Funk, who cried openly during the film, had after
all accepted shipments of gold teeth pried from the victims' mouths into
the vaults of his Reichsbank. Yet he behaved like someone who didn't
know.

I suggest that there is an explanation, one, however, that is not easy
to accept. They knew something, but they did not know what it was
that they knew. Funk obviously knew that people were dying (he had
their teeth); but a war was going on, and people do die in wars. Maybe
the teeth came from civilian victims or military casualties. Similarly,
Conot's euthanasia "experts" were presented with completed questionnaires and did not know what public health or epidemiological menace
required the drastic measure they were implementing, while the institutional personnel who filled out the forms did not know what was
going to be done with them. Perhaps they sensed that something was
amiss; nevertheless, based on the small amount of information available to them, they were unwilling to trust their own judgment. The
higher authorities, on the other hand, did not know the details of human lampshades or Zyklon B—and so on, up and down the line.

The disquieting feature of this explanation is that it renders our
ordinary model of moral decision making moot, at least in part. On that
model, a moral decision occurs at a discrete moment in time, when the

---

86. Conot, *supra* note 1, at 149.
87. *Id.;* Tusa and Tusa, *supra* note 1, at 160–61.

facts of the case are there before us, and the options are demarcated for our deliberation. *In a bureaucratic setting, however, that moment never arrives.* We get partial information and instructions to fill out a form. We may suspect that the form will be badly used, but we don't know enough about what is going on in the other offices to be sure; often, we may not know what our options are. That we do not take responsibility for our actions is based on ignorance, not subservience or cowardice. We may resolve not to be "good Germans" at the moment of truth, but the moment of truth never arrives.

One way of responding to this problem is to insist that ignorance can itself be culpable.[88] Frank's self-accusing response to the concentration-camp film was instructive: "Don't let anybody tell you they had no idea! Everybody sensed that there was something horribly wrong with this system, even if we didn't know all the details. They didn't want to know!"[89] In the same vein, a former Nazi official once related to me a story: A young soldier of his acquaintance returned on leave from the Occupied East, where the *Einsatzgruppen* were shooting and gassing thousands of Jews, and burst into tears in the presence of his sister. She did not ask him why he was crying: she knew that it was something she didn't want to know about. In the same way, the official said, he himself never "knew" about the fate of the Jews, but did know that there was something to know—something that he could have found out but for his own urgent need not to know.

The criminal law recognizes that "willful blindness" is not a defense. If someone offers you a thousand dollars to hide a package in your spare tire as you drive over the border from Mexico, and customs officials find the package—filled with "the thinking man's Dristan"— you will not be able to defend yourself against the charge of drug smuggling by saying that you did not know what was in the package.

The question, of course, is whether the Nazis were willfully blind in this sense. I believe that they were. The top Nazis may not have known what the inside of a death camp looked like, but they knew what the code name "Final Solution" meant. Lower-level flunkies such as Ivan the Terrible, the notorious executioner at Treblinka, may not have known why they were gassing Jews, but they could not help but know that mass killing was mass murder. Whatever blindness such people allege is willful blindness.

---

88. Alan Strudler, David Wasserman, and I have recently attempted to develop this approach as a general response to the problem of fragmented knowledge. David Luban, Alan Strudler & David Wasserman, "Moral Responsibility in the Age of Bureaucracy" 90 *Michigan Law Review* 2348 (1992). This paper is an extended reconsideration of the issues I am discussing in this chapter.

89. Conot, *supra* note 1, at 149.

What this means, however, is that the bureaucratic crimes tried at Nuremberg *did* have localized responsibility; knowledge was not so thoroughly fragmented that anyone was truly ignorant. The Nuremberg crimes were—in our earlier terminology—morally transparent. That, in turn, means that the decentered, agency-less agency implicit in Arendt's "rule by Nobody" and Marx's "real mindlessness of the state" were not the issue at Nuremberg; Arendt's and Marx's models are gross exaggerations of the Nazi regime. The Third Reich was indeed a criminal state, but individuals in it committed its crimes by performing actions that were themselves criminal—issuing and executing orders to commit mass murder.

For this reason, I believe that the Nuremberg trial dealt adequately with the crimes it tried, even though the legal concepts it employed— conspiracy and group criminality—must be supplemented by a "willful blindness" analysis that the Tribunal did not provide.

But even that analysis may be insufficient to deal with the problem of future criminal states in which the bureaucratic mesh sieves information and agency more finely than did that of the Third Reich.[90] Today, soldiers in silos can incinerate thousands of times more people than Ivan the Terrible ever did while sealed off not only from political information but also from any concrete image of what they are doing. If that happens, the legacy of Nuremberg will be insufficient to deal with state criminality.

As long as such a state exists only in Orwellian nightmares, we will be able to evade this problem: we will not run up against the incompatibility of the rule of law and the rule by Nobody. But this brings us to our final problem, the last legacy of Nuremberg: *that the rule of law may require the rule by Nobody.*

---

90. Strudler, Wasserman, and I argue that the "willful blindness" analysis may be extended to cover cases in which individual actions are morally opaque. Luban, Strudler, & Wasserman, *supra* note 88. In our view, individuals working in bureaucratic settings are morally responsible for attempting to ferret out information about the significance of organizational activities in which they are participants. If an organizational employee neglects to attempt to ferret out this information, his or her ignorance is culpable—it is willful blindness.

However, while we believe that employees have a moral obligation to seek knowledge about the significance of their organizational activities, we doubt that defaulting on this moral obligation should give rise to criminal liability. The reason is that it is too difficult to specify a standard of what counts as a reasonable effort to discover the significance of one's organizational activities. Thus, the standard is far too vague to satisfy the requirement of specificity appropriate to the definition of a crime. For this reason, our approach does not provide a concept of individual criminal liability that can stand in for a legal concept of state criminality.

The Tension between Bureaucracy
and the Rule of Law

The problem is that a "rule of law, not of men" bears an uncomfortable resemblance to "rule by Nobody." Officials in both are, in Plato's words, "servants of the law."[91] Now, as long as the actions taken in obedience to the law are morally transparent, we may be able to rely on the conscience of officials to mitigate harsh, thoughtless, ideological, or just plain crazy directives. A servant of the law need not be a slave of rules. That, indeed, is one standard justification offered for the existence of a career civil service; in the United States, for example, it is conventional wisdom that the most important function of the career Foreign Service is to impede politicized administrations from executing their foreign policy brainstorms.

But as industrial society and its state become increasingly complex, differentiation and sheer complexity make the bureaucracies that exercise jurisdiction over the various subsystems opaque to each other. The different offices and agencies know each other only as "black boxes" that produce outputs which others must simply take as pregiven inputs.[92] As a result, bureaucratic actions lose their moral transparency; the individual official never knows the moral character of the act he or she is performing, and this ignorance is no longer willful blindness.

In that situation, bureaucratic consciences become deactivated; and the default condition of bureaucratic conscience is mere bureaucratic conscientiousness—stubborn competency in carrying out an assignment. Now it may well be that bureaucratic conscientiousness is the virtue that makes the rule of law possible, for it impels officials to adhere to rules. But bureaucratic conscience is what makes the rule of law livable: to use Plato's and Aristotle's analogy, it is what allows physicians to change their course of treatment when they find it is killing their patients.[93]

Conscientiousness without conscience is the Orwellian nightmare. In such a regime, the rule of law, bureaucratically realized, becomes the mechanism by which a disastrous set of rules effectuates itself. And that, in turn, is why Nuremberg's attempt to revive individual responsibility by enhancing the rule of law may be self-defeating.

I say "may be" because the reality of the threat depends on the truth of a complicated empirical conjecture: that industrial societies are becoming increasingly complex; that such complexity can be governed

---

91. Plato, *Laws* 715d.
92. Luhmann, *supra* note 13, at 50–51, 103–17.
93. Aristotle, *Politics* bk. 3, ch. 14, 1286a12–16; Plato, *Statesman* 295c–297c.

only with unfettered and arbitrary administrative discretion—a pragmatism that is the opposite of the rule of law—or else a proliferating
bureaucracy that passes over the threshold to rule by Nobody; and that
a state ruled in either of these two ways is likely to take on the criminal
characteristics of the Third Reich (because, for example, the citizens of
such a state become peculiarly susceptible to ideology disconnected
from factuality—the final consequence of the problem of fragmented
knowledge).[94]

If that is so, the high hopes of the framers of Nuremberg will have
been dashed, for the rule of law will have turned out to be its own worst
enemy. But even then the Nuremberg trial will not have been without a
valuable legacy. We, or our children, will have to fight once again to
defeat the criminal state; if we win, we will once again have to pick up
the pieces; and, once again, we will not be likely to do better than to take
the men and women who became cogs in the murder machine and put
them on trial before a tribunal that is as fair as we know how to make it.
Though we cannot always hope for law, we can at least hope for justice.

Conclusion 1987: The Past Is Not Dead; It Is Not Even Past

The fortieth anniversary of the Nuremberg trial was bracketed by
Ronald Reagan's 1985 visit to Bitburg cemetery—where he delivered a
conciliatory and equivocal speech over Waffen SS graves—and Kurt
Waldheim's election to the Austrian presidency in 1986 despite evidence that he had been involved in war crimes and had repeatedly lied
about his wartime involvements. At the same time a vituperative
debate broke out in Germany over the attempt by revisionist historians
of Nazism to minimize both the extent of Hitler's aggression and the
singularity of the Holocaust.[95] If one of the aims of the Nuremberg trial
was to burn the history of Nazism into the memory of mankind, we
must conclude that it failed.

An equally distressing failure of moral memory appeared at the
same time in the World Court case between the United States and
Nicaragua concerning American support for the contras and CIA mining of Nicaraguan territorial waters. The U.S. government, asserting
that the Court has no jurisdiction over the dispute, argued that the U.S.

---

94. That is Arendt's view in *The Origins of Totalitarianism, supra* note 80.

95. For a brief summary of this complex debate, see Judith Miller, "Erasing the
Past: Europe's Amnesia about the Holocaust," *New York Times Magazine,* Nov. 16, 1986, at
30. The Fachschaftsrat Geschichte of the University of Tübingen compiled a useful
collection of documents from this debate, *Dokumentation zur Historiker-Debatte* (1987).

claim to be acting in the "collective self-defense" of El Salvador was nonjusticiable. Curiously, the identical argument had been offered at Nuremberg by defense counsel Hermann Jahrreis, who asserted, "War of self-defense is permitted as an unalienable right of all States; without this right, sovereignty does not exist; and every State is alone judge of whether in a given case it is waging war of self-defense."[96]

Needless to say, the Nuremberg Tribunal rejected this argument, for to accept it was to abandon the trials. When the World Court declined to resurrect Jahrreis's argument in the jurisdictional phase of *Nicaragua v. United States*, the American government provoked a controversy by pulling out of the litigation. Critics within the United States charged that the unilateral American withdrawal was a symbolic assault on the rule of law in international affairs.

The premise of this criticism is precisely the premise of the Nuremberg framers: that the rule of law in international affairs will advance or retreat through expressive and exemplary action such as symbolically significant trials. As Paul Kahn points out, it is a peculiarity of international law that behavior violative of norms can create new norms; he argues that America's actions in the Nicaragua case may mark the breakdown of the U.N. Charter vision as well as of Nuremberg law.[97]

As we have seen, however, the elements of this crisis were nascent in Nuremberg itself. Though the Tribunal repudiated Jahrreis's argument, his appeal to state sovereignty had already been enshrined in Article 6(a) of the Charter. The Allies' refusal to try their own criminals parallels America's unilateral withdrawal from the World Court. And Americans will recognize in the 1987 Iran-Contra hearings that we are far from solving the problem of organizational irresponsibility—the disturbing fact that a state policy can seemingly emerge from nowhere with no author and the equally disturbing fact that our impulse is inevitably to throw responsibility on a conspiracy of mavericks rather than come to grips with the disagreeable notion that a state might itself be responsible.[98]

---

96. 18 *Trial* 86. A brilliant and disturbing analysis of this uncanny parallel between Nuremberg and the Nicaragua litigation may be found in Paul W. Kahn, "From Nuremberg to the Hague: The United States Position in *Nicaragua v. United States* and the Development of International Law," 12 *Yale Journal of International Law* 1 (1987).

97. Kahn, *supra* note 96, at 2–4, 59–62.

98. The secret funding of the contras through the diversion of profits from Iranian arms sales is a direct lineal descendent of the American policy of covert paramilitary operations that formed the subject matter of *Nicaragua v. United States.*

The ambiguous legacies of Nuremberg linger at the margins of our unreliable moral memories; they inspire but also burden the conscience of our politics.

Afterword, New Year 1993

Since I wrote the essay that forms the basis of this chapter, international politics has been transformed by events that no one could have anticipated. Some of these events confirm the darkest fears I expressed in the essay. These include the German rebirth of neo-Nazism, accompanied by xenophobic street violence and anti-Semitism; the catastrophic decay of conditions within Russia, which today resembles nothing so much as the Weimar Republic with a nuclear arsenal; and, above all, the holocaust Serbia and Bosnian Serbs are inflicting on Bosnian Muslims while the European nations stand immobilized by torpor and timidity. To be sure, the past is not dead; it is not even past.

At the same time, however, events beginning with the Persian Gulf war have wrought an immense change in our understanding of international law, a change that may well nudge it in a direction that I wholeheartedly endorse. In one sense, of course, the U.S.-led coalition against Iraq was responding to a classic violation of Kuwait's sovereignty and in no way represented a new understanding of the relative importance of sovereignty and human rights. The coalition, moreover, was hardly engaged in a disinterested or altruistic expedition—the strategic and economic threat posed by Iraq could hardly be ignored, and the expedition was plainly an exercise in calculated geopolitics-as-usual.

In another sense, however, the "gravitational force" of the coalition's response lay elsewhere. It lay in the international community's revulsion at Saddam's ruthlessness and brutality, coupled with a willingness to act on that revulsion. In addition, the Gulf war revived the United Nations as a serious agent in international affairs.[99]

These two phenomena, which arose independently of concerns over sovereignty, paved the way for more unusual developments subsequent to the war itself: the declaration of a no-fly zone in Iraq to protect Iraqi Shi'ites and Kurds from Saddam; the declaration of a no-fly zone in former Yugoslavia; and the U.N.-sponsored American relief expedition in Somalia.

What I find remarkable in each of these three extraordinary developments is the virtual absence of concern over the fact that each

---

99. For a more pessimistic assessment, see Paul W. Kahn, "Lessons for International Law from the Gulf War," 45 Stanford Law Review 425 (1993).

involves a clear-cut violation of national sovereignty, coupled
primary focus on human suffering and human rights that seems to be
the sole legitimate rationale for the policies. Recall again Paul Kahn's
observation that in international law behavior that violates norms can
create new norms; could it be that a norm of violating state sovereignty
in favor of humanitarian intervention is evolving before our eyes?
Could it be that a norm is emerging that authorizes the United Nations
to orchestrate such interventions?

Plainly, it is too early to draw firm conclusions in answer to these
questions. The world's response to Balkan ethnic cleansing will provide
an early test case for the hypothesis that international norms are evolving away from Article 6(a) of the Nuremberg Charter in the direction of
an enforceable Article 6(c).

We must not overlook the metastasis of nationalism since 1989,
which has led to pathologies that range from the funny (Mongolian
liberals rallying around the memory of that liberal paragon Genghis
Khan) to the horrifying (the agony of Yugoslavia). No doubt there is
repulsive irony in the thought that just at the moment that nation-states
are at their most obsolete, the demand for them has achieved its most
feverish and destructive intensity. This painful countervailing development surely offers little reason to anticipate a more cosmopolitan international order.

As I write this afterword, at New Year 1993, the horrifying situation
in Bosnia is highly volatile and unpredictable. By the time this book
appears, the parties will have agreed to an armistice; or the United
Nations or the European powers will have intervened by force; or the
warfare will have sputtered out; or the Serbian "ethnic cleansing" will
have succeeded, and perhaps spread to Kosovo; or something wholly
unanticipated will have superseded the Bosnian holocaust. For the past
year, however, the atrocities have proceeded accompanied by a great
deal of international hand-wringing but no effective action. There is a
reason for that, which takes us directly back to the issues in this chapter.
No one even among those favoring an intervention in Bosnia has proposed the rule change that would enable such an intervention to succeed militarily: permitting the United Nations to wage an offensive war
against ethnic cleansers, if necessary in Serb territory, rather than a
merely defensive response in Bosnian territory. Without this rule
change, the military prognosis is so discouraging that the U.S. and
European leaders have been justifiably reluctant to assume the risk of a
humanitarian intervention.

But of course the rule change would amount to a step away from
the nation-state system and the protection of sovereignty greater than

any in modern history. It would turn the United Nations into a potentially effective world cop and the nations into each other's keepers in a kind of world federation. By posing so enormous a choice, the Bosnian horror may well mark a kind of moral and political watershed that defines the character of world politics for years to come. Either the world relinquishes the system of sovereign nation-states, or it stands in ineffectual witness of genocide. Bosnia, in a way, *is* the legacy of Nuremberg in today's world, with all of Nuremberg's ambiguities compressed tightly within it.

Chapter 8

Concluding Reflections

Modernist legal theory consists in retelling significant legal events in a way that deliberately and conspicuously detaches them from their traditional context. It aims in this way to arouse wonder and to excite our sense of the incongruity of continuing to rely on those traditions in our present emergency. I aimed in the first part of this book to explain modernist legal theory and to defend it, in rather general theoretical terms, against its most plausible current alternatives.

My aim in the second part has been to practice what I preach. Here I have offered examples of my version of modernist legal theory. The legal events I have retold consisted of three trials, trials that throw into relief the dubious features of statist liberalism. Modernism lies in the power of memory and the power of narrative, and I have chosen trials whose stories trouble our political memories.

But this choice raises important questions. Why trials? (Or perhaps, why these trials?) What makes the story of a trial an appropriate form for a narrative elaboration of legal theory? Why do these trials count as elaborations of legal modernism as I develop it in the book's first half?

In this brief conclusion I wish to address these questions, by discussing four aspects of the trials: their character as *foundational* trials, as *political* trials, as *epic* trials, and as *nested narratives*.

Foundational Trials

The trials I have chosen for the final three chapters attracted me because they are *foundational* trials. Each of them aimed not only to effect legal justice in a particular case but also to establish or legitimize a whole regime of justice. This aim is clear in the trial of Orestes, which purports to explain the origin of the Athenian legal system, and in the Nuremberg trial, which was an explicit attempt on the part of the victorious Allies to (re)establish the rule of law in Germany by force of example. But it is equally true of the trial of Martin Luther King. The stakes in King's case were high: on the one side, an effort to eradicate the old order of the American South; on the other, an apologia by the Supreme Court for reasserting the authority of government over the individual conscience.

The trials that form my subject thus partake of a double character: they are efforts to do justice but also efforts to establish the conditions of the justice that is done. This makes them perfect vehicles for exploring the modernist thesis.

Modernism, I argued, is a response to our complex relationship to our own cultural past; in Habermas's apt phrase, the past is now "connected as *prehistory* with our present."[1] In a modernist predicament, we endure a heightened consciousness that our achievements and endeavors are conditioned by a set of contingent cultural givens—what might be termed *enabling conventions*. (Tonality in music and linear perspective in painting are examples of enabling conventions.) At the same time, modernism finds that these enabling conventions can no longer do the job. To persist within their boundaries dooms us to what Clement Greenberg rightly described as "motionless Alexandrianism."[2] This predicament lies at the source of the basic modernist dilemma. On the one hand, since creation apart from enabling conventions is wholly impossible, we can avoid minor, epigonal imitation of the past only by inventing new enabling conventions. On the other hand, enabling conventions cannot simply be willed or decreed into existence: they must prove their power by actually producing work that is as convincing as the best of what came before. Modernism as I understand it provides one way of devising new conventions to meet this challenge: it consists of the attempt to make the problem of our relation to our past the explicit theme of what we do at present. The enabling convention of modernism consists precisely in exposing and criticizing premodern enabling conventions.

My thesis has been that law currently faces a phenomenon analogous to the modernist predicament in the arts. However, instead of losing faith in artistic quality, we are on (or over) the threshold of losing faith in the justice of our legal institutions, or (indeed) in our very capacity to identify justice.

This is where foundational trials come in. They are emblems of the simultaneous creation of justice and of the enabling conventions of justice: they are, in other words, a response to the modernist predicament. A foundational trial spotlights the dialectical relationship between enabling conventions (in this case, a set of adjudicatory institutions) and an achievement within the conventions (here, the ad-

---

1. Jürgen Habermas, *The Philosophical Discourse of Modernity* 13–14 (Frederick G. Lawrence trans. 1987).
2. Clement Greenberg, *Art and Culture* 4 (1961).

judication of a particular issue). To revert to the Wittgensteinian metaphors I borrowed in the introduction to this book, a foundational trial functions as a "hinge" or "riverbed" that guides an entire legal order. Nuremberg could legitimize the rule of law only by convincing us that the trial did justice to the defendants, but we will be convinced that the trial did justice to the defendants only if the procedural and legal institutions that were established for the trial are able to secure our confidence. Such a bootstrap operation is doubtless circular, but it need not be vicious: a trial may convince us of its justice both in its particularities and in the generalities these may suggest. Similarly with the *Oresteia;* the justice of the outcome wins us over only to the extent that the Athenian court is legitimate, but we will be persuaded of its legitimacy only if the outcome of the trial wins us over. When we observe that the trial permanently subordinates women, our confidence in both the trial and the court disappears. Likewise, in *Walker v. City of Birmingham,* the connection is negative: my argument is that the injustice of King's conviction and the illegitimacy of the Court's assertion of exclusive interpretive authority reinforce each other.

Political Trials

The trials I discuss in Part II are not only foundational trials, however. They are also, in a very obvious way, political trials. This was clear enough at Nuremberg and Birmingham, but it is equally true in the *Oresteia,* where Aeschylus deliberately frames the issue as a political contest between the sexes (and wrote the play in part to intervene in a contemporary political crisis threatening the Areopagite court). The defining characteristic of political trials is that they aim at some present or future political end under the guise of judging a past event. Their legitimacy is always questionable, but few doubt that they are sometimes necessary. The injustice of the past must be replaced by justice; but before that can happen, we must deal with past injustices and ancient, corrupting grudges. Unhappily, to deal with these we may have to commit injustices.[3] To establish a new system of justice, Athena

---

3. This paradox forms the basis for one of the most famous problems in jurisprudence, Lon Fuller's "Problem of the Grudge Informer," in *The Morality of Law* (rev. ed. 1964). The problem derives from postwar German cases concerning individuals who, out of spite or other base motives, denounced their neighbors for disloyalty to the Nazi regime, aiming in this way to get the neighbors imprisoned or executed. Postwar German prosecutors were under urgent political pressure to punish the grudge informers but were somewhat at a loss to find a legal pretext for the punishment, after all, it seems wrong to punish someone for reporting illegal behavior to the police, even if the motive for reporting is base and even if the behavior is illegal only in the framework of

must ride roughshod over the ancient law represented by the Furies; to convict the Nazis at Nuremberg, the Allies must try them ex post facto for crimes that had been committed as much by the state as by particular individuals. In King's case, on the other hand, the Supreme Court insists that prior expectations cannot be overthrown and thus undercuts the civil rights movement.

How can political trials convince us that they are doing justice in the particular case, which I have just claimed is a necessary condition for a foundational trial to secure a new legal order? After all, nothing reeks of injustice more than a politicized show trial with a foregone conclusion. The answer must turn on the particular political end that the trial seeks to achieve. If the aim is merely to placate some constituency or to persecute a regime's political opponents, we will rightly condemn the trial. But if the trial rigorously keeps its focus fixed on the case at hand, so that its procedural or legalistic irregularities may be plainly seen to serve natural justice—think of Nuremberg—then its weak legal credentials will not undercut the political end it aims to achieve.

In other words, when the legal injustice of the political trial arises solely because the trial violates the terms of a prior legal order that is palpably inadequate, then the legal injustice of the trial may turn out to be an asset rather than a liability. Its legal injustice stands as a critique of the antecedent legal order. A trial of this sort uses the characteristic methods of a discipline to criticize the discipline itself—Greenberg's definition of modernism. Each of these trials thus exemplifies the modernist problem of "mastering the past" (as the Germans euphemistically describe the problem of creating justice out of the historical rubbish heap).

It is hardly a coincidence that the heyday of artistic modernism coincided with political upheaval and revolutionary movements. Many artistic modernists participated enthusiastically in political movements and intended their artwork to contribute to the causes they supported (which spanned the spectrum from communism to fascism). Others adopted a self-consciously antipolitical aesthetic ideology that was in

---

evil law. The grudge informer cases were initially analyzed by Gustav Radbruch, "Gesetzliches Unrecht und Übergesetzliches Recht," *Rechtsphilosophie* (Erik Wolf & Hans-Peter Schneider eds., 8th ed. 1973). Subsequently they were discussed in the well-known Hart-Fuller debate, where Hart and Fuller agreed that the best approach to the cases was through an ex post facto criminal statute. H. L. A. Hart, "Positivism and the Separation of Law and Morals," 71 *Harvard Law Review* 593, 615–21 (1958); Lon L. Fuller, "Positivism and Fidelity to Law—A Reply to Professor Hart," 71 *Harvard Law Review* 630, 646–47 (1958).

reality simply an unconvincing defensive reaction to the political preoccupations of their fellow modernists. Still others resolved the tension mystically, believing that artistic experience was itself utopian and political. In any event, the modernist response to historical discontinuity in the arts paralleled in many respects the legal response to historical discontinuity displayed in political trials.

Like foundational trials, political trials thus form a perfect vehicle for exploring aspects of modernism. Inherent in the modernist predicament is the possibility, even the likelihood, that we will not attain escape velocity from the flaws of our history and thus that our efforts to reinvent justice will fail. Our history poses us a problem, and nothing guarantees that we will be able to solve it.

This problem has enormous contemporary urgency, which provides some of the edge to these essays. Germany faced the problem at the end of World War II, but it persists on both sides of the Atlantic today. East Europeans, compelled to deal with a leadership class that is at once indispensable and hopelessly compromised, confront the problem in an immediate form. Less obviously, it lies at the root of the fundamental social issue confronting contemporary America. In the wake of slavery, the United States faced the problem of how to create a new order out of an unjust past and failed to solve it. Our racial problems today stem directly from our failure to master the past—from our failure to cope with the mark of Cain that slavery and racism burned into American history. (Or so I have argued in the King chapter.)

Epic Trials

A trial, it has often been remarked, is like a play. But plays can be treated in either a traditionalist or a modernist manner. My accounts of trials exemplify the modernist approach to drama that Brecht and Benjamin called *epic theater*. Epic theater does not aim at a celebratory or empathic rendition of events and characters. Rather, it aims at a cooler, more distant presentation—what Brecht termed an *alienation effect*—designed to make its audience aware of alternative possibilities. Though the performance is meant to be fun (as Brecht repeatedly stresses), the approach is more cerebral than visceral. As Brecht writes, "Whatever [the actor] doesn't do must be contained and conserved in what he does. In this way every sentence and every gesture signifies a decision; the character remains under observation and is tested."[4] To what end? "The task of epic theater," Benjamin writes, "is not so much the development of actions as the representation of conditions. The

---

4. Bertolt Brecht, *Brecht on Theatre* 137 (John Willett trans. 1964).

truly important thing is to discover the conditions of life."[5] By observing and testing the characters, epic theater displaces attention from individual actions to the conditions (including the enabling conventions) that give these actions their sense.

An example of Brecht's will show what Benjamin is talking about. Consider a dramatic scene in which a young woman leaves home to take a job in another city. Brecht observes that for "the bourgeois theater" this is an unimportant scene, at best the setting for a drama that will subsequently unfold. But the epic theater

> concentrates entirely on whatever in this perfectly everyday event is remarkable, particular and demanding inquiry. What! A family letting one of its members leave the nest to earn her future living independently and without help? Is she up to it? Will what she has learnt here as a member of the family help her to earn her living? Can't families keep a grip on their children any longer? Have they become (or remained) a burden? Is it like that with every family? Was it always like that? Is this the way of the world, something that can't be affected? . . . These are the questions (or a few of them) that the actors must answer if they want to . . . demonstrate a custom which leads to conclusions about the entire structure of a society at a particular (transient) time.[6]

In line with this characteristically modernist way of treating drama, my readings of the trials in the second part of the book focus as much on suppressed or unchosen alternatives as on the trials as they actually unfolded. In each case, my purpose is to lay bare and criticize the assumptions (conditions) underlying the legal systems that staged these trials. Thus, the trial of Orestes elected to purchase social peace by subordinating women. Nuremberg compromised its own commitment to international human rights, as well as to neutral procedural justice, by presupposing and protecting the system of national sovereignty and the supremacy of the state. The *Walker* Court responded to the disruptive heroism of the civil rights movement by plumping for an authoritarian treatment of political obligation. In each case, my aim in retelling the story has been to arouse curiosity and reflection about the unchosen alternatives that might have been.

---

5. Walter Benjamin, "What is Epic Theater?" in *Illuminations* 149, 152 (Hannah Arendt ed. Harry Zohn trans. 1969).
6. Brecht, *supra* note 4, at 97–98.

Nested Narratives

Finally, let me call attention to a characteristically modernist feature shared by trials as such. Typically, a trial aims to reconstruct a set of events: it constructs a narrative (its rendition of the facts) out of other narratives (the evidence and testimony). Yet the trial itself is an event whose story can be told in different ways; thus, to retell the story of a trial is to present a story within a story within a story. This structure of nested narratives carries distinctly modernist overtones: Greenberg's definition of modernism as the use of the characteristic methods of a discipline to criticize that discipline could stand easily as a capsule description of the appellate process, which scrutinizes the trial as an event just as the trial scrutinized an underlying dispute. A trial incorporates various narrative levels that typically move at cross-purposes to each other, responding to the conflicting currents that make up the law itself. In the end, my answer to the question, Why are trials the right narratives for legal theory? is simply that trials and their stories are the embodiment of the law's self-criticism.

Communitarian Liberalism

So far, I have said little about how these chapters display the doctrines of what I have called communitarian liberalism. The trials in the second part explore several tensions or dichotomies that permeate contemporary legal theory: statism versus communitarianism (the King chapter); order versus justice and patriarchy versus feminism (the Greek trials); national sovereignty versus cosmopolitanism (Nuremberg); obedience versus resistance (King); centralism versus pluralism (King, once again). In each case, one pole of the dichotomy represents the strands of political and legal history that glorify statism, order, patriarchy, obedience, sovereignty, and centralism—the strands that represent nineteenth-century statist liberalism, the form of politics against which modernism defines itself.

I regard each of these statist values as a historical legacy that is demonstrably inadequate to the world we inhabit. Demonstrably inadequate, because the energies that split statist liberalism apart at the seams shine through the trials themselves. From the mythical identification of legality with patriarchy at the Areopagus, to the wishful thinking about world order at Nuremberg, to the Supreme Court's plaintive assertion of its own authority in *Walker* (where the Court found itself in the nightmarish position of reenacting the condemnation of Socrates), the grand themes of statism rise conspicuously to the surface of our trials. In these nested narratives of trials, statism finds itself on trial and is condemned by the moral challenges it is unable to surmount. That leaves us with a challenge: to lever ourselves somehow out of an unjust and inquiet past. Communitarian liberalism represents a vision that aims to provide the fulcrum for our effort.

Since a number of communitarianism's prominent exponents (e.g., Alasdair MacIntyre, Michael Sandel) view communitarian thought as a form of antiliberalism, *communitarian liberalism* may sound like a contradiction in terms. Liberalism, for these communitarians, stands for the priority of individuals—atomistic, or isolated, or presocial individuals, as communitarian writers like to say—over the community. These antiliberal communitarians reject the idea of presocial individuals as metaphysically false and morally corrupting, and it is this view that leads them to reject liberalism as well. To these writers, liberalism likewise requires neutrality among theories of the good, a neutrality that to them implies a fatal indifference to community values and to the contingent choices by which communities define their collective historical identities.

I, on the other hand, find no contradiction between communitarianism and liberalism, because I deny that liberalism implies either isolated individualism or neutrality among theories of the good. The isolated individualism picture of liberalism's history has been a favorite libel of the European right since the French revolution, but gained currency among academic theorists on the left largely because of C. B. Macpherson's influential 1962 book *The Political Theory of Possessive Individualism*, which offered a persuasive reading of early liberal thinkers from Hobbes to Locke along isolated individualist lines. Macpherson's thesis that political liberalism implies possessive individualism harmonized nicely with the suspicions of the New Left, which followed the early Marx in stressing the connections between political economy and human personality and argued that liberal capitalism fosters estrangement and alienation. The New Left reached its zenith shortly after the appearance of Macpherson's masterpiece, and this political development gave Macpherson's thesis such widespread currency that it became more or less the conventional wisdom of progressive social theory in the 1970s and 1980s.

And yet the history of liberalism—in political practice, not merely political theory—is much richer and more complex than "possessive individualism" suggests.[7] Early liberals extolled competitiveness, to be sure, but their opponent was economic monopoly, not social coopera-

---

7. Stephen Holmes has argued this point repeatedly and persuasively. *See, e.g.,* Holmes, *The Anatomy of Antiliberalism* (1993); Holmes, *Benjamin Constant and the Making of Modern Liberalism* (1984); Holmes, "The Permanent Structure of Antiliberal Thought," in *Liberalism and the Moral Life* 227 (Nancy L. Rosenblum ed. 1989).

tion.[8] To take a more significant point, the attack of liberalism on traditional communities was much more than a purely destructive fragmentation of timeless communal rhythms (which were in any event less timeless and communal than the wistfulness of contemporary antiliberals would have them); it also involved a constructive effort to envision larger communities—provinces and nations, rather than villages and free cities—and thus incorporated cosmopolitan ideals that centered on communities and not only on individuals. Nor, for that matter, should individualism be identified with antisocial selfishness; as Stephen Holmes points out, "individualism can involve a heightened concern for others as individuals, rather than as members of ascriptive groups."[9]

In chapter 5, I discussed the basic thought in Martin Luther King's "Letter from Birmingham Jail": "We are caught in an inescapable network of mutuality, tied in a single garment of destiny. Whatever affects one directly, affects all directly."[10] This is plainly the sentiment of a communitarian, not a possessive individualist; yet King argued from the "network of mutuality" to the pursuit of liberal equality and liberal rights. King is, for me, the most inspiring communitarian liberal of our time (perhaps of all time).

Thus, I mean to contrast communitarian liberalism not only with statist liberalism but with individualist liberalism. I also distinguish it from liberal neutrality. There is, in my view, no reason for liberals to be neutral among theories of the good, and, in any case, no political order *can* be neutral among theories of the good. The liberal's substantive commitment to human equality leads her to reject racist and sexist theories of the good and to enact that rejection into law. But equality is not liberalism's only substantive commitment. Judith Shklar has remarked on the fact that liberals characteristically "put cruelty first"— they regard cruelty as the worst of vices and build this implicit theory of the good into innumerable institutional arrangements.[11]

To be sure, many liberals insist on governmental neutrality toward competing theories of the good because they fear that abandoning neutrality will lead to official intolerance and the suppression of minority viewpoints, unorthodox religions, or unpopular ways of life (homosexuality, for example). They fear that to abandon neutrality would entail, for example, governmental oppression of homosexuals. Let me con-

---

8. Holmes, "The Permanent Structure of Antiliberal Thought," *supra* note 7, at 250.

9. *Id.* at 233.

10. Martin Luther King, Jr., "Letter from Birmingham Jail," in *Why We Can't Wait*, 79 (1963).

11. Judith N. Shklar, *Ordinary Vices* 7–44 (1984).

sider this example briefly to show why communitarian liberalism would entail no such thing.

Historically, liberalism was accompanied by a change in heterosexual marriage practices. With the liberal assault on domineering familial and clan ties, marriage for love—volitional coupling—began to replace the preliberal norms of arranged marriage and marriage for family alliance. But this change is not merely because of a neutralist commitment to autonomy; it is because of a nonneutral, substantive commitment to the intrinsic value of volitional sex and love. To be sure, this commitment did not extend to extramarital sex, nor to gay sex; but, as in the case of many other principled commitments, once the genie emerged from the bottle, it was only a matter of time before conventional limitations began to seem not merely conventional but arbitrary. The communitarian liberal, then, must be the sworn enemy of antigay practices and laws—not because liberals are neutral among theories of the good but because liberals believe that sexual love is a positive human good. Communitarian liberalism does not merely tolerate gays; in a decidedly nonneutralist way, it supports and affirms homoerotic love.

It may nevertheless seem that communitarianism, which emphasizes the value of particularistic local attachments and contingent histories, cannot be reconciled with cosmopolitan concern for strangers outside one's communal sphere. It may seem as well that valuing a contingent history is fundamentally at odds with modernism, the defining characteristics of which are its suspicion of history and its alienation from community.

In my view, however, these seeming incompatibilities arise only when one conceives of a community as pregiven, unambiguous in its norms and shared understandings, "always already there," closed, largely static, and free of tension. This is communitarianism as tribalism (or nationalism), the most destructive myth of our time. Just as I counterpose communitarian liberalism to statist, neutralist, and individualist liberalisms, I counterpose it to communitarian tribalism.

I regard a community as dynamic, as living, to precisely the extent that it is tension-ridden, and, in a phrase, as *never* already there. Cover, in *"Nomos* and Narrative," observes that *nomoi* are inherently schismatic and "jurisgenerative," by which he means that laws and norms inevitably fracture into multiple incompatible interpretations.[12] The ap-

---

12. Robert Cover, "The Supreme Court, 1982 Term—Foreword: *Nomos* and Narrative," 97 *Harvard Law Review* 4 (1983). In a similar vein, Stuart Hampshire argues that the evolutionary branching of natural languages into mutually unintelligible dialects arises inevitably from human creativity. Stuart Hampshire, *Innocence and Experience* (1989). On this theme, see Richard Hyland's remarkable essay "Babel: A She'ur," 11 *Cardozo Law Review* 1585 (1990).

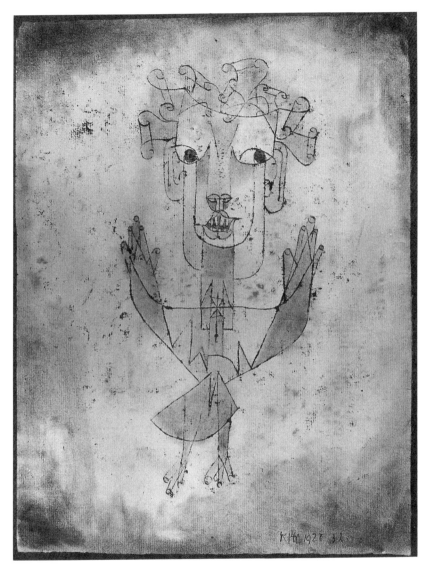

elus Novus, by Paul Klee. (Collection Israel Museum, Jerusalem. Photo credit: Israel Museum.)

propriate musical metaphor for community is not harmony but counterpoint. I regard community not as a given but as a task, as something that still lies ahead of us, and as something to be achieved in large measure through the modernist critique of norms that are arbitrary, precisely because they fall short of full communal reciprocity. Its preconditions are economic and legal fairness, without which the tribalist's vaunted "community standards" in fact have precious little to do with community. That, of course, was King's whole point. Moreover, particularly in our world of mass migrations and shifting demographic patterns, communities must be cosmopolitan and reject the murderous myth of homogeneity.

Admittedly, "communitarian liberalism" is by itself merely a phrase, a promissory note that must be backed by constructive political philosophy. That is something that these chapters, which are largely concerned with the inadequacies of statist liberalism, cannot claim to have provided. Yet I trust that enough of the communitarian liberal vision has shown through these chapters, if only in negative relief, to persuade the reader that there is something there worthy of development.

Doubts nevertheless remain. In chapter 5 I have argued on behalf of a multiplicity of interpretive viewpoints with no special interpretive authority vested in the Supreme Court; I have also defended social protest movements and conscientious disobedience to unjust law. In chapter 6 I have argued for the priority of justice over order and stability, while in chapter 7 I endorse (somewhat cautiously) the promotion of human rights through an activist and interventionist world order. One may well wonder whether any political community can handle so much unruliness.

Perhaps it is impossible; perhaps communitarian liberalism represents an unattainable political ideal. The world around us in 1993 inspires little hope for the prospects of a cosmopolitan and communitarian liberal order. In that case we are condemned to dwell in the ruins of history side by side with the ghosts of past injustice. It is still worthwhile to make the case for communitarian liberal ideals, if only to permit us to understand the character of our failure. But I would like to believe that my writing may serve a purpose that is not merely elegiac.

The Angel of History

In his most famous passage, Walter Benjamin reflects on Paul Klee's painting *Angelus Novus* (which Benjamin owned) in order to imagine the angel of history.[13] This angel always looks backward, so that he is unable to stop contemplating the uninterrupted chain of catastrophes that make up the past. He would like to repair the wreckage, but the powerful winds blowing from paradise hold his wings open and send him sailing backward into the future. The gale, Benjamin bitterly observes, is what we call "Progress." For Benjamin, this word invariably refers to the idea of inevitable and predictable progress, determined by transpersonal forces, that arises in the nineteenth-century philosophers of history. In Benjamin's parable, then, it is inevitable progress, all the fatality in our nature, that blows the fragile human edifice apart; and it is progress that stops our angel from folding his wings and maintaining his position long enough to lend a helping hand. All that he can do is contemplate the past—memorize it as it topples, so that our achievements do not vanish without a trace. That is something, to be sure, but it is not much. Taken as a whole, the picture Benjamin paints seems utterly hopeless.

Perhaps, however, there remains a bit of hope in Benjamin's bleak parable. The angel, unlike us, is a winged being. His wings make him more than human, but in Benjamin's parable it is his wings that make him helpless. Instead of enabling the angel to fly, they catch the gale and leave him splayed out like a butterfly in an album.

We have no wings. Beneath the layers of despair in his story, I take Benjamin to be concealing a challenge. It is a challenge to us who are not winged. Perhaps our very insignificance permits us to make our way upwind, evading the bluster of progress to salvage what we need from the wreckage of history. Hölderlin wrote, "But where danger threatens / That which saves from it also grows."[14] Who can be sure that Hölderlin was wrong?

---

13. Benjamin, "Theses on the Philosophy of History," in *Illuminations, supra* note 5, at 259–60, Thesis 9.

14. Hölderlin, "Patmos," in *Poems and Fragments* at 463 (Michael Hamburger trans. 1980).

Index

Legal cases that are neither quoted nor discussed are omitted from the index, as are purely bibliographical references to the names of individual authors. Incidental mentions of names are also omitted. Italicized page numbers refer to reproductions of artworks.

398